THIRD EDITION

International Management

CROSS-CULTURAL DIMENSIONS

Richard Mead

Blackwell
Publishing

BLACKWELL PUBLISHING

350 Main Street, Malden, MA 02148-5020, USA
108 Cowley Road, Oxford OX4 1JF, UK
550 Swanston Street, Carlton, Victoria 3053, Australia

First published 1994 by Blackwell Publishers Ltd
Second edition published 1998
Third edition published 2005 by Blackwell Publishing Ltd

Library of Congress Cataloging-in-Publication Data

Mead, Richard.
International management : cross-cultural dimensions / Richard Mead. – 3rd ed.
p. cm.
Includes bibliographical references and index.
ISBN 0-631-23177-3 (pbk. : alk. paper)
1. International business enterprises – Management – Social aspects.
2. Corporate culture. 3. Intercultural communication. I. Title.

HD62.4.M4 2005
658'.049–dc22
2004001162

A catalogue record for this title is available from the British Library.

Set in 10/12^{1}/₂pt Rotis Serif
by Graphicraft Limited, Hong Kong
Printed and bound in the United Kingdom
by TJ International, Padstow, Cornwall

The publisher's policy is to use permanent paper from mills that operate a sustainable
forestry policy, and which has been manufactured from pulp processed using
acid-free and elementary chlorine-free practices. Furthermore, the publisher ensures
that the text paper and cover board used have met acceptable
environmental accreditation standards.

For further information on
Blackwell Publishing, visit our website:
www.blackwellpublishing.com

CONTENTS

PREFACE

Members of different cultures express different values and priorities when they make and implement decisions. These values influence work relationships, whether between superior and subordinate, peers, international joint venture partners, managers in headquarters and subsidiary, and others. The international manager needs to recognize and respond to the opportunities and threats that they present.

This book argues that the influence of culture is never stable and its effect on behavior can never be precisely predicted. Furthermore, a range of other factors may also intervene. These include the social and business environments, industry and organizational interests, and the personalities of the people concerned. The problem for the manager is deciding which have priority in any given situation.

Culture is *sometimes* very significant; and on other occasions it is not, and the other factors are more so. The manager needs the skills to recognize *when* culture is significant, to weigh its influence against that of the other factors, and then respond appropriately. This book aims to equip managers with these skills.

A: Who is the Book For?

The book has been written for

- MBA and other management students. The book is recommended for students majoring in international management.
- Managers and students with specialist interests in
  human resources
  project development
  strategic planning
  cross-cultural communication.

The globalization of business means that the new manager is almost certain to work with members of other cultures during his/her career, and to need cross-cultural management skills. This is true for the headquarters manager as much as for the expatriate.

Whether or not all cultures are converging to the point at which the differences are so slight that they can be safely ignored is a theoretical issue discussed in the book. The practical answer for today is that any final convergence is still a long way in the future. Today's manager cannot afford to ignore the obvious differences. These are real, and vitally affect the workplace.

B: What Makes the Book Different?

In addition to covering the core topics common to most textbooks on international management, this book has a number of original features.

Most MBA texts pay little attention to the influence of culture on family companies (chapter 12). But as experts become aware that neither Western nor Japanese models of capitalism explain developments in China and elsewhere in Asia, the topic becomes increasingly important. Informal patronage and *guanxi* also tend to be overlooked, reflecting a Western notion that all business relationships can and should be fully transparency. But the reality is that in much of the developing world (and in some parts of the most developed economies) these arrangements are still accepted as an effective way of managing relationships, and they are discussed here in chapter 9. Whatever the international manager may think of the ethics of patronage and *guanxi*, he/she needs to recognize the circumstances in which they function and to be prepared to cope with their effects. Chapter 11 examines the relevance that political and economic theories of globalization have for the manager.

Each chapter includes a section examining the practical implications of the discussion, and an exercise. Short case studies are included.

C: What's New About the Third Edition?

All chapters have been revised and their content updated. A new chapter is devoted to globalization. Three rather than two chapters now develop the themes of relationships between headquarters and subsidiaries, and international joint ventures. The previous two chapters on dispute resolution and negotiation have been simplified and unified in a single chapter.

The theme of tension between environmental and internal influences was introduced in the second edition, and is here much developed in chapters 1, 11 (on globalization and localization), and 12 (on family companies, illustrating points raised in chapter 11).

Human resource management topics are discussed throughout, and the final two chapters on selecting, training, and supporting subsidiary and IJV staff have been reorganized. Greater emphasis is paid to local management. The new section on *guanxi* recognizes the growing importance of China. Sections on knowledge management are enlarged. The problems of planning and managing in increasingly unstable markets are discussed at greater length than in previous editions.

Many of the exercises and cases are new. The bibliography is radically revised and updated.

Many MBA and other management students have to write a dissertation or report as part of the assessment exercise. This edition includes an appendix on planning the dissertation.

D: How Are the Chapters Organized?

The structure used in the previous edition has been simplified, and the material reorganised in three parts. Part one consists of an introductory first chapter. In part two, chapters 2–10 focus on cross-cultural management, and examine how far culture influences behavior in the workplace and the internal systems of the company. In part three, chapters 11–18 focus on global and strategic issues in international business, and emphasize the influence of non-cultural factors on decision making and implementation. The mix of cultural and non-cultural influences on strategy has implications for international human resource planning, and this discussion concludes the book.

The thematic development of the chapters is as follows.

a Decision making in the company is influenced by factors in the ENVIRONMENT (chapter 1).
b Significant factors in the ENVIRONMENT include national CULTURE (chapters 1–3).
c National CULTURE influences the design and use of STRUCTURES AND SYSTEMS used in the company (chapters 4–10).
d These STRUCTURES AND SYSTEMS are among the factors that influence how the company formulates and implements its INTERNATIONAL STRATEGY (chapters 11–13).
e Implementing an INTERNATIONAL STRATEGY involves making decisions about how to CONTROL INVESTMENTS abroad (chapters 14–15).
f One means of CONTROLLING INVESTMENTS abroad is to use STAFFING (chapter 16).
g An effective STAFFING policy makes decisions about selecting, training, and supporting expatriate and local staff (chapters 17–18).

The ideas discussed in each chapter are developed in a short case. The cases are grouped at the end of their respective parts, namely after chapters 1, 10, and 18. An appendix on report planning precedes the bibliography.

The Instructor's Manual that accompanies this book suggests alternative arrangements by which the instructor can structure teaching courses based on it.

ACKNOWLEDGMENTS

The three editions of this book were written at business schools in three countries – the United States, Thailand, and the United Kingdom.

Most of the first edition was written at the Kellogg School, Northwestern University, Illinois. I owe much to the support given by the then Dean, Professor Donald P. Jacobs. Some chapters were drafted at the Middlesex Business School in the United Kingdom. The second edition was started at SasinGIBA in Thailand, and I continue to be grateful to the Director, Professor Toemsakdi Krishnamra. It was completed at the School of Oriental and African Studies, the University of London, where the Director of the Centre for Financial and Management Studies, Professor Laurence Harris, encouraged me to embark on this third edition.

Professor Robert Taylor commented on a chapter. Anny Wang read various chapters and cases, and also designed the power point slides that accompany the *Instructor's Manual*. Dr Tim Andrews commented on the entire manuscript.

This edition also owes much to suggestions, material, data, and ideas contributed by colleagues, managers, students, and my family. They include, in no particular order: Dr Colin Jones, Peter Van Veen, John Kelly, Derek Condon, Dr Chatri Sripaipan, Dr John Elsom, Pierre Segal, Naoko Kasai, Keith Jackson, Francesco Zancanaro, Sebastian Bruch, Mitsuko Nishiguchi, Helena Hung, Hisako Suzuki, Brad Bamfield, Ray Carter, Takeshi Nagata, John Trzeciak, Paron Mead, Maggie Arden, Yoichi Shigetani, Noriko Yamamoto, Greg Wood, Elizabeth Shi Yu-lin, Nick Zhang Ning, Dr Peter Trim, Peter Barratt, Rowena Chiu, Paul Hudson.

My wife, Dr Kullada Kesboonchoo-Mead, has been most generous in sharing her ideas about a number of topics discussed here, in particular globalization. She led me through the literature and commented on earlier drafts of Chapter 11.

I wish to express my continued appreciation for the enthusiasm shown by all Blackwell staff, and in particular by my publisher, Rosemary Nixon, and Bridget Jennings.

Professor Robert Taylor has been highly supportive of all stages of this project, and has made useful suggestions for each of the three editions. I am extremely grateful. This edition is dedicated to him.

Dr Richard Mead
CeFiMS, The School of Oriental and African Studies, The University of London

PART ONE

Introduction

CHAPTER ONE
International Management and Culture

1.1 Introduction

The book deals with international management, and has three Parts. Part one (this chapter) is introductory. Part two (chapters 2–10) deals with cultural factors. It shows how far NATIONAL CULTURE influences the internal management systems of the organization. Part three (chapters 11–18) emphasizes issues in INTERNATIONAL MANAGEMENT. It focuses on strategic planning and implementation in international organizations, and shows when other factors may be more significant than culture.

When is culture important, and when not?

At one extreme, some management scholars claim that culture must be understood as the predominant force driving *all* decisions made in the company. At the opposite extreme, others reject the notion that culture has any relevance to management at all.

In practice, this question of the importance of culture depends *both* on the particular circumstances of the event being analyzed *and* on the professional interests of the person making the analysis. Here is an example. A communications professor, married to a macro-economist, sees the study of culture as vitally important in understanding what happens within the firm and how the firm communicates with its business environment. The macro-economist is employed by government agencies to analyse and predict trade cycles, and dismisses the study of culture as a waste of time. Given their different professional interests and needs, this disagreement on the importance of culture is not surprising.

This book rejects both extremes. It is argued that culture *is* always likely to be an influence on how the organization makes decisions, communicates, and structures its roles and relationships; but culture is unlikely to be the *only* significant factor. Other possible influences include internal factors such as the organizational strategy and the personality of the Chief Executive Officer (CEO). External factors other than national culture include markets, competition, economic conditions, and so on. A more complete list is given in section 1.2.

The questions facing the international manager are:

▮ WHEN IS CULTURE A SIGNIFICANT FACTOR, AND WHEN IS IT NOT? And when culture *is* significant,
▮ HOW MUCH WEIGHT SHOULD BE GIVEN TO CULTURE AS AGAINST OTHER FACTORS?
▮ HOW CAN CULTURAL ANALYSIS BE APPLIED TO SOLVING A PROBLEM, OR EXPLOITING AN OPPORTUNITY?

The aim here is to develop skills of identifying when culture is significant – and has to be taken into account in making and implementing plans – and when it can be ignored.

The book is principally aimed at management decision making in the private sector. But it also deals with topics relevant to managers employed by international not-for-profit organizations. These include organizations with an extra-national identity (the United Nations, World Health Organization, the World Bank); national organizations such as embassies and cultural organizations (the British Council, Alliance Française, Goethe Institute); and non-governmental organizations (Amnesty International, Oxfam, Medecins Sans Frontières).

1.2　Factors that Influence Decision Making

Here is a list of *some* of the internal factors that influence decision making within the organization:

• the CEO's psychological make-up;
• the organizational strategy;
• resources (financial, plant, staff, technology) already secured;
• organizational history;

- policies and systems;
- ORGANIZATIONAL CULTURE.

The EXTERNAL factors include

- decisions made by competitors;
- decisions made by suppliers;
- decisions made by customers;
- labor markets;
- technology;
- the national, regional, and world economies;
- financial markets;
- local, national, regional, and international politics;
- laws and regulations;
- infrastructure factors (transport, power, etc);
- trade unions;
- consumer groups;
- ethical and religious systems;
- factors in the green environment;
- INDUSTRY INTERESTS;
- NATIONAL CULTURE.

It might seem that the internal and external influences can be easily distinguished – as in figure 1.1. However, this model oversimplifies the true situation. In practice the internal factors are themselves influenced by the wider environment. For example, the formulation and implementation of strategy is bound to be influenced by analysis of market factors, the activities of competitors, and the economic environment. The organizational culture is influenced by the national culture; staff resources by the cost and availability of labor in external markets; and so on.

In practice, the boundary between the internal and external factors influencing decision making in the organization is porous – as is shown in figure 1.2.

When the company is dealing with a subsidiary or joint venture partner operating in another country, decision making is influenced by its own environment *and* the environment of this second player. This second environment may be very different – and the company has even less control over it than it does over its own. The company needs to take into account such factors in this second environment as:

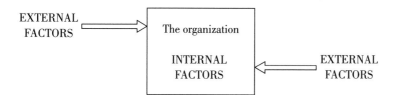

Figure 1.1

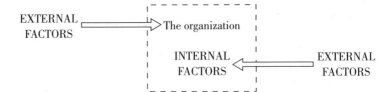

Figure 1.2

- the other country's laws and regulations;
- its economic profile;
- its market conditions and competition from local companies;
- the other national culture.

The company is continually REINTERPRETING its external environment, and reinterpreting its own history, present capacities, and possible futures in terms of how best it can respond to this external environment. The company collects and analyzes information about its external and internal environments, and in this sense it functions as a system for making interpretations; see Daft and Weick (1984) in Weick (2001), pp. 241–58. Then plans are made and implemented on the basis of the interpretations made.

1.3 Using Culture

This chapter is chiefly concerned with one environmental factor, NATIONAL CULTURE. The culture characterizes the national group and influences the behavior of its individual members.

Culture is not the only factor to influence individual values. His or her personality is also influenced by:

- GENETIC TRANSMISSION and development;
- FAMILY members, their personalities, and relationships;
- GENDER STEREOTYPES and beliefs about the behavior characteristic of males and females – attitudes are communicated within the society of how males and females should feel and behave;
- AGE: the individual's values shift as he/she grows older and takes on new social responsibilities.

These factors help mold the individual's PSYCHOLOGY. The manager needs to make psychological analyses in order to recognize and respond to the opportunities presented by individuals in the workplace, and to help each resolve his/her problems and realize his/her potential.

However, it is not practical that the manager base decisions entirely on the needs of individuals; most decisions have to be made in respect of a group – a unit, department, branch, the entire company. In such situations, psychological analysis may be of little help. For example, the manager who needs to motivate a unit of a dozen employees can only afford to invest the necessary resources (of time, labour, research and so on) in tailoring a dozen individual schemes if each employee is of extraordinary value to the survival and success of the company, and each individual has to have his or her needs individually catered for. So, given the economic constraints on applying psychological analysis to a small unit, is it likely that the manager can afford to design an individual scheme for each of, say, a hundred? Or a thousand? Probably, the manager has to treat them as a group with shared identity. This means making a generalization about their values and needs, testing this generalization by observation and experience, and acting on this basis. This is a process of developing and implementing a CULTURAL ANALYSIS.

1.3.1 Cultural analysis gives predictability

On the basis of cultural analysis the manager can assume a degree of uniformity in the values held by group members, and make generalizations about their behavior. These generalizations give a basis for predicting their future behavior in routine situations.

For example, your understanding of Culture X gives you a basis on which to predict how Culture X negotiators might respond to your offers, concessions, and refusals; how Culture X managers might respond to more or less centralized control; how the Culture X workforce might respond to a new incentive scheme.

A Chinese American entrepreneur, Lu Hua Si, argued that basing business dealings with the other culture (in this case, China) on the basis of past performance

> ... will always lead to the wrong path. It is being able to make decisions under conditions of great uncertainty, knowing that your decision is based on assumptions about the future rather than facts, that gives the best chance of success. Of course, the assumptions must take into consideration how the Chinese will make their decisions. This is where knowledge of the culture is immensely important.[1]

However, the predictive worth of cultural analysis is limited. First, the manager can never precisely calculate the influence of culture against that of other factors in the environment – for example, economic factors. Second, in extraordinary and non-routine situations (such as in a war or revolution, or in natural disasters like floods or earthquakes) individuals typically feel a primary need to safeguard their own interests, and less need to conform with group expectations. Third, every society produces persons whose psychological make-up makes them untypical, and persons who are simply inept at understanding their culture and accepting its norms. Every society produces social outsiders, criminals, and lunatics.

In sum, models of culture analysis give the manager invaluable instruments in his/her work of interpreting and predicting the behavior of the workforce, but models that are never one hundred percent reliable.

1.3.2 Defining national culture

Scholars have produced hundreds of definitions of "culture." Hofstede's (1984) definition is still the best known to management scholars and is used here. Culture is

> ... the collective programming of the mind which distinguishes the members of one human group from another.... Culture, in this sense, includes systems of values; and values are among the building blocks of culture. *(p. 21)*

This implies that:

- A culture is particular to one group and not others.
- Culture is learned, and is not innate. It is passed down from one generation to the next.
- Culture includes systems of values.

Sections 1.3.3–1.3.6 examine the implications of this definition. Section 1.3.7 deals with aspects of culture that the definition does not cover. The focus is on national cultures; the definition does not entirely fit for organizational culture, which is discussed in chapter 4.

1.3.3 Culture and the group

The first point raised above is that a culture is particular to one social group and not others. This means that:

- different social groups have different cultures; and
- different social groups may respond to similar situations in different ways.

For example, the staff of an American organization were asked to contribute to a medical charity. Each person made his or her decision about how much to contribute on an individual basis, and did not consult with any other person either before or after the collection was made. A few weeks later, it was suggested that the Panamanian subsidiary subscribe to the same charity. Members were unsure about how much each should give, and consulted in groups and with their superiors to decide on a figure. Each person at each level of the company hierarchy contributed the same sum, but higher levels contributed more, and the CEO most.

This shows two different groups responding to the same situation in very different ways – one by deciding on the basis of individual interests, the other by deciding on the basis of collective and hierarchical interests.

The notion of national culture assumes that the cultures of, say, the Japanese, Americans, and Portuguese have their particular characteristics shared by members, and are distinct. This generalization is useful if you have to compare the three countries. Assume, for example, that you are trying to decide in which to situate a new plant, and you need to take into account the likely behaviors of the workforces. But homogeneity within the national culture cannot always be taken for granted. According to Barber (2001),

> less than 10 percent (about twenty) of the modern world's states are truly homogeneous and thus, like Denmark or the Netherlands, can't get smaller unless they fracture into tribes or clans. In only half is there a single ethnic group that comprises even 75 percent of the population. As in the United States, multiculturalism is the rule, homogeneity the exception. Nations like Japan or Spain that appear to the outside world as integral turn out to be remarkably multicultural. *(p. 9)*

In the case of Japan, sub-cultures include Korean Japanese, and the people of Okinawa, for whom home rule is an issue. At the heterogeneous extreme, American society includes a range of sub-cultures claiming Caucasian, Black, Asian, Hispanic, Native American, and other loyalties. In some aspects of life, these loyalties may override mainstream "Anglo-Saxon Protestant" values. If you have to choose whether to site your new factory in Boston or Miami you cannot assume cultural uniformity, and in the case of Miami, where the workforce are likely to have Spanish as a first language, you might need to refer to models of Hispanic culture. Immigrant sub-cultures are significant in many other countries (for example, in Brazil, the United Kingdom, and Australia), and elsewhere regional sub-cultures (for example in Spain, Italy, and Russia) may have local influence.

If you are trying to decide whether a new investment should be located in, say, Japan or the United States, a comparison between their national cultures is useful. If you have to decide between Okinawa and Tokyo, or Boston and Miami, analysis of the national mainstream may not help you. Even grosser oversimplifications are common. Politicians and journalists like to distinguish between, say, "Asian culture" and "Western culture," but in Asia, the cultures of Japan and Iran may have as little in common as do the Western cultures of, say, Greece and Sweden. In the United Kingdom, a Hindu correspondent made the point in a letter written to a newspaper editor after the 11 September 2001 attack on the World Trade Center:

> Sir – Once again, I see that you are writing articles on Muslims and then suddenly referring to Asians [article reference . . .]. If you continue to use the term "Asian" then please refer to the citizens of this country as Europeans, as this will have the same validity. . . .[2]

The authorities may have political motives for imposing cultural homogeneity. The bureaucrats governing the European Union would like to impose cultural uniformity because this seems likely to ease their problems of exerting control. But increasing numbers of European peoples are worried by bureaucratic regulations over which they have no influence, and resent being stripped of their cultural identities. In 1996, the *Economist* (a pro-EU journal) reported that:

> a poll done last year for the European Commission found that half the people of Britain, Portugal and Greece thought of themselves in purely national terms; so did one third of the Germans, Spaniards and Dutch. And this was in a part of the world where there is an institution – the EU itself – explicitly devoted to the encouragement of "Europeanness".[3]

The electoral successes of nationalist parties in France, the Netherlands, Austria, and Denmark since 2000 suggest that the need for local identity is alive in Europe.

After the handover of Hong Kong to China in 1997, the government worked to integrate the political and cultural systems of the ex-British colony with the rest of China. But Hong Kong people refused to give up their sense of a separate identity. And when anti-subversion laws were proposed in June 2003, up to 500,000 took to the streets in protest – despite an assurance from the Chinese premier, Wen Jibao, that the legislation "absolutely will not affect the different rights and freedoms that Hong Kong people enjoy under the law." However, two days later the proposed laws were withdrawn. And rather than weakening resistance, Beijing insistence on a "two countries, one system" formula for incorporating Taiwan into the mainland appears to be strengthening the Taiwanese sense of an independent identity and local culture. In Tibet, the continuing resistance to Beijing rule demonstrates the same point. These examples imply that Chinese claims for the inevitability of uniform Beijing rule are overstated, and that the international manager might need to treat Hong Kong, Taiwan, and other Chinese cultures as distinct.

To sum up: the limits to the "culture group" that you wish to analyze are influenced by your reason for making the analysis. Sometimes you need to compare national cultures, sometimes sub-cultures, industries, and organizational cultures. In general this book focuses on national cultures, and this is usually the reference of the term "culture" here. The text makes clear when organizational cultures and other sub-groups are differentiated.

1.3.4   Culture is learned

The second implication of Hofstede's definition is that your culture is not programmed into your genetic structure. You learn it. In the case of a national culture, you learn most intensively in the early years of life. By the age of five you were already an expert in using your language. You had learned how to communicate different language functions appropriately; for example, how to:

- interact with other members of your family;
- elicit rewards and avoid punishments;
- negotiate for what you wanted;
- cause and avoid conflict.

Your behavior as a small baby might have been indistinguishable from that of babies in any other society. But very quickly you learned to mold your behavior to the particular constraints of your culture group, and to recognize the meaning of messages communicated by other members of the group.

Here is an example. Koreans learn in their childhoods to be cautious of claiming "my" relationships; rather than "my mother" and "my house," the well-behaved child soon learns to refer to "our mother," "our house". A Korean explained:

> "we try to avoid saying the word 'my' something. And when we have to, we use a very polite form. When we are introducing something [as a topic] we use 'our' – 'our parents,' 'our book.' 'My' sounds very selfish."

When Koreans visit English-speaking countries, they compensate.

> "When Koreans come to England, they often say 'parents' [rather than either 'my parents' or 'our parents']. They know that 'our parents' is wrong in English but they don't like to say 'my parents.' So they miss [the possessive adjective] out."

The Korean preference for the plural possessive adjective ("our" rather than "my") reflects the collectivist values of the culture; Koreans are brought up to believe that they are united by common ancestry and descent from the same two original parents. Second, this shows Koreans are aware of differences between their own and Anglo cultures.[4]

Cultural values are passed on to you first by parents and family, then by other members and institutions in the culture group. These include friends, other adults, schools, media, and religious organizations. In different societies, these different agents play different roles in teaching the culture. In Japan, the mother is mainly responsible for early rearing, while in Scandinavian countries, the parents play more equal roles. In many Islamic societies the mosque plays a greater part in educating the young than might the church in many Christian societies. In some areas of the PRC, it is still common for small children to be brought up by grandparents, leaving parents free to join the labor force.

Much of the child's learning is unconscious. When you began learning your mother language you were not aware of being inducted into the group culture. And so these values become second nature, and massively influence your behavior in later life. Because your cultural values are acquired so early and without conscious application, they are extremely deep-rooted.

1.3.5 *Values*

Hofstede defines culture as including systems of VALUES. Values are defined here as assumptions that members of a culture group make about how they should behave and do behave. The person may never articulate these assumptions, or even think of them; we have seen that persons start learning their cultural values in early childhood, at a preconscious level. As such these values are ingrained and are slow to change.

Because they are taken for granted as the right way to behave, values strongly influence what behavior occurs. Here is an example. In an Indonesian business school, students waited after class for all members of their friendship circle to collect before they went off together for lunch. A group of Americans was studying in the school at the same time. They noticed the Indonesian behavior and challenged it in class. Didn't this waste time? The Indonesians answered that giving precedence to group loyalty was how they "ought to behave," and they took this courtesy for granted. An individual overlooked by his friends would feel betrayed, and this would have negative effects on them all. Then they challenged the Americans; how long do you wait for your friends after class? Two minutes at the most. To the Indonesians, this showed coldness and unfriendliness.

Members' behavior directly reflects their values. In this case, the Indonesians' high collectivism influenced more than how they organized their lunch-hours; it influenced all their social and work priorities, loyalties, and relationships between groups. Whereas Indonesians hoped to achieve their goals through membership of and loyalty to a powerful group, the Americans expressed theirs in a drive to succeed on an individual basis. But until the two groups began to analyze each others' behavior, neither had thought to question their fundamental values.

1.3.6 Beliefs

Hofstede says that culture *includes* values, which raises the question of what else is included. Culture is also influenced by conscious BELIEFS. But these are often less reliable than preconscious values as guides to what really motivates behavior in the group.

The individual's beliefs indicate how he/she thinks that things are, or ought to be. (You may wish to separate beliefs, attitudes, opinions, and so on, but these distinctions are not necessary here.) The point is that people often do not behave according to their beliefs, and so they are only weakly predictive of future behavior.

For instance, most people in most countries profess some religious belief, and all religions condemn killing and theft. But murders occur in all countries, and most of us have committed some forms of theft at some time or another. Here is an example from the workplace. Most managers agree that communication initiated by subordinates is useful and important, and many may claim that "my office door is always open, and you can come and discuss your problems at any time." Often, they believe this. But how many managers do you know for whom this is true? What often happens is that

- he/she is too busy and asks you to come back at some other time; *or*
- he/she tells you that your problem is trivial and that you are wasting time; *or*
- he/she hears what you say, but is thinking of something else; *or*
- he/she listens, and promises to help, but forgets.

In these cases, behavior does not correspond with conscious belief, and the belief gives weak predictions of behavior.

A survey conducted in Singapore found wide differences between public attitudes – which were "progressive" – and "traditional" domestic attitudes.

> An overwhelming 97 per cent of the respondents felt that the government should treat men and women equally and 77 per cent said that it actually does. At the same time, 78 per cent of men and 77 per cent of women agreed that husbands must always be the household head.
>
> In 83 per cent of households surveyed, the wife cooks, 77 per cent wash toilets, 80 per cent wash dishes and do the laundry and 78 per cent do the ironing.
>
> It shows that "there is no watertight link between what people say they believe and how they act," the *Straits Times* said.[5]

To sum up: although culture includes beliefs (and attitudes, opinions, etc.), these are less reliable than values in predicting behavior. For this reason, the book focuses on values. But there is one point that must be borne in mind. Because (most) people are not good at describing their deepest values, these are not easily accessible. The analyst cannot expect to learn much by asking direct questions such as "what are your values?"

Robertson et al. (2001) examine the differences between beliefs and values in Saudi Arabia, Kuwait, and Oman. They find the same belief system operating in these countries, and that is deeply rooted in the common religion, Islam. But values differ significantly:

> Saudis tend to have a stronger work ethic than Kuwaitis do, and are more independently motivated in the workplace.   *(p. 236)*

> Saudi Arabia may have a stronger emphasis on individuality in the workplace.
>   *(p. 240)*

1.3.7 *Values and religion*

The example presented by Robertson et al. above shows that the relationship between cultural values and beliefs derived from RELIGION is complex. Even when the same religious forms are shared by a range of cultures, this does not guarantee common values expressed outside religious practice. Religion expresses the culture and also influences it. The religion practiced by the group expresses a system of ethical belief, and is idealistic, rather than descriptive of how they actually behave.

Religious belief does not necessarily influence behavior. For instance, Buddhism teaches moderation and the importance of seeking a middle way between extremes. But here is an educated Thai noting the contradiction between the behavior and religious beliefs of his townspeople:

> Characteristically, the Muang Petch people are suited to be nak-leng (patrons). Killing and revenge is the name of the game, not necessarily based on any particular principle except for defending one's honour in the old way. We're quite extreme people which is strange considering that the people are mostly devout Buddhists.[6]

Most of the major religions are shared by a number of national cultures:

- *Christianity* is the most widely practiced. The majority live in Europe and the Americas, and numbers are growing rapidly in Africa. Protestant Christianity emphasizes the individual's responsibility for his or her own actions, and in the Anglo cultures has had a major effect on business values associated with individualism and independent thinking.
- *Islam* is practiced mainly in Africa, the Arab countries, in parts of Southeast Asia, Afghanistan, and in some countries and regions comprising the former Soviet Union – for example, in Chechnya.
- *Hinduism* is most common in India. Beliefs emphasize the spiritual progression of each person's soul rather than hard work and wealth creation.
- *Buddhism* has adherents in Central and Southeast Asia, China, Korea, and Japan. Like Hinduism it stresses spiritual achievement, although the rapid economic development of these regions shows that this does not necessarily impede economic activity.
- *Confucianism* has adherents mainly in China, Korea and Japan. The emphases on loyalty and reciprocal obligation between superiors and subordinates, and honesty in dealing with others, have influenced the development of family companies in these regions.

The fact that the same religious form may be practiced across a range of national boundaries means that differences in belief (between, say, Christianity and Islam) give an imprecise reflection of national cultural differences (between, say, Peru and Morocco). And the fact that majorities in different countries (say, Peru and Poland) have a common religion does not make them culturally identical.

1.3.8   Other aspects of the culture

We have seen that values are expressed in everyday behavior, and bear a complex relationship with religious belief. They are imprecisely reflected in other aspects of the culture, including:

- the group's material culture;
- technologies;
- political and economic ideology.

The MATERIAL CULTURE of arts and crafts immediately reflects the producers' individual psychologies, and only indirectly the values of the culture group. The cultural meaning may be difficult to discern, even to a skilled sociologist or art critic. In general, the international manager is not expected to have these skills. However, he/she who can demonstrate some knowledge of and interest in the local arts and crafts (including the local cuisine) is more likely to make a favorable impression.

The material culture includes TECHNOLOGIES. Modern technologies are used across all cultures and this fact is sometimes used as evidence to argue that all cultures are converging. But this ignores the important differences that occur in how technologies are used in different cultures. For example, information technology may be used on a group basis in the more collectivist cultures, but on an individual basis in the more individualist cultures.

When the international manager finds the same technology used in different cultures, he/she asks, for each culture,

- who selects the technology in this culture?
- who uses the technology?
- what status and values are associated with its use?
- what other activities co-occur with this use?
- when is the technology used?
- where is the technology used?
- what is this use of technology intended to achieve and why is it used?

When different cultures typically provide different answers to these questions about the same technology, cultural analysis is needed to explain the differences.

POLITICAL IDEOLOGY: Political leaders commonly legitimize their regimes by claiming that their system accurately reflects the majority culture. But in practice, the ideology may give a very distorted version of the culture.

A political system represents a set of beliefs, and in the long term can succeed only when it reflects values in the national culture. A revolution in the political structures does not necessarily reflect a change in the underlying value system. Adedaji (1995) was making this point in the context of the official "transition to democracy" in Nigeria (1992):

> democracy cannot be decreed. Unlike instant coffee, there is no instant democracy. You cannot move from totalitarianism to democratic practice from one day to another. Democracy is more than just the ballot boxes, the political parties and all the institutional trappings. It is a way of life, a culture and a lifestyle at all levels of society and in all spheres of human endeavour. *(p. 95)*

The implication is that democratic models that suit, say, the United States or the United Kingdom, may not be appropriate elsewhere in different cultural settings.

1.4   Cross-Cultural and International Management

In different circumstances, managers perform a range of different roles. These include leading, acting as figurehead, communicating information, negotiating, allocating resources, handling disturbances, planning, overseeing implementation of plans, evaluating. Factors that influence which of these roles a *particular* manager exercises, and how much emphasis he or she gives to them, include:

- his/her personal psychology;
- his/her functional responsibilities;
- the organizational culture and history of the company;
- industry factors (e.g. banks have relatively greater needs for hierarchical structures and controls than do advertising agencies; advertising agencies need structures that facilitate rapid creativity);
- NATIONAL CULTURE (e.g. in some cultures the manager is expected to emphasize control and direction elsewhere, to facilitate, and participate).

The national culture of the workforce influences how they respond to the structures and systems planned and implemented by management. This means that a workforce in one culture may respond differently to a workforce in another. That is, in different cultural and industrial contexts, different management roles are emphasized. The international manager must be prepared for these different responses, and he/she adapts to the different contexts.

Gooderham and Nordhaug (2004) define INTERNATIONAL MANAGEMENT as the generation and transfer of knowledge across initial settings, organizations, and countries (p. 1). O'Connell (1998) defines the notion as the planning, staffing, and control of international business activities (p. 320). These activities occur between business units that are located in different countries, whether joint venture partners, headquarters and subsidiary, principal and agent, supplier and customer. Both emphases – international management as a knowledge-based activity and as a function-based activity – are applied at different points in this book.

CROSS-CULTURAL MANAGEMENT is defined here as development and application of knowledge about cultures in the practice of international management, when the people involved have different cultural identities. These people may or may not belong to the same business unit.

The two terms do not correspond entirely. Some international managers in senior positions may have no face-to-face interactions with the other-culture workforce; many home-based managers deal with immigrant groups assimilated into a workforce that serves domestic markets.

1.4.1 Cross-cultural management skills

A SKILL is defined as the ability to demonstrate a sequence of behavior that is functionally related to attaining a performance goal (Torrington, 1994, p. 98).

Communication skills are often ranked as most important in qualifying the manager for positions of international responsibility. In addition managers need to be adaptable to the other culture and capable of leading its members.

The core assumption of cross-cultural skills learning is that the manager cannot expect to force-fit members of another culture into his or her own cultural norms. They cannot easily be made to accept his or her perceptions of reality as superior to values in their own culture. This is not an ethical matter so much as practical. The organization that attempts to impose its behavioral norms upon unwilling employees from another culture faces an uphill battle. This means that headquarters can never completely replicate its structures, systems, and organizational culture in the subsidiary based in another national culture.

The first half of this book focuses on those management systems in which these interpersonal skills are most in demand. The manager needs to master skills associated with:

- the organization culture;
- motivation and reward systems;
- recognizing and resolving disputes;
- establishing and implementing formal structures;
- recognizing the significance of informal structures;
- formulating and implementing plans for change.

In general the book focuses on the needs of international managers in expatriate positions – working outside their own countries. The sections below deal with the needs of managers working with mixed groups of immigrants and locals.

1.4.2 Managing cultural diversity

Cultural diversity in a work group provides both opportunities and difficulties. When managed successfully, it brings economic benefits. The company's ability to attract, retain, and motivate people from different cultures can give it competitive advantages in cost structures, physical structures, creativity, problem solving, and adapting to change.

Cultural diversity presents major opportunities for synergy. Group work is synergetic when the output of two or more individuals or groups working in cooperation is greater than would be the combined output of their working separately. Here is an example from a firm manufacturing cellular phones. The challenge is to design a new model that suits the needs of consumers in the country of the subsidiary, Country X.

The local sales-force know about local needs, what market segments are likely to purchase the product, how much these customers will pay and what advertising channels can be used to communicate with them. But they lack understanding of modern research methods and of headquarters' resources for designing new products. The headquarters marketers have access to the technology and can report on R&D conducted elsewhere, but they have no local expertise and contacts. Pooling their various expertise, the teams develop specifications for a phone designed to meet the needs of the growing youth market in Country X.

The solution is reached through a synergetic process; neither team could have made the creative jumps on its own or by adding its outcomes if working apart.

1.4.3 Factors influencing group creativity

Factors associated with the task influence by how much the diverse group is more creative than the homogeneous single-culture group. Diverse groups outperform homogeneous groups on complex problem-solving tasks, but may be less successful in performing routine tasks. Diverse groups need time to resolve difficulties of working together. In experiments conducted over 17 weeks, Watson et al. (1993) found that when groups were newly formed, the diverse groups were immediately less successful but caught up, and eventually outperformed the homogeneous groups in some respects (identifying problem perspectives, generating solution alternatives). In general both performed equally; but where the task was open-ended and a range of possible solutions was desirable, diverse groups performed better.

Over time, the experience should help break down racial, gender, functional, and organizational prejudices in diverse groups. But the effects can never be precisely calculated and the creation of a diverse group always carries an element of risk. A successful group is profitable both in terms of immediate results and the creation of goodwill for the future. If it fails, negative stereotypes are reinforced.

Factors associated with the industry and organization culture are also important. Citigroup, the largest US financial services company, decided to form a team composed of their New York and London managers. Relations between the groups were not immediately cooperative, in part because the industry attracts individualistic, ambitious, and materialistic employees with a high tolerance of conflict. Further, the two offices had different organizational values.

> The New York-based managers complained of excessive bureaucracy from their London colleagues who accused the New Yorkers of "shooting from the hip". They were unable to resolve conflicts and resorted to personal criticism and scapegoating.[7]

The team was diverse in other ways. It included five nationalities and a third were women. A project identified needs for interpersonal sensitivity, greater flexibility, less extreme assertiveness, greater attention to networking and to constructive organizational politics. The results were impressive. Nevertheless a senior vice-president acknowledged that managing diversity is:

> "not so straightforward. If we're going to take advantage of diversity in thinking and problem-solving and serving clients, and in new product development, we've got to understand more about each other and how we work together. We can't leave that to chance."[8]

Diverse groups are more likely to succeed when members:

- value the exchange of alternative points of view;
- cooperate to build group decisions;
- respect each other's experiences and share their own;
- value the opportunity for cross-cultural learning;
- are tolerant of uncertainty and try to overcome the inefficiencies that arise when members of different cultures work together.

In sum, a diverse group is more likely to be creative when the members are tolerant of difference and perhaps no more than moderately competitive, *and* the task is organized so that diversity is an advantage. The task is non-routine and open-ended. Top management gives its moral and administrative support, and allows time for the group to overcome the inevitable process difficulties. Diversity training is provided. The commitment of group members is rewarded.

The potential benefits of diversity are demonstrated by two studies conducted in the banking industry. Ng and Tung (1998) collected data from 98 respondents of seven branches of a Canadian bank. They found that the culturally heterogeneous branches experienced lower levels of absenteeism and achieved higher productivity and profitability than did culturally homogeneous branches, although at the cost of job satisfaction. Field research by Richard (2000) in banks in the United States showed that cultural diversity can add significant value to the company. Under appropriate conditions it contributes to firm competitive advantage and to corporate financial performance.

1.4.4 The alternative: ignoring diversity

The Citigroup example above makes clear that managing diversity can be difficult. The alternative, of ignoring it, may be even more injurious. This means that management:

* ignores cultural differences within the workforce;
* down-plays the significance of cultural differences.

This refusal to recognize diversity occurs:

* in cases of ignorance – when management lacks the awareness and skills to recognize diversity;
* when management recognizes diversity but lacks skills to manage it;
* when the negative effects of recognizing diversity seem likely to cause greater problems than ignoring it;
* when the expected benefits of recognizing and managing diversity do not justify the expected costs;
* when the work offers no opportunities for deriving advantages from diversity.

In the workplace, strategies for ignoring diversity may work when culture groups are assigned different tasks and, beyond sharing essential resources, are otherwise independent. But when groups and group members are reciprocally integrated and need to collaborate, deep-seated ambiguities arise from not recognizing different value systems held by different staff groups.

1.5 Implications for the Manager

How can the material covered in section 1.4 above be applied to your organization? Answer for your company or business school.

1 In what departments/classes are a range of cultures represented? What cultures are represented?

2 In each department/class, is cultural diversity managed or ignored?

3 If cultural diversity is managed:
- what tasks are allocated to the diverse groups?
- what benefits arise from diversity?
- what problems arise?
- how could the diversity be better managed?

4 If cultural diversity is not managed, why not?
- Do you think it should be? Why/why not?

1.6 SUMMARY

This introductory chapter has focused on the importance of understanding culture.

Section 1.2 examined FACTORS THAT INFLUENCE DECISION MAKING in the business environment. The relationship between internal and external factors is complex, and problems of responding to external factors are further complicated when the company is making international investments and is operating in more than one national environment. National culture is only one of the factors involved, and the manager needs skills of distinguishing when it is, and is not, significant. Section 1.3 saw that models of CULTURE are useful because they give the manager bases for predicting behaviour within the culture group. A definition, commonly applied by managers, was discussed and its implications discussed. A culture is specific to a group, and is learned by its members. A culture includes systems of values, and values were defined. Section 1.4 examined the scope of CROSS-CULTURAL AND INTERNATIONAL MANAGEMENT. The cross-cultural manager needs specified interpersonal skills, as expatriate and when managing a culturally diverse group.

1.7 EXERCISE

Cultural values that are thought desirable and normal in one culture might be undesirable and deviant elsewhere.

1 Rank each of the values below in terms of how you think your culture group estimates it, from "strongly agree" to "strongly disagree."

  (a) Men should be competitive

     strongly agree : agree : disagree : strongly disagree

  (b) Women should be highly competitive

     strongly agree : agree : disagree : strongly disagree

  (c) Managers should participate with their subordinates

     strongly agree : agree : disagree : strongly disagree

  (d) Good work relationships are more important than task efficiency

     strongly agree : agree : disagree : strongly disagree

  (e) Powerful people should have privileges

     strongly agree : agree : disagree : strongly disagree

  (f) The manager should have all the answers to subordinates' questions

     strongly agree : agree : disagree : strongly disagree

2 Compare your answers with those of some other student, from another culture and explain the differences you identify.

Notes

1 "Management: China's Young Visionaries," *Business Week Online*, October 11, 2000.

2 "Letters to the Editor," *The Daily Telegraph*, November 8, 2002.

3 "The man in the Baghdad café," *The Economist*, November 9, 1996.

4 In this book, the expression "Anglo cultures" refers to the mainstream cultures of Australia, Canada (outside Quebec), New Zealand, the United Kingdom and the United States.

5 Associated Press: "Singaporeans don't practise what they preach on equality," *The Nation* (Bangkok), December 25, 1994.

6 Piya Angkinand, "Of fear and honour," *Bangkok Post*, January 25, 1991.

7 Alison Maitland, "Bridging the culture gap," *Financial Times*, January 28, 2002.

8 Alison Maitland, "Bridging the culture gap," *Financial Times*, January 28, 2002.

CHAPTER ONE **International Management and Culture**

CASE   THE BOSTON BANK

This examines the problem of deciding when culture is a significant factor in the environment

Peter had worked for several years in an advertising agency before joining a small Boston bank as a human resource manager. In the week after he joined, the bank was acquired by a Japanese bank. Senior Japanese staff arrived and soon exerted their authority.

Peter noticed three aspects of their behavior that seemed to him strange – at least, in terms of his previous experience. He was not sure how to explain them.

First, relations between staff at all levels were relatively formal, and responsibilities to superiors were differentiated rigidly.

QUESTIONS
What factor/s explain(s) these hierarchical relations?

1   The industrial culture of banking.
2   Japanese culture (compared to American culture).
3   Japanese economic policy.
4   Some other factor in the marketplace.

Discuss your answer, and decide what response/s Peter should have made.

(a)   Train the American staff to understand Japanese cultural values.
(b)   Train the Japanese staff to understand American cultural values.
(c)   Start looking for another job.
(d)   Nothing.
(e)   (Some other).

Second, all the Japanese were male, and were patriarchal in their relations with female employees.

QUESTIONS
What factors explain these patriarchal attitudes?

5   The industrial culture of banking.
6   Japanese culture (compared to American culture).
7   Japanese economic policy.
8   Some other factor in the marketplace.

Discuss your answer, and decide what response/s Peter should have made.

(f) Train the American staff to understand Japanese cultural values.
(g) Train the Japanese staff to understand American cultural values.
(h) Start looking for another job.
(i) Nothing.
(j) (Some other).

Third, the Japanese management showed no interest in long-term planning, and discouraged their American subordinates from strategic planning.

QUESTIONS

What factors explain this lack of interest in long-term planning?

9 The industrial culture of banking.
10 Japanese culture (compared to American culture).
11 Japanese economic policy.
12 Some other factor in the marketplace.

DECISION

Discuss your answer, and decide what response/s Peter should have made.

(k) *Train the American staff to understand Japanese cultural values.*
(l) *Train the Japanese staff to understand American cultural values.*
(m) *Start looking for another job.*
(n) *Nothing.*
(o) *(Some other).*

Then, six months after the purchase, Japanese management announced that they were re-selling. It then became clear that this had always been the main purpose in making the purchase, and that management had not wished to invest in strategic planning that might prejudice the sale.

DECISION

Suppose that you had been Peter, and you had known about this planned resale at the time of the original acquisition, how would you have responded?

Review your choice of (k)–(o).

PART TWO

Culture and Management

CHAPTER SIX   **Needs and Incentives**
The workforce is most productive when workers are motivated to achieve company goals. Management may choose from a range of both monetary and non-monetary incentives, such as the possibility of doing interesting work and feeling a sense of achievement. Culture plays a part in deciding why a particular incentive is motivating.

CHAPTER SEVEN   **Dispute Resolution and Negotiation**
Disputes arise from a range of factors including argument, competition for scarce resources, and misunderstandings. Tolerances of conflict vary across cultures, and behavior that causes conflict in one culture may be acceptable in some other. Participants negotiate both as a means of resolving conflict and of sharing resources.

CHAPTER EIGHT   **Formal Structures**
Formal structures determine roles and relationships within the company, and determine what communication options are more or less acceptable. A structure is influenced by factors that include the work being done, the national culture, and needs for organizational culture. Formal structures can be bureaucratic and impersonal.

CHAPTER NINE   **Informal Systems**
Informal systems may have a greater influence than do formal systems in deciding how management decisions are made and implemented. Patron and client are bound by long-standing ties of loyalty and obligation. Patronage networks reinforce in-groups and exclude outsiders. Cultural variations include guanxi in Chinese societies.

CHAPTER TEN   **Planning Change**
Planning to make change has a political dimension in the sense that it needs the commitment of other people. If they are persuaded that the proposed change lies in their interests, the plan may be accepted and implemented. Otherwise, the plan is unlikely to achieve its goals. Some planning models demand heavy investments of time and information, and under some business conditions long-term planning may be impossible.

Comparing Cultures

2.1 Introduction

The different spatial perceptions held by Majorcans and German settlers in Majorca sometimes lead to disputes.

"The islanders do not have a strongly developed sense of private land ownership and happily roam over each other's boundaries.

"The Germans, on the other hand, are intensely prickly about such matters and militantly defend their boundaries.

"The German sense of private property is somewhat different to the one here," said Eduardo Puçhe, a local councillor. "Some of the conflicts have reached the courts."[1]

This gives an example of different national groups understanding the world in different ways. The difference can cause conflict.

Cultural attitudes to space influence demands for work space, and in a cross-cultural situation the different groups may have conflicting expectations of their environment. Majorcans are happier to work in an open-plan office and each German prefers the privacy of his or her own office. A company employing both cultures might need to take this difference into account when planning office accommodation.

This chapter deals with cultural difference. It focuses on comparative analyses of culture and asks how they can be applied by management.

2.2   Comparative Models

International managers depend upon comparative models of culture. For example, they use models that tell them that Culture A is more collectivist than Culture B; that Culture C is more individualist than Culture D; that needs to control nature are higher in Culture E than in Culture F. Why are comparative models so much used? International managers need to make decisions about one nation in comparison to another:

- Where do I invest? In the Czech Republic or China?
- How far can I adapt my Japanese incentive system to my workforce in Thailand?
- Should I expect a matrix structure designed for a Swedish workforce to function effectively in Mexico?

The models discussed in this chapter enable the user to make comparisons between different cultures, and any one culture is described in relation to another culture or cultures.

Comparative models have a number of weaknesses. First, they lack the descriptive depth that an anthropologist might demand in respect of any one particular society, but they do provide descriptive breadth; as we shall see, Hofstede's (2001) comparative model compares 50 national and three regional cultures. Second, a cultural dimension carries different associations when used to describe different cultures, and hence there can be no *exact* point of comparison. For instance, the notion of individualism means different things in the United States and in China because the total cultural contexts differ. Because individualism is expressed slightly differently in the United States and China, a statement such as "the culture of the United States is more individualist than the culture of China" gives only a rough and ready guide to the two cultures. Third, the mainstream values in the national culture do *not* accurately reflect the values of sub-cultural minorities, or the values practiced in different industries and organizations. Fourth, comparative models (like all models) can never take account of how far non-cultural factors may influence a particular event. Nevertheless, the examples discussed below show that when applied within their limitations to specific tasks, comparative models have significant strengths.

2.2.1   Kluckhohn and Strodtbeck

Kluckhohn and Strodtbeck (1961) designed an early comparative model, which has been widely influential. It claimed that members of a culture group exhibited constant "orientations" towards the world and other people. Different cultures could be compared on the basis of their different orientations.

Table 2.1

Orientations	Range of variations
1 What is the nature of people?	Good (changeable/unchangeable) Evil (changeable/unchangeable) A mixture of good and evil
2 What is the person's relationship to nature?	Dominant In harmony Subjugation
3 What is the person's relationship to other people?	Lineal (hierarchical) Collateral (collectivist) Individualist
4 What is the modality of human activity?	Doing Being Containing
5 What is the temporal focus of human activity?	Future Present Past
6 What is the conception of space?	Private Public Mixed

The model distinguished six basic orientations. These asked about the culture group's perceptions of the human condition, and presented a range of variations (possible answers) in response to each orientation (table 2.1). Many later scholars have applied the basic principles.

2.2.2 Applying the Kluckhohn-Strodtbeck model

The Kluckhohn-Strodtbeck model offers valuable insights, but the model is based on anecdotal evidence only, and so the illustrations given in table 2.2 are subjective.

You may or may not agree with the subjective applications of the model shown in the table. However, you can test it further by using it to assess your own culture or a culture you know well. When using it, you will experience uncertainties in making a precise evaluation. For example, supposing that, in a culture oriented to dominating nature, not-for-profit organizations seek harmony with nature. Do they reflect the values of a sub-culture, or does it indicate a change in the culture?

Whatever your opinion, this early comparative model continues to influence how some management scholars think about culture. Scarborough (1998) compares Western

Table 2.2 Implications for management

Orientations	Variations	Implications for management
1 What is the nature of people?	GOOD	Optimistic about other people's motivations and capacities; Theory Y; participation encouraged; trust; direct communication valued
	EVIL	Pessimistic; Theory X; suspicion of peers and subordinates, and of negotiation partners; secretive
	MIXED	Use of middlemen and consultants; a discrepancy between optimistic attitudes and behavior – for instance, the values of open communication are proclaimed – but the message may be vetted by a lawyer
		Example: Mainstream United States culture is optimistic insofar as that any achievement is thought possible if worked for, and humanity is ultimately perfectible – as the millions of self-help books and videos marketed every year demonstrate. But the dependence upon legal remedies to resolve conflict indicates pessimism
2 What is the person's relationship to nature?	DOMINANT	Control and planning (particularly when also "optimistic" – above); imposing one's will on the natural environment, and on the business environment; working to mold the organizational culture
		Example: In cultures with this orientation, the need to dominate natural forces is expressed by attempts to plan and mold the organizational culture and employees' experience of the work environment
	HARMONY	Coexistence; search for common ground; aversion to open conflict within the workplace; respect for different others
	SUBJUGATION	Fatalism; ready acceptance of external control; aversion to independent planning; pessimism about changing the organizational culture
3 What is the person's relationship to other people?	LINEAL (hierarchical)	Respect for authority, and for seniority as determined by age, family, gender; tall organizations; communication on a hierarchical basis

Table 2.2 (cont'd)

Orientations	Variations	Implications for management
	COLLATERAL (collectivist)	Relationships within the group influence attitudes towards work, superiors, other groups. Members of other groups are treated with suspicion. Structures and systems that remove the individual from the group, and that break down group boundaries, are disliked
	INDIVIDUALIST	People primarily perceive themselves as individuals rather than as members of a group. A need for systems that maximize opportunities for personal achievement and status. Interesting work is more likely to be valued. Competition is encouraged. Egalitarian self-images; informal
		Example: In mainstream United States culture, self-identification is achieved through action and performance. Because other persons must be able to recognize this achievement, it has to be visible and measurable. In business, a financial statement provides one measure of success
4 What is the modality of human activity?	DOING	Performance valued, and hence financial and other measures of performance are valued. Work is central to the individual's life; practical orientation. Ambiguities frustrating performance cause anxiety
		Example: In the United States, the failure over several weeks to decide on a winner of the 2000 presidential election caused tension, and a rush of people needing psychiatric help. One psychiatrist commented "The election is causing ambiguity. We are used to there being a winner and loser."[2]
	BEING	Status is derived by birth, age, sex, family, connections more than by achievement. Feelings are valued. Planning is often short-term; spontaneity is valued
		Example: Buddhist cultures believe in reincarnation, which means that the individual is born into his/her present status and circumstances by virtue of actions performed in a previous life, and that struggle is pointless. By avoiding sinful acts and maintaining harmony, you help your chances of being born into a higher position in your next reincarnation

Table 2.2   (*cont'd*)

Orientations	Variations	Implications for management
	CONTAINING	Focus on self-control; striving for balance between feeling and doing; self-inquiring
5 What is the temporal focus of human activity?	FUTURE	Future planning is prioritized; past performance is less important; the concept of change valued. Career planning and training are valued
	PRESENT	Immediate realities are prioritized, and used as the basis of planning; long-term plans are liable to modification; an emphasis on contemporary impact and style
	PAST	The past is used as the model when planning for the future; respect for precedence; need for continuity; respect paid to age
		Example: A Japanese-American manager suggests "If you're having any trouble with a government department in Japan, take along someone who is really old. Japanese bureaucrats respect old people. When I had a problem, I took along a pensioner who used to work for my company and he explained my situation."[3]
6 What is the conception of space?	PRIVATE	Respect for personal ownership; what is private is valued; private meetings are valued. Strangers are kept at a distance
	PUBLIC	Activities conducted in secret are held in suspicion. Social proximity is taken for granted; public meetings are valued
		Example: The introductory case in section 2.1 shows differing perceptions of private and public space
	MIXED	Private and public activities are distinguished

and Chinese cultural differences and finds in Western culture "an aggressive, active approach to nature, technology and progress" and "reliance on reason and the scientific method" whereas Chinese culture embodies "passive, fatalistic submission" and "reliance on precedent, intuition, and wisdom" – reflecting orientations of the person's relationship to nature, and of the temporal focus of human activity.

2.3   Comparing the Influences of Context

Suppose that a visitor enters your office and remarks "It's cool today." The context influences how this utterance should be interpreted. If the room is cold he might be asking you to turn up the heating. If he had complained the previous day about the hot weather, he might mean that the cool was an improvement. If he had enjoyed the heat, the cool might disappoint him.

We interpret and create messages in reference to shared information. This information includes values in the culture, which link members of the culture group and influence how they refer to their contexts when maintaining relationships. That is, members' experiences of context influence how they communicate, and different culture groups respond to their contexts differently.

Hall (1976) distinguished between high-context and low-context cultures. Members of HIGH-CONTEXT cultures depend heavily on their shared experience and interpretation of their cultural environment in creating and interpreting communications. Members of the culture group learn from birth to interpret the covert clues given in these contexts when they communicate, and so much meaning is conveyed indirectly. In languages such as Arabic, Chinese, and Japanese, indirect styles of communication and the capacity to interpret non-verbal signals and indirect illusions are prized. But in LOW-CONTEXT cultures, the environment is less important, and non-verbal behavior is often ignored, and so communicators have to provide more explicit information. Samovar and Porter (1995) distinguish it this way:

> A high-context communication or message is one in which most of the information is already in the person, while very little is in the coded, explicitly transmitted part of the message. A low-context communication is just the opposite; i.e., the mass of the information is vested in the explicit code. *(p. 101)*

2.3.1   High-context cultures

High-context cultures have the following characteristics.

▪ RELATIONSHIPS (both positive and negative) are relatively LONG LASTING, and individuals feel deep personal involvement with each other.

▪ Because so much is communicated by SHARED CODE, communication is economical, fast, and efficient – in a routine situation. High-context cultures fully exploit the communicative context:

> The Japanese talk around the point. [They] think intelligent human beings should be able to discover the point of discourse from the context, which they are careful to provide. *(Hall, 1983, p. 63)*

▪ Communication in high-context cultures employs a far wider range of expression than is usual in Anglo cultures. The Japanese can communicate widely using non-verbal signaling, and non-language utterances constituting HARAGEI or "belly language."

> One Japanese told me that he often wonders of his non-Japanese colleagues, "Why can't they just figure it out by looking at my face?" – because that of course is what Japanese do with each other. . . . Non-word sounds, such as hissing, grunting, growling, and sighing, are just one more way that Japanese communicate without using actual words.
> *(Kopp, 2001, p. 30)*

▮ People in AUTHORITY are PERSONALLY RESPONSIBLE for the actions of subordinates. Loyalties between superiors and subordinates are reciprocal. A Thai employee related:

> "when I was working in a commercial bank in Bangkok there was one mistake in a transaction that I dealt with. My direct boss then took care of the problem solving even though she did not deal with the transaction directly before. It is quite usual for a direct boss to take responsibility for a subordinate's action in Thailand. I think it is reasonable for a subordinate to have high loyalty to such a boss."

▮ AGREEMENTS (between members) tend to be SPOKEN rather than written. This can mean that a written contract is only "best guess." After a contract has been signed in Japan, the Japanese may request further changes. This can prove difficult for their American negotiation partners.

> The American reaction is one of indignation or distress because Americans regard a contract as binding, a stable element in a changing and uncertain world.
> *(Hall, 1987, pp. 128–9)*

This difference is reflected by the different functions of the legal profession in the two societies. The US boasts over 700,000 lawyers – one for every 365 Americans. In 2000 Japan had only 14,433 – one for every 8,576 citizens (Nishiyama, 2000, p. 111). American law is essentially adversarial, whereas Japanese lawyers are more often asked to mediate and resolve difficulties.

▮ INSIDERS and OUTSIDERS are closely DISTINGUISHED; outsiders include, first, non-members of the family, clan, organization, and then foreigners. Nationality can be an emotive issue. In Singapore, the problem of defining national membership and its obligations was illustrated by the case of a woman who had lived there for 23 years, but had been repeatedly denied Permanent Resident status, although her son was a citizen.

> It is a sob story but one that raises larger issues about the ties that bind Singaporeans to Singapore. What does citizenship mean in this nation-state? Should it be a purely political and economic question – or is it ultimately a matter of the heart?[4]

▮ CULTURAL PATTERNS are INGRAINED, and slow to change.

2.3.2 Low-context cultures

Low-context cultures have the opposite characteristics.

- RELATIONSHIPS between individuals are relatively SHORTER in duration, and in general deep personal involvement with others is valued less.
- MESSAGES must be made EXPLICIT, and the sender can depend less on the receiver inferring the message from the context. Members depend less on using non-verbal communication codes. Low-context Anglos tend to feel that explicit logical structures are best for presenting ideas.
- AUTHORITY is DIFFUSED throughout the bureaucratic system and personal responsibility is difficult to pin down.
- AGREEMENTS tend to be WRITTEN rather than spoken. Low-context countries treat contracts as final and legally binding. The obsession with legal precision may bewilder members of high-context cultures. A Chinese negotiator commented:

> "The Americans spend much effort on one word or one sentence in the contract. Sometimes, they even argue non-serious items for a whole week. Then they have to ask approval from their lawyers. Their lawyers are picky and like to find bones in eggs."

- INSIDERS and OUTSIDERS are LESS CLOSELY DISTINGUISHED. This means that foreigners find it relatively easier to adjust. Immigrants find it easier to take nationality – particularly if they have skills.
- CULTURAL PATTERNS are faster to CHANGE.

2.3.3 Applying Hall's model

Hall's model is built on qualitative insights rather than quantitative data, and does not rank different countries. But, in general, high-context cultures include Japan, China, Korea, Vietnam and other Asian countries, and some countries around the Mediterranean and in the Middle East. Low-context countries include the United States, Scandinavian countries, and Germany. But no country exists exclusively at one end of the scale or the other, and all countries show high-context cultural behavior and low-context cultural behavior at different points. The low-context Anglo countries include associations with restricted membership such as Rotary and the Masons, which are higher context organizations than their surrounding culture. These offer members the opportunity to build long-term power and influence both in the association and more generally in society.

France exemplifies a country whose culture is a mix of high- and low-context situations. Insiders and outsiders are distinguished and great importance is associated with speaking the language correctly. But the impersonality of bureaucratic organizations is more typical of low-context cultures.

The model is useful in understanding *why* different cultures might communicate differently, for example in developing business relationships, negotiating with insiders and outsiders, and implementing contracts. It helps explain why family companies in high-context Southeast Asian cultures differ so widely from their equivalents in low-context Anglo cultures.

Hall does not supply numerical data and, hence, comparisons between national cultures can only be made on a subjective basis. He can only support his theory with anecdotes. In general, anecdotes can serve a useful function in illustrating and illuminating arguments, but do not provide hard data from which to develop a model that can be applied.

2.4   Comparing Status and Function

Cross-cultural research conducted by André Laurent examined attitudes to power and relationships. Laurent (1983) analyzed the values of managers in nine European countries (Switzerland, Germany, Denmark, Sweden, United Kingdom, Netherlands, Belgium, Italy, and France) and the United States. Adler, Campbell, and Laurent (1989) collects additional data from the People's Republic of China, Indonesia, and Japan.

The research treats management as a process by which managers express their cultural values. Three points are examined here:

1   How far the manager carries his/her status into the wider context outside the workplace;
2   The manager's capacity to bypass levels in the hierarchy;
3   The manager as expert in contrast to the manager as facilitator.

2.4.1   Managerial status in the wider context

In response to the statement "through their professional activity, managers play an important role in society," the percentages *in agreement* were as follows:

Denmark	32%
United Kingdom	40%
Netherlands	45%
Germany	46%
United States of America	52%
Sweden	54%
Switzerland	65%
Italy	74%
France	76% (Laurent, 1983, p. 80)

These findings show that in France and Italy the manager carries his status into activities outside the workplace. But Danish and British managers are less able to apply their organizational status to influencing their non-work relationships. The British manager who is also a member of a local football club may play under the captaincy of his works foreman; his French or Italian equivalents would be much less likely to face this situation.

An Indonesian manager explained why his culture differed from American culture on this point. He perceived that in the United States, the boss and a low-level employee can be relatively much closer to each other outside the workplace.

"They still respect each other, because they separate the relationship at work from the personal relationship. But in Indonesia, if the person is respected in the office, he will be respected also out of the office in his private life. In the culture he is the boss, wherever he is, and the staff will think that he is the boss, even outside office hours, and they don't have to behave differently than they usually do in the office."

The general implication is that the expatriate manager who expresses his/her status as though at headquarters may confuse subordinates who have different expectations of authority.

2.4.2 Bypassing the hierarchy

The values ascribed to hierarchical structuring affect what information is communicated, how, and to whom. In response to the statement "In order to have efficient work relationships, it is often necessary to bypass the hierarchical line," the national groups responded thus, *in disagreement*:

Sweden	22%
United Kingdom	31%
United States of America	32%
Denmark	37%
Netherlands	39%
Switzerland	41%
Belgium	42%
France	42%
Germany	46%
Italy	75% (Laurent, 1983, p. 86)
People's Republic of China	66% (Adler et al., 1989, p. 64)

These figures have clear implications for the design of cross-cultural projects. For instance, Swedish employees bypass hierarchical lines when direct contact with knowledge sources located elsewhere in the company promises to produce greater efficiency and speed. Swedes are relatively happy working in matrix structures, in which the subordinate reports to two managers on the same hierarchical level. But suppose that they are working in an Italian company; their Italian boss perceives this lack of respect for the hierarchy as insubordinate and threatening. And Italians are unlikely to accept a matrix structure.

On the other hand, Italians working in a Swedish firm seem to lack motivation and initiative when they refuse to approach a knowledge source in some other unit. Italians find security in knowing precisely the rights and limits of their authority. They know who communicates with whom on what topics, and how these communications will be handled. Hence the Italian company tends to be pyramidic, with clearly differentiated hierarchical ranks and power centers. But the Swedish company may have a number of power centers.

2.4.3 The manager as expert vs the manager as facilitator

Adler et al. (1989) asked managers from 13 countries to respond to the statement "It is important for a manager to have at hand precise answers to most of the questions that his subordinates may raise about their work." Percentages *in agreement* were:

Sweden	10%
Netherlands	17%
United States of America	18%
Denmark	23%
United Kingdom	27%
Switzerland	38%
Belgium	44%
Germany	46%
France	53%
Italy	66%
Indonesia	73%
People's Republic of China	74%
Japan	78% (Adler et al., 1989, p. 69)

In a traditional Asian organization, the superior should be able to provide specialist answers to technical questions. Because subordinates cannot easily challenge the advice, they tend to value it above suggestions given by peers, whatever its quality.

The Asian manager who cannot answer questions loses status. Because the unity of the group depends on their superior's maintaining his/her hierarchical position, his/her loss of status would endanger the security of the entire group, and so also the interests of its individual members. So it is in their interests to maintain their superior's status. This may mean that they restrict questions to topics on which they know that the superior is technically competent.

At the opposite extreme (say, in Sweden) it is more important that the manager should be able to tap sources of expert power, perhaps elsewhere in the company, than give all the technical answers him/herself. The Swede is less inhibited about approaching an outsider for advice.

Whereas the Swedish manager uses hierarchical structuring to facilitate problem solving and organization, the Indonesian values it as a means of signaling who has authority over whom. So, when planning a project, the Swede first identifies the necessary functions then looks for the right people to fill them. But the Indonesian places most value on social harmony, and assesses the potential of a project on the basis of who will be involved in the different positions.

2.5   Comparing Values in the Workplace

Hofstede's research goes further in showing how national culture affects the values of the workplace. This book focuses on the 1984, 1991, 1997, and 2001 versions of his IBM study. The findings demonstrated that:

- work-related values are *not* universal;
- when a multinational headquarters tries to impose the same norms on all its foreign interests, their local values are likely to persist;
- local values determine how headquarters regulations are interpreted;
- by implication, a multinational that insists on organizational uniformity across its foreign investments is in danger of creating morale problems and inefficiencies.

Hofstede's research compared work-related values across a range of cultures. He investigated the attitudes held by 116,000 employees in branches and affiliates of IBM, in 50 countries and three regions (East Africa, comprising Ethiopia, Kenya, Tanzania, and Zambia; West Africa, comprising Ghana, Nigeria, and Sierra Leone; and Arab countries comprising Egypt, Iraq, Kuwait, Lebanon, and Saudi Arabia). Comparisons between the different cultures were plotted across at first four, later five dimensions, largely independent of each other. These are:

1 *Power distance*: the distance between individuals at different levels of a hierarchy.
2 *Uncertainty avoidance*: more or less need to avoid uncertainty about the future.
3 *Individualism versus collectivism*: the relations between the individual and his/her fellows.
4 *Masculinity versus femininity*: the division of roles and values in society.
5 *Long- versus short-term orientation*: temporal orientation towards life. (This dimension was developed in 1987, later than the four base dimensions, and was tested in 23 countries.)

A breakdown of the countries and regions covered in the study is shown in table 2.3. The abbreviations given correspond to the findings presented in figures 2.1 and 2.2 below.

2.5.1   Power distance

Hofstede's findings for power distance are shown in figure 2.1 on the horizontal axis. This shows power distances least in Austria and Israel and greatest in Malaysia.

The power distance dimension measures how different national cultures cope with inequalities in society and their effects on the workplace. No country is entirely free from hierarchies, which may arise from physical and mental differences, social status, legal rights, wealth, power, and education. But while some nations accept them and

Table 2.3 Key to the countries and regions

Abbreviation	Country or region	Abbreviation	Country or region
ARA	Arab-speaking countries	ISR	Israel
	(Egypt, Iraq, Kuwait,	ITA	Italy
	Lebanon, Libya,	JAM	Jamaica
	Saudi Arabia,	JPN	Japan
	United Arab Emirates)	KOR	South Korea
ARG	Argentina	MAL	Malaysia
AUL	Australia	MEX	Mexico
AUT	Austria	NET	Netherlands
BEL	Belgium	NOR	Norway
BRA	Brazil	NZL	New Zealand
CAN	Canada	PAK	Pakistan
CHL	Chile	PAN	Panama
COL	Colombia	PER	Peru
COS	Costa Rica	PHI	Philippines
DEN	Denmark	POR	Portugal
EAF	East Africa (Ethiopia,	SAF	South Africa
	Kenya, Tanzania,	SAL	Salvador
	Zambia)	SIN	Singapore
EQA	Equador	SPA	Spain
FIN	Finland	SWE	Sweden
FRA	France	SWI	Switzerland
GBR	Great Britain	TAI	Taiwan
GER	Germany F.R.	THA	Thailand
GRE	Greece	TUR	Turkey
GUA	Guatemala	URU	Uruguay
HOK	Hong Kong	USA	United States
IDO	Indonesia	VEN	Venezuela
IND	India	WAF	West Africa (Ghana,
IRA	Iran		Nigeria, Sierra Leone)
IRE	Ireland (Republic of)	YUG	Yugoslavia

Source: from Hofstede (1997, p. 35)

even encourage them (for example, by giving their elites privileged access to political power, good medical services and university education, and low taxation), others try to minimize them (for example, by taxing the rich at higher rates than the poor and giving all the same access to social services). In the Scandinavian countries, inequalities are reduced by educational policy:

> In Norwegian schools, grades no longer exist for pre-teen students and the message in classrooms throughout the region is that to be average is to be safe.[5]

Uncertainty avoidance index

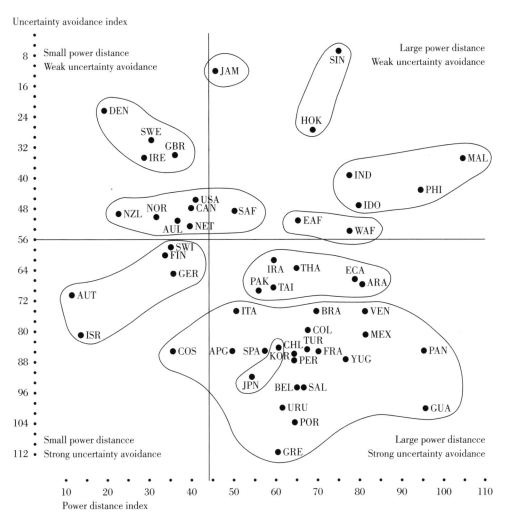

Figure 2.1   Uncertainty avoidance × power distance
Source: from Hofstede (2001, p. 152)

An Australian political scientist noted that:

Australians have always had a tendency to cut down tall poppies, our sporting heroes excepted. We are extremely cynical about most of our leaders.[6]

When the German tennis champion Boris Becker returned to Germany from the tax haven of Monte Carlo, he was convicted of tax evasion.

He told *Die Zeit* magazine that he was disappointed by the way he had been treated. "Stars here are first destroyed so that they can fit into the system."[7]

Hierarchies are seen as convenience arrangements rather than as having existential justification. Managers see themselves as practical and systematic and admit the need for support.

Subordinates expect to be consulted when important decisions are made, and prefer a participative superior with whom they can disagree without feeling at risk. They dislike close supervision. They find it easier to cooperate with each other, and interdependence is stressed. In the wealthier lower power distance cultures, technical education is used to acquire expert power rather than to signal social status.

In countries where power distances are relatively high, the opposite values are found. Hierarchies are more respected. In China, for example:

> when keeping an appointment, the Chinese visitor may arrive 25 to 30 minutes early if the host is a person of senior age and high status, because the visitor wants to show respect for the host by not keeping him waiting even a second. This may be strange to a Westerner, but the Chinese quite naturally accept social inequality.
>
> *(Zhou, 2000, pp. 18–19)*

In the Cameroons in 2002, African Nations Cup soccer players were late returning to their European clubs because they were made to return to their capital

> . . . to meet the country's president, who, unfortunately, was busy and could not see the squad until later in the week. The players' passports were taken away, ensuring that they could not leave until the presidential handshake had been received.[8]

Managers are expected to make decisions autocratically and paternalistically. Less powerful people feel themselves dependent on the more powerful. Employees manage their work according to what the manager wants – or what they intuit he or she wants.

Managers show relatively little consideration but like to see themselves as benevolent decision-makers. Employees find it easier to cooperate with superiors than with peers, unless under the direction of a powerful superior respected by all. Coercive and referent powers are stressed over reward, expert, and legitimate powers. Children treat parents with respect.

2.5.2 Uncertainty avoidance

Everywhere, life is uncertain. No one can be entirely certain of the future, or about relationships with others. This dimension measures how far cultures socialize their members into tolerating uncertainty about the future and ambiguous situations.

In cultures where needs to avoid uncertainty are higher, members appear anxiety-prone and devote more energy to "beating the future" and stabilizing relationships in the workplace. In Japan, the unwillingness to take risks (Hofstede, 2001, p. 161) is shown by the 54 percent of household assets being held in cash and bank deposits compared with only 10 percent in the US and 21 per cent in the UK.

Expert managers are preferred to facilitators, and clear rules and precise job descriptions are expected. Subordinates are given little opportunity to take their own initiatives. Individuals are relatively less entrepreneurial. Job security, career patterning, and detailed retirement plans are expected. Opponents may be accused of deliberately spreading confusion and rumours. In Kuwait, a politician warned that:

> ... since the countdown for elections has started ... rumours will fill the arena, along with contradictions and irresponsible statements which will not benefit Kuwait.[9]

Members of cultures with lower needs to avoid uncertainty experience lower levels of anxiety and job stress. They may be more willing to take risks, and be less resistant to change. Swedes, for instance, suppress emotion, and see shyness as a positive trait and talkativeness as a negative one.[10] In business life they prize the rational above the sentimental; Swedish firms are avid appliers of new technology and ruthless in scrapping what is old and inefficient. Trade unions, which are often represented on the boards of companies, may accept job cuts if there are rational arguments to back them.[11]

In these cultures, managers are of lower than average age in higher level jobs. Little virtue is attached to loyalty to the boss. Managers may be generalists and build their careers on facilitating skills. (A hospital manager in the north of England had previously managed a railway company and in the job before that, a theme park.) Interorganizational conflict is considered natural, even desirable, and compromise is an accepted route for reconciliation. The manager breaks formal rules and bypasses hierarchical structures if necessary. Foreigners are accepted as managers with relative ease.

Until recently, the occupational elite in Japan could still hope for life-long employment with one employer, which helped meet their needs for security. In response to a question about cultural problems that arise when dealing with American and Japanese employees, the CEO of Nomura Securities explained the firm's different employment systems:

> the American employment system at Nomura is by contract. Under that system, we are prepared to pay the best possible price now. The Japanese employment system, in contrast, is very traditional – step-by-step. Our Japanese employees give up part of today's salary to enjoy guarantees of future employment and income. Every few years, everyone gets promoted at the same time. If our American employees would accept the Japanese system, we would be glad to offer it. But as of today, no American has signed up for it.
>
> *(Schrage, 1989, p. 74)*

Of course, in an ideal world everyone would be able to have high salary *and* security, but in a world when only one of those options was possible, the Americans – being willing to accept future uncertainty and needing to express their achievement in high rewards – chose salary; and the Japanese – having greater needs to avoid uncertainty – bought security at the price of salary.

2.5.3 *Individualism versus collectivism*

This describes the relationship between the individual and the group to which he/she belongs. The more individualist cultures stress individual identity. The person is expected to achieve for him/herself, and to satisfy his/her own needs. Individual achievements and rights are respected; in business, managers are expected to work hard for their rewards, but those who do not deserve their salaries may be censored. A 2003 MORI poll conducted in the United Kingdom found that:

> 78 per cent of Britons think that company directors are overpaid and 80 percent think that they can not be trusted. Ordinary people are outraged by what they see as excessive executive rewards that seem to bear no relation to performance.[12]

Competition is expected. In the United States, the law courts serve the function of testing individuals' rights both against authority and each other. For example, George W. Bush and Al Gore contested their rival claims to have won the Presidential Election of 2000 through the court system up to the Supreme Court.

Individual decisions are valued above group decisions, and the individual has a right to thoughts and opinions which differ from those held by the majority. The manager aims for variety rather than conformity in work and does not have strong emotional connections with the company. He/she is loyal for as long as this suits his/her interests; that is, loyalty is calculative.

Individualism may be expressed by rebellion against conformity, even when the rebellion is symbolic. A television commercial advertised "Hugo. The fragrance from Hugo Boss. Don't imitate, innovate."[13] Like any advertisement, this attempts to create a mass response from consumers all conforming to an image of individuality.

Social philosophies in individualist cultures tend to reflect universalistic concerns with society, rather than the needs of a particular group or family. Political correctness reflects a sense that one should be "fair" to all, and can lead to dreary conformity. The positive side is that by 1995, 80 million Americans were volunteering their unpaid labor in various causes.[14] They might otherwise have spent this time in increasing their personal wealth. But this statistic suggests a capacity for great altruism, and contradicts the opinion of a Japanese manager: "in Japanese we interpret individualism to mean selfishness." In practice, individualism can *not* be equated with greed – which arises in any cultural context.

In the more collectivist cultures, the opposite conditions apply. Group interests prevail over individual interests, and the individual derives his/her social identity from the groups of which he/she is a member – including family, school class, work unit. A premium is placed on loyalty to group members, which may be placed above efficiency. Andrews and Chompusri (2001) comment:

> The collectivist nature of Thai business culture is . . . expressed in the manner "insiders" and "outsiders" are tightly distinguished in organizational sub-culture. Loyalty is expected between group members – as within a family – because they are considered to share the same world-views, and communicate more efficiently in routine situations.   *(p. 81)*

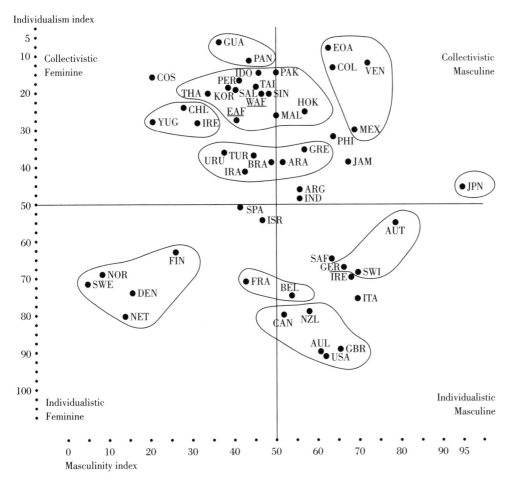

Figure 2.2 Individualism/collectivism × masculinity/femininity
Source: from Hofstede (2001, p. 294)

This distinction between insiders and outsiders was voiced by a Thai ex-prime minister after the crisis of 1997:

> "Those in a position of responsibility for the Kingdom's administration should offer only constructive criticism," [General Prem Tinsulanonda] said. . . . "If foreigners think that people in this country are not united, then trade and investment which are essential to our economic recovery will not take place."[15]

But the greater the loyalty to the group, the greater may be competition with other groups. An example from Vietnam shows units within a single organization (city government) in competition – resulting in organizational paralysis.

Rivalry between institutions is endemic whether it is between party and government, between the centre and city, or between every conceivable combination of offices within the city itself. . . . At the root of this rivalry is a struggle to maintain control over regulatory, inspection and licensing responsibilities and to head off encroachments by rival offices.[16]

2.5.4 *Masculinity versus femininity*

In "masculine" cultures, sex roles are sharply differentiated. Some occupations are reserved for men, and some for women. For example, few men are primary school teachers and few women senior politicians. In Japan, few women reach the top levels of management, and they are normally expected to stay at home after marriage and bring up the children. A 1999 survey found that men with children under six years old spend 17 minutes a day caring for them, while women spend an average of 2 hours and 39 minutes.[17] The social ideal is performance, and the maintenance of economic growth has top priority. Employees may think time spent on company business is more valuable than time spent with the family; the manager expects staff to work on Saturdays rather than stay at home, and they are happy to do this. Men are supposed to be competitive and assertive, and women tender and able to take care of relationships.

In the more feminine cultures, sex roles are less sharply distinguished, and men and women have more equal access to the same jobs at all levels. For example, both may be senior politicians, airline pilots, nurses, or primary school teachers. In a family, the better paid parent might go to work, whether male or female, and the parent with less earning power stays at home to bring up the children. Modesty in both sexes is valued. The company should not interfere in its employees' private lives. Achievement is measured in terms of human contacts, rather than of power and property, and motivation is less. Members stress relating to others rather than competing. Individual brilliance is suspect and the outsider and anti-hero are regarded sympathetically.

In 1995 in Norway – a highly feminine culture in Hofstede's terms – a shelter for abused women opened its doors to men who had been battered and tyrannized by their wives or girlfriends. This opened up a debate over whether the government-sponsored shelters should help anyone in need regardless of sex, or whether men should start their own – thus discriminating.[18]

2.5.5 *Long- versus short-term orientation*

The long-term orientation (LTO) dimension was developed only in 1987 when researchers working in the Confucian cultures attempted to develop a culturally based research instrument that correlated with Hofstede's original model. They failed to identify a dimension equivalent to uncertainty avoidance because, Hofstede argues, uncertainty and its antithesis "truth" are not major concerns in the region whereas they are in the West. And researchers using the original four dimensions in the West had failed to identify the importance of "virtue" which is of greater concern in Pacific Asia.

Hofstede (1991) described the principles of Confucianism thus:

- the stability of society is based upon unequal relationships between people;
- the family is the prototype of all social organizations;
- virtuous behavior towards others consists of not treating others as one would not like to be treated oneself;
- virtue with regard to one's task in life consists of trying to acquire skills and education, working hard, not spending more than necessary, being patient, and persevering. (p. 165)

The values observed in the long-term orientation dimension are labeled "Confucian" because, at both poles, the values seem to be taken straight from the teachings of Confucius. Cultures with a long-term orientation demonstrate the values of persistence; ordering relationships by status and observing this order; thrift; and having a sense of shame. Cultures with a short-term orientation demonstrate values of personal steadiness and stability; protecting one's face; respect for tradition; reciprocation of greetings, favors, and gifts.

Hofstede (2001) lists the index values for the 23 countries as shown in table 2.4.

Table 2.4   Long-term orientation dimension index

Score rank	Country or region	LTO score
1	China	118
2	Hong Kong	96
3	Taiwan	87
4	Japan	80
5	South Korea	75
6	Brazil	65
7	India	61
8	Thailand	56
9	Singapore	48
10	Netherlands	44
11	Bangladesh	40
12	Sweden	33
13	Poland	32
14	Germany (F.R.)	31
15	Australia	31
16	New Zealand	30
17	United States	29
18	Great Britain	25
19	Zimbabwe	25
20	Canada	23
21	Philippines	19
22	Nigeria	16
23	Pakistan	00

Source: from Hofstede (2001, p. 356)

2.5.6   The weaknesses of Hofstede's model

Over the years, Hofstede's model has been enormously influential. Very many academic papers on cross-cultural issues cite his work in the bibliography. But he has also attracted criticism (see Roberts and Boyacigiller, 1984), and his achievements are still much debated; a recent paper by McSweeney (2002) doubts the plausibility of a series of assumptions built into the study. He is answered in a useful paper by Smith (2002).

First (like all national cultural studies), it assumes that NATIONAL TERRITORY and the limits of the culture correspond. He does not argue that all members of a nation share their culture to the same degree but that the culture reflects central tendencies, representing a statistical average based on individuals' views. Nevertheless, there must still be some assumption of cultural homogeneity within the national group. But this is bound to vary, and the spread is bound to be greater in countries which include a range of sub-culture groups or with socially dominant and inferior culture groups: the United States, Brazil, Switzerland (French, German, Italian, and Romansch cultures); Belgium (French and Flemish cultures); Spain (Basque, Catalan, and Castilian). The break-up of Yugoslavia during the 1990s and continuing resistance to unified control among the different national cultures comprising the European Union demonstrates the futility of trying to create tight political units from disparate cultures. Smith (2002) is generally sympathetic to Hofstede's work, but admits that:

> It is very possible that societies differ in the degree to which they hang together in a unified manner. *(p. 56)*

Second, Hofstede's informants worked within a SINGLE INDUSTRY (the computer industry) and a single multinational. This raises the question of how far each IBM unit can be considered culturally typical of the country in which it is based (see McSweeney, 2002, p. 101). It can be argued that the values of IBM employees are typical only to a small group (educated, generally middle class, city dwelling); other social groups (for instance, unskilled manual workers, public sector employees, family entrepreneurs, etc.) are more or less unrepresented. Also, it seems unlikely that in each country the same segment of the population chose to work for IBM. At the time this research was conducted, IBM represented established bureaucratic capitalism in the United States, and American employees might be looking for a long-term career in a safe high-status occupation. But elsewhere different employment pools might be attracted. In rapidly developing countries, employees might be young graduates needing to gain experience and credentials in a Western multinational before leaving when still young to start their own firms or return to the family business.

Third, there are questions of BIAS in the QUESTIONNAIRE RESPONSES. McSweeney (2002) argues that the:

> Administration of the survey and the ownership of its results were IBM's; some of the questionnaires were completed within groups and not individually. *(p. 103)*

Further, some respondents had foreknowledge that their managers might develop new policies on the basis of the survey results. This possibility of bias is compounded by a general difficulty afflicting cross-cultural survey research, the respondents' sense of their relationship to the survey instrument. In some cultures there seems to be a greater willingness to treat the questionnaire objectively; elsewhere, the notion of confidentiality is treated with skepticism and respondents provide answers that they hope will match the expectations of their superiors.

Fourth, TECHNICAL difficulties; intuition suggests that some of the connotations listed above overlap. For instance, we find:

Small power distance:	Large power distance:
Powerful people try to look less powerful than they are (Hofstede, 1997, p. 43)	Powerful people try to look as impressive as possible
Feminine:	Masculine:
Everybody is supposed to be modest (Hofstede, 1997, p. 96)	Men are supposed to be assertive, ambitious, and tough

Suppose that you come to a country of which you have no prior knowledge and you observe that managers normally defer to subordinates who possess particular expertise. Are you observing the effects of small power distances, or of high femininity?

2.5.7 *Defining the dimensions: e.g. individualism/collectivism*

Typically of comparative models, the model actually says very little about any one culture except in terms of other cultures; Culture X is more individualist than Culture A, but less individualist than Culture B. This would not be problematic if the phenomenon of individualism meant precisely the same in both Culture A and Culture B, their differing only in terms of quantity. This point applies to all other dimensions; do "uncertainty avoidance," "power distance," and "masculinity" have precisely the same meaning in all national cultures? Hofstede's data provide one reason for saying not; each score represents the mean for a bundle of approximately 32 values questions associated with the dimension, not a single question. Any comparative study has problems in defining dimensions in terms that can be applied in different contexts. The individualism/collectivism dimension is examined here by way of illustration.

We have seen that Hofstede applied the Anglo concept of individualism – that is, in terms of the need to achieve and competitiveness. But other emphases are possible. Schwartz and Sagie (2000) suggest that the many variations in the meanings of these terms can be explained by different political systems and stages of economic development (see Smith 2002, p. 129). Writing from a Polish perspective, Czarniawska (1986) referred to American individualism in the United States as a choice made in preference to cooperation. Brummelhuis (1984) explains the Thai concept in terms of avoidance and distrust of authority.

> The individual's preoccupation is not so much with self-realization and autonomy as with adaptation to the social or cosmological environment.   *(pp. 44–5)*

In other words, he or she resorts to individual solutions as a reaction to social pressures and as a means of escaping them. This defines individualism in negative terms, and differs from the highly positive definition usually applied to American culture.

Likewise, "collectivist" behavior in one context might have different connotations elsewhere. For instance, Japanese collectivism is organization-based whereas Chinese collectivism is family-based. In a Japanese multinational, Japanese management might perceive that the Taiwanese employee who places his family interests above those of the company is disloyal to their shared identity and cannot be fully trusted.

2.5.8 Is Hofstede out of date?

It is sometimes argued that whether or not Hofstede's model is valid, it is now out of date. An obvious example is presented by the break-up of Yugoslavia, which he treated as a national unit. On the other hand, Sondergaard (1994) discussed 61 works replicating Hofstede's model and found that the four base dimensions are "largely confirmed." Smith, Dugan, and Trompenaars (1996) studied 8,841 informants from "business organizations" in 43 countries, including Bulgaria, Czechoslovakia, Hungary, Rumania, the former USSR, and other formerly communist countries. Their work confirmed two of Hofstede's dimensions – individualism/collectivism and power distance. To represent values that then predominated in Eastern Europe, these dimensions could be redefined as loyal/utilitarian involvement with groups and conservatism/egalitarian commitments. Smith (1994) concluded that:

> There are no indications that the cultural diversity mapped by Hofstede is in process of disappearing. Recent studies show just as much diversity as those done earlier. *(p. 10)*

Lowe (1996) examined Hofstede's question "do American theories apply abroad?" in the context of Hong Kong and found that often they did not, despite the popularity of the American MBA. Merritt (1999) conducted a replication study of Hofstede's base four dimensions with 9,000 male commercial airline pilots in 18 countries. The dimensions of power distance and individualism/collectivism were replicated successfully. The dimensions of uncertainty avoidance and masculinity/femininity showed only moderate replicability – for technical reasons associated with the industry.

In sum, the evidence for arguing that Hofstede's findings are no longer applicable is inconclusive.

2.5.9   The strengths of Hofstede's model

The weaknesses are dwarfed by the strengths of Hofstede's work in comparing cultures and applying cultural analysis to practical management problems.

■ The INFORMANT POPULATION (IBM employees) is relatively CONTROLLED across countries, which means comparisons can be made. This is a strength despite the difficulty of generalizing to other occupational groups within the same national culture (see section 2.5.6, the second point.) The problem of representation is real, but this would occur in any international organization selected as an informant pool. And worse problems arise if one attempts to use a range of pools. At an extreme, data derived from, say, American IBM employees, Japanese advertising executives, Spanish bank staff, employees of a Vietnamese family trading, lack any occupational common basis and hence useful comparisons cannot be made.
■ The DIMENSIONS tap into deep cultural values and make significant comparisons between national cultures.
■ The connotations of each dimension are RELEVANT to management. The comparisons that can be made are of immediate interest to the international manager concerned with establishing and implementing management structures and systems.
■ No other study compares so many other national cultures in so much detail. Simply, this is THE BEST THERE IS.

2.5.10   Applying Hofstede's model

Hofstede's model is most useful when its limitations are respected. It cannot be applied to describing individual psychology or organizational culture. It does *not* present detailed analyses of individual cultures. It does *not* distinguish between, say, entirely individualist and entirely collectivist cultures. It offers sets of comparisons. To take an example, Thai culture is *more* collectivist (and less individualist) than, say, Australian culture; but *more* individualist (and less collectivist) than, say, Malaysian culture.

In practice, the research findings may have to be modified to the *specific* situation and needs. The manager who needs to understand a particular setting might always be wise to supplement comparative findings by the single-culture research conducted by anthropologists. In addition, he or she is likely to be concerned with making decisions for a specific industry and organization, and for this needs an understanding of industry standards and the organizational culture.

Finally, the manager needs to take into account how far the target situation equates to Hofstede's informant pool – IBM. Members of an organization participating in the same industry are likely to share many of the same characteristics, and the manager might feel more inclined to take the IBM findings on trust. On the other hand the national culture reflected in an organization far removed from IBM might demand greater attention in checking how far they can be generalized. For example, the IBM findings might be relatively accurate when applied to some other computer manufacturer hiring from the same labor pools and located in the same urban environment, but be more questionable when applied to, say, a food producer based in a rural area of the country.

Here are some guidelines as to how Hofstede's findings might be applied. First, review the similarities *and* differences between your situation and that of Hofstede's research sample (within the same country), and decide how the differences affect your application of the model to the target workforce. In particular:

- look for sub-cultural and regional differences;
- look for industry differences;
- look for differences arising from the organizational culture.

Second, Hofstede's research indicates which orientation *most* members of a culture group are likely to adopt in routine situations. It does not make hard and fast predictions that apply in all circumstances. You are chiefly concerned to explain behavior in normal circumstances and not in exceptional times.

It is a mistake to assume that his research profiles describe only the values accepted by the power elite or by those who seem most likely to benefit from their expression. In practice, the majority endorse their shared culture, even though an outsider might perceive that they are its victims. The implication is that members' cultural values must be inferred from their behavior in routine circumstances and not be their ideals of how they think they should behave and their attitudes, or by the outsider's values and attitudes.

2.6   Implications for the Manager

Compare an organization that you know well in *your own culture* (Organization A) and a similar organization in *some other culture* (Organization B).

1 Review Hall's explanations of high- and low-context cultures (section 2.3) and apply it to the two organizations. What differences do you find in the following?
   (a)   Management–staff communications in Organization A and Organization B.
   (b)   Relations between peers in Organization A and Organization B.
2 Which of these is more likely to be rewarded or punished in Organization A and Organization B?
   (a)   The individual follows his/her job specification to the letter, whatever the task.
   (b)   The individual departs from his/her job specification when this seems more efficient.
   (c)   The individual follows authorized reporting procedures, whatever the task.
   (d)   The individual departs from authorized reporting procedures when this seems more efficient.

3 In which organization:
   (a) Is the manager more likely to participate with his/her subordinates as an equal?
   (b) Is competition in the workplace more likely to be tolerated?
   (c) Are hiring and promotion decisions more likely to be based on group membership?
   (d) Are male and female jobs distinguished?

How far do your answers reflect Hofstede's comparisons for the two cultures in which the organizations are based?

2.7 SUMMARY

This chapter has discussed how far national cultures can be effectively analyzed on a comparative basis, and has examined various models making cross-cultural comparisons.

Section 2.2 dealt with the KLUCKHOHN-STRODTBECK model of CULTURAL ORIENTATIONS. Section 2.3 examined HALL's notion of CULTURAL CONTEXTS, which shows how cultures vary in the way their members define and utilize the context when communicating and developing relationships. Section 2.4 examined LAURENT's concepts of CULTURE, STATUS, and FUNCTION. Section 2.5 discussed HOFSTEDE's work. The parameters of power distance, uncertainty avoidance, collectivism/individualism, masculinity/femininity, and long-/short-term orientation were discussed. Despite the weaknesses of this model, it is the most comprehensive and most used of all. Its strengths deserve respect.

2.8 EXERCISE

Use the models discussed in this chapter to decide whether the behavior described in the last sentence of each of the following might be *typical* or *untypical* in the culture, and explain your answers.

1 In the United Kingdom, you discover that a junior employee is the daughter of an influential politician, and so you promote her to a senior job. She is a poor communicator and unqualified. Nevertheless, this promotion is happily accepted by (almost) all other employees.

2 At company headquarters, you form a mixed-culture work team consisting of Japanese men and Swedish women, and chaired by a woman. These persons have been temporarily borrowed from your subsidiaries in Tokyo and Stockholm. The team is neither compatible nor productive.

3 You are posted to a newly acquired subsidiary in Turkey. You discover that your peer's subordinates are unwilling to come to you for advice even though they know that your

technical skills can help them solve their professional problems.

4 In Australia, the great majority of your employees opt to take relatively low salaries in return for guarantees of life-time employment.

5 In Nepal, an employee asks for your help to solve a family problem with his brother-in-law because you are "an important person in the community."

6 In Sweden, your subsidiary is losing money. You decide to introduce new technology, which means scrapping the previous technology and retraining many in the workforce. The outcomes of making the change are uncertain; the technology might be a great success, but if it fails, all will suffer. The workforce quickly accept your proposals.

Notes

1 Justin Webster, "Germans outrage Majorcans with plans for political party," *Sunday Telegraph*, September 6, 1998.

2 Philip Delves Broughton, "Shrinks clean up in election mess," *Daily Telegraph*, November 22, 2000.

3 I am indebted to Ms. Laurie Sugita for this example.

4 Tan Harn How, "Getting to the heart of citizenship," *The Straits Times*, November 9, 2002.

5 Tyler Marshall, "The Scandinavian good life: would a few hurdles hurt?" *International Herald Tribune*, December 15, 1988.

6 "Australians elect to go Howard's way," *Daily Telegraph*, March 4, 1996.

7 AP, Hamburg, "Becker regrets going home," *Daily Telegraph*, November 15, 2002.

8 Christopher Davies, "Arsenal counting on Campbell to stand tall," *Daily Telegraph*, February 19, 2002.

9 "No cancellation of power, water bills," *Kuwait Times*, February 11, 1996.

10 "Cool as a Swede," *The Economist*, May 6, 1989.

11 Alan Elsner, Reuter, "Research says Sweden can banish emotion from life," *Bangkok Post*, January 30, 1989.

12 Tom Lloyd, "Personal View," *Daily Telegraph*, July 14, 2003.

13 Commercial for Hugo Boss. Music TV, aired in December 1998.

14 George F. Will, "Sprawling, metastasizing, undisciplined, approaching self-parody," *International Herald Tribune*, January 30, 1995.

15 "Time to button our lips," *The Nation* (Bangkok), December 20, 2001.

16 Martin Gainsborough, "The Ho Chi Minh City elite," *The Vietnam Business Journal*, November 23, 2000.

17 Juliet Hindell, "New age for Japan's fathers," *Sunday Telegraph*, May 2, 1999.

18 "European topics: Norwegian men beating at door of shelter for abused women," *International Herald Tribune*, March 2, 1995.

CHAPTER THREE
Shifts in the Culture

3.1   Introduction

In Brazil, the largest tribe of Amazonian Indians has been pushed close to extinction as the result of contact with outside people. (Watson et al., 2000). Time and time again the Guarani have been forced to abandon their settlements in the Southwest of Brazil. They have a history of being exploited and murdered by colonists, the Brazilian army and police, traders and ranchers, and even those Brazilian agencies supposed to protect Indian rights. In the past 200 years they have lost about 95 percent of their ancestral territory, and have declined in number from about 1.5 million to 27,000 today.

   Indian land ownership rights are not acknowledged by the Brazilian government even though they are established in international law. The sites which they now occupy are too small to support their traditional occupations of hunting and gathering, and too dry to sustain farming. The water is too polluted for fish. Forced to find work to prevent their families starving, many of the men have been recruited by sugar cane factories for as little as $10 a week. Used to a barter economy, they have found it hard to adjust to the rules of the market.[1] Alcoholism is widespread, and many women are forced to prostitute themselves.

The Guarani culture has been devastated. Community and family structures have broken down, and sacred rituals come to a halt. Most serious, the sense of hopelessness and loss of identity has led to a wave of suicides, particularly among the young. More than 280 Guarani have taken their own lives in the past 10 years, including 26 children under the age of 14 who have poisoned or hanged themselves.

This example indicates the damage that outside intervention can inflict on a once healthy culture. The case of the Guarani is extreme (although not as extreme as that of many other Brazilian tribes, which have been entirely exterminated; see Watson et al., 2000). However, it is not unusual. In Africa, Asia, and elsewhere, many examples can be found of cultures that have been severely damaged by pressures for change. The concept of the "failed state" has emerged to explain those societies that have become unable to manage their own affairs, and are under the control of international authorities.

In modern Anglo cultures it is often taken for granted that material change is always to be desired. But material change can affect the culture, and it cannot be taken for granted that the effects are always positive. Under what conditions does change lead to growth in the culture, and under what conditions is it destructive?

This chapter examines problems of identifying the positive and negative effects of material and economic change on the culture, the causes of cultural shift, and the implications for the international manager.

3.2   Recognizing Significant Shifts in the Culture

In all areas of life, including the workplace, people must adjust to transition. Today's manager has to develop skills of identifying those events that cause shifts in the value system, and to predict how these cultural shifts will influence the business environment.

Because changes in the business environment may have a direct impact on the manager's company and its relations with markets, he/she needs to understand shifts in the culture. For example, these shifts may lead to changes in:

- service and product markets (demands for consumer goods, and for technologies);
- industries (old industries disappear, new industries are born);
- the labor market (old skills fall out of demand, new skills are at a premium; new social groups seek employment – e.g. in many economies, increasing numbers of women are entering the managerial workforce);
- needs of the workforce (employees need different relations with superiors, peers, and subordinates; new structures and systems are needed to organize and motivate performance);
- relations with the green environment (new regulations may have to be imposed in order to protect natural resources);
- social structures, which mean that new social agencies are developed and old agencies take on new responsibilities.

Changes in work patterns and technologies force changes in the traditional extended family and a weakening of traditional family ties. In Malaysia, increasing numbers of children are "experiencing a sense of loss and support" and are running away from home. These "unknown disappearances" rose from 1,500 in 1992 to 4,000 in 1995.[2]

Social breakdown means that governments and not-for-profit organizations have to invest more in family welfare, marriage counseling, and tackling social problems among the young.

3.2.1 Stability and change

Cultures need both stability and change in order to develop. On the one hand, excessive stability removes the need for experiment and creativity; on the other, excessive change can lead to fragmentation and total breakdown – as the introductory case demonstrates.

For centuries, scholars have tried to find the optimal balance between stability and change. Conflict theorists such as Marx, Mills, Dahrendorf, and others perceived all social systems to be in continual conflict; and the point of conflict is reflected in the society's predominant values. Functionalists such as Parsons and Merton described change as an adjustment process and focused on the natural capacity of social systems to adapt to strains and stresses in order to find a new stability. Social systems are functional when all parts are related and integrated.

The approach followed here is functional. Figure 3.1 indicates why shifts in the culture affect the business. It shows:

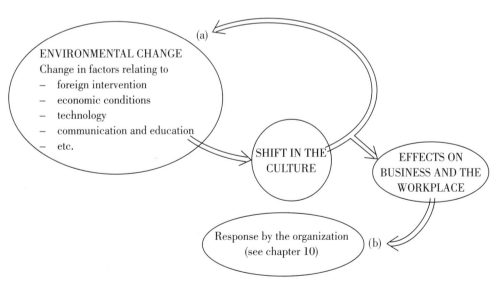

Figure 3.1 The process of change and shift

■ CIRCULARITY in change factors. The arrow labeled (a) indicates that environmental changes cause shifts in cultural values, which lead to new perceptions of the environment and its further change. The model shows a continuing PROCESS of adjustment. For instance, labor costs in the United States increased to the point that American electronics producers moved their manufacturing facilities to Mexico. Because females were more dextrous and docile than males, managers recruited more females. This change in the labor force caused role reversal and disruption, and forced men to emigrate to find work. The culture of male dominance was undermined as traditional distinctions between "man's work" and "woman's work" eroded. Women had more control over family income and demanded new goods and services, which presented new opportunities to manufacturers.

■ The COMPANY RESPONSE. The arrow labeled (b) indicates that a shift in the culture may force the company to make a conscious response. Any response made depends on how perceptive management is in identifying the change, and what impact the change has upon the company's interests.

3.2.2 *Why the manager needs to understand cultural shift*

The manager seldom deals directly with abstractions of change in the value system. Rather, he/she responds to concrete factors such as new market developments, new labor supplies and demands, new efficiencies in the labor force. These changes may reflect shifts in the deep culture. The company that recognizes significant shifts in the deep culture, and also perceives how these impact upon the market, is well equipped to cope with strategic opportunities and threats.

Suppose that economic events have caused a narrowing of power distances throughout society and a need for greater informality. When the new values are expressed in a demand for more casual clothing, opportunities arise for a clothing manufacturer. These new values have less immediate impact on the business of an insurance company. However, the demand for insurance *is* boosted by events that stimulate a sense of anxiety – for instance, rising crime and disease rates, and a perceived increase in natural disasters such as earthquakes and floods.

Cultural shift also affects the internal arrangements of the company. Again assuming a narrowing of power distances, employees might respond more positively to closer relationships between superiors and subordinates. How far should a particular company go to develop new structures and systems that reflect the new realities? These factors are significant:

■ The INDUSTRY. Some industries, such as the media, are more sensitive to this cultural adjustment than are others, such as government.

■ The company's ORGANIZATIONAL CULTURE and history.

■ The COST of making change. If your skill resources are in great demand, and if radical change is the only way to keep them, you may have no alternative. But if your labor resources are easily replaced, you might limit change to cosmetic (and cheap) reforms.

■ The NATURE of the cultural shift. Is this fundamental and long-term, or is it superficial? If fundamental, then a response must be planned and implemented.

The company alienates its members when it continues to operate procedures and structures that reflect outmoded values, just as it loses customers when it goes on producing outmoded goods and services. On the other hand, it makes another expensive mistake if it over-commits in accommodating shifts that later prove short-lived.

3.2.3   Problems in recognizing significant shift

Problems arise in distinguishing significant and deep-rooted shifts from superficial movement. Media stories tend to portray all economic, social, and technological change as important. Stories of change attract attention and sell newspapers, and stories of continuity do not. Journalists work under time constraints which mean that they do not usually have the time to analyze the long-term implications of the events they report. Journalism can lead the observer into mistaking the values of a sub-culture for a shift in the mainstream culture, and to assuming that a shift in the sub-culture reflects a general movement.

Here is an extreme example. Mainstream American culture is individualist, but this story about a Los Angeles street gang, the Crips, might suggest to an uninformed outsider that it has grown more collectivist.

> It is notoriously difficult to leave the gang once initiated – a procedure that can include murdering an innocent bystander to prove one's mettle. Gang members pledge lifelong service and consider fellow members closer than family. They are often murdered if they leave.[3]

In practice, of course, the Crip sub-culture is very far removed from the main-stream culture – at least in this respect – and the mainstream continues to be highly individualistic.

Finally, appearances might suggest that Culture X has shifted but if neighboring cultures have also shifted in the same direction, the movement in Culture X may be less significant.

Hofstede (1983) repeated his research 4 years after the first study and his data showed that of the 50 countries now reviewed, at both times 19 showed increases in individualism, and only Pakistan, which alone had grown poorer, showed a move towards collectivism. Although the extremes of individualism and collectivism were converging, countries that had achieved fast growth were shifting most towards individualism. Hofstede (1997) commented "the cultures shift, but they shift together, so that the differences between them remain intact" (p. 77). That is, Japan, for example, may appear to be more individualist; but if all the other cultures have also moved towards greater individualism, the comparative differences are the same.

3.2.4   *Change and the manager's roles*

A final reason why the manager needs to understand the relationship between change in the environment and cultural shift is that the process affects his/her own identity as a manager.

The manager is no longer restricted to planning, organizing, coordinating, and controlling – which is how the French industrialist Henri Fayol described managerial functions in 1916. Since then, the manager has had to become more than expert and autocratic. He/she has had to respond to and control a range of new factors in the environment – new economic and market forces, new relations with customers and suppliers, new technologies, new relations with skilled workforces, new managerial experiments with different management styles and structures.

The environment has grown so complex that no manager can hope to control all sources of information. In this age of uncertainty and discontinuity the modern manager has had to acquire skills of facilitating other people to find and manage their own sources of information. This has long been the case in cultures where the manager is expected to be a facilitator rather than an expert. Describing American managers, Mintzberg (1975) identified the new roles of figurehead, leader, liaison, monitor, disseminator, spokesman, entrepreneur, disturbance handler, resource allocator, and negotiator. A quarter century later, Blumen (2002, p. 90) stressed similar qualities: managers "negotiate, persuade and integrate."

The problems of dealing with new uncertainties are more severe in cultures that still give greater emphasis to the manager's qualities as an expert. A Taiwanese commented that if a manager does not know the answer to a technical question, he/she "must say nothing or find a way of not answering" – anything rather than admit ignorance. Such skills are increasingly in demand where technological developments outpace the manager's capacities to keep his/her expertise up to date. Developing and operating these new technologies force the manager to introduce new responsibilities and relationships in the company, but the conservative pull of culture makes it difficult for members to adjust their communicative styles (see Mead and Jones, 2002).

Role confusion causes stress, which is acute in societies experiencing rapid economic change and cultural shift. It can be severe among local management in multinational companies. Perhaps most stressed are those senior local managers who have to respond to the different needs and values of expatriate top management above them, and to subordinate local staff below. These managers have the "invisible" role of negotiating and interpreting between different levels of the company.

Managerial stress is compounded by radical adjustments to the company workforce. In the United States, IBM shrunk from 406,000 employees in 1987 to 202,000 in 1995, then changed direction and recruited 21,000 in 1996. Hughes Electronics reduced its workforce by a quarter between 1985 and 1995, then added 8,000 the next year. The new levels of stress in middle class life mean that the manager faces greater uncertainty over the value of his/her specialty and status.

3.2.5   The speed of culture shift

Problems of recognizing those culture shifts that promise to have long-term effects on market and workforce values are complicated when the deep values of a culture change slowly.

Why are cultures often slow to shift? First, any change can be painful. People's values are reinforced by habit and a fear of too much novelty. Second, individuals start learning their values in earliest childhood (recall section 1.3.4). At this age culture is learned without conscious effort, and conscious resistance. This learning is extremely deep rooted, and so the individual is slow in modifying his/her unconscious values in later life. This has general implications; not only individuals but the groups to which they belong cannot easily shift their unconscious values.

However, in the recent past there have been notable examples of cultures apparently making radical shifts in a short space of time. One example is Japan.

3.2.6   Factors that cause the culture to shift

The culture may shift in response to significant changes in the business environment. Some of these factors are listed in figure 3.1. This chapter continues by examining the influence of the following:

- economic change (section 3.3);
- technology (section 3.4);
- foreign intervention (section 3.5).

The effect of foreign intervention on local identity is discussed in greater detail in chapter 11, which is devoted to the economic and cultural affects of globalization.

3.3   How Economic Factors Influence Shift

The possession of wealth does not in itself lead to economic development. The most populous country in Africa, Nigeria, has received approximately $300,000 million in oil revenues since its independence, but is probably now poorer than when oil was first discovered there in the 1950s.

> Because these revenues were controlled entirely by the government, participation in government became the royal road to fast and fabulous illicit wealth. . . . enterprising Nigerians – of whom there are many – concentrated their efforts on gaining political influence rather than on more productive activities.[4]

However, in some circumstances a correlation occurs between wealth and individualism. The wealthier countries tend to be more individualist; for example, the United States

Table 3.1   Real per capita GDP (1980–2000)

Japan	+54%
Singapore	+169%
Hong Kong	+105%
Taiwan	+210%
Korea, Rep.	+229%
Malaysia	+115%
Thailand	+142%
Philippines	−1%
Indonesia	+75%

Source: Penn World Table, IMF. http:/pet.econ.upenn.edu/

and the United Kingdom are both wealthier and more individualist than Guatemala and Panama. But this correlation is not exact and an obvious exception is made by the wealthy but relatively collectivist Japan. And it also seems to be the case that as a country becomes more developed, it also shifts towards greater individualism. In turn, a new spirit of individualism generates new wealth.

This, at least, is the hypothesis. It is very difficult to prove. Table 3.1 gives economic data showing percentage increases in GDP between 1980 and 2000. Can hard evidence be found to prove that the shift to individualism has been greater in Korea than in, say, Thailand and Japan? Can it be shown that in these 20 years Philippines culture has not changed significantly in this respect? And even when a general correlation is found, can we be sure that increased GDP has caused the decline in collectivism and that other possible factors do not count?

An entrepreneurial private sector may earn greater rewards. Neither Hong Kong nor Singapore is rich in natural resources, yet both have moved from third-world to developed status within two generations.

Four years after completing his original research, Hofstede (1983) repeated it, and concluded that in the 50 countries then under investigation, in all but Pakistan an increase was found in individualism and this seemed to follow an increase in wealth. Although the extremes of individualism and collectivism were converging, those that had achieved the fastest economic growth were shifting most strongly to individualism.

However, it must be borne in mind that the model is comparative. This means that although Thai culture, say, is growing more individualist, Thailand is not likely to approximate to the United States in the immediate culture – because American culture is also growing more individualist. In absolute terms, the relative difference may have changed only slightly.

3.3.1   The effects of economic change in Japan

At the end of the Second World War, Japan was faced with massive problems of economic reconstruction. In order to rebuild and prosper, companies had to depend upon the whole-hearted commitment of their staff, and gave commitment in return. This relationship of mutual dependence and obligation perfectly expressed a culture of organizational collectivism, relatively high needs to avoid uncertainty and stress, and relatively high power distances.

The conventional Japanese office-worker or "salaryman" built a reputation for loyalty to the company and his boss to the point of giving up evenings, weekends, and even vacations in order to serve their interests. This loyalty was expected. In 1967 Hitachi sacked an employee who refused to work overtime. The case went to court and after several years the Supreme Court came to a ruling, in favor of the company; "employees are obliged to work overtime, even against their will, if the request is reasonable."[5] In return, the company did its best to protect him against redundancy, and in some cases (but perhaps in never more than 40 per cent of all companies) awarded guarantees of lifetime employment to management staff. The relationship worked.

Nevertheless, values were beginning to shift. Not only younger managers were adopting new attitudes to work. A 1991 survey conducted by an employers' association found that only three per cent of the 250 managers surveyed still favored such traditional practices as long hours and the arbitrary transference of employees to distant posts where they might be separated from their families.[6]

By this time the Japanese economy had grown to the point at which it seemed likely to dominate the world economy for decades to come. But only a few years later it went into recession and, by 1998, employees were being laid off and companies were failing. Bankruptcies had never occurred on this scale before. In September 1998, Japan Leasing, a unit of the failed Long-Term Credit Bank of Japan, went under with debts of 2.18 trillion yen. In October 2000, Chiyoda Mutual Life Insurance became the nation's biggest corporate bankruptcy to date, with a 2.94 trillion yen debt. These failures meant that the private sector could no longer guarantee its side of the contract, and massive numbers of salarymen were made redundant. In a culture with high needs to avoid uncertainty, and where growth had been continuous since 1947, the effects were devastating – particularly among middle-aged male managers. This is shown by leaps in the suicide rates. In 1990, 5,200 middle-aged men killed themselves; in 1998 around 10,000 committed suicide.

3.3.2   The new workforce in Japan

In sum, new economic conditions had made the old values untenable. The effects of change were magnified by the new generation entering the workforce. They had no experience of the struggle for survival after 1945. The exposure to Western values through the media and personal contacts made with Westerners meant that they did not fit the traditional model, and were developing other priorities.

The 1980s generation were known as the SHINJINRUI, or new human beings. According to a contemporary account, the Shinjinrui was more direct than the traditional Japanese.

He acts almost like a Westerner, a *Gaijin*. He does not live for the company and will move on if he gets the offer of a better job. He is not keen on overtime, especially if he has a date with a girl. He has his own plans for his free time, and they may not include drinking or playing golf with the boss.[7]

The employee's involvement with the company was becoming less moral and more calculative – in Hofstede's terms, apparently reflecting higher individualism. By 2001, the break with the past culture of deference to elders had grown more obvious. Every year the Japanese have a national holiday celebrating the coming-of-age of their young people who turn 20. Held in every municipality, these ceremonies began after 1945 as a way of inspiring young people with hope for the future and commitment to social structures. But in 2001:

> when the mayor of Takamatsu city stood up to address a coming-of-age ceremony . . . he expected the ritual to be conducted with its usual pomp and solemnity. Instead Shozo Masuda had to deliver his speech while drunken members of the audience approached his party podium and fired party crackers at him.
>
> Across Japan other dignitaries suffered similar affronts as 1.5 million Japanese marked the day on which they officially become adults. Young people ignored, heckled and even shouted abuse at mayors and governors who presided over ceremonies designed to mark their passage into maturity.[8]

In the past, young graduates had aimed at working for one of the giant corporations that dominated the economy. By the end of the century, a rising generation were beginning to challenge this orthodoxy and start their own companies, often in information technology fields. This change seems to have been influenced both by rising affluence and the realization that it was no longer necessary to commit to a lifetime of company drudgery in order to guarantee survival, and also because the large companies were no longer able to guarantee a lifetime job even if one wished it. Among the young it was no longer fashionable to secure a salaryman job, and entrepreneurial successes were widely reported.

The new rejection of the big corporations is also shown by the increasing numbers of young Japanese who prefer to work on only a part-time basis. Between 1982 and 1997 the numbers of part-timers increased from 500,000 to 1.51 million, 80 percent of whom were in their twenties.[9] However, at the same time the Tokyo Metropolitan Government was holding seminars to persuade middle-aged people to take up full-time jobs, which showed that not everybody was sympathetic. The officials had an economic incentive for resisting the trend to part-time work; tax revenues were falling at a time when the population was greying. It was possible that the welfare system might collapse.[10]

3.3.3 In Japan, shift between the sexes

In 1945, women made up about 22 percent of the total labor force. This figure increased rapidly after 1975, and reached 40 percent in 1999 (The Ministry of Public Management Statistics Bureau, 2000).

After 1945, most Japanese females had been expected to marry in their early twenties, then stay at home and rear children, and this usually meant giving up the career. This was typical of a highly masculine culture, in Hofstede's (1997) terms, in which male and female roles were sharply divided. In this situation it was economically realistic of Japanese companies to hesitate in recruiting and training unmarried women to managerial posts when they are likely to quit the job on marrying. However, that situation is now changing, and women are being given greater opportunities to develop managerial careers.

Some observers expected rapid change. However, expectations in the past had been raised and then disappointed. The boom years of the 1980s had seemed to suggest that traditional patterns of job discrimination were breaking down, and that Japan was moving towards a more feminine orientation in which sex roles were less strictly differentiated. In 1989, a female role model arose in the public sector:

> the success of the Iron Butterfly, Takako Doi, the Socialist Party leader, created a "Madonna Boom" in Japanese politics, with parties rushing to enlist women candidates.[11]

And when Mr Junichiro Koizumi became Prime Minister in 2001, he:

> . . . immediately underlined his intention to break with the past by appointing five women to the cabinet, including the first woman foreign minister.[12]

The private sector seemed to follow suit. The financial press warned that, at senior levels, the labor shortage could only be solved by hiring more women managers, and it seemed certain that women would soon take their places in the top boards of directors. In addition, companies eager to impress their foreign clients made a point of dispatching women managers to overseas posts. Because many overseas postings were still unpopular and regarded as akin to banishment, the companies perhaps welcomed the excuse not to send their male managers, and thus kill two birds with one stone.

However, expectations of radical change were premature. By 1992 the recession and stock market collapse had meant that firms were shedding staff and making fewer appointments. Women suffered disproportionately.

> Toyota Motor will reduce its intake this year of young male high school graduates by 7.4% to 1,580, while the number of women graduates is to fall by 25.6% to 570. Nomura Securities will halve its annual intake of women from last year's [1991] 800 and the total number of women workers is likely to fall to 3,000 in 1997 from the present 5,000.[13]

And Mr Koizumi's female ministers began to lose their jobs.

Environmental influences on both the hiring and firing of female managers included external factors. Finance companies entering the booming market chose to be represented by expatriates, who hired Japanese women. As the boom slowed, head offices had calculated the cost and canceled their expatriation policies. Expatriates were replaced with locals – usually males. These local males tended to dismiss the females and replace them with males. The recession over the past ten years has seen a move towards more traditional recruitment policies, at least in the traditional manufacturing industries. The newer industries – fashion, software, and advertising, for example – are more liberal.

3.3.4 *The Japanese future*

On January 18, 2000, a Commission on Japan's Goals for the Twenty First Century reported to the Prime Minister, Keizo Obuchi. In order to survive in a globalized world, Japan needed to drastically change its culture. The Commission stressed the need for "individual empowerment." In the past, the emphasis on loyalty, patience and hard work had bred the production-line workers needed for Japan's transformation after 1945, but in the new climate, qualities of spontaneity, innovation, and ambition were needed. The emphasis on homogeneity and uniformity in both the educational system and workplace should be curbed. Reward structures should recognize individual excellence. The Japanese had to accept more foreigners and cultural influences from abroad and not simply stick to "the identity of the past."

This report reflected a growing dissatisfaction with the hierarchies in government and business, the repression of innovation, and complacency in public life. Suddenly it seemed that cultural shift was possible:

> A decade-long recession has forced people to reassess their world. The process is simultaneously a national identity crisis and an awakening. The powers-that-be are scrambling to react to pressure from a dissatisfied public. Individuals are not waiting for solutions from above, but are asking questions and coming up with their own answers.... "We all know that we are facing a crisis and that we have to change," says Kawai Hayao [the chairman of the Commission]. "It is a great opportunity for Japan to take real action."[14]

This illustrates a general point, that people are most likely to perceive the need for change – and act on it – in response to crisis, when the cost of continuing without change is prohibitive. Undoubtedly, Japanese culture *is* shifting – as are the cultures of other industrial nations. But the shift may not occur as rapidly as some observers expect, and the old values are unlikely to disappear soon. Shift is not a simple linear process, and this section shows that steps in one direction are followed by side-steps. We are too close to events to map development with certainty. However, it seems likely that the new values will have marked Japanese characteristics, and the Anglo manager who has assumed that the new Japan will replicate Anglo culture, and structured a Japan-based subsidiary on this basis, might be making an expensive mistake.

3.4 How New Technology Causes Shift

Financial wealth is only likely to influence the process of social change and cultural shift when it contributes to economic development. In practice, this means that the wealth is applied in technological development. Technology causes a shift in the culture when it causes people to significantly change how they live and work.

Technological development has three main stages:

1   the acquisition of existing technology (e.g., transferred by a joint venture partner);
2   the adaptation of existing technology to local needs;
3   the creation of new technology.

Innovations made at the third stage are most radical and are most likely to lead to people modifying their behavior, which causes a shift in the values by which their behavior is governed. Acquisition alone does not necessarily motivate change. Saudi Arabia has shot from dire poverty to phenomenal wealth in a few years. The first oil revenues were earned in 1933, and by 1996 estimated revenues were $47.8 billion – more than any other OPEC oil producer. Yet the country is not a significant technology producer.

In general, where individuals and companies cannot depend on the state for support and are given opportunities to enrich themselves, attitudes towards applying and creating technologies tend to be more entrepreneurial. In the innovative economies of Southeast Asia, where local companies are increasingly moving to stages 2 and 3, social change appears to have been more profound than in many of the oil-rich states.

3.4.1   *Fear of change; fear of technology*

Technology brings social change, which may be welcomed by some, but feared by others. Values in the culture influence attitudes towards technological innovation; Hofstede's model shows that cultures with high needs to avoid uncertainty are less likely to welcome a new technology. Political factors may also be significant, as in the case of the development of the internet in the People's Republic of China. The government welcomes the commercial opportunities offered by a healthy internet system, particularly as China enters the World Trade Organization. Commercial modernization sends a powerful message to potential investors. On the other hand, some Chinese leaders worry that surrendering control over the flow of information will threaten Leninist orthodoxy and rule by the Communist Party. For example, during the Student Democratic Movement in 1989, fax machines – the new communications technology of the day – were widely used by the protestors to transmit information, pamphlets, and demands to the foreign press. The protestors came close to toppling the government.

A startling demonstration of the power of information technology was provided by the religious sect Falun Gong one day in 1999, when 10,000 adherents surrounded the Communist Party leadership compound. The demonstration had been organized in total secrecy using e-mail, and the leadership were deeply disturbed. They banned the sect and imprisoned many members, and even executed some. This efficient use of the technology was recognized by *AsiaWeek* magazine when it named the founder of Falun Gong, Li Hongzhi, "the most powerful communicator in Asia" in 2001.

At various times the Chinese government has also attempted to block web sites of some foreign newspapers (such as the *New York Times*), human rights groups (Amnesty International), and Taiwanese agencies.[15] But these attempts at censorship have not been very effective. The problem of control has been complicated by the number of Chinese authorities with responsibilities for regulating internet use. Rocca (2000) cited 17, among which the Ministry of Information Industry was pre-eminent. In sum, the problem for the Chinese authorities has been how to use the new information technologies in order to foster economic growth, and still to keep tight control of political expression.

3.4.2   How technology influences values at a micro level

Within the company, the development and implementation of new technology empowers it to develop a number of strategic alternatives. These include:

(ai)   creating the same numbers of old products or services more efficiently;
(aii)   creating greater numbers of old products or services;
(b)   creating new products or services;
(c)   developing new organizational structures and systems.

In practice, most companies pass through these steps in sequence: *either* ai then aii, *or* aii then ai, *or* ai or aii, followed by b, then c. That is, the experience of using technology to achieve current production goals gives an impetus to planning new production goals; and this leads to thinking about modifying processes within the company in order that these and future goals may be better achieved.

The changes made at step c may be implemented in order to achieve a strategic goal – for example, re-engineering relations within the hierarchy. When information crucial to operating procedures is transferred to technology, the functions of supervisors – who previously supplied this information – are weakened, and a level in the hierarchy may be eliminated. When the company sheds its supervisors, it loses a level of junior management. This flattening of the organization influences members' relationships with superiors, subordinates, and peers in ways which may not be foreseeable.

The implementation of an innovative technology may not only modify relationships but also influence work-related values. However, the international manager cannot assume that technology exerts the *same* pressures on all cultures, and cannot assume that in all cultures, relationships are modified *in the same way*. That is, he or she cannot infer from the universality of the technological revolution that all cultures are converging.

3.4.3   Communicating about the new technology

Before a technology can be successfully adopted, management tries to overcome the anxieties of those who will use it. This means explaining:

- *What* the technology is; its functions;
- *Why* it is being introduced (i.e. how its use can help the company achieve its goals);
- *How* it should be used (i.e. instructions for operation);
- *Who* will use it (the operators);
- *How* its use benefits the operators;
- *What* skills the operators must apply (if necessary, what new skills they must learn);
- *When* it will be used;
- *Where* it will be used.

If these points are not adequately communicated to persons who need to know, the technology is unlikely to win their commitment and may be inadequately applied, possibly incurring repair costs.

3.5   How Foreign Intervention Causes Shift

Intervention by an outside power may cause a major shift in the culture. Occupations by Western colonialists profoundly influenced the cultures of many less developed economies during the nineteenth and early twentieth centuries. In some cases, the effects were entirely negative. The introductory case of the Guarani people shows how interventions by, first, the colonial Spanish and then by a local non-indigenous power – traders supported by the Brazilian government – have almost extinguished the culture. But usually the effects are not so drastic, and mix positive and negative effects.

Some experts argue that cultures are CONVERGING and that economic development is leading all countries to adopt the same value system adopted from the Anglo cultures. Others argue that culture is so powerful a force that it will continue to shape managerial values, and that in some respects cultures are DIVERGING. A third school argues that CROSSVERGENCE can occur. In these cases, a unique set of work values is formed as a result of the interaction of internal values and external pressures. Andrews and Chompusri (2001) apply this notion to analyzing shift in an organizational culture. Here we are interested in how it applies at a national level.

Robertson et al. (2001) found that whereas work values in Saudi Arabia are diverging,

> . . . Oman and Kuwait are at a crossvergence point and are developing their own unique cultural paradigms as a result of a combination of internal and external factors. *(p. 241)*

The lack of crossvergence or convergence in Saudi Arabia is of interest, given that country's recent experience with external powers. The short- and mid-term effects of the 1990–91 Gulf War are discussed here.

3.5.1   *Intervention in Saudi Arabia*

Saudi Arabia was a front-line antagonist and host to a massive Allied army (led by the United States). And as foreign troops flocked in during the run-up to war, many Saudi and non-Saudi citizens were convinced that changes in social values were imminent. Middle-class and Western-educated Saudis hoped that the confrontation would prompt the Saudi ruling family to side more openly with those who favored the liberalization of religious, social, and political institutions. They expected sex roles to be influenced. Traditionally, women had played very little part in the segregated labor market. But now, King Fahd suggested they be allowed to replace expatriate women as nurses, clerks, and medical technicians. But a year later, after the fighting in which Saudi Arabia had played an important part on the winning side, the country apparently returned to routine.

In the immediate aftermath the impact made by Western culture "was just about nil," according to a Western diplomat.[16] Open access to Western media was allowed for only a short time. The ultra-religious morals police, or *Mutawah*, returned to harassing both those Saudi and foreign women they considered insufficiently covered in public places, and the authorities reneged upon promises to employ women in a wider range of occupations.

3.5.2   Why intervention did not cause Westernization

In the Saudi Gulf War case, many observers expected that the mass intervention by Western forces would cause an immediate crisis in the local culture, and that liberal Western values would emerge from the process of adjustment. These observers included both outsiders and some "expert" insiders. Why were their expectations disappointed? These factors inhibited the shift.

1   The presence of Allied troops in large numbers was short-lived – less than a year. They were quarantined away from large urban centres. Contacts between Saudis and troops were restricted, and there was no cultural contamination.
2   This quarantining was deliberate and planned; uncontrolled change had been feared by both Saudi *and* Western authorities.
3   Saudi political structures are capable of integrating tribal and social differences. If a sufficient number of Saudis had understood and supported the "progressive" cause, and if the contradiction between traditional and modern value sets had been acute, the old values might have been more challenged. Hence the question of adjustment between alternative or conflicting value sets did not arise.

A year after the War, a Saudi diplomat said:

> "Saudi Arabia is really undergoing real change." "But," he added, "Americans flatter themselves if they think they provoked it. The change is Saudi Arabia working on its own dynamic."[17]

In retrospect, his analysis seems to have been both right and wrong. Certainly the intervention did not cause a rush to Westernization; but it did have an effect, and that was to drive at least some Saudis in the opposite direction. In the wake of the events of September 11, 2001, it became evident that the person responsible, Osama bin Laden, many of his al-Qa'eda terrorists, and financial supporters, were Saudi nationals. Revulsion at the allied presence in the country of the Prophet and the birthplace of Islam had led to a return to traditional fundamentalist values – and in some other Muslim countries besides Saudi Arabia.

The long-term effects of outside intervention are difficult to predict, and may be entirely opposite to those planned.

3.5.3   *The conditions under which intervention is influential*

This analysis gives a lead to understanding the conditions under which intervention by "outsiders" *will* significantly influence the culture, namely:

1   The outsiders are respected.
2   They have regular contacts with significant groups within the local society; they create relationships and build role models. If any attempts are made to block these contacts, these tend to be unsuccessful.
3   Leading members of the local society want change, and local political and social structures seem incapable of implementing these changes.
4   The outsiders are perceived to offer the desired change.

Conditions 2, 3, and 4 were *not* present in the case of the Allied intervention in Saudi Arabia, discussed above. Condition 1 applied only in that the outsiders were respected for their technical and military skills; the developing support for Osama bin Laden demonstrated that the outsiders' life-styles and philosophies were *not* respected.

Intervention is most likely to succeed when the outsiders offer a specific change and when locals support this change. If this support does not exist as a prior condition, the intervening outsiders must invest in training and developing it. History is littered with cases in which these conditions were not met, and when outside intervention was not immediately welcomed.

3.5.4   *When intervention was decisive*

The predominant importance of conditions 3 and 4 above are illustrated by an earlier example, from Japan.

By 1853 Japan had defended itself from Western cultural influences for almost three hundred years; foreign visitors were forbidden, and no Japanese who left the islands could claim re-admittance. This isolation only ended when an American sailor, Commander Perry, entered Tokyo Bay and refused to leave. Perry's "black ships" profoundly shocked the value system. By denying its authority, Perry caused the Shogunate to lose so much face that political change was inescapable. He precipitated the Meiji restoration and the collapse of Japanese feudalism.

Why did this intervention serve as a catalyst for culture shift in Japan, when the Gulf War appears to have had no corresponding effect in Saudi Arabia? Western power was respected (condition 1). There already existed an organized opposition to the Shogunate and a sense of moral revulsion towards the values that it represented, and the powerful lords well understood the need for political liberalization and economic development (condition 3). Relations with the Americans and other foreign powers seemed likely to produce support for this development (condition 4). Only condition 2 seems not to have applied; there were necessarily few contacts before Perry's arrival.

The American intervention did not create the conditions for change; it lit the fuse to a bomb already primed by growing resentment to the feudal court. And the failure of the Allied forces to play a similar role in Saudi Arabia is partly explained by the relative absence of any such political and moral contradictions among the mass of the Saudi people.

3.5.5   Globalization as foreign intervention

Globalization represents a further aspect of intervention from abroad. In theory it implies the free movement of political, economic, and cultural resources between countries, each society influencing and being influenced by every other society. In practice, Western values predominate. For example, American values impose on Peru to a far greater extent than Peruvian values impose on the United States. In practice, globalization has effects that have not been predicted, and may be violently opposed by those who feel threatened and perceive that their local economic, political, and cultural systems are under assault. These issues are considered more fully in chapter 11.

3.5.6   Intervention on a company level

This analysis of intervention by one country in the affairs of another country has lessons for the multinational company, in which headquarters intervenes in the organizational culture of the subsidiary, or the foreign parent of an international joint venture company intervenes in that venture. The intervention is most likely to cause a long-term shift in the organizational culture when:

1   The outsiders are respected – both as individuals and as representatives of the headquarters or parent. Their interventions are perceived to meet existing needs and as likely to profit the subsidiary of venture.
2   They have regular contacts with significant groups within the subsidiary or joint venture; they create relationships and create role models.
3   Influential managers in the subsidiary or joint venture champion the change proposals made by the outsiders, and the local organization is able to implement them.

These issues concerning change in an organizational culture, and control in international organizations, are discussed in later chapters.

3.6 Implications for the Manager

Under some conditions, environmental changes may affect behavior and lead to shifts in cultural values.

1 Identify significant economic and other events that have occurred within *your own culture* during the previous few years (for instance, intervention by some other country, economic recession or boom, technological innovation, educational innovation).
   (a) How have these affected people's behavior, if at all?
   (b) How have these affected your relationships with:
       – other persons in your organization?
       – family, friends and social acquaintances?
2 Do you expect these behavioral changes (if any) to cause a shift in the culture of *your* country?
   (a) If you answer *yes*, what shift do you expect?
   (b) Do you expect it to be superficial or long-term?
   (c) Should your organization plan a deliberate response?
   (d) If you answer *yes*, what response should be made?
3 Identify significant economic and other events that have occurred within *some other culture* that you know well during the previous few years.
   (a) How have these affected the behavior of members of *the other culture*, if at all?
   (b) Do you expect these behavioral changes (if any) to cause a long-term shift in the culture of *the other country*?

3.7 SUMMARY

This chapter has examined how changes in the environment cause shifts in the culture. In general terms, section 3.2 examined the problems of RECOGNIZING SIGNIFICANT SHIFTS IN THE CULTURE, and responding appropriately. Section 3.3 examined the conflicting evidence for how ECONOMIC CHANGE might cause CULTURAL SHIFT. It focused on the post-war development of Japan and saw how the changing economic picture has influenced attitudes towards women in the managerial workforce. Section 3.4 dealt with the influence of NEW TECHNOLOGY at the macro level of the country and the micro level of the firm. Section 3.5 focused on the effects of FOREIGN INTERVENTION, and examined the conditions under which intervention may have long-term effects (as in Japan) or no long-term effects (as in Saudi Arabia). General rules were deduced to explain when shift does occur, and briefly applied this to the intervention of headquarters or the international joint venture partner in the subsidiary or venture.

3.8 EXERCISE

This exercise helps you practice predicting the effects of economic change on cultural values.

- The Kingdom of Darana is landlocked and historically of little interest to the outside world (the Kingdom was never colonized). The United Nations lists it among the world's 20 poorest countries. It has a population of six million, of whom about 500,000 live in the capital, Daranaville. There are no other large cities.
- Social and political life in the Kingdom is controlled by a traditional elite of 16 families who benefit from extensive land holdings. They are proud of their country's history and independence, and their custom of giving lavish hospitality to strangers. Those families who can afford to, send their children to Western countries for secondary and university education.
- Primary education is good: 87 percent of males and 63 percent of females are literate. The one university teaches basic technical skills.
- The largest single employer is the civil service. Seventy-seven percent of the workforce is employed in the agricultural sector. There is a small clay mining industry. Otherwise, the private sector consists of small family businesses.
- The typical company is marked by wide power differentials between ownership, middle management, and the workforce. Females are employed in junior secretarial functions.
- Other than among the elite, 91 percent of the female workforce in Daranaville is employed in the production of domestic ceramics (an all-female specialization), other craft occupations, and as housewives and domestic servants.

Then it is discovered that the local clay has unusual qualities of heat-resistance and tensile strength, of major value to the kitchenware, auto, aero, and space industries. This clay is unknown elsewhere in the world.

The government is inundated by offers from a range of foreign companies in extraction, manufacturing, and service industries. Companies from France, Japan, the United Kingdom, and the United States secure rights. An economic boom is promised; one prediction foresees average per capita income growing by 20 percent every year for the next ten years.

1 Predict the long-term effects on Daranese values.
2 How can the government protect Daranese interests while also exploiting this bonanza to the national advantage?
3 What human resource policies should a foreign company adopt, assuming that it expects to have a long-term presence (at least ten years) in the Kingdom? In particular consider policies for:
   (a) recruitment;
   (b) training;
   (c) motivating, rewarding, and disciplining.

Notes

1   Christina Lamb, "Rising suicides cut a swathe through Amazon's children," *Sunday Telegraph*, November 19, 2000.

2   "Runaway minors problem black mark on KL record", Agence-France Presse, *The Nation* (Bangkok), December 23, 1996.

3   Simon Davis, "Death row gang chief named for peace prize," *The Daily Telegraph*, November 22, 2000.

4   Anthony Daniels, "Did riches lead to ruin?" Review of Maier, K. (2001), *Sunday Telegraph*, January 14, 2001.

5   "Free, young and Japanese," *The Economist*, December 21, 1991.

6   "Free, young and Japanese," *The Economist*, December 21, 1991.

7   Ronald E. Yates, "Juppies," *Chicago Tribune*, 24 April, 1988.

8   Peter Hadfield, "Japan dismayed as teenagers insult dignitaries," *Sunday Telegraph*, January 14, 2001.

9   Fumihiro Hayasaka, "Tokyo wants part-timers to carry load," *Mainichi Daily News*, November 23, 2000.

10 Fumihiro Hayasaka, "Tokyo wants part-timers to carry load," *Mainichi Daily News*, November 23, 2000.

11 Robert Thomson, "Future dims for Japanese women," (*Financial Times–Bangkok Post* service), *Bangkok Post*, August 31, 1992.

12 Colin Joyce, "Five women in Japan's cabinet," *Daily Telegraph*, April 27, 2001.

13 Robert Thomson, "Future dims for Japanese women," (*Financial Times–Bangkok Post* service), *Bangkok Post*, August 31, 1992.

14 Jonathan Sprague and Murakami Mutsuko, "Japan's new attitude," *AsiaWeek*, October 20, 2000.

15 Eric Eckholm, "China cracks down on dissent in cyberspace," *New York Times*, December 31, 1997.

16 Rone Tempest, "Change Comes, at Its Own Pace, in Saudi Arabia," *International Herald Tribune*, September 4, 1991.

17 Rone Tempest, "Change Comes, at Its Own Pace, in Saudi Arabia," *International Herald Tribune*, September 4, 1991.

CHAPTER FOUR
Organizational Culture

CHAPTER OUTLINE

4.1 Introduction

Bosham University College (BUC) is situated in the south of England. It competes with a much larger university serving the same student catchment area. BUC is the smaller, and has a reputation for being more friendly. In addition, students are attracted by its reputation for relatively small class sizes and higher teaching standards. It offers a range of first degree programs in the social sciences, and taught masters programs in anthropology, sociology, and politics.

On the first day of the academic year, new students are invited to an induction meeting. This year, the first part of the meeting was addressed by administrative staff, who advised students on the facilities and rules and regulations. The second part was chaired by faculty representatives, who discussed the teaching timetables and described assessment procedures. Officers of the students' union led the third part and talked about student clubs, accommodation, and welfare.

A new Principal was appointed during the long vacation and that evening he addressed the collected faculty and administrators for the first time. "In the next few weeks I shall complete my plans for a new strategy," he told them. "I am not yet in a position to spell out all the details. However, I can say that I want greater attention to be paid to timekeeping. From henceforth faculty are normally expected to be on the premises throughout the working week, even when not teaching."

His address was greeted unenthusiastically. Afterwards one professor remarked to the registrar "He does not understand. That is not the way we do things here."

In sum, BUC has a culture which is unique, although this is influenced by factors common across the industry. The culture comprises a number of sub-cultures, which express the different interests and experiences of their members. The new CEO is unlikely to inspire more than compliance until he pays greater attention to members' perceptions of their organizational identity.

This chapter discusses aspects of organizational culture, and examines how far it is influenced by national culture.

4.2   Defining and Analyzing Organizational Cultures

The study of "organizational culture" is difficult because the term has no one accepted meaning. Definitions are many and varied; they may include the organizational structure and rules, values, feelings, norms, the organizational "climate." Lewis (1998) argues that this lack of consensus means that the concept has little practical value, and that the various definitions used have not been applied successfully to improving performance.

In many local organizations outside North America and Europe, management focuses on indoctrinating the workforce in order to align the individuals' interests with theirs; they do not articulate a concept of organizational culture, but their practice is similar to that of Western companies who are very much attuned to it.

In general, this book uses the term organizational culture in preference to corporate culture; the former term includes the notion of culture in private, state, and not-for-profit sectors, whereas the latter is restricted to the private sector. The book assumes that every organization in whichever sector has its unique culture that can be defined and analyzed.

Which definition of "organizational culture" is most appropriate? That may depend on the use to which it is being put, and the analyst's point of view and needs. A top manager, an academic, a consultant, and a business journalist, will each have different interests in the organization and probably need to apply different definitions of the concept of organizational culture, even to the same organization.

In general, most definitions fall between two extremes:

1   *Definitions that focus on structures, systems, and regulations.* These are formal systems in the sense that they are planned and implemented by management. In this chapter, these are referred to as STRUCTURAL definitions.
2   *Definitions that focus on the members' sense of "how we do things here."* These perceptions influence how they experience their relationships with each other and with management, and are referred to here as EXPERIENTIAL definitions.

This difference is important. The first set, the structural definitions, imply that top managers are able to create and manipulate the organizational culture in order to achieve management goals, and they achieve this by setting policies by which to control the organization. These responsibilities are reflected by a Chairman and CEO of the Gillette Company:

> A successful multi-country business also requires a strong corporate culture to provide uniform standards of business conduct everywhere in the world. A strong corporate culture, which can be codified in a formal Mission and Values Statement, instils in all managers the same perspective, the same ground rules to apply in decision making.
>
> *(Alfred M. Zeien, quoted in Puffer, 1996, p. ix)*

Section 4.3 deals critically with the concept of the organizational culture as a set of structures and systems imposed by top management.

At the opposite extreme, experiential definitions imply that the values of members are influenced by a range of factors, including national culture, industry values, and market factors, which may be far more powerful than company policy and which lie outside management control. Section 4.4 examines the relationship between the organizational culture and the wider environment, paying particular attention to national culture.

In practice, the organizational culture is influenced *both* by management practices *and* by the national cultural influences on its members. Any one organizational culture can be viewed from either perspective – either as the influence of structures and rules, or as the expression of experience. Managers usually prefer the first because it prioritizes their professional activities, justifies their planning activities, and plays down factors over which they have no control. The academic might prefer the ethnographic definition because it helps in the understanding of the company as a social value system which can be objectively analyzed.

4.2.1   The definition used in this book

This book examines both the structural and experiential definitions. In practice, the members' experiences are formed both by their attitudes towards the work and sense of appropriate behavior *and* by the influence of the structures implemented by top management. Tensions occur when management controls do not correspond to the expectations of other members. If management tries to impose policies and systems that appear not to take into account the cultural realities of the situation, disputes arise. The introduction above outlined a situation in which a negative culture might arise.

This definition fits with Trompenaars' (1997) three aspects of organizational culture:

1   the general relationship between employees and their organization;
2   the vertical or hierarchical system of authority defining superiors and subordinates;
3   the general views of employees about the organization's destiny, purpose and goals and their place in it. (pp. 138–9)

Point 1 stresses the importance of the relationship between management and employees – which varies between cooperation (when management goals and employee perceptions coincide) and, at the other end of the spectrum, conflict (when goals and perceptions are far adrift). Point 2 implies that top management has the capacity to influence the culture by manipulating the structures and systems. But point 3 indicates that management control is never total, and the perceptions shared by employees may not correspond with those that top management is trying to impose.

Organizational culture embraces both the structural and experiential aspects. This balance:

- reflects both management goals and employee experiences; *and*
- recognizes that misunderstandings, disagreement, and conflict between management and workforce are always possible.

Not surprisingly the differences between how management and workforce think about their organization can lead to misunderstandings and disputes. These can be severe in any organization. They are particularly severe when top management and workforce have different national cultures (for example, in a multinational operation when top management are expatriated from headquarters located in the one national culture and other staff are recruited locally in the country of the subsidiary and belong to the local culture).

4.2.2 Analysis: positive/negative organizational cultures

Different organizational cultures can be compared when a common system of analysis is used. Two simple models are used here. First, the organizational culture is assessed in terms of how far it is POSITIVE or NEGATIVE. The culture is POSITIVE when its members support and trust top management and workforce and top management share a commitment to the organization. Their relationships are good (note Trompenaars' first point in section 4.2.1). This occurs when:

- *Official relationships are considered reasonable.* Top management communicate effectively and fairly with members. Grievances are listened to, and given a fair response;
- *Members perceive that they have a stake in company outcomes.* When the company benefits, they benefit (and when it fails, they fail). Profits and losses are shared fairly;
- *Demands for productivity are considered reasonable.*

When the opposite conditions apply and relations with management are unproductive, the organizational culture is NEGATIVE.

4.2.3 Analysis: strong/weak organizational cultures

The second model being used is to analyze the culture in terms of how strong or weak it is. The organizational culture is STRONG when:

- *It is cohesive.* Group members share the same values, beliefs and attitudes.
- *Members can easily communicate between themselves.*
- *Members depend upon each other in meeting individual needs.*

The strength of a culture is shown by the uniformity in members' perceptions of their working experiences.

When the opposite conditions apply and relations between members are not cohesive, the organizational culture is WEAK.

4.2.4 The four alternatives

The positive/negative, strong/weak models generate four alternative cultural descriptions:

(a) A positive, strong culture.
(b) A negative, strong culture.
(c) A negative, weak culture.
(d) A positive, weak culture.

These alternatives can be mapped diagrammatically, as shown in figure 4.1.

4.2.5 A positive and strong culture

When the culture is positive and strong, relations between management and workforce are good. Communication is easy, open, and fruitful, morale is high, and productivity

	POSITIVE	NEGATIVE
STRONG	a positive, strong	b negative, strong
WEAK	d positive, weak	c negative, weak

Figure 4.1

climbs. Manpower Scandinavia provides an example (Harung and Dahl, 1995). The company first operated in Norway, then Denmark, and now Sweden. By 1995 it had been certified to meet European quality standards (ISO 9002), the first in its trade in Norway and one of the first service companies ever.

> Management focused on developing, maintaining, and ensuring that the organization members have healthy and productive values. In other words the pivotal strategy is to ensure that the culture is strong. *(Harung and Dahl, 1995, p. 13)*

Unconditional customer satisfaction was guaranteed and defects were close to zero (97 percent customer satisfaction).

Management normally hopes to create a positive, strong culture. If this is not possible, management wants a positive, weak culture – that is, a culture in which relations between management and workforce are good, even if the workforce itself is disunited.

4.2.6 A negative and strong culture

Management most fears a negative, strong culture. Employees are united in their alienation from official structures, their disbelief in management messages, and their perceptions of management dishonesty. In the 1980s one branch of General Motors offered an extreme example.

> The original GM plant in Fremont, California, was built in 1962 as a state-of-the-art facility. However, angry workers called it the "battleship" partly because of its drab greenish-tan color, partly because of the endless conflict that raged there for twenty years. Sick-outs, slow-downs, and wildcat strikes frequently disrupted production, and daily absenteeism usually reached 20 percent. Alcohol and drugs were freely available on the premises. *(Wilms et al., 1994, p. 101)*

Management weakens a strong culture by reducing the cohesion among members. Dependencies and regular contacts between members are lessened by introducing:

- information technologies, which substitute for face-to-face communications;
- flexi-time systems;
- work-at-home schemes;
- shared office space, meaning furniture is no longer dedicated to the particular individual – he/she is expected to work at any workstation available.

In addition, some specialist units can be axed by assigning their responsibilities to outside consultants, who are contracted to the organization on a short-term basis and make no investment to the organizational culture.

4.3   Controlling the Organizational Culture

How can management modify the organizational culture? A structural definition of culture assumes that management can directly influence culture in the direction it wants by modifying structures and systems. An experiential definition suggests that although new structures may sometimes influence the culture, management has no control over the direction of this change. Hesselbein (2002) comments on his experience:

> Our focus was not on changing the culture – though this was a result. Our focus was on building an organization committed to managing for the mission, managing for innovation, and managing for diversity.   *(p. 2)*

The consultants' work on developing the structures of the company resulted in the members' rethinking their experience of working for it. While such a positive change is never certain, the chances of success are improved when the workforce already trust management. If the workforce do not trust management, then they are likely to respond positively to structural innovation. Hence, if the culture is already positive, management may find it relatively easy to make change; but if the culture is negative, the process will be very difficult.

On the other hand, when management adopt a structural approach and perceive the culture as a tool by which they can achieve strategic goals, they develop systems with the explicit aim of manipulating values. When the structural changes made are superficial, the assessment of success is also likely to be superficial. But acceptance cannot be taken at face value. Compliance by the workforce does not necessarily indicate genuine commitment (Ogbonna and Harris, 1998).

4.3.1   Modeling the change process

When management adopts a structural approach, it invests more in policies designed to give control over the culture. Figure 4.2 models the change process. Whether the present culture is mapped at d, c, or b, management prefers it to move to a. If, in the worst case, the present culture is at b, management might aim to first move it to c (where the workforce continue to be alienated but are unable to build a united front against management) and then to d (where the workforce support management even though disunited), and only then to a.

The meaning of a structural approach is that in developing policies to control this process, management applies a structural interpretation of the concept of organizational culture (see section 4.2); it manipulates those factors over which it has some control, and ignores or downplays those factors over which it has no control. This section distinguishes these two sets of factors and examines the limitations of this definition.

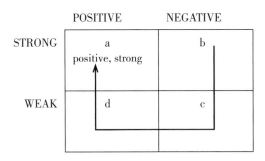

Figure 4.2

4.3.2   *Factors over which management has most control*

Below we examine those factors over which management has *most control*, and some of the implications are discussed below. (Factors over which management has less control, or no control, are examined in section 4.4.)

▌ STRATEGIC FACTORS (see also chapter 13): for example,
  • strategic goals;
  • strategic plans.
▌ FORMAL STRUCTURES (see also chapters 5–8): for example,
  • responsibilities and relationships;
  • systems for communicating, motivating, resolving disputes;
  • sub-structures;
  • leadership;
  • size and composition of the workforce.
▌ TECHNOLOGY: for example,
  • acquisition and development of technology;
  • knowledge as technology;
  • training programs.
▌ The OFFICIAL PROFILE projected to members and to the environment, for example, by
  • official symbols, including the mission statement;
  • official rituals, ceremonies, history.

4.3.3   *Strategic factors and the organizational culture*

Chapter 13 deals in detail with strategic planning and implementation. In short, management plans and implements a corporate strategy that aims to maximize financial assets and the company's position in the marketplace. The company depends on its members operating efficiently. In most industries and markets the company prefers to retain and develop at least the core of its existing workforce rather than continually fire and hire – this may only be an option for a company which requires very basic skills that are easily hired from the labor market.

This dependence on a core forces management to take the organizational culture into account when planning and implementing new strategy. For example, a strategy that requires the workforce to acquire new technical skills may affect the relationship between workforce and management as measured in terms of a more or less positive and negative culture, and relations between members of the workforce as measured in terms of the culture's strengths and weaknesses.

4.3.4   Structures have sub-cultures

The organizational culture usually includes a number of sub-cultures. These may correspond to structural units and departments. There might be a need to compare the hierarchical sub-cultures of:

- *Top management*, which is chiefly involved in relations with the environment and planning strategy; as against *middle management*, which designs and implements policies conceived to achieve the strategic goals set by top management; as against *lower management*, which manages the routines within the policies; as against different levels in the non-managerial *workforce*.
- *Headquarters* as against *subsidiary/joint-venture*.

Secondly, organizational sub-cultures can be compared and contrasted on a horizontal basis; for example, the sub-cultures of:

- the marketing department, the finance department, the engineering department, and so on;
- different subsidiaries.

The analysis of organizational sub-cultures can show how different structures coexist in the organization, and how their members perceive themselves, their relationships with other structures, the company, and its environment. We can distinguish:

- core organizational perceptions that are shared by all members of the organization from those that are not shared;
- the perceptions of different structural units (for example, divisions, departments, shifts, work teams, and so on);
- conflicts in perception (in the case of perceptions that are not shared by all);
- the perceptions of groups within different units – including headquarters and subsidiary.

Why is this analysis needed? Managers and consultants make comparisons and contrasts between organizational sub-cultures in order to assess organizational relationships and differences in efficiency. Analysis can reveal that the culture is positive in Department A, say, and negative in Department B, and indicate where investment is needed. Analysis shows cultural diversity is welcomed when it enables top management to identify non-essential staff and essential staff who can be developed, and when cultural differences influence personal creativity.

4.3.5 Leadership

The leader recognizes opportunities and threats before others do, and is already planning how to maximize the first and avoid the second when others have still not seen the need for change. Here is one example. When John Bond was appointed chairman of HSBC, few saw the need for a new direction. He was faced with:

> ... a bank management that had every right to feel content. HSBC, after all, had grown its assets by 20% to 25% annually for three decades and consistently racked up a return on equity that put it near the top of any ranking of bank competitors. That's the kind of performance that tends to inhibit change. Bond needed a convincing rationale to shake things up. Enter the Internet, which is turning the global banking industry on its head. Bond sensed a solution to HSBC's years of unfocused growth. ... Bond pushed Internet development and has been willing to spend heavily to make it happen – $2 billion last year alone. He also showed he has a good eye for talent and an unexpected willingness to take a chance.[1]

In Anglo companies, a new CEO is not normally expected to continue his or her predecessor's strategy other than in the short term during the transition period. Bond was typical of new CEOs in that he marked his accession by giving the company new strategic emphases. This means attempting to modify the organizational culture to achieve the new strategic goals.

However, the leader who marches too far ahead of unpersuaded followers, and fails to communicate his or her vision, brings confusion and may damage the company as much as the leader who becomes too comfortable with existing ways and fails to recognize the need for change.

The successful leader understands how the company is positioned within its business environment, recognizes needs for change, and communicates these needs effectively to members. This example shows a leader who failed to communicate appropriately, with serious consequences for the morale and value of his company. Neal Patterson, founder and CEO of an American healthcare company, Cerner Corporation, decided that staff were not contributing sufficiently, and e-mailed his managers:

> "We are getting less than 40 hours of work from a large number of our employees. ... As managers, you either do not know what your employees are doing or do not care. In either case, you have a problem and you will fix it or I will replace you. Never in my career have I allowed a team which worked for me to think they had a 40-hour job. I have allowed you to create a culture which is permitting this. No longer."

The e-mail was posted on a Yahoo! financial message board, and then Wall Street analysts began receiving calls from shareholders. The callers wanted to know whether a crisis had occurred in the company, and raised questions as to whether this was a CEO with whom they could be comfortable. The value of stock dropped 22 percent in three days.[2]

Section 6.4.2 examines how a successful leadership style motivates members.

4.3.6   Recruitment

The company influences the development of a positive culture by recruiting persons who show the psychological and professional characteristics needed to achieve strategic goals.

Psychometric and other personality tests are widely used in the West to select persons who seem likely to "fit in" and contribute to the culture. In collectivist cultures, informal means of recruitment may still be more important than formal means. In Korea, school culture plays a major part; recruitment by "culture-matching" is a convergence of selection by the employer and self-selection by the applicant in which they match their respective school cultures. According to Soon (1995):

> the typical advice students receive from their knowledgeable alumni is said to include "Go to Lucky Gold Star if you want to live like a human being, but go to the Samsung Company if you want to develop your talent." *(p. 57)*

A company that projects a positive culture in the business environment attracts potential applicants looking for an employer with a culture that seems likely to satisfy their professional and psychological needs. Schneider (1988) cited a human resources manager at Olivetti:

> those Italians who want autonomy go to Olivetti instead of IBM. He described the culture of Olivetti as being informal and non-structured, and as having more freedom, fewer constraints, and low discipline. *(p. 239)*

Those who preferred greater formality and structure chose IBM.

4.3.7   Technology and the organizational culture

Technology may be tangible or intangible:

▮ Narrowly, the term refers to tangible PRODUCT TECHNOLOGY – machines, tools, and materials (e.g. a computer).

▮ More broadly, the concept includes intangible PROCESSES and technical systems needed to operate, maintain, and repair the product technology (e.g. the skills to operate, maintain, and repair the computer).

■ More broadly again, the concept includes intangible MANAGERIAL TECHNIQUES and systems.

■ Most broadly, the intangible elements include experiential or tacit KNOWLEDGE that members bring to and create in the workplace – it may not be specified in their job descriptions but management hopes to identify and apply it (see section 13.3.2).

This ambiguity in the definition need not be a problem if the degree of specificity intended is always made clear.

In this context, we are most concerned with the middle two levels. Technology influences the organizational culture insofar as it affects members' relationships with each other (on the strong/weak dimension) and with management (on the positive/ negative dimension).

Typically, technology is introduced in order to facilitate or improve production. A new production technology gives capacities to:

• produce an existing product, at the present quality, in greater volume; *and/or*
• produce an existing product at a higher quality, possibly modifying it; *and/or*
• produce a new product.

At some point in this process, a fourth capacity occurs. Relationships between members are modified, and this influences the organizational culture. This modification might be planned or unplanned. A new technology influences the structural relationships between members involved in the task which it facilitates, and hence influences their needs to communicate with each other. For example, the technology might demand that certain stages of the task are now performed by individuals working alone whereas before they had worked in groups – or it might demand that groups replace individuals. The characteristics of the communication between members, and their dependencies on each other, directly affect the strength or weakness of the organizational culture – as we saw in section 4.2.3 above.

The influence on the organizational culture is more direct in the case when a new information technology is acquired. For example, an increased dependence on a computer system can weaken the members' dependencies on a supervisor. In the event that the underworked supervisor is made redundant, the new technology has the indirect effect of flattening the organizational structure. This dependence on technology may also weaken dependencies between members on a horizontal axis. Persons involved in the same or similar tasks have less need to communicate. This has the effect of weakening the culture. A top management threatened by negative and strong values may be inclined to select a technology that moves the culture from b to d in figures 4.1 and 4.2.

4.3.8   *The learning company*

Companies increasingly depend upon their members' knowledge as a source of competitive advantage. Companies that deliberately set out to identify and apply this knowledge are said to be LEARNING. The learning culture is reflective in the sense that members learn from their experiences.

Knowledge should not be mistaken for information immediately available through information technologies. Knowledge is defined here as the capacity to select relevant items of information and to understand how these can be applied, and includes:

▮ knowledge of the INTERNAL arrangements of the company;
▮ knowledge of the EXTERNAL environment.

This book focuses on the knowledge of the environment. This is derived from the employees' skills, experiences, and memories of strategic alliances and foreign operations. Here is an example. An oil company heard that the United States was about to auction more oil leases in the Gulf of Mexico, and immediately began planning an expensive seismic survey.[3] At the last moment, an executive recalled that the company had previously surveyed the area and had even drilled some inconclusive wells before giving it back to the government. Thus the employee's memory saved the company from repeating the exercise and making an expensive mistake.

The company takes the decision to develop a learning culture when it operates in an environment in which:

• change is increasingly rapid;
• essential skills are scarce (and expensive) and the knowledge held by members represents an important commodity.

In this environment, the company is under growing pressure to exploit the knowledge of its expert employees. The other side of the coin is that it cannot afford to lose experts, whose knowledge represents an important resource with long-term strategic implications. Investments are made in retaining and motivating these people, and to develop and apply their knowledge throughout the company.

The company needs to develop a positive and strong culture in which members feel aware of their mutual dependencies and able to communicate freely. The structural implications are, first, control can no longer be strictly maintained within departmental boundaries, and tight departmental structures may need to be reengineered away. Secondly, the company may decide to appoint a dedicated "knowledge officer" to develop and organize its knowledge bank.

4.3.9 *Official symbols and the organizational culture*

Top management builds a positive culture by using symbols to create commitments by the workforce to company goals. Management creates symbols that express management perceptions of core values, and projects these symbols throughout the company. The official symbols are designed and applied to create shared interpretations of the company, its operations, and its position within the environment.

Management symbols include

- rituals and ceremonies – an award is made to the employee of the month;
- myths – "how we brought home the deal with Amex;"
- history – the early years, epic struggles, heroes, and villains;
- language – in-house jargon used by insiders that distinguishes them from outsider non-members;
- the mission statement – discussed below.

4.3.10 The official profile expressed in the mission statement

The MISSION STATEMENT defines the company by answering these questions:

- WHO are we?
- WHAT do we do?
- WHERE are we headed?

Mission statements vary greatly in length and content. They might explain the company philosophy, promote ethical policy, celebrate successes, and discuss strategic goals (so long as this does not help competitors). They project the corporate image to a range of persons with interests in the company: these include the media, analysts, customers and suppliers, other persons in the environment, and company members. When addressing the members, mission statements aim to fill the following functions (discovered by Baetz and Bart (1996) in their analysis of Canadian statements):

- guide strategic planning;
- define the scope of operations;
- provide a common purpose;
- guide leadership styles;
- promote a sense of shared expectations among all levels of the organization.

All these functions are directed at building a positive and strong organizational culture. Of course, mission statements often sound clichéd and unoriginal – have you ever read a mission statement that did *not* claim that the organization's chief asset was its members? Nevertheless, the best do provide interesting reflections about their values, experiences, and future plans. When management wishes to signal a change in the organizational culture, it changes the statement. To show that the customer was respected and to redirect its organizational culture to be more consumer oriented, Nissan changed its slogan from "Distinctive Technology" to "Feel the Beat."

4.4 Organizational Culture and National Culture

Management can never exert total control over the organizational culture because it does not have total control over all the factors that influence members' attitudes to their work. These contributory factors include:

1 Members' informal systems, including:
   • informal communication, gossip;
   • informal relationships, including friendship and patronage relationships (see chapter 9);
   • informal rules and norms for surviving and getting along in the workplace;
   • observed practice.
2 Factors in the business environment, such as:
   • economic factors;
   • market forces and competition;
   • industry factors.
3 The national culture, including values associated with working and the workplace.

Although management may attempt to police members' informal systems, it can probably exert no influence on the national culture.

4.4.1 *Comparing national culture and organizational culture*

Which has greater influence on members' values and behavior, national culture or organizational culture? The question is important because it leads us to investigate the degree of control that the headquarters of a multinational company can realistically exert on its subsidiary abroad, located in some other culture.

If organizational culture has a stronger influence on members' values than their national culture, then headquarters management can directly determine the behavior of subsidiary staff. If, on the other hand, national culture has the stronger influence, then headquarters has to take local values into account when imposing strategies, systems, and structures; and how subsidiary staff interpret and implement these policies is strongly influenced by their culture.

Headquarters might always hope to override local national values but this is not always practical, and the attempt may be time-wasting and damaging to local morale. This does not mean that a headquarters' value system can *never* be transferred abroad. Certainly if the cultures are close, or if members already have experience in the values of the national culture of headquarters, the transference may be relatively simple. An example of the second point occurs when, say, an American bank operating in Indonesia recruits Indonesian graduates of American universities. However, in other circumstances (and depending on the values being transferred), staff may need to be trained in the new systems and indirectly in the values they express, perhaps over considerable time.

As a first stage in assessing the relationship, we ask how far Hofstede's definition of national culture (discussed in section 1.3) can be applied to organizational culture.

> ... [It is] the collective programming of the mind which distinguishes the members of one human group from another.... Culture, in this sense, includes systems of values; and values are among the building blocks of culture. *(Hofstede, 1984, p. 21)*

These inferences were drawn for a national culture:

1   A culture is particular to one group and not others.
2   It influences the behavior of group members in uniform and predictable ways.
3   It is learned, and is not innate.
4   It is passed down from one generation to the next.
5   It includes systems of values.

These inferences apply to organizational culture (as defined in section 4.2.1) in that:

- every organization has its own culture, and no two are quite the same;
- management hopes that by building and analyzing the organizational culture it can predict the attitudes and behaviour of the workforce in routine situations;
- members of the organization have to learn its culture.

But the applications of points 1 and 5 are less straightforward. The values of the national culture are taught by family, friends, school, media, and others. In the organization, perceptions of who is responsible for essential teaching differ according to the definition made of organizational culture. Management hopes to act as the primary "teacher" by applying the formal tools discussed in section 4.3 in order to build and sustain the organizational culture. However, the alternative definition indicates that experiential culture of the workforce is passed on informally, through example, gossip, and so on.

So far as point 5 is concerned, values in the national culture are learned from the first weeks of life, and most of this learning is unconscious. It is held at a deep level in the psyche, and provides the individual with values that determine his or her behavior throughout life.

On the other hand, the learning, and impact, of organizational cultures is relatively shallow. This is because:

- The individual experiences a succession of organizational cultures throughout life (e.g. the cultures of primary school, secondary school, university, first workplace, second workplace and so on, religious associations, social clubs, retirement home – and many others). These cultures may have common elements, but in other elements may be in conflict.
- The individual usually joins the organization from free will, and, usually, is equally free to quit. Members who cannot adjust their perceptions and behavior to the prevailing culture of their organization are likely to quit at an early stage.
- At different times, elements of one organizational culture may be in conflict (e.g. when a new CEO leads the company towards new strategic goals, and attempts to create new cultural priorities in order to meet these goals).
- National cultural values are learned so early in childhood that the individual is unaware of his or her cultural conditioning. However, organizational values are

learned much later, and in general are only assimilated at a conscious level. The individual learns many of these organizational cultures in his or her maturity, and adopts an objective and critical attitude towards the learning.

You acquire and shed a series of organizational cultures in the course of your working life. But you cannot shed your national culture.

In sum, at a very superficial level, the defining parameters of national culture can be applied to organizational culture. However, the two notions of culture are *not* the same and should not be confused.

4.4.2   The influence of organizational values

This leads to the question, are organizational values ever so powerful an influence on behavior as national culture? The point is important because if they *are*, employees can be conditioned to expressing values that contradict national values. For instance, in an individualist national culture, employees of Company X can be conditioned to placing a premium on group harmony and avoiding confrontation – connotations of a collectivist culture. But if national values are always likely to overrule contrasting organizational values, there may be little point in investing heavily in systems designed to modify the organizational culture. In this case, headquarters control over the organizational culture of a foreign-based subsidiary is always insecure.

The evidence is ambiguous. There is no doubt that organizational values do influence the employees in the long term, and generate patterns of uniformity among organizational units, regardless of geographic, functional, or business boundaries. But this does not mean that they operate as deeply as do the values of national culture, or significantly modify the national culture when the two are in conflict. In practice, the influence on the individual may be determined less by management controls than by the length of time he or she stays in the organization. The "job-hopper," who moves rapidly between companies, is unlikely to be much influenced by their cultures. On the other hand, the person who stays with one company for all his/her career may be significantly affected. Small family companies can indeed impose this degree of control on members born within the organization.

4.5   Implications for the Manager

Answer each of the questions for:

• an organization that you know well in *your own culture*; *and*
• an organization that you know well in *some other culture*.

1 For each organization, decide whether its culture is (i) STRONG or WEAK, (ii) POSITIVE or NEGATIVE.

(a) What factors make it strong/weak?

(b) What factors make it positive/negative?

(c) How might it be made stronger?

(d) How might it be made more positive?

2 In each organization, what sub-cultures can you discern? What values do the following sub-groups share?

(a) top management;

(b) middle management;

(c) junior management;

(d) shop floor;

(e) different functional groups;

(f) different plants/subsidiaries;

(g) headquarters staff, expatriate staff, and local staff in subsidiaries abroad.

3 In each organization, look for evidence of top management attempting to change the culture.

(a) Are these attempts succeeding? If so, why?

(b) Are these attempts failing? If so, why?

4 In each organization, look for evidence that:

(a) values in the national cultural are a more significant influence on behavior in the organization than is the organizational culture;

(b) organizational culture is a more significant influence than are values in the national culture.

4.6 SUMMARY

This chapter has discussed the concept of organizational culture. Section 4.2 dealt with problems of DEFINING AND ANALYZING ORGANIZATIONAL CULTURE. The problem for the manager is to select a definition of organizational culture that can be usefully applied to the specific situation. A distinction is drawn between definitions that emphasize management's capacity to control the culture, and those that focus on the members' experience of the culture, outside management's direct control. Cultures can be analyzed in terms of their strong/weak and positive/negative characteristics.

Section 4.3 examined those factors over which management has CONTROL and which can be used to manipulate the culture; these were strategic factors, formal structures, technology, the official profile. An organizational culture can be analyzed in terms of component sub-cultures, a point that has implications for analyzing relations between component units of a multinational company.

Section 4.4 examined the relationship between ORGANIZATIONAL CULTURE AND NATIONAL CULTURE. Whether or not values in the organizational culture can supplant the national culture is an important question when the multinational headquarters decides on policies for controlling a subsidiary through its culture.

4.7 EXERCISE

Comment on the following case.[4]

1 Analyze the problems and suggest solutions.
2 What does this tell you about Mr Feraro's beliefs and values?
3 Suppose you were a consultant. What advice would you offer Mr Feraro?

Luigi Feraro is an active entrepreneur. Ten years ago he established an electronics company in Singapore and continues to be Chief Executive Officer. The national identities of the current management team and their length of time with the company are listed:

General Manager:	Swiss	7 months
Finance Manager:	British	29 months
Production Manager:	Italian	32 months
Marketing Manager:	Singaporean	25 months
Personnel Manager:	Singaporean	18 months
Administration Manager:	Malaysian	15 months
Engineering Manager:	Taiwanese	9 months
R&D Manager:	Dane	3 months
Transportation Manager:	Singaporean	8 months

The company started with a staff of three – Feraro and two Singaporean business friends, Hervey Tan and Michael Swee. But after a series of bitter rows, the two Singaporeans left. Feraro says:

"They left to start their own business together. In some product lines we are directly competing. Even so, I owe them a lot. They were hard workers. Whatever I told them, they got on and did. Usually I couldn't have done better myself. Another thing I learned from them was the value of internationalism in a country like this. It was their idea. When we make a new staff appointment, the first question we ask is how can the applicant help make this a more international firm."

However, the team has found it difficult to work together successfully. Meetings are not successful. The Western staff tend to contribute far more than the Asian staff, who sometimes even find it difficult to communicate among themselves. Feraro complains:

"I've tried to inspire them, to give them my enthusiasm. I set them off in the direction I want them to take, but they never seem to take off. I encourage them to take initiatives but frankly, they usually come up with ideas that are impractical. When that happens, I'm the one that has to straighten things out. And although each one of them can be good on his – or her – own, they can't work as a team."

In an attempt to generate a stronger culture, Feraro asked his Finance Manager to arrange a series of social events for the top management team and their spouses/significant others. The first event involved dinner on a luxury cruiser, touring around the island. Two senior French managers, visiting from a Brussels company with which Feraro-Kayel hoped to do business, were invited. By the end of the evening, they had broken into a number of small groups – the Italian, Taiwanese, and Dane together; the Swiss, Briton, and Malaysian together; and so on.

Notes

1 Assif Shameen, "Hold on tight," *AsiaWeek*, 26 January, 2001.

2 Philip Delves Broughton, "Boss's angry e-mail sends shares plunging," *Daily Telegraph*, April 6, 2001.

3 Tom Lester, "Accounting for knowledge assets," *Financial Times*, February 21, 1996.

4 This case was suggested by material produced by Professor Fredric Swierczek, the Asian Institute of Technology.

CHAPTER FIVE

Culture and Communication

CHAPTER OUTLINE

Introduction	Non-Verbal Communication
Appropriate Communication	Implications for the Manager
Across Cultures	Summary
One- and Two-Way	Exercise
Communication Styles	Notes

5.1 Introduction

These stories all raise questions about the relationship between the content of messages and their length.

- The Ten Commandments required 300 words, and the American Declaration of Independence, 1,300 words. However, the European Union regulations regarding the export of duck eggs needed 26,900 words.

- "The large bureaucracies are drowning in their own communications. I get maybe 160 e-mails a day of which 100 are of no use to man or beast, but I have to read them because that is the nature of bureaucracy." *Senior consultant in an international consulting firm.*

- Computer technologies were originally expected to reduce the need for paper, and eventually to bring about the paperless office. But the opposite has occurred. As more people routinely make hard copies of ingoing and outgoing messages, the use of e-mails has led to an increase in paper consumption by perhaps 40 percent. On the subject of the quantity of messages transmitted, one writer described a day in which she pressed the send/receive button to be greeted by 52 new e-mails, of which 15 were of interest. Since June she had collected 3,387 e-mails: "My Hotmail

address has been killed in action by junk mail which was outnumbering anything interesting to a ratio of about 55:1."[1]
- Between 2001 and 2002, one Singaporean company sold 45,000 business and 200,000 personal e-mail addresses for Singaporean $120. Another has been selling 75,000 business and 350,000 personal addresses for Singaporean $59.90. Many targets of the unsolicited mail suffer quietly. Boutique owner Sandy Lee, 34, is fed up with the several dozen unsolicited messages that land in her in-box every day. Asked what she does about it, she said: "What to do – delete!"[2]

More communication does not necessarily mean better communication, and quantity alone does not necessarily create greater involvement in the receiver. A message that does not involve and persuade the receiver is a failed message. This chapter deals with the conditions under which communications succeed.

5.2 Appropriate Communication Across Cultures

A message is most likely to be efficient and to achieve its purpose when it is appropriate to its context. This means that it should be designed for a particular context, and can be interpreted in that context.

Suppose that a poorly dressed stranger approaches you in the street and says "Have you any spare change?" Superficially this appears to be a request for information to which you might answer "Yes I do" or "No I don't." In practice, most people would guess from the physical situation and his obvious poverty that the stranger is actually asking for money – although no explicit request has been made.

Suppose that a second stranger approaches you in the street. This man looks prosperous and carries a paper-case, and he says "Have you any spare change?" The contextual clues do not support the earlier interpretation, that he is a beggar asking for a handout. If you are unable to find an alternative explanation and to attach any purpose to the message, you conclude that this behavior is irrational.

We create and interpret messages in terms of their context. When we understand the context, the purpose and meaning of the message becomes clear. If we don't understand the context, the purpose is obscure. Here is another example: a short conversation.

A: "Telephone."
B: "I'm in the bath."
A: "Okay."

These six words tell us very little until we know the situation, which is that A and B were occupying an apartment consisting of a bedroom, living room, bathroom, and kitchen. A telephone rang in the living room. A, in the bedroom, heard it ring and shouted at B, whom he assumed to be in the kitchen, asking her to go into the next room and answer the telephone. B shouted back that she couldn't because she was in

the bath and therefore could he answer it instead. He agreed. In full form the conversation might be paraphrased as follows.

A: "The telephone in the living room is ringing. I'm in bed and I don't want to get
up. So if you're in the kitchen please could you answer it."

B: "I'm not in the kitchen. I'm having a bath and it's easier for you to answer it than
it is for me."

A: "Alright, I accept your explanation. I'll answer it." [A goes to answer the telephone.]

In this example the key factors in interpreting the purpose of the message relate to the
physical situation. But in other cases other factors may be as – or more – important.
These are described below.

5.2.1   *The context of communications*

The set of contextual categories below helps the user decide whether a message is
appropriate and likely to be persuasive, and can be used both in creating a new message
and interpreting a message already transmitted. The contextual categories answer the
questions:

▪ WHAT content is communicated by the message?
▪ WHO communicates?
▪ TO WHOM is the message communicated?
▪ WHEN is the message communicated?
▪ WHERE is the message communicated?
▪ HOW is the message communicated?

The model shown in table 5.1 does not explain how factors in the national culture
and organizational culture influence expression of the six categories. The significance
of these contexts is explored throughout the remaining sections in this chapter.

5.2.2   *Appropriate and inappropriate selections*

The selection made of any one category influences the appropriate selection of all
others. For instance, when a senior person becomes associated as ADDRESSOR with the
CONTENT of a communication, it derives status from his/her importance. In Japan in
2001, a Prime Ministerial commission reported on how the country should redirect its
culture and institutions in order to meet the challenges of the future (see section 10.1;
The Prime Minister's Commission on Japan's Goals in the 21st century, 2000). The ideas
were not radical and had been discussed for many years before, but the commission
received massive publicity both within Japan and abroad because Prime Minister Obuchi
associated himself with its work. He participated in 11 of the four committee and
40 subcommittee meetings. He expressed the hope that the working practices and

Table 5.1   The contextual communication model

WHAT is communicated?	What is the appropriate CONTENT of the message?
WHO communicates?	Who is the appropriate ADDRESSOR to send the message? For example, a routine message is more likely to be communicated by a manager below the level of CEO.
TO WHOM is the message communicated?	Who is the appropriate ADDRESSEE? The addressee(s) might consist of a single person; a number of people – a group, department, organization; people inside the organization or in the environment; any combination of these.
WHEN is the appropriate TIME for communicating the message?	For how long should the message be communicated? Does the message need repetition, and if so, for how long?
WHERE is the appropriate location for communicating the message?	LOCATION includes physical and organizational situations.
HOW is the message communicated?	What is the appropriate MEDIUM? For example, print, e-mail, text, conversation?
	What is the appropriate LANGUAGE?
	What is the appropriate STYLE? For example, how should content be selected and sequenced? What degree of ambiguity is acceptable? Should the communication be one-way or two-way (see section 5.3)?

minutes of all proceedings should be made available through e-mail and fax, and met for two hours with a group of young persons who had submitted proposals.

If you choose to communicate strategy to the stockholders, this influences your choice of communicator – almost certainly the CEO, supported by senior officers of the company.

If one category is inappropriate, the message lacks persuasiveness and may fail. For example, appropriate content communicated to the appropriate audience, in the right style and medium, at the right place, at the right time but by the wrong person fails to persuade. Suppose that headquarters has agreed a new strategy for the subsidiary. This is presented to subsidiary managers in a weekend conference held in a five-star hotel. In these respects, the arrangements are appropriate. Unfortunately, the person selected to make the presentation is a junior headquarters manager. The senior subsidiary managers are insulted. They expect to be addressed on such an important topic by the CEO in person, and interpret this selection of addressor as a signal that headquarters has no confidence in their operations.

Similarly, suppose that the CEO does attend, but has only time to meet his managers for an hour; or the conference is located in a two-star hotel; or is timed for a holiday weekend. The result of any one of these inappropriate selections is to damage management morale.

A message that is communicated inappropriately may be misunderstood or be AMBIGUOUS (understood differently by different receivers). Managements sometimes practice deliberate ambiguity – for example, leading the marketing department to believe that "this company is marketing-led and depends centrally on your efforts" and the production department to believe that "this company is production-led." But this can be a dangerous strategy that undermines trust and morale when representatives of marketing and production meet and compare their impressions. In general, management should aim to communicate as clearly as possible. This means that a message loses credibility when it is communicated:

* with an inappropriate content (see section 5.2.3); *and/or*
* by an inappropriate addressor (see section 5.2.4); *and/or*
* to an inappropriate addressee (see section 5.2.5); *and/or*
* at an inappropriate time (see section 5.2.6); *and/or*
* in an inappropriate location (see section 5.2.7); *and/or*
* in an inappropriate medium, language or style (see section 5.2.8).

The choice of WHEN and HOW the message was communicated might have been appropriate if the WHAT – the content – had been good news. In the circumstances of bad news, the WHEN and HOW were inappropriate. It was hardly surprising that those TO WHOM the message was communicated responded negatively.

5.2.3   Content

The content of the communication consists of the information that is communicated. But "information" may mean very little unless it is given for a purpose, and this purpose is clear. The usual purpose of giving information is to persuade. Even a casual, friendly greeting serves the function of trying to persuade the addressee that you are a friendly person who intends good will.

The examples of the meetings described in the introduction to section 5.2 make the point. The literal meaning of the words used by the second stranger is quite clear, but the PURPOSE which they are intended to serve is obscure, and so the message fails as communication. That is, content has meaning when the addressee understands:

▮ the CONTEXT within which it is transmitted;
▮ the PURPOSE for its being transmitted.

This has implications for international business. Business deals can go wrong when one person does not understand why certain information is being given or requested – or is not being given – and because his/her informational priorities do not correspond to those of the other side. For instance, Anglo companies face problems in planning joint ventures with organizations in the People's Republic of China because the two sides' perceptions of what information is needed do not coincide. The Anglos complain about the lack of hard data and of coordinated information systems, which may indicate cultural disagreement over that data is significant. Perhaps, from their own point of view, the Chinese *are* supplying significant information. Of course, it *might* simply indicate a lack of interest in playing Anglo information "games" when several other firms are competing for the same business. If you do not understand the situation, you are unable to decide which explanation fits.

So a message is persuasive when the addressor selects information that the addressee perceives as relevant – in terms of his/her needs. This information must be presented at the appropriate level of explicitness; and important points should be appropriately highlighted – so far as possible, in terms of the expectations of the other culture.

5.2.4 Addressor

A management message is efficient when the person for whom it is intended (the addressee) believes that it is being communicated by the appropriate addressor, and that this addressor has credibility and can be trusted.

Suppose that you, as CEO of your company, decide to re-engineer operational processes in the production department. Who should give the employees this message? You? Your secretary? The production manager? A supervisor? What factors influence your decision? Who is the appropriate addressor if you decide to change the timing of the lunch break?

Senior managers prefer to communicate positive events that reflect well on their performance. Hence they may prefer to delegate the communication of bad news to subordinates. Giving bad news has negative implications, and no one wants to be associated with an unpopular cause. When Shoko Asahara, founder of the Aum Shinrikyo terrorist group, was first put on trial and charged with 11 deaths and more than 3,700 injuries following the gas attack on the Tokyo metro system, his 12 defense lawyers asked to remain anonymous because they did not support Aum.[3]

However, the top manager who remains silent for too long in a time of trouble is also likely to be criticized. For example, a CEO who leaves all responsibility for firing redundant staff to a subordinate may appear cowardly. Hence, managers may have a delicate task in calculating for how long they can afford to stand aside from bad news and when they have to get involved.

5.2.5 Addressee

You cannot take for granted that the norms governing addressor–addressee relationships in your culture apply elsewhere. Suppose that you have an idea for a new product. In a culture where power distances and needs to avoid uncertainty are slight, you as a junior manager might feel secure approaching the CEO to make your suggestion. In a culture where it is acceptable to bypass lines of authority (see the discussion of Laurent (1983) in section 2.4), you have no inhibitions about seeking the opinions of colleagues and superiors elsewhere in the organization (assuming that you trust them not to steal your idea). But in contexts where these conditions do not apply, you might have no option but to first discuss your idea with your immediate superior.

5.2.6 *Time*

Concepts of time affect:

- when messages are communicated;
- the length of time devoted to a communication;
- the number of times a message is communicated;
- the time allowed to elapse between a message being received and the response (in Japanese companies, the subordinate is expected to respond immediately to a spoken message from the *Sacho* (boss));
- how often one should communicate. (Many Anglo companies report their financial status every quarter. Is this frequency always necessary given that the energy and time spent might be better invested in maximizing the long-term value of the business? And in practice, when a company is facing financial disaster and investors really want to be kept informed, communication often tends to dry up completely.)

Hall and Whyte (1961) distinguish the following:

- ▌ SCHEDULE time, which refers to the time by when a job should be completed.
- ▌ DISCUSSION time refers to the length of time that should be spent in discussing business.
- ▌ ACQUAINTANCE time determines how long you need to know the other person before he/she will do business with you. In a low-context culture acquaintance time might be cut back to a single meeting and the identity of your company may be more significant than your personal identity. In a high-context culture you may need to invest time in building an "insider" relationship.
- ▌ APPOINTMENT time deals with the issue of punctuality. How late can you afford to be before you should make an apology? The Japanese should be five or ten minutes early. The Anglo manager may be up to five minutes late for an appointment without feeling it necessary to apologize. Some Scandinavians are more particular; an appointment for ten o'clock means ten on the dot. But in Latin American or Arab cultures, precise punctuality is less valued.

5.2.7 *Location*

This parameter determines:

- where business is appropriately communicated;
- what sort of business is communicated in different locations;
- the symbolic meaning that the choice of location imparts to the communication.

The space where the individual works, the ease with which others can gain access, and how the space is furnished, communicate messages of power and status. In American companies the CEO typically occupies a top-floor office (often on a corner), distancing him/herself from the workforce, and aides compete for an office nearby. But the manager of a Federal Express subsidiary in Mexico managed to keep closer tabs on delivery workers by converting a plush conference room next to his office into an employee cafeteria.

"In Mexico, people will work harder for you if they can see you, if work becomes a personal thing between you and them," says Mr Duenas. Federal Express's rate of late delivery has fallen to less than 1%.[4]

5.2.8 *Language, medium, style*

Language, medium, and style determine *how* a message is communicated.

What LANGUAGE is appropriate when dealing with a joint venture partner from another culture when you don't share a first language? What language is appropriate when communicating between headquarters and foreign subsidiary, within the subsidiary, and at different levels of the hierarchy? The selection is decided by such factors as:

- the addressee's language;
- needs for formality or informality;
- organizational policy, culture;
- the language associated with the task (for instance, English has evolved as the language of computer science, and even non-English-speaking computer analysts are bound to use English terms);
- the status of the language in the particular industry (in China, for instance, some public relations firms use English to communicate among their own staff);
- the official status of the language (in some countries, use of the national language is protected by law).

The manager can select from a wide range of MEDIA when choosing the appropriate form for communicating a message. He/she can use speech (in formal and informal meetings, telephone, video, etc.); text (by reports, memos, fax, e-mail, the net, etc.); pictorial forms; or combinations. The selection is decided by situational factors such as

- the number and identities of the addressees;
- the complexity and importance of the message;
- the message function, and whether routine or original;
- distance – opportunities to ask for and make clarifications;
- the need for accuracy and legal considerations;
- the availability of appropriate technology;
- expense.

We saw in section 2.3 that Hall's low-context cultures are in part characterized by a greater dependence on written text, whereas high-context cultures tend to be largely oral, and their members may give text a much lower priority. This gives rise to difficulties when members of a culture at one extreme have to communicate with an organization whose members belong to the other.

Anglo managers make heavy use of text when communicating internally, partly to give some guarantee of legal protection. This means that an Anglo working in a high-context company may be frustrated by the extent to which his/her e-mails and written messages are ignored unless they have been introduced orally.

However, in high-context cultures where personal relationships are more trusted, a face-to-face interaction may be preferred, even though it takes more time. The extreme is illustrated by the problems facing Chinese banks (increasingly influenced by Anglo business culture) when attempting to negotiate loans to the growing numbers of small businesses.

> One applicant, the owner of a factory that makes pickled vegetables, visited [the office of a bank lending supervisor] recently with his ledger: a single piece of handwritten paper folded in his breast pocket. Other would-be borrowers often pile receipts on Binbin's desk in lieu of a balance sheet. Even those who kept books "usually have two or three" Binbin says. "They figure out what we want and write it down."[5]

A Thai financial analyst reports that:

> "I have to write memos (call reports) to the boss after I meet customers. Memos are important for investment bankers. [But] talking with colleagues and superiors about what I do is easier. I can express my feeling to them.... By talking like this, we can know by his face. From memos, we cannot know his real feeling."

That is, a written mode is selected only when there is no alternative. In these cultures, a text may be seen as cold and alienating unless it is used to support a spoken interaction. Indonesian middle-managers report that although they may commit plans for a new policy to writing, they always take the opportunity to discuss the content first with their superiors. The low-context American manager might reverse the process, first writing in order to establish legal ownership of the idea, then proceeding to discussion. In general, the international manager needs to consider when speech or text is most appropriate to the needs of an addressee in the other culture.

The notion of STYLE is the third factor associated with how a message is communicated. It encompasses a range of features, including the length and structure of the message. The introduction gives examples of text messages that are expressed in far greater length than is appropriate to their content; perhaps only EU bureaucrats would value 26,900 words on the subject of duck eggs. The same point applies in speech, and misunderstandings arise when different cultures associate different meanings to extended or reduced messages. For example, Japanese communication style causes problems for Americans because:

Japanese tend to use fewer words. In the US, we tend to think that the more detailed, explicit, and lengthy a communication is, the more complete and thus better it is. In contrast, a common Japanese expression describing ideal communication is *ichi ieba ju wo shiru* (hear one, understand ten). The idea is that if the speaker and listener are on the same wavelength, then it's not necessary to explicitly state everything in words.

(Kopp, 2001)

Formal speech and written styles are appropriate in contexts where authority differences are exaggerated, and less so where they are diminished. In the low power distance Anglo cultures the manager may try to motivate staff by adopting a less formal style and thus creating a closer relationship with them. This tactic can backfire when applied by the Anglo manager in high power distance cultures in circumstances when subordinates expect to occupy a significantly lower place on the hierarchy. They may find it difficult to adjust to the superior lowering him/herself, and so instead of improving, morale suffers.

The use of an informal style further risks confusing a non-native speaker of the language who does not have experience of the idioms and slang used by native speakers. A word may have different connotations in different cultures. To a Frenchman, the word "*eventuellement*" means maybe and probably not, whereas its English equivalent implies that something will definitely happen in the end. Anglo negotiators are happy in searching for a "compromise" – which does not imply a willingness to "compromise" their values – but in Iranian terms, the concepts are less easily separated and the notion of "compromise" implies betraying basic principles.

Such differences occur within one language. The Briton resolves to "table a motion" when he puts a motion before a meeting for discussion; the American interprets this to mean that the motion is delayed. In sum, an inappropriate choice of style leads to misunderstandings and unnecessary ambiguities.

5.3   One- and Two-Way Communication Styles

The participants' decision to use a one- or two-way communication style reflects their relationship and their needs to communicate – which may be task-based. Figure 5.1 models a *one-way* communication between participants A and B, the Addressor and Addressee.

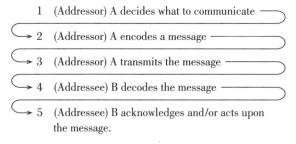

1   (Addressor) A decides what to communicate

2   (Addressor) A encodes a message

3   (Addressor) A transmits the message

4   (Addressee) B decodes the message

5   (Addressee) B acknowledges and/or acts upon the message.

Figure 5.1   One-way communication style

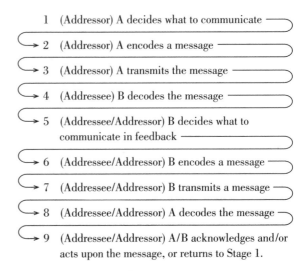

1   (Addressor) A decides what to communicate

2   (Addressor) A encodes a message

3   (Addressor) A transmits the message

4   (Addressee) B decodes the message

5   (Addressee/Addressor) B decides what to
    communicate in feedback

6   (Addressee/Addressor) B encodes a message

7   (Addressee/Addressor) B transmits a message

8   (Addressee/Addressor) A decodes the message

9   (Addressee/Addressor) A/B acknowledges and/or
    acts upon the message, or returns to Stage 1.

Figure 5.2   Two-way communication style

Participant A plans and makes all significant utterances. B may contribute attention markers and acknowledgements during A's communication ("yes," "I see," "of course," and so on) and otherwise responds only by taking any appropriate action. It is implied that the message given B is straightforward, and B does not need to ask for clarification.

Figure 5.2 models a *two-way* communication between A and B. This time, both A and B contribute significantly to the conversation. Each utterance in the conversation may be expressing one of a range of functions, which include:

- requesting and giving information, an opinion, etc.;
- asking for and giving clarification;
- making and responding to a query;
- inviting and suggesting an alternative;
- agreeing and disagreeing;
- requesting and giving support.

Figures 5.1 and 5.2 model the extreme points on a continuum, and in practice most communications occur at a median point on this continuum. Nevertheless, the question then arises as to what factors influence a move in one direction rather than the other.

5.3.1 How the task influences the choice of a one- or two-way style

Task-based factors influencing the choice of style are listed in table 5.2.

Table 5.2 Factors influencing choice of style

One-way style	*Two-way style*
Task urgency	Lack of task urgency
Simple task	Complex task
Routine task	Non-routine task
Close-ended task	Open-ended task

TASK URGENCY can be a factor in all work, and in some tasks – for example, surgery, firefighting, military exercises – is inherent. The key task demands immediate responses to formalized instructions. A one-way style is more efficient so long as all members of the work team share precise understanding of the instructions. Prolonged two-way discussion threatens to impair their efficiency and is avoided so far as possible. But in another situation when no longer engaged in the urgent task – for example, when relaxing off-duty or discussing policy – the medical staff, firefighters, and soldiers might prefer a two-way style.

A SIMPLE TASK is defined as a task comprising few stages. An example might be painting a wall, and A, the person requiring the work to be done, needs to give only a simple instruction to Painter B. A COMPLEX TASK comprises a range of stages, for some of which there may be acceptable alternatives. For example, Manager A has to meet clients abroad and requests his Assistant B to confirm the meeting venue, check the time of flights, and when a flight is agreed to make flight and hotel reservations.

A ROUTINE TASK is one which B has performed many times before or knows from observation of others; and B needs only a minimal instruction from A. A NON-ROUTINE TASK is new to B and A must be prepared to answer queries, provide clarifications where necessary, and to check B's understanding.

The routine/non-routine dimension may override the simple/complex dimension. When the participants are used to performing a complex task, a short one-way communication may be sufficient to trigger its completion. To develop the example above, when Manager A has for many years been visiting his clients on a regular basis (say, every first Monday of the month), always flies at the same time and stays in the same hotel, and Assistant B has been working with him for all this time, perhaps A need give only a brief reminder that the normal procedures apply this month too. On the other hand, if Painter B has never before performed this apparently simple task, A and B may need to participate in a two-way discussion to ensure that the lessons are learned.

A CLOSE-ENDED TASK has one possible satisfactory outcome. For example, I could ask you to wash the plates and stack them. AN OPEN-ENDED TASK has a number of possible outcomes, any of which may satisfy the task goals. For example, a company decides to adapt and manufacture a foreign technology to suit the local market. A number of departments are invited to send representatives to a meeting to discuss the project; these include marketing, R&D, production, finance, sales. Each one of these representatives contributes knowledge and ideas that the others may not initially share, and the communication has a multi-party two-way style. The contributions include questions, clarifications, opinions, information, arguments, and counter-arguments. The final negotiated outcome is unlikely to suit all parties' interests entirely. Other adaptations of the imported technology are equally possible, and might be equally – or more – successful.

In sum; a prejudice has grown up that one-way communications are inherently "bad" and inefficient. This discussion has tried to show that whether or not a communication pattern is efficient depends upon how far it is appropriate, given the task being performed and who is communicating with whom. In some contexts, one-way communication is more useful than the discursive alternative.

5.3.2   Getting the choice wrong

The virtues of two-way communication between top management and lower levels are often taken for granted. Writing for American managers, McNerney (1995) urges:

> . . . you should certainly share the bad news with employees. Doing so will elicit their ideas on how to improve the situation. . . . Companies that fail to share information – particularly bad news – with their employees . . . miss out on the valuable insights their workers could offer to reorganize work, develop new products and improve the business.   *(p. 3)*

This assumes that the employees are prepared for the relationship. In the United States where power distances are narrow, this assumption is often valid. Employees expect to be consulted, and might be seriously alienated if management employed a one-way style in situations that affect their livelihood. But this does not apply everywhere, and a wrong choice of style may give the addressee serious difficulties in interpreting the meaning of a message.

An American company acquired a fruit-processing plant in Puerto Rico and, concerned about productivity levels, hired a firm of American consultants. The consultants advised that they increase motivation by involving the labor force more directly in planning the company's future. Supervisors were given the job of soliciting opinions and proposals from the employees – many of whom subsequently quit.

> Queried by researchers as to their reasons for exiting, the employees said it was apparent that their supervisors did not know what they were doing any more, for they kept enquiring what their employees thought. Therefore the obvious conclusion was that the company must be in trouble and would soon fold.   *(Woodworth and Nelson, 1980, p. 63)*

Power distances in Puerto Rico are relatively large compared to the United States, and the employees were used to being addressed by their supervisors in a one-way style. They were puzzled and discomforted by the two-way style imposed upon them. In sum, the international manager cannot take for granted that his/her choice of style to communicate a given content is appropriate elsewhere. Local employees may need to be trained to recognize and respond to meaning when communicated in a style different to that which their culture group considers appropriate to perform the particular task.

5.3.3 How culture influences the choice

When patterns of communication in an organization between A and B are normally one-way and the superior, A, normally takes the role of Addressor, it can be deduced that the organization is hierarchical. When this occurs regularly in a national culture, it can be deduced that power distances are high.

Where power distances are great and where members place a priority on preserving social harmony, the superior's rights to delegate are associated with authority. Subordinates are wary of asking for clarification of ambiguous utterances lest this involve the superior in loss of face – by implying that he/she communicated inadequately the first time. Comments and suggestions might also suggest a challenge.

Here is an illustration. The CEO and his Assistant belong to a high power distance culture, in which the subordinate Assistant works hard to identify and serve his/her superior's needs. They are situated in the office.

CEO: "I don't have the figures from sales."
Assistant: "Yes sir." [*Calls the sales department and requests that the figures be submitted.*]

The Assistant interprets the CEO's comment as a directive: "Get me the figures from sales." Where this meaning is inappropriate to the context, the Assistant needs to try again, interpreting it as a *wh-* question requiring an answer: "Where are the figures from sales?" If this is inappropriate, he/she might respond as though to a question requiring a *yes/no* answer: for example, "Have you seen the figures from sales?" Only if this meaning is clearly *not* intended dare the Assistant interpret it, at face value, as a statement, perhaps requiring an acknowledgment such as "Oh?" or "Nor me." (See Sinclair, 1980.)

When the participants come from a low-context culture the Assistant is less inclined to intuit his superior's needs. He is less inhibited in giving feedback responses that make the CEO's meaning explicit. These include:

CEO: "I don't have the figures from sales."
Assistant: (a) "Oh?" [providing acknowledgment];
           (b) "No, they haven't been issued yet" [answering a *yes/no* question];
           (c) "They were e-mailed across this morning" [answering a *wh-* question];
           (d) "I'll call for them now" [*calls, and requests the figures*].

This basic model could be made more complex, for example to include options for making a comment: "They're late again," ask for clarification, reinterpret, and so on. But the basic point is clear. To the extent that the context, including the cultural context, does not provide clues as to how the message should be interpreted, the possibilities for ambiguity are vastly multiplied.

How does the Assistant decide which interpretation to make and which response is most appropriate? We look now at the situational factors that help him or her decide.

5.3.4 Clues that help interpretation

Where power distances are low in a low-context culture, the sensible way to resolve this uncertainty is for the Assistant to ask for clarification. But in cultural and organizational contexts where a request for clarification is punished, the Assistant has to rely on other cues in order to disambiguate the CEO's utterance and identify its purpose. What clues are available? They include:

- clues from the specific task;
- clues from the situation (in this case is the utterance made in a location where the figures are easily accessible?);
- clues from the organizational culture (what is normal practice in this company?);
- clues from your experience of this individual (the history of the relationship, his/her psychology, gender, etc.);
- clues from non-verbal signaling (see section 5.4);
- clues from the national culture.

In a high-context culture, the employee invests effort in observing his/her superior, intuiting needs, and predicting appropriate responses from past experience. In turn, the considerate superior avoids behaving unpredictably. But in a low power distance and individualist culture, employees need invest less in understanding the boss's psychology. The other side of this coin is that typical relationships with the workforce in his/her own country lead the manager into making assumptions that may not be justified in an expatriate post. For instance, many Japanese working in the United States:

> ... get quietly frustrated with American underlings. Americans, a Japanese boss often feels, need more supervision than their Japanese counterparts, who try to intuit their superior's desire.[6]

The local American employees spend more time in debating instructions and appear less competent than Japanese employees back home.

5.3.5 Unofficial channels for communicating upwards

In all cultures, "unofficial channels" may be used in preference to the formal structures for conveying information around the organization. In a study of the use of business information in Canadian and Chinese companies, Vaughan (1998) discovered that in both cultures informal sources were more important and better used than the formal sources.

The use of these channels is common in high power distance cultures where it is difficult to communicate unwelcome news and criticisms up the hierarchy. For example, a subordinate wishes to draw the attention of his boss to illegal activity in the workplace. He may choose to send an anonymous note, or to talk to a cousin who passes the information on to a friend of the boss.

In some high-context cultures where the expatriate is not assimilated into social structures, he/she may act as a conduit conveying messages between ranks of locals. His/her equivocal status gives locals the opportunity to pass informal messages around the hierarchy. An American working in a Thai company commented:

> "Exchanging gossip with someone's secretary or driver can often be much more informative than going directly to a top executive, as he may feel uncomfortable expressing dissatis-faction directly. . . . Likewise, most of the Thai executives in my firm use my secretary to convey messages to me or ask my feelings about something rather than communicating with me, even though their English may be better than my secretary's. . . . If she gets it wrong, [that is] her mistake, not theirs."

The Japanese achieve the same ends by making rules for after-hours eating and drinking. Japanese culture is relatively tolerant of drunkenness, and once in the bar subordinates can express opinions that would not be tolerated back in the office. Subordinate–superior messages that are inappropriate in the official setting (during working hours, in the office) can be communicated appropriately when different temporal and locational factors apply (after working hours, in the bar).

5.3.6 *When task and culture conflict*

When values in the culture influence the choice of style in one direction and factors associated with the task influence it in another, which is likely to prove the stronger? It seems that, initially, culture is the stronger. For example, an Anglo manager working in the high power distance culture of Indonesia encourages his Indonesian staff to contribute suggestions for a new strategy. He tells them that no penalties are attached to "wrong" answers, and he knows from another source that they have opinions. But they keep silent. Their culture of saying nothing to a respected superior that might be interpreted as a challenge overrides the organizational priorities that he is trying to develop.

However, we cannot assume that culture is *always* the major determinant. Long-term changes in the task do affect style priorities. People adopt new patterns of behavior when the old are no longer appropriate or effective. For example, members may modify their communication style when the company adopts a new strategy which obliges them to:

- change from performing close-ended problems and participate in open-ended tasks;
- take up responsibilities "pulled down" from a higher level in a job-enrichment program.

In other words, economic forces compel the company to develop new products and apply new technologies; these lead to changes in processes and work relationships, which may propel the use of new communication styles which are appropriate to the new tasks. The work that people do influences how they communicate about it.

5.3.7   One- and two-way texts

So far we have focused on communications expressed through spoken messages, but the same general points apply to written text. In short, a written message transmitted as an order or piece of information that does not invite or expect a response expresses a one-way style; a message that invites participation by the addressee (made either by another text or by a spoken contribution) invites two-way communication.

The addressor/sender chooses the form of text most likely to influence the addressee/receiver to react appropriately. At one extreme e-mail messages might be tagged "urgent," with the purpose of eliciting an immediate response which can include action. At the opposite extreme, chat-lines are designed for two-way communication. Some written reports provide routine information only (and this purpose might be flagged "For information only" or "File"). Other reports are written with the purpose of generating open-ended activity. Spoken and written messages are frequently combined. For example, a report can be intended to generate two-way discussion in face-to-face meetings, and might be labeled "Discussion document."

5.4   Non-Verbal Communication

A transactional model demonstrates how non-verbal signals can contribute to a spoken communication. The participants, A and B, communicate in a context of NOISE. Noise consists of:

- Situational CLUES: factors in the task and physical and cultural contexts that help the participants encode and decode the message. Hall's model (discussed in section 2.3) shows the relatively great importance of cultural clues in high-context cultures and their lesser importance in low-context cultures.
- DISTRACTORS HEARD: unrelated communications and noises that distract the participants from encoding and decoding the message. These might include utterances made by other persons present, doors opening and closing, cars, radios and television, overhead aircraft, and visual signals – all of which may either distract or provide stimuli for the communication.
- DISTRACTORS SEEN: unrelated sights, light/darkness, color.

Encoding and decoding is also facilitated by NON-VERBAL SIGNALS, which pass between the participants in a continual stream. These are discussed further in section 5.4.1.

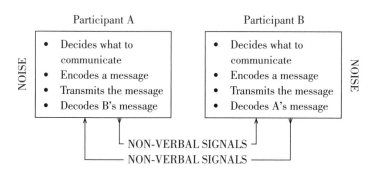

Figure 5.3

This transactional model, summarized in figure 5.3, shows both participants simultaneously sending and receiving (encoding and decoding) messages. Thus it differs from the linear two-way model given in figure 5.2, which implies that B only contributes when A has completed his turn, and A then contributes only when B has completed. The transactional model recognizes that we often make decisions about sending a message and its content *during* the other person's contribution, and not simply on its completion. And so planning what to encode in your next contribution is influenced by what he/she is communicating to you and how you decode it.

5.4.1 *Non-verbal signaling*

When interacting with others, we all make non-verbal signals that convey meaning. By some estimates, 75 percent of all communication is non-verbal (Trompenaars, 1993, p. 69). The interactional model in figure 5.3 takes account of these signals, which supplement and modify the participants' spoken communication to take into account the importance of non-verbal contributions.

These are transmitted whether or not the person is speaking, and are usually involuntary. They are both transmitted and interpreted unconsciously. This means that in any face-to-face interaction, you are sending messages to the other person which are creating impressions of your sincerity, trustworthiness, commitment, etc., and neither of you is fully in control of how the transmission and interpretation processes operate.

These signals have different meanings in different cultures. For example, Anglos greet a new acquaintance by smiling, but the French keep a serious expression. When the French meet a smiling Anglo they may react against his/her apparent insincerity.

The following factors are discussed briefly:

- stance;
- gesture;
- eye movement;
- voice quality.

STANCE includes how and where you position yourself in relation to the other person. Stance conveys messages that differ across cultures. In many societies standing with hands on hips might indicate informality and is neutral for mood. In Indonesia it may be interpreted as a sign of bad temper.

Here is a second example. A Briton and an Egyptian met at a stand-up reception to discuss a proposed business deal. Each unconsciously adopted the posture which his culture associates with good manners. Egyptians value physical proximity, which allows them to assess the other person's sincerity, and tend to stand face to face, at perhaps only 18 inches distance. But when conversing with strangers, the British are used to standing about four feet apart, often at right angles to each other. In this case, the Briton responded to the Egyptian's proximity by moving away and to one side. The Egyptian reacted by moving closer in front. The Briton moved again. This pattern continued throughout the evening.

The Egyptian came away from the reception sensing that the Briton was distant and untrustworthy, and the Briton felt the Egyptian to be pushy. Each interpreted the other's stance subconsciously and negatively, but was unable to rationalize his own sense of disquiet. The opportunities for doing business, which would have benefited both, were not pursued.

GESTURE includes how you use your hands, head, shoulders to reflect and reinforce or substitute for verbal messages.

Many cultures accept physical contact in a business greeting. Anglo males usually resist embracing in public, which is normal in Latin cultures. In Latin America a kiss on both cheeks is accompanied by placing a hand on the other person's shoulder and is known as the "*abrazzo.*" But contact is not universally appreciated. In Malaysia:

> Prime Minister Mahathir Mohamad has ordered Malaysian women serving the government overseas to shake hands with foreigners at official functions after receiving reports that Muslims were not doing so.... "Some Muslim women, both married and single, feel it wrong to touch the bodies particularly of men who are not their relatives," a senior government official said.[7]

Physical contact with strangers is avoided in many Asian cultures.

> Australians have reached the conclusion that "G'day mate, how's it going?" followed by a hearty slap on the back is no way to do business in Asia. The blunt greeting has in the past been an endearing formula for winning contracts in many parts of the world. But in Asia, it can be as insulting as a slap in the face.[8]

EYE MOVEMENT includes length of gaze, maintaining eye contact, dilation, and blinking. Eye movement is always significant and some cultures consciously ascribe great importance to feelings communicated by the eyes. These may be avoided, or welcomed.

The traditional Indian woman avoids looking into the eyes of a man to whom she is not related; on the other hand, the Egyptian stands close in order to "read" the other person's eyes. In both Arab and Indian cultures a subordinate averts his/her gaze when communicating with a superior. In Anglo societies eye contact is crucial to confirm interest and the manager expects it, and is likely to interpret a refusal to make contact as evasiveness.

A Japanese executive who had worked in the United States for a lengthy period experienced difficulties on returning home:

> In New York Mr. Kashimadid a lot of business on the telephone. In Japan, he must personally visit people in order to conduct any important business – "so they can see my eyes."[9]

In Japan, and more generally in high-context cultures, face-to-face communication and eye contact are particularly important in initial business contacts.

VOICE QUALITY. Different cultures associate different communicative meanings to such qualities of the human speech as voice quality, tempo, pitch variation, and volume. They respond differently to variations in these qualities.

In Latin American cultures, wide pitch variation (ups and downs) indicates emotional commitment to the topic. In West Africa, a wide pitch range is expected among males. Many Oriental cultures prefer a more monotonous style, which indicates respect. Until recently, Japanese women were expected to speak in a high pitch in the workplace. One woman explained:

> "when you are with a customer, you want to be polite. If you're being courteous, your voice naturally rises."

5.5   Implications for the Manager

Compare an organization that you know well *in your own culture* with a similar organization *in some other culture*.

1   Assume that you are planning appropriate messages in the two organizations, intended to achieve similar purposes (for example, messages used to communicate a promotion; a reprimand; a query for technical information; a directive; a policy change.) What differences occur in your selections of:
   (a)   appropriate addressor?
   (b)   appropriate addressee?
   (c)   appropriate content?
   (d)   appropriate language, medium, style?
   (e)   appropriate time?
   (f)   appropriate location?

What cultural and other factors explain these differences?

2 In each of the two organizations, how typical are two-way communication styles between superior and subordinate? With what tasks are one-way styles usually used? With what tasks are two-way styles usually used? How far do these factors explain why two-way styles are/are not selected? Consider:

(a) task factors;
(b) cultural factors;
(c) any other factors.

5.6 SUMMARY

This chapter has reviewed aspects of cross-cultural communication that concern the international manager. Section 5.2 dealt with the notion of APPROPRIATE COMMUNICATION in different CULTURAL contexts. A message is persuasive and effective when it is perceived as appropriate. Appropriateness depends on WHAT content is communicated, by WHOM, to WHOM, WHEN, WHERE, and HOW – that is, in what medium, language, and style. The concept of style was further developed in section 5.3: ONE- and TWO-WAY COMMUNICATIVE STYLES. This saw that selection of an appropriate style is influenced by factors associated with the task – whether it is urgent or non-urgent; simple or complex; routine or non-routine; close-ended or open-ended. The influence of national culture was also examined. Section 5.4 dealt with NON-VERBAL COMMUNICATION, and emphasized that non-verbal signals may have different meanings in different cultures, and are often made and interpreted unconsciously.

5.7 EXERCISE

This exercise examines how the cultural context influences WHAT information is communicated, the choice of person TO WHOM it is communicated, and HOW it is communicated.

Figure 5.4 shows part of a small engineering company, Acme. *You* are Assistant Marketing Manager C. You have been with Acme for six months. Your relations with D and E are neutral, neither good nor bad. B is also a new-comer, appointed to this position nine months ago.

1 SITUATION

In your own time, you recently attended a trade exhibition at which Acme was not represented. You were interested by the display made by a competitor, and believe that it offered lessons which Acme could apply. (This would not involve serious modifications to your current marketing strategy.)

Acme is in a national culture where:

- power distances are high;
- relationships are highly collectivist;

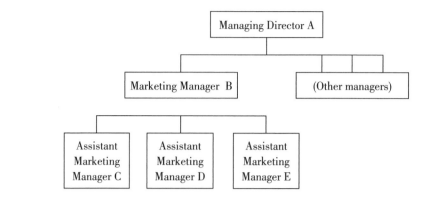

Figure 5.4

- needs to avoid uncertainty are high.

QUESTION A: To WHOM should you communicate your ideas?

(i)   no one?
(ii)   inform B?
(iii) inform A?
(iv)   inform D and E; then all three of you inform B?
(v)   inform D and E; then all three of you inform A?
(vi)   any other alternative?

QUESTION B: Depending on your choice of (i)–(vi), HOW should you communicate?

(a)   by a short e-mail message?
(b)   in a long written report?
(c)   in a casual conversation, face-to-face?
(d)   in a casual conversation, by telephone?
(e)   in a formal meeting?
(f)   any other alternative?

2   SITUATION

As for situation 1, *except* that Acme is in a culture where:

- power distances are small;
- relationships are highly individualist;
- needs to avoid uncertainty are low.

QUESTION C: To WHOM should you communicate your ideas?
   As for situation 1, (i)–(vi).

QUESTION D: Depending on your choice of (i)–(vi), HOW should you communicate?
   As for situation 1, (a)–(f).

3   SITUATION

It is apparent to you, as a recent recruit, that the workload in the marketing department is too heavy. Too much time is spent on unnecessary routine and the opportunities for creative marketing are greatly restricted. All staff at your level and at subordinate levels are demoralized.

Acme is in a culture where:

- power distances are high;
- relationships are highly collectivist;
- needs to avoid uncertainty are high.

QUESTION E: To WHOM should you communicate your ideas?
    As for situation 1, (i)–(vi).

QUESTION F: Depending on your choice of (i)–(vi), HOW should you communicate?
    As for situation 1, (a)–(f).

4 SITUATION
As for situation 3, *except* that Acme is in a culture where:

- power distances are small;
- relationships are highly individualist;
- needs to avoid uncertainty are low.

QUESTION G: To WHOM should you communicate your ideas?
    As for situation 1, (i)–(vi).

QUESTION H: Depending on your choice of (i)–(vi), HOW should you communicate?
    As for situation 1, (a)–(f).

Notes

1 B. Barrow, "Last post for unwanted mail," *Daily Telegraph*, November 13, 2001.
2 Tan Tarn How, "Hit by spam," *The Straits Times*, November 14, 2002.
3 "Murder trial of doomsday cult leader grips Japan," *The Guardian*, April 25, 1996.
4 Matt Moffett, "Culture Shock: Moving to Mexico," *Asian Wall Street Journal*, September 24, 1992.
5 Matthew Forney, "Betting on the Wrong Horse," *TIME Asia*, February 17, 2003, 161/6.
6 John Schwarz, Jeanne Gordon, and Mark Veverka, "The 'Salaryman' blues," *Newsweek*, May 9, 1988.
7 "KL order to women," AFP, *The Nation (Bangkok)*, August 14, 1992.
8 Brian Timms, "'G'day Mate' not working in Asia," Reuter, *The Nation (Bangkok)*, January 5, 1989.
9 E. S. Browning, "Unhappy Returns," *The Wall Street Journal*, May 6, 1986.

CHAPTER SIX
Needs and Incentives

6.1 Introduction

Each person has his or her personal needs for work, and needs for work are many and various. The need for financial reward is an obvious one and employers and employees usually find it easier to discuss their contractual relations in terms of money than, say, the appreciation given for work done – which, we will see, is sometimes very important. But people value money for different reasons, some of which may be symbolic. A British businessman describes why money was important to him. Mr. Duffield was a successful entrepreneur, at one stage married to the daughter of an even more successful businessman.

> "Money is how you keep the score," said Mr Duffield. "I am very competitive. At the time I married [his former wife] I think her father thought I married her for her money. Actually I loved her. What I have always wanted to prove to myself and to her father, if he was still alive, is that I did marry her for love. I thought that if I had more money than her, that would prove it. I needed to prove it to myself, mainly to myself."[1]

This chapter examines a range of factors that motivate performance. The first half deals with the analysis of needs. The second half focuses on the application of this analysis in an incentive system. There must be a close relationship between the two. An incentive system directed towards meeting needs that employees do not experience is bound to fail.

It is argued throughout that the individual's needs are influenced by factors associated with his/her personal situation (age, experience, and so on) and with factors in the environment, including culture. People living in different economic and cultural systems have different needs, and an incentive system that motivates performance in one situation may be useless in some other. This means that an incentive system designed for the headquarters of a multinational organization, say, may be inappropriate when implemented in a subsidiary.

6.2   Needs

When the individual perceives that his/her needs are likely to be satisfied by a particular activity, he/she will commit to this activity, at least until the need is satisfied or the activity seems unlikely to achieve satisfaction.

However, not all needs are of interest to the company. Some needs may be neutral to company goals and relate entirely to the individual's private life over which the company has less control than in the workplace. Some may be positive, but do not match with company goals; for example, "I feel a need to work slowly and carefully so that my output carries only a 1 percent margin of error; as a result I produce only 100 items a day. The company tolerates a 5 percent margin so long as I can produce 1,000 items." In extreme cases, the contradiction may be negative: "I am motivated by a need to destroy company plant and products, and management may have no alternative but to dismiss me and to improve any conditions under its control that have caused the destructive behavior."

Incentive systems are far more likely to achieve company goals when they also promise to achieve the individual's goals. This means that the manager needs to first identify workforce needs that correspond to company needs, then to design incentive systems that offer opportunities to satisfy these needs in ways that help achieve the company goals. For example, if the company needs production of 1,000 items a day, it aims to stimulate individuals' need to achieve this output.

6.2.1   Perceptions of needs

What do you need from your work? Research by Kovach (1987) aimed at discovering what "job reward" factors were really valued by employees. His findings suggest that conventional stereotypes – that workers are most motivated by offers of a pay rise – may be far from the truth. The informant pool consisted of industrial employees, including unskilled blue-collar and skilled white-collar workers, in American manufacturing companies. The research was conducted in 1946 and again in 1986.

Table 6.1   Ten "job reward" factors ranked first for 1986, then, in parentheses, for 1946

1	Interesting work	(6)
2	Full appreciation of work done	(1)
3	Feeling of being in on things	(2)
4	Job security	(4)
5	Good wages	(5)
6	Promotion and growth in organization	(7)
7	Good working conditions	(9)
8	Personal loyalty to employees	(8)
9	Tactful discipline	(10)
10	Sympathetic help with personal problems	(3)

These rankings (table 6.1) show that over 40 years, most priorities did not change significantly between 1946 and 1986. But why did "interesting work" become so much more important? And why had "sympathetic help" declined in importance? In 1946, the year after the Second World War, American society was suffering strains and shortages. In 1986 firms were required by law to provide personal support that in 1946 might have been available only on an informal basis. We cannot answer these questions definitively, but they do raise issues of how far needs and motivators are influenced by the world outside the workplace – the economic, political and cultural contexts.

Your needs are partly influenced by your personality. They are also influenced by your membership of different groups, and by factors in the wider environment.

6.2.2   Sub-group differences

Perhaps surprisingly, "good wages" were ranked below four other factors in both 1946 and 1986. But this does not mean that wages were not of prime importance to *any* of the informant pools. These findings generalize the needs of different sub-groups – for example, different age groups, skill groups, and both genders. Informants aged under 30 listed good wages, job security, and promotion and growth as their first three choices.

Among Kovach's older workers job security continued to be listed high, although declined in importance over time – perhaps because they no longer had to support young children, and had built up adequate investments to carry them through retirement. The best-paid ranked wages tenth, and "interesting work" their top priority. It is likely that the best-paid were also the most highly educated and trained.

Few differences were found between the preferences of men and women. Women ranked "full appreciation of work done" in first place, while men placed it second. However, this does not mean that gender differences are never significant. In other cultures and other industries, the work needs of men and women may be far apart.

The practical importance of this research is that management can apply the analysis of needs in designing an incentive system. Members of a group that prioritize their needs as above are more likely to be motivated by opportunities for "interesting work" as the main consideration than "good wages" or "sympathetic help." Of course, this does not mean that the company can afford to ignore needs for wages and help.

The implication is that an incentive system designed for one group of employees and proved effective with them may be less effective when applied with another group who have different characteristics, different relations with their environment, and prioritize their needs differently. For example, opportunities that motivate older workers approaching retirement may be unattractive to new workers struggling to support a young family.

Within a single culture, these groups may have different needs:

- different age groups;
- different educational groups (e.g. university graduates and school leavers);
- different functional specializations (accounting and engineering staffs);
- genders;
- ranks.

Factors that influence needs, based in the wider environment, include the following:

- the economic and political context;
- industry norms;
- organizational culture;
- national culture.

These last four factors are briefly discussed in the following sections.

6.2.3   The economic and political context

Members of a society suffering economic hardship or political disturbance typically place greater priority on their security needs than do members of a society that is economically and politically secure. Onedo (1991) found that samples of Australian and Papua New Guinean managers both regarded a sense of achievement as their most important needs but the Papua New Guineans were more dissatisfied with their levels of security and placed security needs higher than autonomy needs.

6.2.4   Industry norms

Long-term employees in stable and conservative industries are more likely to be motivated by the security which attracted them to the industry in the first place. Employees in new and relatively insecure industries – such as in some areas of finance and communications – may be prepared to trade career security in return for immediate financial rewards. To a degree, workers select the occupation that seems most likely to supply the incentives that appeal to their personalities. Chow (1988) found that public sector managers in Hong Kong most valued job security, and private sector managers most valued opportunities for high earnings. Both sectors valued opportunities for promotion. The national culture might be irrelevant; that is, these findings might be duplicated among public sector and private sector workers elsewhere.

In Greece, Bourantas and Papalexandris (1999) studied employees in public and private organizations, and found no differences in needs for pay and security. This might seem to contradict Chow's findings; but, the authors suggest, public sector employees compensate for their lower pay by the greater opportunities for tenure, while private sector employees accept their lower security by the greater range of opportunities in the job market. Perhaps all employees are attracted by the ideals of generous pay *and* full security (see the discussion of the Nomura example in section 2.5.2), but in practice few jobs offer both and most employees have to choose one or the other.

6.2.5 *Organizational culture*

Section 4.2.2 defined a positive organizational culture as one in which workforce and management share a commitment to the organization. They are motivated by opportunities to achieve strategic goals. In a negative culture, the values of management and workforce do not correspond, and in an extreme case the workforce may be negatively motivated, and act to frustrate management and to sabotage company interests. Similarly, employees are motivated by a cohesive and strong culture in which they communicate successfully with colleagues. How management attempts to motivate the workforce by making appropriate modifications to the organizational culture is developed in section 6.3 below.

6.2.6 *National culture*

The employees' national culture influences their needs, and Hofstede's model can be read as a ranking of motivational factors in different cultures. This model is not only explanatory; it enables the manager to predict what incentives are likely to attract in different contexts. Here are some examples.

More INDIVIDUALIST cultures value opportunities for individual promotion and growth, and autonomy. Hence employees are more likely to be attracted by an incentive system that provides these opportunities. Kent State University (1997) research focuses on the individual's needs for control over events, recognition for achievements, and influence over the environment.

On the other hand, more COLLECTIVIST cultures value opportunities to belong to an influential group. In a strongly collectivist culture, members are not attracted by individual recognition and the opportunity to shine above other members of the group. In Thailand, Rieger and Wong-Rieger (1990) suggest:

> ... the introduction of an individual merit bonus plan, which runs counter to the societal norm of group cooperation, may result in a decline rather than an increase in productivity from employees who refuse to openly compete with each other.   *(p. 1)*

Cultures with HIGHER NEEDS TO AVOID UNCERTAINTY value job security, and may value a guarantee of long-term employment more than the offer of a pay rise. Females may not wish for promotion when this seems likely to bring them into conflict with male colleagues, and so are demotivated from making the effort to win promotion. Cultures with LOWER NEEDS TO AVOID UNCERTAINTY value job variety.

Cultures with WIDER POWER DISTANCES value opportunities to work for a manager who shows loyalty to subordinates and gives clear instructions. A Japanese manager with long experience of working in China noted that "Chinese workers care about the reputation of their boss more than the result of the business." Cultures with NARROWER POWER DISTANCES value opportunities to work for a manager who maintains a consultative relationship with subordinates.

More FEMININE cultures strive for tender, welfare societies and focus on domestic values. They tend to value shorter and convenient working hours. More MASCULINE cultures value opportunities to compete for promotion – but males may not be motivated by competition with females.

6.2.7   *Identifying needs*

The company can only develop an incentive system that gives employees the opportunities to satisfy their needs when it identifies these needs accurately. This may not be straightforward.

Besides analyzing employees' perceptions of their needs – discussed in section 6.2.1 above – Kovach (1987) also reported on rankings made by these employees' direct supervisors. The supervisors were asked to order job rewards as they believed that their subordinates would rank them (see table 6.2). Their ranking remained almost the same for 1946 and 1986 (recall table 6.1).

This ranking does not correspond with the rankings made by employees. Why were the supervisors so inaccurate? Possibly they failed to understand their subordinates' needs – but many must have once worked themselves at the same levels with the same

Table 6.2   "Job reward" factors

1	Good wages
2	Job security
3	Promotion and growth in organization
4	Good working conditions
5	Interesting work
6	Personal loyalty to employees
7	Tactful discipline
8	Full appreciation of work done
9	Sympathetic help with personal problems
10	Feeling of being in on things

experiences of need. Perhaps they were projecting their own needs. Or perhaps they were reflecting the management values that they now represented.

Kovach's findings demonstrate that managers may fail to accurately identify the real needs experienced by their subordinates. An inaccurate needs analysis can hardly be applied to the design of an incentive system that is optimally motivating.

These findings have an important implication for the international manager. Kovach's informants were all American; and if managers fail to perceive, or to act upon, the needs of subordinates with whom they share the same cultural profile, they are even more likely to mistake the needs of members of another culture. That is, the manager posted from headquarters to a foreign subsidiary may have even greater difficulties in understanding the needs of the local workforce, and thus difficulty in designing an incentive system that is optimally motivating.

6.2.8   Hierarchies of needs

Needs are frequently described in terms of a hierarchy. The most influential hierarchy produced is still that designed by Maslow in 1954. This continues to influence theories of motivation and the design of incentive systems.

Maslow describes needs on five levels:

- Level 5 (highest): Self-actualization and achievement needs.
- Level 4: Esteem needs – both self-esteem and the esteem of others.
- Level 3: Belonging and social needs.
- Level 2: Safety and security needs.
- Level 1: Physiological (existence) needs.

Cartwright (2000) proposes a new highest and sixth level – the "unattainable," namely, what the individual strives for and can never entirely satisfy. Because this level is unreachable, it suggests that however many other goals the individual achieves, eventually he/she cannot be entirely satisfied.

Needs at Levels 1–3 are basic needs which are satisfied by extrinsic outcomes external to the person, such as food, money, praise from others. The ego and self-actualization needs at Levels 4–5 (or 4–6, if Cartwright's suggestion is accepted) are satisfied by intrinsic and internal outcomes, such as a sense of achievement and competence. These spring from personal feelings of worth and cannot be given by someone else.

A satisfied need is no longer motivating, and you satisfy needs progressively. This means that when you have satisfied needs at one level you try to meet those at the next level up, and a higher level need is usually only experienced when those below have been met. Assume that a man needs to buy a car. He knows that if he completes his job he will be rewarded with the money with which to buy the car, and so he works. When the effects of behavior are valued, the individual continues to repeat that behavior; and so he continues to work until his monetary needs are satisfied. When he has enough money he stops working – unless, of course, he finds a new need.

This implies that the model is not only hierarchical but also sequential. It helps explain why Kovach's (1987) older and better-paid employees, who have satisfied their "deficit" needs on Levels 1 and 2, should place a premium on work that is interesting. It explains why the younger and most poorly paid, who are not yet secure in satisfying their physiological and safety needs, should most value good wages.

6.2.9 *Maslow and money*

Most people will admit to needing money, but for different reasons. The case in the introduction gives an example of someone needing money for a very individual reason that reflected his personal circumstances – to impress his wife's father.

Maslow's model does not include "money," which might suggest that he does not think that needs for money are important, or can be applied in an incentive system. In practice though, money plays a part at every level. The model helps us recognize how monetary reward functions as a means to an end, rather than an end in itself.

Money enables us to purchase the necessities of life, thus satisfying needs at Level 1. And when we have consumed sufficient food and drink, any extra money is invested in accommodation to meet safety and security needs at Level 2. Purchasing an expensive car, a house in a good locality, restaurant reservations, and new clothes serves to impress others and build relationships. Thus money helps satisfy social needs at Level 3.

But the simple relationship described above is obviously inadequate. People buy cars, houses, restaurant reservations, clothes, for more than their utilitarian worth. They also serve as symbols of success. In China in 2002 many employees seemed to have the same ambitions as do many Anglo workers – for instance, the ambition to drive a good car.

> With over 10 per cent annual growth, the capital market in Shanghai is flowing into automobiles, the second icon of a successful lifestyle after housing.[2]

Your ownership of an expensive car tells the world: "I have achieved, I am a success." And in Thailand, Bangkok

> ... has more Mercedes per capita than any other [city] in the world; car hunger is driven by low interest rates on long-term hire purchase schemes and advertisements that emphasise "prestige" and "the demonstration of your achievements", not comfort or reliability.[3]

Elsewhere, wealthy people who wish to project an image of sympathy with natural environmental causes may prefer a cheap car, and even cycle to work – as do many in the Netherlands – and, there, invest in some other symbol.

Needs are satisfied by intrinsic outcomes at Levels 4 and 5, and the size of your pay packet has other symbolic values. It justifies your sense of self-esteem, and reflects your achievement. It serves as a means of keeping score with other people (are you more or less successful?) and with yourself (have you achieved more this year than last?).

In a developed economy, top executives can earn salaries of many millions of dollars a year. In the United Kingdom, Dr. Martin Read earned £27 million[4] from Logica in 2001, and Philip Green was paid £201 million in dividends[5] from his family-owned company, BHS, in 2003. These sums projected powerful messages to the media, their colleagues, employees, customers, and competitors. No one needs so many millions in order to meet existence needs, yet these executives might feel humiliated if it were suggested that next year their compensation should be reduced by, say, a million dollars. The deprivation would not be physical but psychological.

6.2.10 Maslow across cultures

Section 6.2.6 showed how your national culture influences your perceptions of needs. The questions then arise, how far do models of needs reflect the cultures of their writers, and how far can they be applied in different cultures and in different economic and political contexts?

Maslow's "self-actualization" at the top of the pyramid reflects the individualism of American culture. Nevis (1983, p. 21) proposed a variant model appropriate to the collectivist culture of the People's Republic of China.

- Level 4 (highest): Needs for self-actualization in the service of society.
- Level 3: Safety and security needs.
- Level 2: Physiological needs.
- Level 1: Belonging (social) needs.

How far does this model reflect abiding values in Chinese culture? The data were collected in extraordinary times, in the final years of the Cultural Revolution, when group loyalty was essential. A few years later, the continued influence of collectivism was demonstrated by Mann's (1989) analysis of Beijing Jeep, a joint venture between AMC and Beijing Automative Works, in which some workers willingly gave up their pay rises in order to appease the resentment of less productive colleagues.

A period of reform followed, and in the new economic and political situation, the political priorities of the Cultural Revolution were no longer motivating. In 1991 Tung argued that although Chinese enterprises still depended on a combination of rule enforcement, external rewards, and internalized motivation, these elements were differently emphasized.

> In periods of greater political openness, external rewards were paramount. During times of political retrenchment, ideology and internalized motivation have assumed a greater role.   *(p. 342)*

The process of rapid change continued. *Time* reported in 1993 that it was acceptable to preach "To be rich is glorious," and a Beijing entrepreneur was quoted as saying "The only thing we believe in today is making money."[6]

Other scholars argued that the cultural gulf was still too wide to allow immediate application of Western systems. Easterby-Smith et al. (1995) found such significant differences between Chinese and United Kingdom companies in approaches to rewards, appraisal, and the assessment of potential that they doubted whether the principles of human resource management could be applied at all, even very generally.

Jackson and Bak (1998) also questioned the relevance of concepts of motivation based on individualism. They characterized Chinese culture as collectivist with a great respect for authority and hierarchy. This led them to recommended that Chinese employees in international joint ventures can only be motivated by incentives that reflect these cultural attributes. Their recommendations included:

- clear communication of job descriptions, rules, and procedures, which reduced risk and ambiguity;
- rewards for loyalty;
- pay commensurate with rank and standing;
- a strong corporate identity;
- effective induction and training programs;
- the development of positive local and expatriate role models;
- clear opportunities for career development.

The old Communist ideals of egalitarian pay schemes had not been entirely abandoned. Sun (2000) perceived that the transition to "pay for labour" schemes was only gradual, and that older workers brought up to believe that equal, undifferentiated pay was more "fair" were least comfortable with the new policy of paying "to each according to his labour." Nevertheless, entry to the World Trade Organization in 2001 and greater exposure to Western business systems seems to mean that Western values are increasingly likely to motivate Chinese employees.

We may infer from this example that:

- in any one culture, needs change over time;
- needs are influenced by the political and economic environments;
- Anglo models of needs do not necessarily apply in other cultural contexts (i.e. an incentive system based on an Anglo model may not necessarily be effective elsewhere).

6.3   Designing Incentives

Management applies its analysis of needs in an incentive system. This aims to stimulate desired productivity by offering employees the opportunities to satisfy their needs in ways that help to achieve company goals.

When needs have been analyzed, management decisions have to be made about how much to invest in implementing an incentive system, and how far the different needs of individuals and groups can be accommodated.

6.3.1 Cost

The design and implementation of an incentive system costs money. The financial investment is direct when employees are offered wage rises and bonuses in return for greater productivity; it is indirect when, for example, facilities are refurbished in order to create a more positive atmosphere and managers are trained how to develop new relationships with the staff. A company only invests in its incentive system to the extent that this promises to increase profits.

The size of the investment in building motivators is determined by labor market factors; the value added by scarce labor and the cost of hiring in the labor market. When numerous companies are competing strongly for a small supply of labor and the company depends on holding the loyalty of its key employees, it invests more in identifying their needs and providing opportunities by which these can be satisfied. When supplies of the labor required are plentiful, the company invests less. Here are two examples.

1 Aamax Company manufactures paper cups. The cups are made from lengths of pre-cut paper, that are pressed out and glued. Profits are modest. The work is unskilled, and the labor market offers a large pool of people happy to take a position. Those who cannot cope with the work or do not like it are easily replaced. The company has little interest in whether they enjoy the work or not. There is no need to invest in motivating them – and profit margins are so thin that if a significant investment were made, the company would soon be forced into bankruptcy.
2 Bamax Company manufactures rocket guidance systems. A small group of highly trained rocket engineers is employed. The engineers cannot be easily replaced from the labor market. A successful project can earn massive profits – but the success rate would decline significantly if these elite employees left the company (worst of all, to work for a competitor). It is vitally important that they be retained and so the company is prepared to invest large sums in motivating them. This includes building their commitment to work that is "fun" and gives a sense of achievement.

In sum, good wages, guarantees of long-term employment, offers of promotion, attractive physical conditions, and pension schemes all carry a price tag. The company will not spend more on designing and implementing an incentive system than it can expect to benefit from in terms of continued and increased productivity.

6.3.2 How far can incentives be designed to meet needs?

We have seen that individual needs differ. Employee A is motivated by opportunities to earn more; B by increased responsibility; C by a title; D by a good relationship with management; E by the use of a company car; and so on. In practice, a company employing a large workforce cannot design a different incentive system for each individual, tailored to his or her particular needs profile. And so it is unlikely that the company can ever provide optimal motivation for every individual.

On the one hand, management is under pressure to generalize needs, and to assume that members of a group share some common needs. This approach makes savings, but is bound to provide inaccurate reflections of some individuals' needs, and perhaps is fully accurate for no one person. On the other hand, a company competing for labor in an expanding economy may decide that it has to invest in greater attention to individual needs in order to secure and retain those skills that are in great demand. In 2003:

> Businesses worldwide are placing greater emphasis on cost control and talent management to differentiate people, and tailoring payments for each employee to stimulate productivity.[7]

The models of needs discussed so far (Kovach, 1987; Maslow, 1954) suggest that individuals may give priority to non-financial needs from their work, which suggests that these may be used as motivators. These include opportunities to do interesting work, win appreciation of work done, feel that they are in on things, and so on. The company applies these alternatives when:

- they are as effective as the wage rise;
- the costs they incur are less (including the costs of implementation);
- they are implemented consistently over time, and when applied to different individuals and groups they are credible.

The following subsection considers monetary incentives. The alternatives are discussed in sections 6.4 and 6.5.

6.3.3   Wages and bonuses as motivator

In practice, the conditions for successful motivation through non-monetary incentives are often difficult to meet (see sections 6.5.2 and 6.5.3 for examples of problems that arise). Companies find it easier to motivate and reward using salaries, bonuses, stock options, and the like. They apply a system of monetary rewards both as a recognition of past performance and as an incentive to future performance for three reasons:

- First, it is relatively simple to administer. Pay packets can be easily calculated and paid to a large number of employees.
- Second, the individual employee is easily able to convert financial rewards into the goods and services that satisfy his/her particular needs. People need money to exchange for a range of items including food, clothing, housing, entertainment, educational and medical services, and status symbols.
- Third, a salary rise sends out signals about the status of the company and the individual rewarded.

The worth of a bonus as an incentive depends on industry and company factors. When the same bonus is paid every year it becomes taken for granted, as though an element of the basic reward structure. This has two effects. First, the bonus no longer motivates greater effort in the future; and second, any decrease in the level paid – perhaps caused by adverse trading conditions which the workforce are unable to control – causes disappointment and may be demotivating. When Sanyo (Thailand) was forced by an economic downturn to cut its end-of-year bonus from 5.75 months in 1995 to 3 months in 1996, workers burned down a warehouse containing 500 new refrigerators and started fires in the production facility and company headquarters.[8]

A bonus paid to one unit in the organization but not to others is likely to demotivate those others. In 2001, after a relatively unsuccessful year, British Telecom awarded a ten-day vacation in Australia to 21 members of its accounts team and their partners. An engineering manager commented:

> "They're being rewarded for doing their jobs, only what they should be doing. Last year our team won an industry commendation, and management didn't give us a chocolate bar. So we say, why should we do anything to help these accountants?"

The financial services industry, on the other hand, is very sensitive to market swings; profits vary enormously from year to year. Experienced employees soon learn why their bonus payments fluctuate. Hence when companies in this industry pay a low bonus that fairly reflects the state of the market and their lack of success, these employees accept the fact and are not necessarily demotivated.

Stock options can be relatively cheap, and in Asia are gaining popularity as a means of encouraging long-term commitment.

6.4   How Structures Motivate

Employees are influenced by factors associated with their company, its goals and mission, and its organizational culture. They are more productive when they work in structures that motivate them.

Companies commonly work to build positive structures that give employees the sense that their interests and management interests are aligned. Day et al. (2002) argue that employees are less motivated by excessive financial incentives than by a culture that promotes the individual's sense of commitment to the company, and to thinking not only about present circumstances but also about innovatory systems to develop in the future. The disadvantage lies in the difficulty in creating such structures. Day et al. admit that "we don't thoroughly understand how companies can build such a culture."

6.4.1   Teamwork structures

Managers increasingly recognize the importance of relationships between colleagues. Teams are developed to give employees the opportunities for:

- group decision-making;
- increased autonomy;
- shared responsibilities;
- a greater sense that they are shaping their own working lives.

The difficulties are that:

- The cost of reorganizing work on a teamwork basis may be greater than the revenue generated.
- The tasks may demand individual work and cannot, therefore, be restructured.
- Middle management often feels threatened by lower-level autonomy.
- Reward systems are not changed, and employees continue to be paid on the basis of individual performance.
- The new structures do not fit in the cultural context. Teamwork is usually better suited to a collectivist culture than to an individualist culture. This does not mean that it cannot work in an individualist culture, but management should be prepared to resolve the difficulties that might occur.

6.4.2 *Leadership*

Vroom's (1964) expectancy theory recognized that the extent to which the individual feels able to achieve the targets set influences whether they try, and how much effort they invest in it. The leader has the function of setting a high target and then inspiring his/her followers to achieve it.

The attributes of good leadership are not constant. The roles adopted by the successful leader vary in different contexts. In any society and organization, members have their own expectations of appropriate leadership behavior, and the successful leader must make some concessions to his/her followers' expectations. The leader must also be responsive to the needs of the organizational culture. A successful bank CEO, for example, may not be suited to lead an advertising agency. The manager competent to lead one activity may be incompetent in some other activity. Here we consider the significance of national culture.

Hofstede's (2001) data indicate that successful leadership styles vary between cultures. For example, where power distances are small, the ideal boss is a resourceful democrat and subordinates expect to be consulted. Where power distances are large, the ideal boss is a benevolent autocrat or good father, and subordinates expect to be told what to do.

Suutari (1996) examined the experiences of Finnish expatriates in different European countries, and his anecdotal evidence indicated different perceptions of appropriate leadership.

An expatriate in Germany stated that a Scandinavian "softness" was not appropriate, and one had to be more authoritative in order to receive subordinates' respect. An expatriate in France had to become less participative because he could not get any opinions from

French subordinates and nothing happened if he did not make the decisions himself. An expatriate in Great Britain was told to be more rigorous and use a more directive style.

(p. 701)

In Thailand, good leadership is sometimes associated with moral qualities. Chamlong Srimuang, an ex-general, ex-politician, and devout advocate of Buddhist values, founded a Leadership Training Centre in which Thai politicians, civil servants, and business people were encouraged to:

> ... "devote, to sacrifice, to think of the majority of the people, not only themselves and their families." . . . "To be a good leader, you have to be efficient. But the other thing is, you have to be good," says Mr Chamlong, clad in the simple denim work shirt and trousers of a traditional Thai farmer. "We are teaching them about the last category: to be good."
>
> [The Federation of Thai Industries chairman commented]: "the qualities of a leader are to be a 'giver' and a 'server' but most of the leaders are not qualified. . . . Most people are 'commanders' and 'receivers'."[9]

At a superficial level Mr Chamlong's concept of leadership as a motivator might not be fit easily into the standard American MBA syllabus. However, it does underline the MBA lesson that a successful leadership style must be appropriate to the context within which it is exercised.

6.4.3   *Learning and training*

Anglo cultures place great importance on personal change and achievement, and opportunities to learn new skills are valued. The employees of technological organizations are motivated by opportunities to develop their technical skills and understanding.

GE is a company that focuses on encouraging learning rather than formal teaching. The Chief Learning Officer explained the company's continuing success by its focus on a culture based on achievement and self-critical reflection on how to improve. Training systems emphasized employees' needs to learn rather than the company's capacity to teach.

> "A learning organisation is full of people that always want to know why. . . . No one is satisfied with just doing good enough," he said.
>
> Corcoran admitted that another critical element of GE's learning culture and continued success had been the type of people it had recruited, from factory workers to highly trained professionals. "We always look for people who are very bright over-achievers."[10]

But there are disadvantages. Learning divorced from formal teaching systems is difficult to measure. Learning that contradicts present practice and policy may not be rewarded – and may even be punished, which does not encourage further experimentation. The danger is that learning is rewarded only when it conforms to what has already been learned and applied. Further, the accent on "learning" is not equally appropriate in all contexts. Opportunities to learn may be less stimulating in a company where employees are primarily interested in securing a reasonable wage. For example, a manager in a Taiwanese garment manufacturer found that production staff much resented being asked to work on new product lines. They were paid on piece rates, and time invested in learning new skills represented a fall in their wages. In this context, the call to new learning was demotivating.

6.5   Work as a Motivator

Kovach (1987) and Maslow (1954) both make clear that factors intrinsic to the work are motivating. People want interesting work that wins esteem and is recognized, and gives feelings of achievement. Two further theories and their applications are discussed here:

- Herzberg's two-factor theory (sections 6.5.1–6.5.5);
- McClelland's achievement motivation (section 6.5.6).

6.5.1   Herzberg

Herzberg's work has implications for multinational companies attempting to transplant management systems across cultures in the expectation that systems that prove motivating in the home country will also be effective in the new cultural context.

Herzberg et al. (1959) and Herzberg (1968) distinguished two types of motivational factors, HYGIENE FACTORS and MOTIVATORS. If the hygiene factors are absent, the employee will be dissatisfied, but their presence does not guarantee satisfaction. The hygiene factors include:

- wages;
- working conditions;
- company policy and administration;
- relationships with supervisors and peers;
- security.

The motivators include:

- intrinsic value of the work, and a sense of achievement;
- responsibility;
- recognition.

6.5.2   Intrinsic value of the work

Employees challenged by interesting work are more likely to stay in their jobs. Employees who do not derive a sense of achievement show frustration, aggression, ill health, and may withdraw from the labor force. Companies can, therefore, benefit from making tasks more interesting.

Defining interesting work, and then structuring it, presents difficulties. Ideas about what makes work interesting vary widely, and are influenced by personal, cultural, and industry factors. Even where there is agreement, the ideal may not be possible to achieve. It is very difficult to make some tasks interesting to all but a few individuals. For instance, how many people derive a sense of achievement from washing dishes in a restaurant? And how can this be made an interesting task?

Section 5.3.1 distinguished OPEN- and CLOSE-ENDED tasks. An open-ended task has many possible outcomes, all more or less satisfactory depending upon the context, and the objectives can be identified only broadly (e.g. planning a new marketing campaign). A close-ended task has one correct outcome, and the objective can be precisely stated (e.g. sell 100 units of a particular product) – either you succeed or fail.

Research conducted in the United States and United Kingdom cultures suggests that when the task is close-ended, performance-based incentives can be clearly formulated. In these situations, incentives influence performance, and are effective. The incentive system can be closely linked to strategic goals, and it gives management close control on performance and output. But where the employee must use complex skills to perform an open-ended task for which the best possible outcome cannot be defined in advance, performance is less easy to measure. Hence, performance-related incentives are less effective. Incentive systems cannot be effectively applied and so are less useful as a means of controlling performance and output.

Kowtha and Quek (1999) tested these findings in the retail sector of Singapore. Their data showed that performance-linked incentives can also be effective in that context. But, they found that problems in measuring the output of complex tasks lessen management control. Although an increase in skill level usually gives more control over output, when there is greater uncertainty in how to perform a task, output control is reduced.

In the Anglo cultures, many people would consider open-ended tasks to be intrinsically more challenging. However, in contexts where needs to avoid uncertainty are high and routine is valued, people may be more challenged by perfecting a close-ended task.

6.5.3 *Responsibility and recognition*

Responsibility only motivates when it is perceived to be real. Promotions and titles are unlikely to motivate if they do not give genuine authority. For example, in Kroll Associates, in 1996:

> . . . status titles were dispensed as an inexpensive way of retaining top staff but, ultimately they failed to prevent dissatisfaction. At one stage the company had seven managing directors in its London office.[11]

Such an arrangement is not credible. When staffs understand that they are being fobbed off with empty status, they become demoralized.

Kovach's (1987) ranking shows that appreciation of work done is needed, and this might appear to be a cheap option compared to paying a wage rise. In practice, it is difficult to deliver effectively on a long-term basis. It may cost nothing to give informal appreciation, but this can quickly lose its effectiveness. There are conditions for it to succeed. First, appreciation must celebrate real achievement (Pettinger, 2001, p. 76). Appreciation of trivial success rings false, and is unconvincing. Second, the appreciation must be sincere, which may mean that it has to be demonstrated selectively. The manager who tells employees "you're doing a very good job" is unconvincing if this message is given to each and every person every day. The repeated banality may actually have a demotivating effect on an increasingly cynical staff.

Appreciation is given on a more formal basis by recognition schemes ("employee of the month," for example) and notices in company publications.

6.5.4 Applying Herzberg

Herzberg's theory has been applied in the following techniques:

- job rotation;
- job enlargement;
- job enrichment.

These are designed to develop the employee's responsibilities in ways that increase his/her sense of worth and motivation.

JOB ROTATION involves planning the employee's time so that he/she performs a variety of tasks. For instance, he/she spends, say, a period working in Process A, then moves to Process B, then moves to Process C. Job rotation introduces variety to the employee's routine, and helps develop a multiskilled work force. In a Japanese finance company in the 1990s, male recruits were rotated to different functions every six months until they had learned something of all the company's main operations. (Female recruits were expected to leave the firm for marriage in their twenties, and no investments were made in rotating them.)

Despite its successes, job rotation does present problems. Not all jobs can be easily exchanged – a high-status specialist is unlikely to accept a move to a job perceived appropriate only for someone of lower status. Second, rotation is expensive. An assistant marketing manager may be transferable to the accounts department only after money has been spent on training. Employees are bound to make early mistakes when rotated to new tasks, and to take time in perfecting the new skills. The more skilled the employee, the greater his/her value in the labor market; and so the employer has to pay more in order to retain him or her.

Employees may also be rotated to perform the same task in different settings. Japanese primary school teachers can expect to be rotated between schools every three years until, in their fifties, they are sent to the district office.

JOB ENLARGEMENT involves reorganizing the job specification so that all the tasks required to produce one unit are performed by the individual. Rather than have Tasks C, D, and E performed by employees P, Q, and R, respectively, all three tasks are allotted to each of P, Q, and R. In theory, the individual derives greater satisfaction from completing all tasks contributing to production and seeing the completed unit than from specializing in a single task.

JOB ENRICHMENT means making a job more interesting and more challenging, which in practice usually means more complex. Job enrichment recognizes the importance of interest as a motivator. First, responsibilities are pulled down from above, and the employee is trained to take new responsibilities for aspects of the task, including scheduling, that previously were performed by a supervisor. Second, earlier work stages are pushed forward into the job. Third, later work stages are pulled back so that the employee is made responsible for up-stream and down-stream activities that were previously handled by other persons. Fourth, parts of the task are pushed down to a lower job level and are performed by lower grades (whose jobs are thus enriched by these responsibilities being pulled down). Fifth, parts of the job are rearranged and reordered.

6.5.5 Making Herzberg work

A job enrichment system succeeds when:

- jobs are structured so that they can be enriched;
- employees welcome change and experimentation;
- employees are confident – they are not worried by fears that the enrichment program will lead to enforced redundancies and sackings;
- the cultural context is sympathetic.

On this last point, the possibilities for job enrichment are greater in a context where:

- employees have low needs to avoid anxiety, and tolerate ambiguity in job descriptions;
- power distances are low, and employees tolerate ambiguity in relationships with superiors and subordinates;
- employees tolerate change in work-group membership;
- experimentation is welcomed;
- bureaucratic practices are flexible.

But what happens when these conditions do not apply?

Job enrichment presupposes that employees are demotivated by the routine of their present jobs, and are more motivated by novelty. Neither may be true. The advantages of job enrichment are diminished or reversed if the changes have unanticipated effects elsewhere in the organization – for example, middle managers lose responsibilities to the workforce, feel their positions threatened, and are demotivated. Enrichment programs seem bound to fail if bureaucratic practices are insufficiently flexible to handle the reorganization of control and communication systems. They fail to have positive long-term effects when employees do not understand the reasons for change or the changes made, or are inadequately trained to manage the changes.

The cultural context is also significant. Job enrichment is less likely to be effective in a collectivist context where a sense of "belonging to the group" is essential, and the successful participant feels him/herself to be in danger of promotion above his/her colleagues. As Jackson and Bak (1998) imply, opportunities for individual achievement and responsibility have little attraction in circumstances where the achievement isolates the individual from his or her group. In other words, an enriched job may not only fail to increase motivation, but also in some circumstances it may actually have adverse effects on creative achievement and motivation.

Job rotation is less likely to succeed where resistance to change is greater and employees prefer specialist to general careers. In cultures where status differentials between roles are significant, problems arise in identifying jobs of equivalent status between which employees may be rotated. In collectivist cultures where group membership is important, members of a group may not welcome the temporary membership of an employee rotated from his/her normal assignments in some other group. The employee in question may interpret this "banishment" from his or her group as a form of punishment.

6.5.6 *McClelland's theory of achievement motivation*

McClelland's (1976) theory of achievement motivation argued that the greater the need to achieve in a society, the greater that society's economic growth and tendency to innovate. The need for achievement is defined as a desire to meet and exceed performance standards, and to succeed in the face of competition.

High achievers seem to have in common:

- a preference for taking moderate risks;
- a need for immediate and frequent feedback on performance;
- a preference for specific performance criteria;
- a dislike for leaving tasks incomplete;
- a sense of urgency.

McClelland argued that motivation to achieve could be taught by focusing on:

- goal setting;
- developing cognitive supports (i.e. thinking in terms that relate to achievement and consciously dismantling those assumptions in the culture that inhibit achievement);

- developing communication norms that focus positively on achievement;
- developing group systems for emotional support.

McClelland's theory is also culture-bound. It associates achievement with the satisfaction of individual needs and responsibilities, and relatively low needs to avoid uncertainty in taking initiatives. Hence it cannot explain achievement in cultures where achievement is associated with group effort and where individual effort is associated with avoiding punishment for mistakes.

6.6 Implications for the Manager

Compare an organization that you know well *in your own culture* with a similar organization *in some other culture*.

1 How do members of the two organizations (at the same level of seniority) rank these rewards for working?
    (a)   good wages;
    (b)   interesting work;
    (c)   good job security;
    (d)   feeling of being involved in things;
    (e)   opportunity to learn;
    (f)   appreciation for work done;
    (g)   promotion and growth in organization;
    (h)   good working conditions;
    (i)   personal loyalty to employees;
    (j)   sympathetic help with personal problems.
    Explain the differences.
2 Rank the rewards listed in point 1 in terms of how effectively they motivate performance within the two organizations. Take into account such factors as:
    (a)   the target behavior required;
    (b)   cost;
    (c)   risk;
    (d)   ease of implementation;
    (e)   any other significant factors.
    Explain any differences in the rankings.
3 What changes can be made to the two organizational cultures in order to improve performance?
4 How might job enrichment programs be applied within the two organizations? For each organization, take into account:
    (a)   the nature of the jobs to be enriched;
    (b)   how factors in the organizational and national cultures favor enrichment programs;
    (c)   the expense of planning, communicating, and implementing the program.

6.7 SUMMARY

Needs and their satisfiers vary across cultures. A need felt in one context may not be significant in another and a successful motivator in, say, headquarters, may be less motivating in a foreign subsidiary.

Section 6.2 examined NEEDS and saw that different segments of the workforce – distinguished for example by age, gender, education, years of experience, and so on – are likely to prioritize their needs differently. It discussed Maslow's hierarchy of needs and examined the implications for monetary rewards and the cultural impact. A case from China was used to show that needs can change over time and are influenced by the political and economic environments, and that a model of needs and derived incentive system designed for one context may be inappropriate elsewhere.

Section 6.3 discussed the DESIGN OF INCENTIVES, and first examined the economic context. Most systems to motivate employees have a financial cost, and the company cannot invest more in motivating its employees than it expects to benefit; the system must show a profit. The alternatives to the obvious solution of a wage rise carry both advantages and disadvantages. Section 6.4 asked how organizational STRUCTURES MOTIVATE, and dealt with teamwork, leadership, and training. Section 6.5 examined the notion that under some circumstances WORK can act as a MOTIVATOR, and discussed the applications and limitations of theories produced by Herzberg and McClelland.

6.8 EXERCISE

This exercise gives practice in analyzing and developing an incentive scheme.

1 Investigate the incentive schemes used to motivate employees in an organization that you know well – for example, your business school.

2 Distinguish different segments: for example, staff aged 20–25, staff aged 50–55, males, females, different professional groups (in a business school, teachers, administrators).

3 What incentives are currently used to motivate each of the segments you choose? Refer to the material in section 6.3.

4 Are the following incentives used? If not, add them to the list you made in question 3.
   (a) opportunities to develop new skills;
   (b) improved facilities;
   (c) greater responsibility;
   (d) study and other visits abroad.

5 From the total list, select three that you think are *now* most effective in motivating each segment.

6 How might these schemes be improved in order to motivate employees more effectively? Design an improved incentive scheme for each segment you have chosen, using the list of incentives prepared in questions 3 and 4.

Notes

1 Sean O'Neill, "Sex in the City case ends in £5m deal," *Daily Telegraph*, November 23, 2000.

2 "Road to China: car fever grips citizens of Shanghai," *Asahi Shimbun*, November 17, 2002.

3 Alex Spillius, "We're on a road to nowhere: Bangkok," *Telegraph Magazine*, January 18, 2003.

4 Peterborough, *Daily Telegraph*, November 8, 2001.

5 Kate Rankine, "Green nets £201m from BHS Payouts," *Daily Telegraph*, November 7, 2003.

6 Marguerite Johnson, "From bad to worse," *Time*, July 26, 1993.

7 Somporn Thapanachai, "Salaries up 6.2% this year and bonuses at 2.8 months," *Bangkok Post*, November 12, 2003.

8 Anucha Charoenpo and Wuth Nontarit, "Workers put Sanyo HQ to the torch," *Bangkok Post*, December 18, 1996.

9 Amy Kazmin, "A Buddhist boot camp for Thailand's elite," *Financial Times*, January 8, 2003.

10 "GE takes training into the 21st century," *The Nation*, November 19, 2002.

11 Stewart Dalby and Richard Donkin, "The gumshow and the City," *Financial Times*, April 1, 1996.

CHAPTER SEVEN

Dispute Resolution and Negotiation

CHAPTER OUTLINE

Introduction	Implications for the Manager
Reasons for Dispute	Summary
Culture and Dispute	Exercise
Resolving Conflicts	Notes
Negotiation	

7.1 Introduction

Here are two disputes.

First, the result of the American Presidential election result was still uncertain on the night on November 8, 2000. The Republican candidate, Senator George W. Bush, appeared to have a lead. His Democrat contender disputed the vote in Florida, and Senator Bush was only declared the winner several days later, after an appeal to the Supreme Court. Nevertheless, that night, Senator Bush issued a statement that emphasized the need for unity after the election was decided. This included the words:

> "I also want to thank the Vice-President's [Al Gore, the Democrat contender] supporters for their hard work and their belief in their cause. I want to assure them that, should the election go the way we think it will, that I will work hard to earn their confidence.
>
> "America has a long tradition of uniting once elections are over. Secretary Cheney and I will do everything in our power to unite the nation."[1]

Second:

> Señor Damaso Ruiz-Jarabo Colomer, Spanish advocate-general of the European Court of Justice, gave an opinion that "deems that political criticism of the European Union and its

leading figures can be akin to the most extreme forms of religious blasphemy. It can therefore be suppressed – and punished – without violating protected feedom of speech."

Ruiz-Jarabo Colomer ventured into blasphemy law in an opinion delivered on 19 October in a landmark free-speech case – number C–274/99 P. It involves a British economist, Bernard Connolly, who argues that he was unlawfully sacked from the European Commission for writing *The Rotten Heart of Europe*.[2]

These cases occurred within a few days of each other, and both involved disputes in political institutions. Otherwise, they differed. In the first, the dispute was controlled by traditional rules that decided how an election should be fought. Also, American culture has relatively high tolerances of dispute; Senator Bush showed confidence in his own position and had nothing to lose in putting the policy and personal disagreements behind him. In the second, the institution felt threatened by a challenge to its legitimacy and resorted to extreme measures in order to discourage other rebels. This EU official showed little confidence in the capacity of his organization to withstand criticism.

This chapter deals with factors that influence how disputes emerge and how they are resolved. One way of resolving dispute is by negotiation; the chapter also deals with commercial negotiations.

7.2   Reasons for Dispute

Disputes arise within companies as well as between them. Members compete for resources, responsibilities, promotions, the use of facilities, and so on. A second category of disputes is argument. Members argue about opinions, ideas, and beliefs: for example, what strategy is appropriate, how structures and systems should be designed and implemented, how tasks should be performed, and so on. (The positive and negative aspects of competition and argument are discussed further in section 7.3.5.)

These competitions and arguments arise for a range of reasons. Members may have genuine differences of interest and viewpoints. Or they have clashing personalities. They try to satisfy their own agendas, which they hide from others. The dispute might arise from misunderstanding; for example, they use information that is inaccurate or incomplete, or they do not share the same information. They communicate inappropriately. They fail to agree on procedures for how disputes should be conducted and ended. In multinational organizations, cultural differences mean that the dangers of misunderstanding are particularly acute.

7.2.1   Proximity to the dispute

People's attitudes towards a dispute depend upon their proximity to it and how closely it affects their interests. When they feel distant from it, they may be indifferent. If we see two people fighting in the street, maybe we watch for a while and walk on after our interest peaks. If they suddenly involve us in the fight, we experience a much wider range of emotions: anger, fear, anxiety, the need to win, or perhaps escape.

For one scholar, this point was demonstrated by the problems that arose in a small family-owned food company in which he was acting as a consultant.

> I asked some managers whether, in their daily work, they experienced any conflicts with subordinates, peers, or superiors. . . . I usually elicited an immediate and flat denial of any conflict whatsoever. This response puzzled me, since I had been called in to help figure out what to do about "severe conflicts" that members of the organization were perceiving or experiencing.   *(Schein, 1987, pp. 66–7)*

Schein finally realized that he and his interviewees were making very different assumptions. He was:

- using the term "conflict" to refer to any degree of disagreement between two or more people;
- assuming that conflict is a normal human condition, always present to some degree.

But they were:

- restricting use of the term "conflict" to severe disagreements;
- assuming that conflict is bad, and reflecting badly upon managerial capacities of the person involved.

So different connotations of the notion "conflict" were made by:

(a)   The consultant (Schein), who was:
- expert in investigating conflict;
- an outsider to the organization;
- a non-participant in the disagreements.
(b)   The managers, who were:
- non-experts in investigating conflict;
- insiders in the organization;
- participants in the disagreements.

And, by implication, a third party:

(c)   The top manager responsible for hiring Schein, who was:
- a non-expert in investigating conflict;
- an insider in the organization;
- a non-participant in the disagreements.

These persons were responding differently to the disagreements because their interests were affected differently. The outsider consultant has nothing to gain or lose, but was trained to make and analyze objective observations. The managers, on the other hand, were involved, and their reputations would suffer if they were unable to exercise control. Top management was sensitive to any problems that affected production. All were American, and so cultural differences were not significant.

7.2.2   *Factors influencing interest*

Factors that influence your interests in a dispute include:

▮ PERSONALITY FACTORS.
▮ STAKE. How badly do you want to win, and how serious would be the cost of losing? In the example above, I have little interest in a street fight between strangers and its outcome. But if the fight spills over and involves me, my stake in the outcome increases rapidly. Similarly, if my neighbour is made redundant, I feel mild sympathy. But if my employer goes bankrupt, I become worried.
▮ EMOTIONAL INVOLVEMENT. The more involved I am in defending my interests or achieving my goals, the more I commit myself to the dispute. In the example above, I am more able to accept my redundancy if my case has been treated with sympathy. I am more likely to fight it if I feel that I have been insulted. The case for Chapter 5 shows an emotional response by people who felt they had been made redundant with no respect.
▮ URGENCY. If I want a problem resolved quickly, I may force a solution, or at the opposite extreme, do so by quickly withdrawing.
▮ PRECEDENT. How does the individual or organization usually behave in these circumstances?
▮ CULTURE. See section 7.3.

These factors are discussed further in section 7.4.2.

7.3   Culture and Dispute

Western cultures have always been interested by the paradox of dispute, and how it can have both positive and negative outcomes. The Greek historian Plutarch, who lived between about AD 46 and 129, wrote that:

> the natural philosophers believe that if the forces of conflict and discord were eliminated from the universe, the heavenly bodies would stand still, and in the resulting harmony the processes of motion and generation would be brought to a dead stop.
>
> *(1973, p. 29)*

7.3.1   *Dispute in the Anglo cultures*

Plutarch's attitude still holds among cultures most influenced by ancient Greek philosophy. Anglo cultures, in particular, perceive some degree of dispute as a necessary condition for creativity and initiative. In the United States:

... creativity and adaptation are born of tension, passion, and conflict. Contention does more than make us creative. It makes us whole, it propels us along the journey of development.   *(Pascale, 1990, p. 263)*

This expresses the Anglo value of individual growth through creative "doing." But other cultures are much less accepting of disagreements.

This does not mean that *any* level of dispute is accepted in Anglo companies. Every organization must impose some limits to aggression, and the person who passes beyond them – for example by bringing a gun to work and shooting up the opposition – may be referred to legal or medical officers. But so long as negative effects can be limited and dispute seems to aid productivity, tolerances are wide.

The tolerance given to dispute in Anglo cultures means that it can arise in any relationship, and therefore persons skilled in their culture have to become adept at compartmentalizing aspects of their relationship. Persons may disagree in some areas while maintaining their friendship in others. In her biography of the British art critic and spy Anthony Blunt, Carter (2001) explains how in the late 1930s Blunt disagreed with the critic Herbert Read and artist Roland Penrose over the work of Pablo Picasso. This war was fought publicly in journal articles. But Read and Blunt belonged to the same club. Blunt later explained:

"We used frequently to meet there by chance, and one would say to the other, 'I hope that you did not take my saying you were stupid and wrong etc. in my last letter in any personal matter,' and we would go and have lunch together."

(Carter, 2001, p. 208)

7.3.2 *Dispute in collectivist cultures*

But in collectivist cultures, aspects of a relationship are less easily compartmentalized and disputes in one area have repercussions in others. Dispute is feared as likely to destabilize the harmony between individuals, within a group, and between groups. Rather than welcomed as a positive stimulus, it may be regarded as anything but healthy. For example, hostile takeovers which are accepted in American business as necessary and normal are disliked in Japan. During the boom years, they almost never occurred. Ishizumi (1990) reported that when an American finance company attempted to take over a Japanese high-tech company, it was unable to find a local securities firm prepared to act as tender offer agents. The recession is now forcing the Japanese to conform with globalized Anglo standards, but sometimes unwillingly.

In Thailand, a Buddhist critic of Western economics commented:

Modern economics is based on the assumption that it is human nature to compete. Buddhism, on the other hand, recognizes that human beings are capable of both competition and co-operation.

Competition is natural: when they are striving to satisfy the desire for pleasure – when they are motivated by *tanha* – people will compete fiercely.

At such times they want to get as much as possible for themselves and feel no sense of sufficiency or satisfaction.... This competitive instinct can be redirected to induce co-operation of a particular group by inciting them to compete with another group. For example, corporate managers sometimes rally their employees to work together to beat their competitors. But this competition is based entirely on competition. Buddhism would call this "artificial cooperation."

True co-operation arises from a desire for well-being – with *chanda*. Human development demands that we understand how *tanha* and *chanda* motivate us and that we shift our energies from competition towards co-operative efforts to solve the problems facing the world and to realize a nobler goal.   *(Payutto, 1994, pp. 53–4)*

An aversion to overt dispute in Buddhist and other Asian cultures does not mean that disputes do not arise there. (A quick review of Asian history over the past hundred years makes this very clear.) Rather, cultures deal with possible or actual disputes differently. Each develops strategies to prevent or minimize those aspects of dispute that members find most threatening. For example, collectivist cultures discourage OPEN dispute by tolerating LATENT dispute, which is ignored or overlooked. Implicit challenges are smoothed over so that perhaps all involved can deny that any challenge was intended. Communicative style maintains an appearance of harmony.

In some countries, sub-cultural differences may be significant. In Northern Ireland companies, Black (1994) discovered that:

Catholics have a more conflictual view of the employment relationship than do Protestants, particularly in the private sector (though not in manufacturing). Fifty-two percent of all Catholic employees (66 percent of employees in the private sector) agree there will always be a conflict between management and employees because they are really on opposite sides, compared with 38 percent of Protestants.   *(p. 88)*

A greater percentage of Catholic employees agreed on the need for strong trade unions that would represent employees in the (apparently inevitable) disputes.

7.3.3 *Explaining tolerance of dispute by cultural analysis*

Laurent (1983, p. 86) asked managers from a range of countries to respond to the statement: "Most organizations would be better off if conflict could be eliminated forever." Forty-one percent of the Italians agreed, 27 percent of the Germans, 24 percent of the French, 6 percent of the Americans, and only 4 percent of the Swedish respondents wished to eliminate conflict. The desire to eliminate conflict was coupled with a belief that the manager should be able to answer subordinates' questions, and that organizations were threatened by practices such as bypassing an immediate superior to communicate elsewhere or by reporting to two superiors. In such contexts the matrix is seen as likely to cause disputes and is seldom implemented.

Hofstede (2001, and his previous studies) applies the four dimensions to explain different tolerances. At the extremes:

- In COLLECTIVIST cultures, harmony should always be maintained, and direct confrontations avoided. In INDIVIDUALIST cultures, speaking one's mind is a characteristic of an honest person.
- In cultures where the POWER DISTANCE is large, latent conflict between ranks is considered normal – and always expected and feared. Peers are reluctant to trust each other. Where the power distance is small, harmony between the powerful and powerless is valued; peers are relatively willing to cooperate.
- In high UNCERTAINTY AVOIDANCE cultures, disputes within the organizations are considered undesirable; conflict is emotionally disapproved of, perhaps because it is felt that disputants are unlikely to accept compromise readily. In low uncertainty avoidance cultures, conflict in organizations is considered natural – as the quote from Pascale (1990) above shows. Competition may be fierce, but afterwards the opponents find it relatively easy to reconcile again.
- In MASCULINE cultures, disputes are resolved by fighting them out. In FEMININE cultures, conflicts are resolved by compromise and negotiation.

This shows dispute explained by four of Hofstede's (2001) five dimensions, and might appear to exemplify the point made in section 2.5.6, that the dimensions overlap and that this is a weakness. However, it also demonstrates the capacity of the model to discriminate between types of dispute on the basis of the different relationships in which the persons and groups express their disagreements. For example, competition between groups exemplifies collectivism, and between persons, individualism. High needs to avoid uncertainty might be shown by an unwillingness to embark on a conflict until absolutely sure of the other person's capacities and resources; low needs by a willingness to dispute with strangers – for example, through the legal system. Masculinity is shown by a willingness to move quickly to open conflict and giving little consideration to the alternatives.

7.3.4   *Tolerances of dispute vary across cultures*

The notion that tolerances of dispute vary across cultures, means that a disagreement that causes little reaction in Culture A (or may even be considered positive) gives rise to serious conflict in Culture B. The introduction gave an example, and here is a second.

An American manufacturing company operating in Thailand was structured so that five teams reported to their supervisors, who reported to a manager. Then the manager resigned and the company decided to hold a competition between the supervisors to decide which deserved promotion to the vacant post. After 2 months, Supervisor A was promoted. Supervisors B and C perceived that they had lost face before their work teams, who had all been committed to their respective leaders, and immediately resigned. Supervisor D left a few weeks later. Only Supervisor E was prepared to continue. The company had used a competitive system that worked well in the individualist United States. However, by spreading the competition over 2 months in this relatively more collectivist culture where face mattered, it had created a condition of conflict which cost it three skilled supervisors.

7.3.5 *Distinguishing between levels of dispute*

The case above suggests that we need a model for distinguishing between degrees of dispute. Argument and competition were defined in section 7.2. Handy (1985) distinguishes a lower level (see figure 7.1):

- A1 competition;
- A2 argument;
- B conflict.

COMPETITION for resources serves a useful purpose *when*:

- it sets standards;
- it sorts out the best from the field;
- it motivates and channels energy.

Competition is more likely to be beneficial when it is open, in the sense that all competitors stand to profit by developing new ideas and opportunities. It may be damaging when zero-sum (that is, when there can be only one winner who takes all).

An ARGUMENT is constructive and helps people learn *when*:

- the sides are arguing about the same thing – issues are properly framed;
- information to resolve the issue is available;
- personal attacks are avoided;
- the rules for conducting and resolving the dispute are clear and are accepted by the two sides;
- communication is full and accurate;
- differences are resolved, and the resolution is accepted.

CONFLICT occurs when neither participant is prepared to accept a closure to competition or argument, and no superior or third party is capable of enforcing closure. The competition or argument fails to reach a successful outcome and spirals out of control – for example, *when*:

- there is no perception of common interest;
- one or both of the two sides refuses to accept arbitration;
- the responsible superior refuses to arbitrate, or botches arbitration;
- the procedures for deciding a "winner" and closure are obscure or unacceptable;
- the cost of losing is greater than the cost of continuing the conflict;
- personality clashes cannot be overcome;

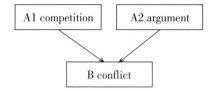

Figure 7.1

- information is inadequate, communication breaks down, and the sides are unable to communicate essential information, or disagree on how it should be interpreted.

The relationship between these types of dispute may be illustrated simply as shown in figure 7.1. The cross-cultural implication is that levels of argument or competition accepted in Culture X may be unacceptable in Culture Y, where tolerances of dispute are lower. The case in section 7.3.4 gives an example of a competition deteriorating into conflict in conditions where this type of dispute is unacceptable.

7.4   Resolving Conflicts

In theory, the manager prevents and resolves conflicts by ensuring that the reasons for factors causing dispute (see section 7.2) are controlled. Specifically, he/she:

- clarifies strategic priorities;
- applies strong but flexible structures;
- sets resource priorities and task descriptions;
- communicates clearly and accurately – avoiding unnecessary ambiguities – and encourages clear and accurate communication from subordinates;
- discourages personal attacks;
- ensures that information is freely available to conduct the argument or competition fairly and, as far as possible, restricts the use of privileged information;
- enforces procedures for controlling arguments and competition that are clear and appropriate to the cultural and organizational context.

These conditions occur in a strong, positive culture, where persons and groups communicate well and are happy to accept their mutual dependencies. They are far less likely in a weak, negative culture, where members feel less responsibility or capacity to halt the deterioration of competition or argument.

7.4.1   How participants resolve conflict

The participants may take their own steps to avoid or resolve conflicts. Thomas (1976) suggested a five-point model, which is shown in a slightly adapted form in figure 7.2.

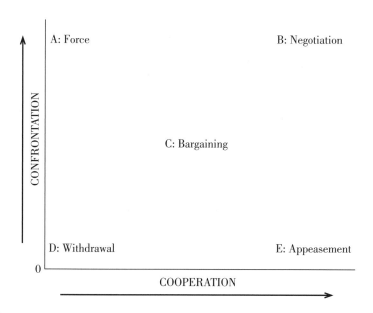

Figure 7.2

The alternatives are anchored by two dimensions, tendencies to confrontation and to cooperation. During the course of a dispute, movement between points is common. For example, both start at A, then move to C; or one continues at A and the other moves to D; and all other alternatives may be tested.

The points in the figure represent the following:

▮ Point A: FORCING your solution on the other side. This position is highly assertive and shows no desire to co-operate. It implies a gamble that the other side will back down – perhaps moving to D or E. If neither is prepared to back off from confrontation, the descent into conflict continues and may eventually be resolved only by group pressure, the intervention of a superior, or mediation by an outsider.

▮ Point B: NEGOTIATE to find a solution that integrates the needs of both sides. New interests may be introduced, and the scale of the negotiation is increased, to the mutual advantage of both. The negotiators are both confrontational in making demands and cooperative in searching for a mutually acceptable solution. (Negotiation is discussed in section 7.5.)

▮ Point C: BARGAIN – for instance, by compromising on a split. For example, I offer a market trader $6 for his product; he demands $12. I reply with $7; he climbs down to $11. Eventually we settle mid-way. If at some point either of us introduces new interests, a simple bargaining process has developed into a complex negotiation. When bargaining, the parties progressively offer compromises that narrow the distance between their initial positions, until they reach compromises that correspond. Bargaining plays a part in negotiation, but in addition the parties offer changes in their initial positions. For example, I offer you $60 for one item of your product and you insist on $120. I change my offer to $70; you demand $110. I refuse to move from $70 but instead offer to buy three items – $210 in total. You are ready to accept $250 for three items and offer spare parts. I accept on condition that you pay haulage and insurance.

■ Point D: AVOID conflict. Avoidance occurs if I refuse to participate and walk out of the door. I neither confront nor cooperate.

■ Point E: ACCOMMODATE and APPEASE the other side. I agree to give the other side everything he wants, on condition that he stops making my life difficult. This position is highly co-operative, and shows no desire to confront.

7.4.2   Factors determining positions

The factors influencing one's interest in a dispute (recall section 7.2.2) also influence the positions taken by the different sides. These, again, are:

* PERSONALITY FACTORS;
* STAKE in the outcome (how serious is the cost of losing, or how much can be gained by winning?);
* the EMOTIONAL INVOLVEMENT of the parties (a side that is emotionally committed to winning is less inclined to cooperate);
* the URGENCY of finding a solution;
* PRECEDENT (how are such conflicts normally resolved in this company, or this industry?);
* CULTURE (how are such conflicts normally resolved in this culture?). The influence of culture is discussed below.

7.4.3   Culture and resolution

Here are examples that suggest how culture influences positions taken in a conflict.

In Anglo cultures, a willingness to confront is valued. Non-assertive strategies of withdrawal and smoothing are equated with admitting defeat; the individual who always withdraws from conflict is likely to be scorned as a "wimp," and the manager who regularly ignores subordinates' disputes will lose their respect. However, a move to B or C may follow quickly.

Avoidance and appeasement are perceived as useful only in coping with the symptoms, and are unable to resolve fundamental issues. Rather than resolve open conflict, they delay it until a time when the effects may be more severe. Before the Second World War, the British and French governments tried to appease Hitler and the Nazi government in Germany. But these efforts were unsuccessful, and in 1939 war broke out anyway.

The Japanese are far more likely to resolve disagreements by compromise and consensus at B or C. Trade contracts avoid stressing rigid performance criteria and typically include a clause such as "All items not found in this contract will be deliberated and decided upon in a spirit of honesty and trust." Third parties may be brought in to mediate agreement and avoid conflict. However, conflict and avoidance are not necessarily exclusive. Both can be the means to another end:

> The end state most desired by Japanese in interpersonal relationships is a condition in which the incurrence of obligations is minimized and the flexibility in fulfilling obligations is maximized. *(Black and Mendenhall, 1993, p. 50)*

In a business negotiation where both sides are Japanese, the winner incurs future obligations towards the loser, and unless these are paid off the disharmony affects not only their future relationship but also the attitudes of observers. The knowledge that the loser may be capable of retaliation at some future date acts as a constraint on winning too clearly.

The Chinese also try to build consensus. Chew and Lim (1995) argue that Confucian values of collectivism and conformity have conditioned the Chinese into developing attitudes towards conflict that are less openly aggressive and emotional than in the West. The writers cite Singaporean research data to show that their values lead the Chinese into preferring compromise to competition as a means of conflict resolution.

In cultures where withdrawal is acceptable, an apparent withdrawal cannot always be taken at face value. It may imply that the "loser" is making a tactical retreat in order to retaliate at a future time when conditions have changed in his/her favor.

In collectivist cultures, other members may try to ignore the dispute or to enforce a resolution. When a peace formula is agreed the disputants down-play their disagreements. If one party continues trying to force its own solution after the group has intervened, he/she risks being expelled from the group.

Because a group is weakened by dispute, in a collectivist culture members try to maintain the appearance of a united front before outsiders. Before King Abdul Aziz of Saudi Arabia died, he drew together his sons Sa'ud and Faisal, who had a long history of personal disagreements. He told them:

> Join hands across my body, and swear that you will work together when I am gone. Swear too that, if you quarrel, you will argue in private. You must not let the world catch sight of your disagreements. *(Lacey, 1981, p. 318)*

7.4.4 *Mediation*

A member of the group, a superior, or outsider may be chosen to mediate between disputants. It is important that both sides accept the mediator as an honest broker, who has no personal interest in one or the other side winning. The mediator acts as a disinterested third party. He/she tries to persuade the disputants to climb down from forcing positions, and encourage a bargained or negotiated solution.

An outsider knows least about the situation, and has to start by asking each sides (together, or separately) to explain his/her understanding of the situation and point of view, and the other side's point of view. This discussion of the facts of the case is useful when it reveals misunderstandings and ambiguities. At a 1995 Asia-Pacific International Court Conference (attended by judges and lawyers from 16 countries) the Chief Justice of Singapore said that:

> ... as Asians were less inclined traditionally towards litigation, courts could turn to mediation as an alternative form of resolving civil disputes. ... This method of settling conflicts is not a "winner takes all" system like a court trial before a judge is, he said.
>
> "In the context of most Asian societies, this is particularly important as it ensures that no one should come away with the feeling that he has lost face." ... He said that in mediation, the parties decide for themselves, and the neutral third party does not impose a decision.[3]

These comments elicited support from other Asians:

> "Mediation? That's the Papua New Guinea way of resolving disputes!" [A Papua New Guinea judge]
>
> "We are starting to look into mediation ... in Brunei. We agree with the concept. The question is: How fast will it be adopted? We have arbitration proceedings, although I think the adversarial approach is here to stay." [A Brunei magistrate]
>
> "Mediation is very suitable for Indonesia, especially with our philosophy of life, *gotong royong* – to join together. We need to settle every case peacefully. Long-term proceedings are costly." [An Indonesian judge][4]

7.4.5 Intervention by a superior

If neither the disputants nor the wider group are able to find a solution, a superior may intervene to find one. The superior can choose from a range of options. He/she can:

- IMPOSE a solution on the subordinates. This shows commitment to resolving the dispute, but unwillingness to become involved as a participant.
- COUNSEL the two sides, providing advice and support, in the hope that they can then resolve their difference on their own – perhaps by negotiation. Counseling becomes more forceful when the disputants are given a deadline by when they must find a solution, or risk punishment.
- AVOID. Avoidance shows the least commitment, but the manager could ignore the conflict when it seems likely that:
  - the two sides can reach a satisfactory solution on their own; *or*
  - involvement will make the dispute worse; *or*
  - involvement will cause him/her a loss of face.
- SEPARATE the two sides – for instance, by postings.

All of these options carry risks for the superior. Imposing a solution and counseling lead to a loss of authority if the disputants ignore the superior. Avoidance looks like cowardice if the conflict gets worse. Even when separation is possible, it signals a failure of control to other members.

The choice of solution is influenced by the cultural factors. Where power distances are high, the manager fears loss of face from becoming embroiled in a subordinate dispute. Where needs to avoid uncertainty are high and a low-level dispute seems particularly threatening, the superior might respond by avoidance. In Chinese cultures:

> . . . supervisors would be expected to display moral strength to deal with a conflict situation and, if circumstances demand, seek an intervention from a third party or from a higher authority. *(Lee and Akhtar, 1996, p. 885)*

In *all* cultures and organizations, the superior has problems in deciding WHEN to intervene. Timing is crucial, and bad timing may make the conflict worse. The superior who waits too long before involving him/herself may cause as much damage as he/she who jumps in too quickly to impose a solution. A lack of action may be interpreted as a signal that an increase in conflict will go unpunished. The manager may sometimes be induced by fear of losing face to hesitate unduly. On the other hand, in Anglo cultures, the manager who wants the reputation of an effective "trouble-shooter" may impose too early. Premature intervention is fruitless when one or both sides still think that more can be gained by forcing than by negotiating and accepting a compromise.

A combination of tactics might work best. During the Bosnian Peace talks in 1995, the Serbs, Croats, and Muslims met in separate rooms and the allied mediators negotiated with each and moved messages between them. The chief American representative, Richard Holbrooke, finally announced deadlines by when they would have to reach agreement or lose allied support for the peace process.

7.5 Negotiation

Negotiation offers a means of resolving a dispute and of exploiting an opportunity. For example, two companies have identified an opportunity offered by developments in the business environment to develop a new product by working together, and they negotiate the terms of an alliance.

Every negotiation expresses a paradox. It involves the participants in both actual or possible confrontation and in cooperation. If there were no confrontation, they would have no need to resolve differences; if they were unwilling to cooperate, they would not try to resolve these differences through talk.

The negotiator is most likely to resolve the contradiction and to achieve a positive solution to this paradox by identifying in advance points at which cooperation is most possible, and at which confrontation is more likely. He/she prepares by:

* developing his/her own priorities and position;
* trying to predict their priorities and position.

These points are related. Understanding their priorities influences your own; and (presumably) they are making a similar analysis of your position.

This preparation means developing a profile of the other company, its context and interests. Relevant factors in the other NATIONAL CONTEXT include:

- Taxation data. To what legal system is the contract valid?
- Financial and economic data (e.g. size of the economy, speed of growth, inflation, economic freedom index, investment policies, subsidies and tax incentives, banking system).
- Infrastructure data (e.g. demographic breakdown; road, rail, air systems, and traffic conditions; access to information technology).
- Labor force data (e.g. skills supplied by the labor market and at what prices; participation of women and minorities).
- Legal data (e.g. legislation relating to employment, safety, ownership, intellectual property, capital transactions; jurisdiction in which the contract is valid).
- Political data (e.g. authorities at national, regional, and local levels).
- Trade unions and professional associations.
- Cultural data; the national culture.

Relevant COMPANY FACTORS in the potential partner include:

- its ownership and legal status; history;
- equity structure; current financial circumstances;
- size;
- strategic interests and scope; labor relations; technology;
- suppliers; customers; partners; competitors;
- organizational structure, systems, and culture;
- commitments abroad.

If you hope to develop a long-term relationship in rapidly changing environments, you need to keep updating this profile on the other company. This means that preparing to negotiate is an ongoing process. By working from a general framework you begin to map in the main points.

- WHERE to negotiate (section 7.5.1).
- WHEN to negotiate (section 7.5.2).
- WHO negotiates (section 7.5.3).
- WHO has authority to decide (section 7.5.4).
- WHY negotiate (section 7.5.5).
- HOW to negotiate (section 7.5.6).

Finally, this section deals with implementation issues.

7.5.1 Where to negotiate

Negotiating at your place may give you the territorial advantage. However, meeting at their place gives you insights into how they manage their operations and their capacities, and enables you to hide from your constituents should you prefer the negotiation to be secret.

Meeting in a neutral territory (a hotel, a chamber of commerce) offers a compromise when both sides are reluctant to give the other a territorial advantage. It also removes negotiators from pressures from their own constituents. When the Western powers required rival Afghan factions to negotiate a government of national unity during the Afgan war of 2001–2, it was decided that no suitable venue could be found in Afghanistan, and Berlin was proposed. Finally, it was decided to hold the negotiations in an even less sensitive site. A London newspaper commented:

> Venues for negotiations are important, and it is significant that Monday's meeting designed to reconcile contending Afghan factions has been moved from the tumult of Berlin to sleepy Bonn. If ever diplomacy needed to be undertaken far from the madding crowd it is this attempt to force Afghan leaders to set aside ancient rivalries and face up to their responsibilities to their people.[5]

Or, you may decide to alternate between your territories; or, both sides negotiate from their own premises linked by information technologies.

7.5.2 When to negotiate

The nature of the opportunity (or problem) over which you are negotiating and the persons involved decide when the time is ripe; and negotiating prematurely, or too late, may be fatal.

The timetable is effected by practical issues such as company routines, when budgets are normally set, and labor contracts signed. If you are traveling to negotiate abroad, are there climatic features that influence your schedule? Are there any religious or national holidays set for that period? In Muslim countries, strict believers fast from morn to dusk during Ramadan. In Chinese cultures, business stops for the Chinese lunar New Year.

Is this a culture in which members expect to negotiate outside regular working hours and over weekends? How much time should you allow to recover from jet lag before going into a meeting? What documentation is needed to support an entry visa – including health certification?

Timing the negotiation also involves planning the schedule; how often should you meet, and at what intervals? How much time do you need between meetings to discuss progress with persons in your organization? What is the likelihood of hold-ups and delays and how much time can you allow for them?

Decision making in collectivist contexts typically takes longer because a consensus has to be built among interested parties within the firm. Once a consensus has been built, negotiators may be very unwilling to make radical concessions that mean going back to consult these various parties again, and creating a new consensus.

Negotiators from the People's Republic of China typically demand large quantities of technical information, and progress may be delayed by time taken in their digesting this. They may also be tactical. A PRC team may decide to spin out the final settlement in order to force impatient Anglos to lower their conditions. They may be genuinely forced to check back with municipal, provincial and national authorities. They may make that decision for themselves. Tse et al. (1994) found that when faced with conflict, PRC negotiators were far more likely to consult with superiors than were their Canadian counterparts.

Any "first time" negotiation requires patience, and negotiating with an organization from some other national culture with whom you have not dealt before may be particularly lengthy. This is particularly true in cultures that place great importance on developing good personal relationships with negotiation partners.

7.5.3   *Who negotiates*

Trust between negotiation partners is all important. Without it, you are unlikely to start talking or to agree on a final settlement. Where trust is high, negotiators are more likely to take a problem-solving approach and to share information, even about their profit schedules. Where trust is low, they depend upon persuasive arguments, threats and other forms of contentious behavior.

Under what conditions will the other side trust you? They must believe in your good intentions. This means they accept that you will:

- negotiate in good faith – it is in your interests to do business with them;
- exchange information that is needed to solve problems;
- not resort to unethical behavior during the negotiation – for instance, by tapping their communications with head office;
- respect the secrecy of information and opinions made in confidence;
- do your best to convince other people in your organization to accept any agreements that you make with them.
- do your best to implement any agreements.

But how do you choose the negotiating team most likely to be trusted in any given situation? A series of questions has to be answered.

First, HOW MANY PEOPLE should represent you? One person or more? A negotiator from the individualist Anglo cultures typically wants to project him/herself as the person with authority who does not need to check with headquarters. But an American team often includes a legal representative. They want to assume that their partners are telling the truth, but include a lawyer in order to remove misunderstandings and to prevent problems arising in the implementation phase. However, many Asians prefer an element of ambiguity in the agreed settlement, which will be dispelled in the course of implementation. They stress compromise rather than conflict in negotiations. It is therefore understandable that Japanese, for example, perceive American practice as hostile and threatening. Many Japanese firms include lawyers in their teams when dealing with Americans and other foreigners – but not with other Japanese.

An organization in the People's Republic of China may be represented by a large team. This may include not only functional experts and administrators, but also representatives of local, provincial and national authorities. Similarly, a Japanese team represents a wide range of units, whose interests must be taken into account.

What AGE is most effective? Anglo companies often select their brighter, more energetic members, but this may be a mistake when negotiating with a Chinese or Japanese team. The Asian team is likely to be led by a senior and older person, who has high status and loses face by dealing as an equal with a younger person. He may play little part in the detailed discussions, but plays an important "figurehead" role. A British negotiator who regularly deals with teams from the People's Republic of China comments that the age of young technologists:

> "... is not an issue when we explain that in the West, the best technologists *are* young. The Chinese understand. That is, until there is a problem, and then they complain 'he's far too young, far too young'."

What company RANK should the negotiator have? The ranks of team leaders, like their ages, should be equivalent. But matching leaders is complicated by the different meanings of ranks in different countries. For example, the title "Vice-President" has far greater currency in American companies than elsewhere. An American company may have 20 VPs when a Japanese company of the same size has one or two.

The staff of one Tokyo firm were disturbed to discover that a visiting American delegation was led by a VP. The visitors were kept waiting for 20 minutes outside the door until their own VP could be found to ceremonially welcome them in. When it turned out that the American VP represented only a service function and was equivalent to a departmental manager in their company, the Japanese felt that they had lost face.

An alternative to using a member of the organization is to use an AGENT. An agent may perform a number of functions beyond negotiating on your behalf. These include:

- identifying organizations with which you might wish to do business;
- making introductions to possible partner organizations;
- arranging negotiations;
- preparing background information and advising on strategy;
- arranging documentation in preparation for a negotiation and for conducting business (e.g. arranging visas, work permits, customs clearance, etc.);
- resolving disputes.

In an international negotiation, an agent who understands the cultures of both sides can be useful when neither side has as much experience. But, according to an Anglo business woman with experience of negotiating in the People's Republic of China,

"... agents tend to get too involved. When he's made the introductions, the company might want him out of the picture. But he wants to carry on – because that's his income. And the Chinese on the other side may get upset if they think that their friend (the agent) is being pushed out too quickly. Maneuvering the agent out of the deal when he's served his purpose calls for delicate handling."

7.5.4   Who has authority to decide?

In many cultures the person who takes the final decision on whether or not to accept the other side's offer is typically the leader of the negotiating team. For instance, company owners in the high power distance cultures of Greece and Latin America wish to keep personal control and not to delegate. Individualist Anglo negotiators similarly insist that headquarters gives them the power to accept or reject. But this is not the case everywhere. The real decision-maker may be absent. An American team negotiating with a family company in Brunei discovered that permission for the deal was given by elderly family members who never appeared at the meetings. In the People's Republic of China the technical representatives often contribute most to the discussions, but distant bureaucrats make the decision.

In transitional economies that have switched from central planning to free-market systems, uncertainty among their teams about who has authority causes delays in reaching decisions. This problem occurs where regulatory controls are absent, or confused, and managers are insufficiently confident to make decisions.

7.5.5   Why negotiate?

When preparing to negotiate, the company needs to be certain about what they hope to achieve from negotiation, and what they predict to be the other side's interests (see Fisher et al., 1997). This means, first, ranking YOUR GOALS in negotiating:

Y1 What you MUST achieve.
Y2 What you HOPE to achieve.
Y3 What you WOULD LIKE to achieve.

Obviously you would like to achieve all Y1s, all Y2s, and all Y3s, but in the real world this is very unlikely. A negotiation from which you achieve all your Y1s, some Y2s, and no Y3s must be accounted a success. A negotiation that wins you Y3s, a few Y2s and no Y1s has failed – however many Y3s.

The next stage is predicting THEIR GOALS:

T1 What they MUST achieve.
T2 What they HOPE to achieve.
T3 What they WOULD LIKE to achieve.

Your analysis of goals tells you where to focus your resources of time and energy, and also helps you decide on concessions that you are able to make in order to secure your goals:

Ya What you are MOST WILLING to concede in order to achieve your essential objectives.
Yb What you are MODERATELY WILLING to concede.
Yc What you are LEAST WILLING to concede.

And, for their side, your predictions of:

Ta What they are MOST WILLING to concede.
Tb What they are MODERATELY WILLING to concede.
Tc What they are LEAST WILLING to concede.

You hope for a match between Y1 and Ta; what you value most, and they are most willing to concede. For instance, your priority is that the goods should be transported by an early date (to meet a seasonal demand) and early transportation presents them with fewest problems (because the goods are already in stock).

Financial goals may not necessarily be the most important. When negotiating an international joint venture, a foreign partner may be primarily interested in gaining experience in the new environment and the local partner in securing the transfer of technology. Or one side or both might prioritize developing a long-term relationship. An enduring relationship offers obvious advantages. It could guarantee a source of supplies on generous terms, and save the costs of finding a new supplier. Trust reduces expense in drafting detailed contracts, and in making economic transactions. However, the negotiator may need to be cautious in accepting at face value the other side's expressed desire for trust, which should rather be earned by demonstrations of good faith. McGuinness et al. (1991) examined German, Swiss, British, Italian, Japanese, and French companies dealing in the PRC, and concluded that despite emphasizing a desire for friendship when opening a negotiation, the Chinese most frequently evaluated relationships in a utilitarian manner that reflected the value of the package.

A company that overvalues promises of long-term relationships may have itself to blame, particularly when product or service quality is an issue. The mistakes can be avoided. It should be common sense to prepare for a negotiation by developing a realistic picture of what the other side can deliver, and how far you have the resources to make a long-term commitment. But this is not easy when understanding is obscured by differences in language and culture.

7.5.6   *How to negotiate*

Like all other communication structures, a negotiation must be appropriate to be effective. The negotiation can be seen as an extended communication created in dialogue by two sides. In practice, it is likely to express a number of communication functions, including:

- developing the relationship between the two sides (particularly if they have not worked together before);
- exchanging information, attitudes, and interests – so far as is necessary to give the communication direction and without giving away confidential information;
- exploring divergent needs, expectations, and assumptions;
- persuasion;
- concession and agreement;
- implementation.

Values in their shared culture or cultural differences count among the factors that influence the stages and style of any given negotiation. Where needs to avoid uncertainty are high, negotiators have a greater need for signals distinguishing stages in the structure, particularly where the relationship is new and therefore stressful. Where these needs are less important, participants are comfortable with an emergent structure.

Particularly in Anglo negotiations, stages cannot be clearly distinguished. Negotiators attempt to persuade each other throughout. Even when first introducing yourself, you hope to persuade the other party that you are a trustworthy person to deal with. Information has to be exchanged in every request for, or offer of, a concession. The activity of creating a relationship is passed over relatively rapidly. Getting to know the other side becomes important in high-context cultures and when the negotiators hope to build a long-term relationship. A Chinese businessman said:

> "I join a negotiation in order to negotiate a relationship. When we feel that we can trust each other, agreeing on the business takes no time."

And when the two sides have developed a sense of each other's interests and their shared experiences, they are quick to resolve issues such as terms of payment, delivery, and quality – details which the Anglo business person tends to prioritize.

In Anglo cultures a concern about the time spent – for example, by looking at your watch – almost always gets things moving along. In other cultures this concern may be interpreted as impatience, which causes apprehension. It may mean that the other person needs greater reassurance, and even more time has to be spent in building trust before the essential business details are discussed.

7.5.7   *Implementation*

In some cultures, the negotiation process effectively ends when the contract is signed; elsewhere, it may not. In Anglo cultures the action of signing a contract symbolizes an intention to fulfill the stated terms. In the United States, the outcomes of marketing negotiations are determined *primarily* by events at the negotiation table. A legal advisor may be included in order to reduce the level of misunderstanding and conflict after signing. The business person with a reputation for constantly attempting to renegotiate contracts is not trusted.

But elsewhere, the contract may not represent finality in the discussions so much as an honest intention to do business along the lines agreed, all other things being equal and in the light of foreseeable events. In Thailand, implementation, rather than signing the contract, is the final stage of negotiation. It involves a continuing process of discussion and adjustment in response to environmental changes which could not have been foreseen at an earlier stage. Anglo negotiators tend to be more legalistic, and to expect that the contract should be implemented as signed *regardless* of the environment.

An American businessman with extensive experience of negotiating with family companies in Southeast Asia reported:

> "When the Chinese negotiate a contract, they never argue at the beginning, they argue when they implement it. In an American negotiation, you argue at the beginning and keep quiet when the contract is signed."

And so the American negotiator cannot assume that once a contract has been signed, his/her responsibilities are at an end. Rather, he/she needs to keep aware of what is happening in all stages of implementation and always be prepared to return to the table.

7.6   Implications for the Manager

1   Disputes (arguments, competition) occur in all organizations in all cultures.
    * Disputes can be positive, and of value to the organization.
    * But when disputes are not resolved (or cannot be resolved) they deteriorate into conflicts which have a negative and damaging effect on the organization.
2   Tolerances of dispute vary. What might be considered trivial and even creative in one context is perceived as highly threatening in another. National culture is one of the factors that influences tolerance levels. It also influences the use of tactics to manage disputes and to prevent or resolve conflicts. These include negotiation.
3   Every negotiation involves the participants in both confrontation and cooperation. The negotiator prepares carefully in order to identify where cooperation is possible, and where confrontation is necessary.
4   The negotiator makes decisions for his/her own side, and predicts for the other side:
    * the best location to negotiate;
    * the best time;
    * the best members of the team;
    * the person(s) with authority to decide on a settlement;
    * the priorities in negotiation;
    * the best styles and tactics.
5   The negotiator also examines possibilities and problems in implementing the negotiation.

7.7 SUMMARY

This chapter has examined how disputes arise and how they are resolved. Negotiation is one way of achieving resolution, and also of exploiting an opportunity.

Section 7.2 discussed REASONS FOR DISPUTE, and saw the importance of how far one's interests are threatened as a stimulus to activity. Section 7.3 dealt with the importance of CULTURE in influencing tolerances of different forms of dispute, and in deciding how far it was considered beneficial or malign. When argument and competition get out of control, they spiral into conflict. Section 7.4 dealt with different ways by which CONFLICTS are resolved. If the disputants are unable to resolve their problems by themselves, a solution may be arranged by the group, mediated by an outsider, or decided by the intervention of a superior. Section 7.5 dealt with NEGOTIATION.

7.8 EXERCISE

This exercise gives practice in preparing for a negotiation, then negotiating. All students should read the case below, then form small groups in order to solve the problems that follow.

NOTE: keep any material that you produce in this exercise. You will need it again when you do the exercise in chapter 15 on international joint ventures.

The Acme Hotels negotiation

You have been appointed to the post of International Officer in your business college. You have just received a letter from a hotel chain in Country X – a tropical country that has a large tourist industry.

Acme Hotels is the leading hotel chain headquartered in Country X. They propose that your college join them in a joint venture to establish a school there for hotel and tourist managers. This will produce staff to work for Acme Hotels and for other hotels in Country X and

neighboring countries. (For a definition of an international joint venture, or IJV, see section 15.2.)

Here are more details of the proposal.

1 Acme Hotels propose establishing a two-year MBA (Hotel Management) program, which your college would validate.

2 Your college would also be responsible for staffing the project with one full-time manager, one full-time assistant manager, and ten visiting faculty.

3 The visiting faculty will be responsible for teaching ten core courses in the first year of the program. These first-year courses are: Introduction to management, organizational analysis, accounting, finance, human resource management, statistics, marketing, sales and advertising, international management, and production management. Each course consists of 40 hours of instruction. A further ten second-year courses will be taught by locally recruited faculty.

4 Acme Hotels expect to recruit 60 students a year.

5 Acme Hotels and your college will share equity on a 50:50 basis, and will be jointly responsible for all financing.

6 The school will be situated in a building leased from Acme Hotels.

This proposal has immediate attractions. It enables you to develop international interests in a country where you do not have experience. If satisfactory financial terms can be agreed, it might be very rewarding. And you are sure that your faculty will enjoy the opportunity to work in Country X.

But there are a number of issues that need to be resolved.

• Formulating a satisfactory financial structure.
• Guaranteeing the standards of student recruitment and of second-year teaching. You have to protect your local market and cannot afford to associate your college's name with a substandard operation.
• Meeting your teaching needs in the college. You are planning a new program on your own campus. If this goes ahead, your staff will be teaching to capacity.
• Timetabling. Your staff must be present in the college during the examination months of May and June. They are normally on vacation between July and September, and your new teaching term begins in October. Acme Hotels propose teaching between August and the following June every year.
• Administrative and secretarial staffing.
• Facilities, including technology, teaching material, etc.

Activities

Acme Hotels have invited you to their headquarters to negotiate a deal.

(a) What more information do you need? Prepare a draft e-mail to be sent to them, outlining your information needs.

(b) Give your draft e-mail to some other group, and ask them to invent appropriate answers that help solve your information needs. Some other group will give you *their* draft e-mail. Invent and supply the information that they need – but be realistic. Put yourself in the position of Acme Hotels, and decide what information you should *not* give the college because it is confidential.

(c) Prepare your college's position for the negotiation.

(d) What position might Acme Hotels prepare? Try to predict their position.

(e) Meet with some other group and negotiate. One group negotiate on behalf of the college, the other on behalf of Acme Hotels.

(f) Switch roles.

(g) The instructor will ask you to explain your results to the full class. If your groups cannot reach a conclusion, say why.

Notes

1 Toby Harnden and Ben Fenton, "One amazing night on the rollercoaster," *Daily Telegraph*, November 9, 2000, p. 3.

2 Ambrose Evans-Pritchard, "Now it's blasphemy to mock Europe," *The Spectator*, November 18, 2000.

3 Brendan Periera, "Try mediation as alternative to settle civil disputes, says CJ," *The Straits Times*, July 21, 1995.

4 Brendan Periera and Lim Li Hsien, "On Chief Justice's Comments," *The Straits Times*, July 21, 1995.

5 Editorial, "The agenda for Bonn," *Evening Standard*, November 23, 2001.

CHAPTER EIGHT
Formal Structures

8.1 Introduction

A Taiwanese bank had branches in Taipei, Taichung, and Kohsung. Organizational structures regulated all aspects of members' work lives. Hierarchies were steep, and any communications (other than the purely routine) needed to be authorized at senior levels; the time taken in obtaining authorization, communicating a message, and waiting for the other party to obtain permission to reply, might extend to days. These features can be explained both by Taiwanese power distances and needs to avoid uncertainty, and by the traditional conservatism of banking everywhere.

Then, in the late 1980s, the development of international banking presented the bank with new business opportunities – but only if it could speed up its communication processes. Top management decided that they had to adapt to the new environment.

The first priority was to synchronize meetings of branches held in the three locations, and the bank adopted a customized telecom system. Colleagues in different branches could communicate and exchange information without a time-lag. The hierarchy could be bypassed whenever necessary. For instance, if an assistant of the Personal Banking Department in the Kohsung Branch found something unclear on the account of a customer, he could at once use the telecom system and ask the counterpart in the Accounts Department located in Taipei Branch. The problem could be solved immediately.

The next development was to establish an intranet system. Every member, from top managers to junior assistants, could use the system and share the same information. Anyone who had any ideas or complaints was enabled to transmit this information directly to the top regardless of the formal barriers. The only condition was that opinions directed to senior levels should be constructive – and top management was empowered to decide what sort of opinions were constructive.

This case shows how an organization tried to respond to changes in the business environment by modifying its structural priorities and flattening the hierarchy. The use of new technologies was not fully effective in this respect. Behavior that reflects deep values in the culture cannot be quickly modified, and in this cultural context subordinates were always likely to self-censor their contributions if they knew that a superior was listening.

This chapter examines how formal structures are designed to facilitate the performance of essential tasks in the organization, and the reporting relationships needed to make this performance efficient. Changes in the task and the introduction of new tasks needing new communication priorities are likely to strain the old structures and perhaps to cause the development of new structures. However, their culture also influences how people adapt to an organizational structure, and culture tends to be a conservative influence. Hence a new structure may be accepted only slowly.

8.2   The Functions of Structure

The Oxford English Dictionary defines a structure as:

> the arrangement or the interrelation of parts dominated by the general character of the whole.

In business, the organization needs structures that will help it coordinate members' activities in order to achieve its strategic goals as efficiently as possible. An efficient structure also builds a strong and positive organizational culture; it meets members' needs for coordination and motivates them so that they are optimally productive. Each individual needs to know how he/she fits into the organization and relates to other members. Too much structuring, which ties members down in red tape, is as likely to be as demotivating as too little.

FORMAL STRUCTURES – discussed in this chapter – are governed by impersonal rules; they express "rule by law." INFORMAL SYSTEMS – discussed in the following chapter – express felt obligations operating between more and less powerful persons and express "rule by personality." In practice, the distinction is not as clear as it might seem. Informal relationships between individuals influence how the formal structure is implemented, and informal systems sometimes correspond with formal structures. However, this broad distinction is sufficient for our purposes here.

A formal structure regulates the following:

▌ The TASKS or duties for which each member is made responsible. Responsibilities are more or less specialized. An employee appointed as a marketing assistant can normally expect to perform marketing tasks and not to act as accountant or transport manager.

▌ The RELATIONSHIP that each member has with other members: for example, who manages whom, who reports to whom, and who works alongside whom. The assistant marketing manager reports to the marketing manager, not to the production manager, an accounts clerk or the office cleaner.

8.2.1 Tasks

Every organization is a distinct unit of economic action, in which a range of related activities or tasks has to be performed in order to achieve its financial goals. The tasks are structured so that they can be integrated with each other, and the use of human, financial, technological, and other resources is coordinated systematically. Thus the company can derive maximum value from the use of these resources.

The contextual communications model, set out in section 5.2.1, can be adapted and applied in a CONTEXTUAL TASK MODEL. The model can be applied separately to different tasks, and so shows how tasks can be described and distinguished from each other. Given a particular task, the model addresses the following questions:

▌ WHO performs the task? Who else is involved? In what capacities?
▌ HOW is the task performed? What happens in performance?
▌ WHAT task typically precedes it? What task follows from it?
▌ WHAT resources are needed to perform the task? (Resources include technology and financing.)
▌ WHERE is the task performed?
▌ WHEN is the task performed? How long does it take to perform? How is the task timetabled?

From your answers to these questions, can you deduce WHY the task is performed? (What is its purpose? How does it help achieve company goals?) If it is *not* possible to deduce the purpose of the task, then the use of resources may be inefficient. Perhaps an inappropriate person is performing it; or it is being performed inappropriately; or it has no clear relation to other tasks; or inappropriate resources are being used; or the location is inappropriate; or the temporal dimensions are inappropriate.

The member's job description makes clear the range of tasks for which he/she is responsible and which he/she needs to perform in order to contribute appropriately. It also implies that he/she is *not* responsible for other tasks *not* listed in the job description, and involvement in these tasks may be considered inappropriate. The accounts assistant who spends his time at a workbench in the production department is behaving inappropriately and risks dismissal – although, of course, this behavior is entirely appropriate for a production assistant.

8.2.2 Communicating relationships

Each individual has different formal relationships with other members of the organization. These do not depend on likes or dislikes but on responsibilities which can be described in job descriptions. The structure shows what routine responsibilities each individual has for communicating with others, and provides formal criteria for deciding which relationships are more or less important at different stages of operations. It has the function of channeling communications, and shows at one extreme what formal communications are essential and, at the other, what formal communications are (usually) unnecessary.

The structure signals priorities for communicating about tasks at three levels:

1   Who *certainly needs* to communicate *with whom*. (The assistant marketing manager needs to communicate with the marketing manager.)
2   Who *may need* to communicate *with whom*. (The assistant marketing manager may sometimes need to communicate with his/her equivalent in the production department.)
3   Who *does not normally need* to communicate *with whom*. (The assistant marketing manager does not normally need to communicate with the firm's legal representative.)

But the structure goes beyond specifying who communicates with whom, and what task-related topics are appropriate. It also implies HOW the communication may be conducted; WHERE; and WHEN the communication may be conducted. That is, the *contextual communications model* given in section 5.2.1 may be used to show how far communications fit the organizational rules.

8.2.3 A taxonomy of structural types

The organization designs and implements task descriptions and communication relationships that are perceived as most likely to achieve its goals as efficiently as possible. Here are some common types of structure. A company may implement different structures in different units.

■   A FUNCTIONAL STRUCTURE (e.g. departments of marketing, finance, production, etc.). This structure is appropriate when the firm produces a narrow range of products or services, and needs to link functional experts together within units.
■   A PRODUCT STRUCTURE (e.g. in a food company, different departments are responsible for bakery products, breakfast cereals preserves; and each of these product departments includes managers responsible for marketing, finance, production, etc.). The company chooses this structure when it produces a wide range of products and services.

▌ A CLIENT STRUCTURE. Departments are organized in terms of the clients they serve (e.g. wholesale, retail).

▌ A MATRIX STRUCTURE. The individual reports to two superiors: for instance, a project manager and a functional mananager. Cultural and industrial factors influence operations of the matrix, and this is discussed at greater length in section 8.2.4 below.

▌ A DIVISIONAL STRUCTURE is adopted by a large company with interests widely separated in terms of geography or product, or both (e.g. Asian division, European division, etc.; toiletries division, food division, publishing division). The divisions have an internal structure (e.g., functional, product, etc.).

▌ A HEADQUARTERS–SUBSIDIARY STRUCTURE. Relationships between headquarters and subsidiaries are discussed throughout chapter 14. Headquarters is usually responsible for planning the company strategy, which the subsidiary implements. In a highly centralized organization, headquarters retains greater control of how the strategy is implemented. In a more decentralized organization, the subsidiary is allowed greater freedom to interpret the strategy in terms of its own needs. Centralization and decentralization are discussed later in section 8.2.6.

8.2.4 The matrix structure

The matrix structure gives a vivid example of how culture affects the design and implementation of a structure. In a simple structure, the individual has an immediate reporting relationship with only one superior. This is shown in figure 8.1, where B and C report to only A.

In the matrix structure (shown in figure 8.2), B reports to *two* superiors, P and Q. These superiors need to balance their decision-making powers in relation to B. They collaborate on planning B's budgets, and how his/her time should be spent.

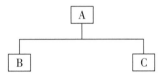

Figure 8.1 Simple structure

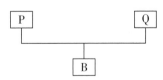

Figure 8.2 The matrix

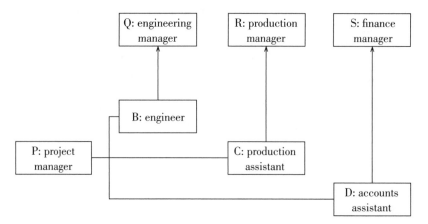

Figure 8.3 A project matrix

The matrix is the chosen structure of many project-focused companies (such as NASA, and many engineering and construction companies), where:

- tasks are non-routine;
- relationships and responsibilities have to be continually changed in order to meet the needs of new projects.

An example is given in figure 8.3, where B is a project engineer and reports to both the project manager and the engineering manager. The other members of the project team (C and D) also have dual reporting relationships – to P, and to their own functional managers.

Members of a matrix structure have to cooperate and share information and other resources in a relationship of trust. This means that they work best in cultures where colleagues trust each other more – that is, in cultures with low power distances and low needs to avoid uncertainty. They succeed in Scandinavian companies, where employees and management might see themselves as peers, control is loose, and manners informal. The matrix serves to reduce conflict and to positively harness the contradictory interests of different departments (for instance, sales and production).

Elsewhere, attempts to implement a matrix may face greater problems. Where members have high needs to avoid uncertainty, they are uncomfortable in dual reporting situations. In high power distance cultures, employees prefer hierarchical lines of control and communication, and are reluctant to trust their peers – as P and Q must, in figures 8.2 and 8.3.

Laurent's (1981) data indicate that "rejection of the dual-boss principle appears much stronger in the Latin cultures [France and Italy] than in others [Northern Europe and the USA]" (p. 108). But even in the United States, success is not guaranteed. A study of American hospitals that had abandoned matrix structures showed that the most common reasons were financing problems, turnover, and staffing problems, and conflicts between physicians and nurses.

Section 8.4 develops this notion that national culture influences how a structure is implemented.

8.2.5 *Structure for control*

Because the structure constrains both the tasks in which members should be involved, and how the members communicate in performing these tasks, it functions as a system for exercising CONTROL.

Tight control is not necessarily the ideal. All control costs money, and exercising tight control often costs more than exercising loose control and does not guarantee greater productivity. One way of controlling the workforce is to implement a structure that uses more managers in proportion to the workforce; but managerial time is expensive, and may constrain rather than encourage creativity. By analogy, it costs a government more to control a lawbreaker by locking him in prison than by giving him a conditional discharge, because incarceration is expensive.

In sum, a company calculates the value of investing in control mechanisms. If tight control is likely to increase profitability and to give protection against internal and external threats, the investment is justified. If the expected rewards do not balance the costs, the company might look for an alternative route to increasing profitability.

Control should be aimed at regulating task performance, and not in developing rules that are perceived as oppressive and hence demotivate the workforce. Here we deal with control in terms of centralized and decentralized structures; this discussion is developed in chapter 14 where we examine structures by which headquarters controls its subsidiaries abroad.

8.2.6 *Centralized and decentralized control*

In a highly CENTRALIZED company, units and individuals depend on decisions taken by the CEO (or a small group). Communication tends to be on a vertical axis between superiors and subordinates.

The advantages are that decision-making is more likely to be coherent and to provide a single interpretation of strategy. Coordination between units can be highly regulated – if this is needed. Centralization may be essential in a company that produces a global product for a global market, and where headquarters needs to retain a high degree of control over subsidiaries abroad. The disadvantage is that top management has greater difficulty in responding rapidly to messages from below and to local events outside the immediate environment of headquarters. In a large and complex company, centralization places excessive responsibility on one person, who cannot be expert in all aspects of the company's activities.

Control is DECENTRALIZED when the opposite conditions apply. For instance, a multinational company might diversify in order to produce for different markets. It decentralizes its country-based subsidiaries, giving each the authority to make marketing and policy decisions previously made by headquarters, and building structures for greater communication between them. Decentralization may be achieved by widening spans of control, giving managers greater control over budgets, and in a foreign subsidiary, appointing from local as opposed to headquarters staff.

The advantages of decentralization are that units have greater capacity to make their own decisions and respond immediately to events in their local environments. This can have the effects of giving lower levels greater responsibilities, motivating them, and stimulating their capacities to manage. It has the disadvantages that activities are less easily coordinated, and may be replicated by different units. An example of what can go wrong comes from the BBC:

> [A former executive] said that the BBC was wasting huge sums through inefficiency and duplication. Once he had sent a BBC crew to Moscow at a cost of £15,000, only to discover another crew had already arrived.[1]

8.3 Bureaucracy

Thus far we have dealt with structure with a narrow focus, concentrating on roles and relationships. This section broadens the discussion, and examines the BUREAUCRATIC network of rules and regulations which influence how the individual uses his/her time and energies in all aspects of work. Although the terms "bureaucracy" and "bureaucratization" have taken on negative connotations, Weber and other sociologists used them in a neutral sense to describe how modern organizations should work.

The term "bureaucracy" is used here to categorize the rules used to regulate members' behaviors. Every organization applying formal rules that restrict the activities and relationships of its members is a bureaucracy. Degrees of bureaucratic structuring vary, first in that some give members greater freedom of choice than do others; and secondly, some make the rules explicit, and some expect members to infer the rules from their observation and experience. There must always be a degree of flexibility – for example, perhaps all organizations tolerate a degree of social chat which is unrelated to work ("How was your weekend . . . ?", "Look what I bought in the sale . . .") but limits are imposed. Very few organizations can exist for long without some regulations identifying what activities are expected and permissible, and those that are not permitted.

"Bureaucracy" is sometimes thought to refer only to organizations in the state sector. But bureaucratic rules are designed to make members' behavior predictable and to reduce uncertainties and inefficiences; and this need for order applies also in the private sector. All organizations have some needs for bureaucratic rules.

8.3.1 *Weber's model of bureaucracy*

The earliest and greatest of the writers on bureaucracy was the nineteenth-century German scholar, Max Weber. Rules determine:

▮ WHO joins: ENTRY to the organization.
Entry qualifications typically include age, educational achievements, and professional expertise. Different qualifications are required for different jobs and ranks.

▮ WHAT the member does: JOB DESCRIPTION.
The member is expected to perform specified tasks and not to meddle in the duties allocated to others (see section 8.2.1). The accountant cannot choose to spend one day marketing, the next in sales and the third on the production line. If he/she wishes to change jobs, the bureaucratic procedures must be followed.

▮ WHO works with WHOM: RELATIONSHIPS.
Formal relationships with superiors, subordinates, and peers are regulated. The member cannot choose to spend one day as a secretary, the next as CEO, the third as canteen manager. Relationships influence his/her options for communication (see section 8.2.2). If he/she wishes to change position in the hierarchy, the bureaucratic procedures must be followed (e.g. when applying for promotion).

▮ HOW the member works: PERFORMANCE SPECIFICATIONS.
There are rules and procedures for doing the job. Behavior that breaks these rules may be punished.

▮ HOW work is regulated positively: REMUNERATION and INCENTIVES.
Pay and allowances (including sick pay and pensions) are paid for satisfactory service, depending on the member's job description, rank, and length of service. Performance is motivated by incentive systems (e.g. bonus payments, company car – see chapter 6).

▮ HOW work is regulated negatively: PUNISHMENT.
Rules make clear what behavior can be punished and what punishments can be imposed. Punishment is rule governed and should not be arbitrary – as when people are punished differently for the same offence.

▮ HOW members move up to higher ranks: PROMOTION.
Criteria for promotion include length of service, good performance, and qualifications.

▮ WHEN the individual works: TIMETABLE.
Rules set the length of the working day and week, opportunities for breaks, flexi-time, vacations, etc.

▮ WHEN the member leaves: EXIT FROM THE ORGANIZATION.
Many organizations have rules regulating by when staff must retire – usually 60 or 65. In public sector organizations, rules determine how staff are made redundant and how they are compensated. Exit may be enforced as a punishment for certain offences.

8.3.2 *How far does the model apply in practice?*

Weber's model of bureaucracy expresses his notion of an "ideal" organization. It is RATIONAL in the sense that it is based on rational, sensible rules, and IMPERSONAL in the sense that relationships are decided by the individual's formal rank and responsibilities. Relationships are rule-governed and apply to all members, whatever their identity (social status, family membership, etc.) outside the company. The individual is employed to serve the company's interests and not to serve any other member.

How far does this ideal apply in practice? Perhaps no organization can ever match it entirely. Human beings are all swayed by emotional and irrational pressures at some points in their working lives, and we are all likely to respond differently to people we know and to complete strangers. The bureaucratic practices in a ten-person company and a ten-thousand-person company are sure to differ. On the other hand, even the ten-person company is likely to follow some aspect of bureaucratization, at least in discriminating between task and communication priorities.

What factors determine which aspects of bureaucracy an organization needs, and how it implements them? Culture, discussed in section 8.4, is one factor but it is not the only one, or even the most important. Other factors are discussed below.

8.3.3   The characteristics of the industry

A structure that meets the needs of any one industry may not suit the others. For instance, a traditional government ministry, a private law firm, a hospital, a bank, a single-product manufacturer, and a multi-division firm will all have different structural needs. The ministry and law firm lie at opposite extremes. The ministry operates through a mechanistic and centralized structure. Responsibilities and relationships must be precisely formulated, and a hierarchical structure is appropriate. An early study of US government public personnel agencies and finance departments found that when administrative authority was invested in expert personnel, there was a tendency to generate tall hierarchies with narrow spans of control (Blau, 1968). The law firm may consist of partners who work relatively independently of each other, with a minimum of administration. Goals are formulated loosely; to provide legal services, perhaps in a specific area of law. Knowledge-based organizations, such as hospitals, depend on the inputs of independent specialists who route their communications directly, rather than through superiors. This has the effect of flattening the organization. But banks – which are also knowledge-based – need centralization in order to standardize rules and so give legal protection, and to reassure clients. Joint venture partners control the joint venture through agreed specifications and deadlines, and depend upon trust relations. Licensing and franchising firms control their franchisees through formal financial agreements and monitoring of service standards.

8.3.4   The strategic response to the environment

Top management is responsible for assessing opportunities and threats in the business environment and for deciding how the organization should respond to them. This means taking account of factors that include:

- customer demands;
- the pressure of competition, market share, and strategies followed by competitors and/or new entrants;
- possibilities for strategic alliances with other organizations;

- new technologies;
- availability of resources, finance, staff.

Management develops the bureaucratic systems that enable the members to achieve the strategic goals as efficiently as possible, making optimal use of the resources available.

8.3.5 Personality of the top manager

In any organization the top manager has considerable power to interpret the rules. A strong single owner is free to decide on strategic goals and how these should be achieved, and hence to set structural priorities. In the entrepreneurial organization, influence spreads from the central figure along functional and specialist lines. The founder of a family business may give preferential treatment to his/her children when making appointments.

8.3.6 Organizational culture

At certain points in operations, informal norms agreed by the workforce may be more powerful than formal rules. For example, it is generally accepted that the workforce finish work an hour early on the last day of the working week, even though the rule says that everybody should continue until the normal time. Top management recognizes that attempting to enforce the rule would cause unrest, and that the damage to productivity would greatly outweigh the gains from the additional hour's work. Also, it is accepted that a manager can ask staff to work unpaid overtime in order to complete an urgent project. In a positive culture, management and workforce cooperate to interpret the rules flexibly, to the advantage of all.

8.3.7 Size

A small three-person company and a multi-division multinational company have different needs for rules. A new company may have very few members, and responsibilities and relationships are flexible. As numbers grow, the structure becomes more formalized. If structural adjustments are *not* made, chaos follows. A Thai company grew from two to 300 employees in 3 years. The entrepreneurial founder devoted far more energy to seeking new business opportunities than to sorting out internal problems. As the company mushroomed, units increasingly disputed their areas of responsibility. The human resources department and the production department both demanded to train production staff. After 3 years, he was forced to channel his energies into arbitration, and, eventually, into a structural overhaul.

8.3.8 Technology

Whether or not this is intended, the introduction of technology affects relationships between members, and in time this leads to a modification of the existing formal structures and possibly the design of new structures. For example, when a computer rather than a supervisor is used to communicate standardized data, operating procedures and quality controls, supervisors become redundant. This has the effects of reducing human interaction and of removing a managerial layer – a point made by Hammer and Champy (1993) in their program for re-engineering. The use of information technology (IT) leads to standardizing processes. Supervisory rules are replaced by covert control administered through the organization culture. When expert information is located within the technology, human specialists are replaced by generalists. And this "de-specialization" of functional departments means that formal boundaries between them can be dismantled. Those experts remaining find that their status is enhanced, and expertise and accomplishments (rather than span of control and seniority) decide how they are rewarded.

8.3.9 Labor-force factors

Needs for structure are also influenced by factors associated with the labor force. Experienced and educated workers may be better able to plan and manage their own tasks – and may strongly resent overmuch supervision. Inexperienced employees need more supervision. In some developing countries, workers have migrated to find factory work in cities. Migration causes family units to break down, and family strife may be reflected in uneasy work relationships.

In Thailand, companies including Bata, Nike, and Dr. Scholl have tried to resolve this problem by relocating to the villages – from which their workforce come. When young people no longer migrate to Bangkok, families are kept intact and wages benefit the local economy. Absenteeism and staff turnover rates are reduced.

> Bata, with about 400 of its 2,400 Thai workforce scattered around Buri Ram in the impoverished northeast, usually has to employ one supervisor for every 12 workers in factories, but needs only one for every 48 in village-collectives.[2]

The implication is that there is no simple answer to the old question of the ideal span of control. An "ideal" span is one that achieves optimal results in practice, and this depends on a range of cultural and non-cultural factors.

8.3.10 Complexity of the task

The complexity of tasks allocated to members of the organization influences their needs for supervisory control and how they communicate. Figures 8.4 and 8.5 show that the same FORMAL relationship between A, B, and C can be implemented differently in different contexts, and have different outcomes. Different implementations are influenced by factors associated with task and culture. The complexity of tasks allocated to members influences their needs for relationships on both horizontal and vertical axes.

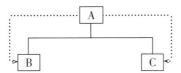

Figure 8.4 Communicative focus 1

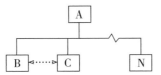

Figure 8.5 Communicative focus 2

For figure 8.4 assume that:

- the task is close-ended – there is only one way of correctly performing it, and one correct outcome;
- A has expert knowledge of how the task should be performed;
- B and C do not have this expert knowledge;
- in this cultural context, close supervision is welcomed (chapter 2 showed that where power distances are large, supervision is positively evaluated, and the superior is expected to be directive).

A invests time and energy in giving instructions, advice, and checking B's and C's understanding. B and C may take little or no part in planning the task, deciding on operating procedures, and performance criteria. A controls the information flow. The (dotted) lines indicate the communicative focus, on a vertical axis.

In narrow power-distance cultures, which do *not* welcome close control, close supervision is *not* positively evaluated and a participative superior is preferred. For figure 8.5 assume that:

- the task is open-ended and there are many possible outcomes;
- B and C know more about how to accomplish the task than does A;
- B and C must collaborate in order to accomplish the task.

In this context, efficient communication between B and C is of prime importance and either's relationship with A is of less importance. Hence in this context, a broader span of control is possible. A gives less supervision to each subordinate, and so can supervise more of them (N).

Section 8.4 shows the same formal structure can be implemented in different ways, and that one factor additionally influencing implementation is national culture.

8.4   Culture and Bureaucracy

Culture also influences needs for structure and how it is implemented. Hofstede's model (2001) provides a guide to the work relationships valued and disvalued by members of the culture group, and to different types of tasks valued and disvalued. This may be interpreted as a guide to needs for structure. For example, in an Anglo culture (lower power distances, individualist, lower needs to avoid uncertainty) we might expect to find structures that are relatively flat, facilitate communication between all levels and units, reward members for taking initiatives, and promote on the basis of achievement. In this context, these are likely to be more effective than structures that are deeply hierarchical, discourage communication outside the vertical axis, reward members on the basis of group achievement, and promote on the basis of years' seniority – all other factors being equal.

Culture also influences how bureaucratic structures function in practice. Lincoln (1989) made comparisons between Japanese and American companies. Other than that the Japanese had more hierarchical levels, the companies were not significantly different. In both, employees were *less* committed and *less* satisfied in taller firms, and *more* so in flatter firms. But relations between superiors and subordinates differed markedly in the two countries. These differences reflected cultural differences; and did not show up in organizational charts when compared on the basis of structural forms showing the patterning of responsibilities and relationships. For instance, American subordinates were:

- far less likely to socialize with superiors and work-groups outside work hours than were their Japanese equivalents;
- less tolerant of close supervision, and they resented narrow spans of control.

And while:

> American manufacturing employees keep their distance from supervisors, Japanese employees seek such contact and through it develop stronger bonds to the work-group and the organization as a whole.   *(Lincoln, 1989, p. 96)*

Until the recent past, top management in Japanese companies focused on providing "top-down" strategic guidance, which gave a framework within which policy details were formulated. Levels below contributed "bottom-up" interpretations of policy (for instance, quality circles had the function of suggesting process modifications, which were reviewed at higher levels). These could eventually lead to process development and, perhaps, stimulate strategic development – although this decision was taken by top management and the quality circles never counted strategic planning among their responsibilities. Thus influence moves in both ways. But this does not mean that formal authority is delegated downward. Strategic decision-making processes tended to be centralized, regardless of organizational size and technology.

How far has this structural arrangement changed since the economy went into recession and Japanese companies have begun to reinvent themselves so that they function more efficiently in new global markets? In practice, factors in the national culture are always likely to inhibit radical change – as the introductory case suggested.

The employee is motivated by a structure that reflects his/her values with regard to work relationships – but on condition that the structure is applied appropriately in the cultural context. Culture influences how Weber's bureaucratic "ideal" is implemented in practice, which means that the same elements of structure may be implemented differently in different cultural contexts. Hofstede (2001, pp. 376–8) distinguishes four bureaucratic tendencies, which correspond to the four quadrants modeled by the power distance and uncertainty avoidance dimensions. The four types are labeled:

- marketplace bureaucracy (see section 8.4.1);
- full bureaucracy (see section 8.4.2);
- personnel bureaucracy (see section 8.4.3);
- workflow bureaucracy (see section 8.4.4).

8.4.1 The marketplace bureaucracy

The marketplace bureaucracy typifies organizations where needs to avoid uncertainty and power distances are low (see figure 8.6). Members depend more upon personal than bureaucratic relationships to achieve results – and may feel free to bypass the hierarchy and cross departmental boundaries. Formal structures and functions may be ambiguous, and members are not sure of the precise limits to others' authority. They negotiate for influence on the basis of individual expertise and need, creating alliances by trading support. The underlying assumption is that "if you scratch my back, I'll scratch yours." Support staff play a key role in helping the different parts of the organization adjust to change. Job-rotation and matrix structures are commonly implemented.

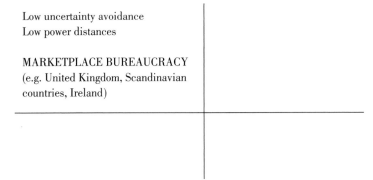

Low uncertainty avoidance
Low power distances

MARKETPLACE BUREAUCRACY
(e.g. United Kingdom, Scandinavian
countries, Ireland)

Figure 8.6

High uncertainty avoidance
High power distance

FULL BUREAUCRACY
(e.g. Belgium, France, Portugal,
Guatemala)

Figure 8.7

8.4.2 The full bureaucracy

The full bureaucracy (figure 8.7) lies at the opposite extreme. It comes closest to Weber's model of making members' behavior predictable and reducing uncertainties. Responsibilities and relationships are standardized and impersonal, and emphasis is given to staff roles (technocrats who supply ideas). Members understand the limits to their own and other people's authority and responsibilities. They respect the unequal distribution of power and have a strong need to avoid ambiguous procedures. Centralized structures and routine tasks are more readily accepted – Hofstede (2001) likens these organizations to pyramids. Vertical communication is the norm, and departments perhaps communicate with each other only at the highest levels.

8.4.3 The personnel bureaucracy

Personnel bureaucracy (figure 8.8) flourishes where power distances are high and needs to avoid uncertainty are low. Hofstede (2001) likens organizations in this quadrant to the family. They often have a simple structure built around a strong leader who controls by direct and close supervision, and authority is associated with this person. The leader may be perceived in terms of his/her social position and personal qualities rather than of the responsibilities associated with his/her bureaucratic rank – the opposite to the full bureaucracy.

In a United Nations report, Ross and Bouwmeesters (1972) described patterns of authority in tropical African organizations. Where delegation of authority does occur:

> ... it is usually confined to relatives (in private enterprises) or persons with whom top managers have political ties (in public enterprises). ... mistrust of those not related by ties of kinship or ethnicity limits the possibilities of delegation and teamwork.   *(p. 72)*

Ranks are tightly differentiated and in a family company, non-family members have few opportunities for promotion. The manager must demonstrate expectation in order to hold the loyalty of subordinates, and must behave according to their expectations

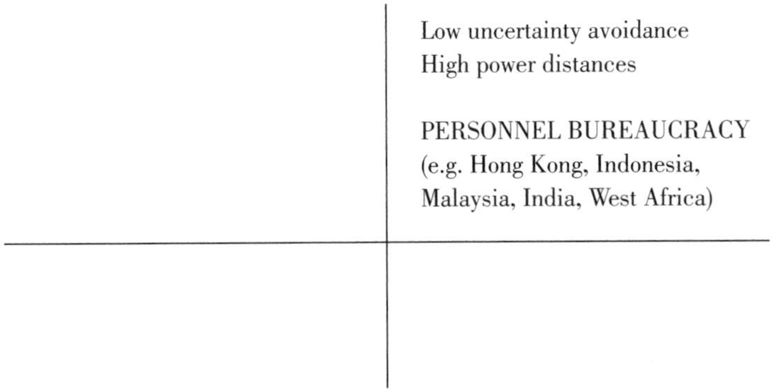

Low uncertainty avoidance
High power distances

PERSONNEL BUREAUCRACY
(e.g. Hong Kong, Indonesia,
Malaysia, India, West Africa)

Figure 8.8

of his/her rank and role. Any "stepping out of place" may be disruptive. Writing in an Indian newspaper, an Indian manager made the point:

> lack of knowledge of one's role and that of others one comes in contact with is one of the foremost causes of employee and organizational ineffectiveness. . . . Relationships often fail due to misunderstandings and lack of role clarity, as can be seen in the example of the old employee trying to play the role of adviser to a new employee who misinterprets this as being "bossed" by one who has no business to do so![3]

This is the antithesis of the approach taken by those (for example, Swedes and Britons) who agreed most strongly with Laurent's (1983) proposition that bypassing the hierarchical line is often necessary (see section 2.4.2).

8.4.4 The workflow bureaucracy

Structures in workflow bureaucracies (figure 8.9) depend heavily upon professional bureaucrats occupying senior posts in the operating core where the productive work is centered. Emphasis is laid on standardizing operating procedures. Hofstede uses the metaphor of the well-oiled machine. Needs to avoid task uncertainty is high and so specifications for job performance are tightly controlled. On the other hand, power distances are relatively low. In Germany, within large companies, executives and workforce may share common canteen facilities, whereas in Russia different facilities may be provided for up to six different grades. German unions, management, and government find it relatively easy to cooperate and avoid conflict – for instance, in organizing training programs and implementing new technologies.

8.4.5 Applying these models of bureaucracy

Hofstede argues that the dimensions of uncertainty avoidance and power distance are the most crucial in determining organizational structures and systems.

High uncertainty avoidance
Low power distance

WORKFLOW BUREAUCRACY
(e.g. Israel, Germany,
Costa Rica)

Figure 8.9

The model is not making rigid predictions. First, it does *not* mean that bureaucratic models are the same across all countries in the same quadrant. For instance, the United States and the United Kingdom both fit within the marketplace quadrant, and have much in common. But decision making in American companies tends to be more authoritarian and in the United Kingdom more ad-hoc with short-term horizons.

Second, it does not mean that all organizations in the same quadrant are of the same type. Not all organizations in, say, Ireland follow the market bureaucracy model or all those in, say, Belgium follow the full bureaucracy model. In both of these countries you could expect to find examples of all four models. Small family companies can be found across the world, and a multinational might try to replicate significant features of its structure wherever it establishes subsidiaries.

Like must be compared with like. The model is not discredited if unlikes are compared. An advertising agency in Portugal *may* show more of a tendency for marketplace behavior than does a government department in Denmark, but this proves nothing. Hofstede's model tells us only that the Portuguese advertising agency is likely to be more fully bureaucratic than is an agency in Denmark; and the Danish government department more of a market than is the Portuguese government department.

Third, the model defines the tendencies of sets of culture (within one quadrant) in relation to other cultures (in other quadrants). It is used misleadingly when applied to a single firm. It is misleading to say: "IrishEngineering is a typical marketplace bureaucracy." More useful is to say: "IrishEngineering typifies manufacturing companies within Ireland, where the marketplace bureaucracy model is predominant."

Fourth, in *all* cultures people want to work in the organization whose bureaucracy meets their psychological needs. A government ministry satisfies needs for routine, and ordered and long-term relationships. Individuals who prefer novelty and change, and value uncertainty, are more likely to commit to, say, advertising, market research, or technological research industries. Some industries cater to both personality types; in banking, routine is offered by the domestic lending department, and excitement by the trading department.

8.4.6 Different needs for structure

Different cultures have different needs for structure in order to function efficiently. This means, first, the same structure may be implemented differently in different cultures, and a multinational company cannot expect that even a simple structural arrangement will yield the same results in different national subsidiaries. Perhaps the members of Culture A are highly collectivist, and they will give more emphasis to those aspects of the structure which foster the development of group loyalties. Members of Culture B give greater respect to high power distances than do members in Culture C, and supervisors in the two subsidiaries have different relationships with their juniors.

Second, when people complain about an organization being "too disorganized," or "too bureaucratic" and having "too much red tape," they are often expressing a sense that the formal structures are inappropriate. When formal structures (whether inadequate or excessive) fail to serve their needs, they make increased use of informal structures, including patronage arrangements (discussed in the next chapter).

8.5   Implications for the Manager

Compare an organization that you know well *in your own culture* with a similar organization *in some other culture*.

1   In each of the two organizations, which of these are rewarded? Which are not?
   (a)   The member follows his/her job specifications to the letter.
   (b)   The member departs from his/her job specification when this seems likely to accomplish the task.
   (c)   The member always follows official reporting procedures.
   (d)   The member bypasses the hierarchy when this seems likely to accomplish the task.
2   In each of the following, which organization is more active?
   (a)   Differentiating the functions performed by members.
   (b)   Imposing formal systems for controlling performance.
   (c)   Imposing formal communication systems.
3   For similar departments in the two organizations, compare and contrast the following:
   (a)   RELATIONS BETWEEN PEERS. How easily do they cooperate? Over what issues do they come into conflict? How much do they socialize outside the workplace? What factors *other* than culture influence their relationships?
   (b)   RELATIONS BETWEEN SUPERIOR AND SUBORDINATES. How much supervision do the subordinates require? How much freedom do they have to plan, implement and evaluate their own work? How easily can they communicate bypassing the hierarchy? How much do superior and subordinates socialize outside the workplace? What factors *other* than culture influence their relationships?
4   How far can differences between the organizations be explained by differences in their national cultures? What other factors explain these differences?

8.6 SUMMARY

This chapter has examined those factors that influence formal structure. Most emphasis has been given to cultural factors.

Section 8.2 dealt with the needs for and FUNCTIONS OF STRUCTURE and focused on how tasks and communication responsibilities are structured in order to achieve the organizational goals as efficiently as possible. The structure gives members information about what communications are necessary or preferred, and what communications are discouraged or even prohibited in routine circumstances. This section then examined structural types, and saw how implementation of the matrix in particular was influenced both by task and cultural factors. The advantages and disadvantages of centralization and decentralization were examined.

Section 8.3 discussed needs for BUREAUCRATIC STRUCTURE and argued that a wide range of factors influences how structures are implemented in different contexts. Section 8.4 focused on how the factors in the national CULTURE influence needs for different types and degrees of structuring, and on how structures are implemented in practice. Hofstede's model shows that a country's culture influences implementation.

8.7 EXERCISE

This exercise role-plays a resolution to a conflict, and then the design of structures aimed at preventing such a conflict recurring in the future. This is a pair and class activity.

1   The class divides into pairs. Each pair consists of:
    • the sales manager;
    • the production manager.
    You work for a small engineering company.

Sales manager. The production manager never cooperates with you when you have a rush order. You have to fight with him/her every time you want to make a change in the production schedule. You can't understand why

he/she won't be more cooperative. After all, if you can't cooperate to keep the customers happy, you could both lose your jobs! You have requested a meeting with the production manager in order to resolve this problem.

Production manager. The sales manager never cooperates with you when there's a rush order. Every time he/she expects you to change the production schedule, and entirely overlooks the problems you face in procuring materials, tooling up, organizing work details, etc. If you have to rush an order ahead of schedule to get it finished, you cannot guarantee quality, and other scheduled jobs are delayed, which affects other customers. After all, if you can't cooperate to keep your customers happy, you could both lose your jobs! The sales manager has requested a meeting with you today in order to resolve this problem.

2 *Each pair*: develop any further data you need about a recent incident in order to give your role-play greater realism.

3 (a) *All sales managers*: meet together to discuss your problems and strategy.

(b) *All production managers*: meet together to discuss your problems and strategy.

4 *Each pair*: role-play and negotiate a solution to the immediate problem.

5 (a) *All sales managers*: meet together to discuss the solutions you have just negotiated. How can such problems be prevented in future, assuming that the company is operating within:

- a market bureaucracy?
- a full bureaucracy?
- a personnel bureaucracy?
- a workflow bureaucracy?

(b) *All production managers*: meet together to discuss the solutions you have just negotiated. How can such problems be prevented in future, assuming that the company is operating within:

- a market bureaucracy?
- a full bureaucracy?
- a personnel bureaucracy?
- a workflow bureaucracy?

6 *All pairs*: role-play as follows. Design a structure/formal rules/informal rules which will prevent such problems recurring in the future – given a specific cultural context or contexts. (Choose one or more of the four bureaucratic contexts above.) Your recommendations will be passed on to top management for their decision.

7 *Full class discussion*. Compare and contrast your recommendations.

Notes

1 Sandra Barwick, "BBC in-fighting turns into torrid series," *Daily Telegraph*, August 27, 1996.

2 Suzanne O'Shea, "A city sagging beneath its own success," *Daily Telegraph*, October 29, 1996.

3 Dr. V. V. R. Sastry, "Know thy role," *Times of India*, May 29, 1991.

CHAPTER NINE

Informal Systems

CHAPTER OUTLINE

9.1 Introduction

In the fifteenth century, the Italian city state of Florence was taken over by a family that was never formally acknowledged as its rulers, but nevertheless remained in control for many years.

> The Medicis of Florence operated a vast network of friends, dependants and clients, powered by an elaborate system of mutual favours, all of it directed to controlling the results of elections. They did not need the offices of power. They owned the office-holders.[1]

The Medicis were the most successful bankers in Italy. They applied their massive resources to rewarding their friends and overcoming their enemies. For example, they were initially under attack from the Albizzi family, led by Rinaldo do Meser Maso. Rinaldo took over effective control of the Florentine government and secured the arrest of Cosimo de' Medici, the first of the great Medicis and supposedly the richest man in the world. The charges against Cosimo were confused, but the government was pressured to banish him. Then the Medicis rallied their client families and powerful supporters who included the Marquis of Ferrara and the Pope, both customers of the bank. The government discovered that no other banks would lend them money. Popular feeling turned. In desperation, Rinaldo tried to stage a coup d'état, but his supporters deserted him. Cosimo was recalled, and Rinaldo and the leading Albizzis were now the ones to be banished.

This historical example has many parallels in business and political conflicts today. This chapter examines how individuals build up and exploit informal power and sees how this can be used to influence and duplicate formal structures. The main focus is on patronage.

9.2   Informal Relationships

The previous chapter discussed why organizations – both public and private – establish formal bureaucratic structures in order to regulate members' responsibilities for tasks and relationships. These structures are intended to make the organization efficient so that it reaches its strategic goals, and to motivate members. They are rule-governed and impersonal in the sense they can be applied equally to all qualified persons, regardless of the emotional relationships between them. Perhaps every organization tries to enforce this rational "ideal" in some respects, but none – or very few – achieve it in all respects. Different organizations have different needs for formal structures and so give different emphases to different rules. Any implementation of the structures is continually being modified by likes and dislikes which are not based on formal qualifications and so may appear non-rational – at least to the outsider, and sometimes even to members.

Informal systems also serve the function of meeting individual needs, but these may only coincidentally correspond with the needs of a formal organization in which the participants may share membership. Participants are selected for their personal qualities and capacity to give loyalty rather than for their formal, paper-based qualifications. The relationships express obligation, and the participants utilize their resources, including economic resources, social contacts, and power, in meeting these obligations to each other. These informal systems are rooted in the power of PERSONALITY.

Three types of informal and personalized relationship are discussed here. They have in common a number of characteristics, chief among which is that they are not fully legal or contractual – which distinguishes from formal relationships. They are:

▮ FRIENDSHIP (discussed below);
▮ PATRONAGE (discussed in section 9.3);
▮ GUANXI (discussed in section 9.6).

9.2.1   Friendship

FRIENDSHIP relationships include:

(a)   Horizontal relationships between peers based on affection rather than on service and mutual obligation.

(b) Vertical relationships between superior and subordinate. Resources – such as birthday presents – may occasionally be exchanged, but not in expectations of support and loyalty, and they do not commit the parties to further obligations. Such relationships may be only of short duration.

(c) A friendship clique – for example, persons who were in the same class at school. After graduation, members typically help each other by arranging reunions, parties, and helping find work. For instance, an employee informs his friends when his company is recruiting. Perhaps he asks the recruitment manager to give their applications special attention, and arranges for them to meet other influential members of the company.

It becomes clear below that the line between friendship and patronage is imprecise, particularly in vertical relationships between superior and subordinate and friendship cliques, as is the line between friendship and guanxi in respect of horizontal relationships.

9.3 Patronage

Patronage relationships include a patron and at least one client. They are vertical: the patron plays a relatively senior role – both within the relationship and in other interactions. The patron rewards the client's loyalty and service, and the client reciprocates. Each contributes from those resources that he/she controls, and has a need for those that the other controls. The relationship reflects the social distance between the two, and provides each with an opportunity to bridge this distance and so to satisfy the need.

Patronage provides means to DISTRIBUTE RESOURCES. These resources include:

■ ECONOMIC resources, such as money, employment, choice of work detail, a contract.
■ SOCIAL and POLITICAL resources, such as loyalty, support and protection. The patron protects the client against outsiders, including impersonal bureaucracy. Clients reciprocate by participating loyally in the patron's family ceremonies – for example, a birthday, wedding, or funeral.
■ SEXUAL favors. For instance, a politician rewards his client mistress with political and business influence – with which she can reward her family and own clients.

The manager who gives precedence to his/her personal relationships with subordinates is behaving like a patron, even though these clients may have been formally appointed to their positions.

9.3.1 Reciprocity

Patron and client exchange resources in order to meet their interests. The patron needs the client's loyalty and service, and the client needs protection, opportunities to work, and so on. Thus patron and client are mutually dependent. The relationship is unequal in terms of rank, but that is unimportant so long as the principle of reciprocation is maintained.

Exchanges are made between DISSIMILAR resources. That is, a vote is not usually exchanged for a vote. Because they play different social roles the patron and client have access to different resources. Normally, the patron controls greater resources than does the client. Given this, a problem arises: how can patron and client have a "reciprocal" relationship when one controls so much more?

The relationship should not be perceived as a simple commercial transaction, and reciprocity does not mean that the items exchanged have equivalent cash value. When the patron is rich and powerful and the client poor a material balance is impossible. It is more important that there should be a symbolic balance. Each side expects to obtain what is not otherwise available and contributes something valued by the other.

9.3.2   A stream of exchanges

A patronage relationship sets up expectations of a stream of exchanges for an indefinite period. For example, a patron in a company arranges that his client manager receive training; the client takes on additional work in the weekends and evenings; the patron arranges the client's promotion; the client acts as informal personal assistant to his/her patron; the patron attends the client's wedding; the client pays respects to his patron on his birthday; and so on. The introductory case showed clients coming to the patron's assistance in a time of crisis.

The comparative worths of the resources being exchanged may never be explicitly measured, and the contribution made by one side does not enforce that an immediate and equivalent contribution has to be made by the other. Conditions such as "if you find my son a job, I'll vote for you in the next election" are unstated; patron and client are *not* bound as seller and buyer.

9.3.3   Duration

A patronage relationship takes time to develop. Because it is not governed by impersonal rules that can be enforced by law, each side makes sure of the other's trustworthiness before making a commitment. Once developed, a patronage relationship may continue for the lifetimes of the participants – and even over many generations.

You cannot buy in and out of patronage relationships as easily as you change your orthodontist or management consultant. For a client to deny a justifiable request for service, or to refuse reciprocation, or to seek a new patron, may be interpreted as betrayal. The client who betrays his or her patron risks social estrangement and a reputation for unreliability, which makes it difficult to find a new patron. Similarly the patron who fails the clients may lose them and hence lose a power base.

By creating the conditions for loyalty and rewarding it, patronage creates relationships based on MUTUAL OBLIGATION. This obligation means that each side can be confident that, in time, a favor given will be reciprocated – materially or symbolically.

Hence the distribution of a resource may not be immediately reciprocated (except perhaps by expressions of loyalty and solidarity), but it does build up future credit.

9.3.4 Insiders and outsiders

Patronage relationships commonly extend beyond a single patron and client and involve a number of people tapping into different sources of power and influence. These linkages build into a NETWORK of influence based on the patron. The net protects members against non-members or outsiders.

Patronage is both an INCLUSION and an EXCLUSION mechanism; economic and social resources are channeled to the favored few and kept out of the grasp of outsiders, however well-deserving. Insiders and outsiders are distinguished on the basis of their relationship with the patron, not on the basis of formal qualifications. For example, the patron-manager accelerates the promotion procedures of members of his/her "supporters club" while non-members find that their own promotion prospects are delayed.

Members of a university-based friendship clique (as introduced in section 9.2.1) behave like a patronage network when they control access to jobs within an organization, which they channel to junior classes, and so deny employment opportunities to persons with other backgrounds. The organization may benefit in that it secures a homogeneous workforce with similar qualifications and knit by bonds of friendship and shared experiences; it may lose in that alternative perceptions and unorthodox viewpoints are excluded and not heard. Whether such control is inherently unethical is an open question; but, like all patronage, it creates the conditions for corruption.

9.3.5 Relationships in formal structures
and patronage networks

Table 9.1 summarizes the differences between formal systems and patronage networks.

9.4 Patronage, Society, and Culture

In *all* societies there are *some* cases in which patronage thrives – those in which it supplies members' needs more effectively than do the formal alternatives. Patronage thrives in occupations which give a priority to social connections, and for this reason, it is endemic in politics. All governments operate systems for rewarding their supporters and cementing this support. In the United States, every incoming administration establishes systems for distributing patronage to campaign supporters; the President rewards his most powerful allies with posts in the Cabinet and ambassadorships.

In the United Kingdom in 2001, it was noted that after 5 years in power the modernizing Prime Minister, Tony Blair, had:

Table 9.1 Formal structures vs. patronage networks

	Formal structures	*Patronage networks*
Qualifications to join:	Bureaucratic criteria	Social relationships
Scope of influence:	Restricted by task/role specifications	Unrestricted
Source of influence:	Rules	Control of resources
Seniority/juniority determined by:	Bureaucratic criteria	Perceptions of status, control of resources
Purpose:	To serve the needs of the organization and its customers	To serve the needs of members of the patronage network
Relations to other members of the organization determined by:	Organizational structure	Membership or not of the patronage network; in- and out-groups
Decision to reward/ sanction determined by:	Performance of formal tasks; position in the structure	Needs to reciprocate and for future exchange; personal relationship
Typical style of communication:	Formal	Informal

already appointed nearly 250 peers [members of the Lords, the upper house of Parliament], which is thought to be the fastest rate of patronage ever. It equates to half of all Labour peers and a third of the entire membership of the Lords. Political patronage is not in itself a bad thing, but it needs to be kept within bounds.[2]

The political patron is able to influence the opinions and actions of his/her client with little fear of contradiction, and the relationship is not accessible to the normal democratic pressures.

Patronage networks provide the individual with a precise place in the social jigsaw. They give social identity and function. The opportunity to belong to a powerful patronage network is always likely to prove attractive in cultures where stable group membership is most valued and group exclusion is most feared. This section looks at the social and cultural conditions under which patronage thrives.

9.4.1 The social conditions for patronage

Anglo cultures adopt strong attitudes against patronage, and treat it as at best undesirable, and at worst evil. However, many people in the world today depend on patronage in order to secure a living. In some situations it may represent the most practical alternative to anarchy. An article dealing with the 1994 genocide in Rwanda argued that in many African countries:

control of or participation in the government is the *only* hope of personal enrichment: hence ethnic hatreds are exacerbated, because the state is an abstraction which is not the object of anyone's primary loyalty.

And a man who, being in a position of power and influence, fails to help his relatives, villagers and tribesmen, is regarded not as incorruptible, but as cold-hearted and unfeeling – a wicked man, in fact.[3]

Patronage is more likely to be accepted in social contexts where:

- public officials do not protect individual rights and liberties;
- officials are corrupt;
- welfare services have few resources;
- individuals do not have easy access to welfare services;
- available services are delivered too inefficiently to be effective;
- individuals do not have opportunities for social and occupational mobility – they cannot escape from traditional relationships.

Several of these conditions explain the rise of one of the best-known instances of organized patronage, the MAFIA in the United States. The Mafia originated in Sicily among small landowners anxious to protect their estates against royal (and alien) authority. When large numbers of Sicilians migrated to New York and the United States in the nineteenth century, the *padrone*, or sponsor, advanced money for the immigrant's passage and found him work – in return for a fee. Most of these immigrants knew no English and did not understand the new society. They were defenceless and alienated. They could communicate with neither welfare agencies nor potential employers. They had very few opportunities for mobility outside their own community, and hence were forced to depend on the *padrone*. The Mafia emerged from the *padroni* system as a set of linked criminal gangs. The early scenes in the film *The Godfather* show the patronage relationship between a Mafia chief and his dependent clients.

In countries where government is unable to impose its mandate on the people and to satisfy their needs, criminal gangs may substitute. In 1995 in a South African community, youth gangs:

> "... rule by both a reign of terror as well as buying favours or silence," [a criminologist] said. "Quite often, when people get into trouble or need a small loan ... they go to the gangs."
>
> Gang leaders control entire apartment buildings, paying tenants' rent and utility bills in exchange for the right to use the homes to store guns and drugs.[4]

Economic recession is not necessarily a condition. India was enjoying a boom when this example occurred:

> A prominent gangster is patron to many clients – even though he lives in exile. He is credited with enormous clout over Indian politicians, police, customs officials, the directorate of revenue and intelligence, and the income tax authorities. . . . Businessmen, film producers, builders and actors regularly fly to Dubai to attend his parties or to ask him to solve

problems. One oft-told tale involves a dispute of about $1 million. It was first referred to a leader of Maharashtra state. He looked through the court case and said, "I'll refer it to the *Bhai* (brother) in Dubai. He'll settle it in your favour in ten minutes. Here it could take months, and I can't even guarantee it'll be settled."[5]

This gangster patron has a reputation for greater efficiency than the state legal system, and his services are recommended – even by a senior servant of the state.

9.4.2   *The cultural conditions for patronage*

The examples show that patronage flourishes in a culture of strong vertical dependency relationships, and hence high power distances. In a collectivist context, insiders (members of the patronage network) are naturally distinguished from outsiders.

Insofar as they demonstrate a respect for loyalty to the superior, a conservative distaste for social change, and a perceived (and perhaps actual) need for protection against abstract authority, patronage networks reflect needs to avoid uncertainty.

Patronage is founded on a personal relationship, which places a premium on face-to-face contact. Where social mobility is low, patron and client meet on a relatively regular basis, and feelings of trust and loyalty are developed and maintained through face-to-face interactions. This is not an absolute condition and there are cases of patronage relationships where the participants meet only occasionally. But in general such dependency relationships develop where there is only limited physical and social mobility and where potentially competing relationships are few.

Patronage links may also be exploited in order to restrict mobility. Research conducted by Wong Siu-lun (1986) into Hong Kong cotton spinners showed that, in an unstable labor market:

> the owner of a family business who feared losing his/her skilled labor to competitors was naturally inclined to develop personal links of obligation with them. These were patriarchal business leaders. They conferred welfare benefits on their employees as favours, took a personal interest in their subordinates' behaviour not directly related to work, and dis-approved of trade union activities. *(p. 313)*

These personal links inhibited the employees from leaving to join existing competitors or from setting up on their own as new competitors.

The other side of the coin is that where the labor market provides opportunities for employees to move to better paid jobs and to secure the qualifications needed, informal patronage ties become less important.

9.5   Government–Business Patronage

In essence, a patronage relationship occurs between individuals rather than between institutions. Nevertheless it links them when the individuals belong to different institutions and use it in order to advance their institutional interests. Government and business are linked by patronage when the businessperson plays the role of client to a powerful patron in politics or the government bureaucracy.

The political/bureaucratic patron:

- steers government contracts towards his/her client businessman;
- secures government funding;
- provides inside information about government policy;
- supports legislation favorable to the businessman;
- opposes unfavorable legislation;
- gives protection against other arms of the bureaucracy attempting to implement legislation which threatens the businessman's interests;
- gives protection against business competitors (helps the businessman secure a monopoly position;
- acts as a consultant and middleman.

The client businessman reciprocates by:

- making straightforward payments – perhaps disguised as "consultancy fees";
- giving favorable stock options;
- paying election expenses (in cases when the patron is an elected politician);
- demonstrating loyalty and respect (for instance, by inviting the patron as guest of honor to family celebrations);
- providing leisure opportunities, such as holidays and golf weekends.

These relationships have been labeled differently: for example, "cronyism" in the Philippines, or "sweetheart deals" in the United States. They have in common that they discriminate against those who do not belong to the circle of influence. In the eyes of the outsider, these relationships are unfair. After the 1997 financial crisis, they were judged to fail the new criterion of "transparency." They are particularly non-transparent to foreign companies which are trying to break into a close-knit local market, and which are incapable of developing the long-term personal links essential in developing a patronage relationship.

Such relationships occur in all societies. They are particularly prevalent where rapid economic and social change is being experienced. That is, where:

- development programs offer unusual opportunities for personal enrichment;
- concepts of collective responsibility by state officials are weak;
- systems for disciplining state officials are weak;
- codes governing the conduct of state officials and their relationships with business people are inadequate or not enforced;
- monopolies, and a lack of competition, are tolerated.

These relationships convey obvious benefits to both parties when both parties are able to satisfy the other's needs. However, they also have weaknesses.

- When the official steers contracts towards a business client, free trade is stifled.
- The benefits of competition are restricted – although, in a culture with strong needs to avoid uncertainty this may be accepted.
- Consumers are forced to pay monopoly prices.
- The bureaucratic patron loses legitimacy when the relationship is condemned as unfair or corrupt by outsiders.
- Either party may find him/herself locked into an unprofitable arrangement when the other's influence wanes.

An example of the last point occurred in Indonesia. As the political fortunes of President Suharto went into steep decline in 1996, many foreign investors began to dump stock in which the Suharto family were major investors. And:

> overnight, in reaction to the surprising challenge to President Suharto, the nation's most favored business partners became political pariahs.   *(Ford, 1996, p. 28J)*

Bambang, the President's son, was unable to provide his business clients with protection and so he lost influence. This became clear when his bid, as CEO, to take Bimantara Citra public was held up in parliament. Ford (1996, p. 28N) commented that:

> a company that once relied on the long serving president's grip on power may now depend for survival on how quickly he descends the throne.

So the businessperson and government official may both benefit from a patronage relationship in the short term, but if one or the other is disgraced, the other may hurry to sever the link.

9.5.1 *Linking mechanisms*

Individuals in organizations may be linked by patronage ties (for instance, between a purchasing manager in Company A and sales manager in Company B). The sales manager studies his "patron's" tastes and interests, and finds ways to satisfy them. The purchasing manager reciprocates by ordering from Company B.

Relationships must be built slowly and carefully. After a few years a Thai manager was assigned by her company to develop informal links with a Thai Board of Investment (BOI) officer, who was empowered to award raw material import licences. At this time the Thai economy was still booming.

> "It is widely known that BOI has a long list of promoted companies to handle and [its staff are overloaded]. One officer has to take care of about 50 companies. As a result, without a personal relationship with the officer who is in charge of your project, you would be always at the bottom of the list when seeking permission in any matter. Time is money so everyone tries to get his documentation approved as fast as possible. . . . The ways to create a personal relationship are firstly to find friends who used to be this officer's

[class mate at school or university, or] to find someone who knows him and introduce you. . . . In my case I was introduced to BOI people by a member of a consulting company. . . . We visited BOI almost every day to follow up the case and try to establish a personal connection. . . . One surprising thing was that our [German] President used to learn Thai from a BOI staff member in Frankfurt and this relationship was always referred to . . ."

When dealing with BOI, she took care to avoid offering a straight bribe or any favour "against the law. It would be considered as corruption." But her company's relations with the Customs Department were assigned to a shipping company whose staff were known to bribe customs officers.

This case demonstrates how complex and multi-layered patronage-building can become. None of the alternatives considered or implemented for building the desired relationships was created "cold." Each was designed to exploit some previous social connection, bridging different contexts: school and university friends, friends of friends, a connection made by a consultant, a connection made by the Company President, a long-term arrangement between the shipping agency and the Customs Department. And when she dealt with this BOI officer this Thai manager took along her assistant:

"so, if I leave the company, [the assistant] is still the link with him. [And if the assistant leaves too] she takes these experiences and personal relationships to her new job."

Thus the manager does her client assistant a favor which will be reciprocated with loyal service, even if they should be working for different companies.

In this case, the patronage relationship could be transferred so long as the BOI officer (patron) is properly introduced to the assistant (new client) while the manager (old client) was still in office. But in other contexts such a transfer may not be possible.

9.6 Guanxi

Informal GUANXI relationships constitute a major social dynamic in the People's Republic of China, Taiwan, Singapore, and in Chinese societies elsewhere.[6] The theoretical question that arises is how far guanxi is a Chinese variety of patronage (patronage with a Chinese name), and how far it should be regarded as a distinct phenomenon. The practicing international manager has to make up his/her own mind, perhaps deciding on the all-embracing interpretation in some situations, and discriminating in others.

Guanxi has been defined as:

. . . the set of personal connections which an individual can draw upon to secure resources or advantages when doing business or in the course of social life.   *(Davies, 1995)*

This definition is broad, and in practice the term is used with many different meanings. At one extreme it may indicate no more than that the individuals concerned are favorably inclined to each other, and that a basis exists for a relationship. At the other extreme it might refer to the relationship and even that the individuals share member-ship of an informal association.

Guanxi relationships are used in order to secure personal, business, and political advantages, and are important in all aspects of business life in the Chinese world. The businessperson approaching local government with an application to establish a new company hopes that a guanxi relationship with someone in authority will make the procedure much shorter and smoother. When he decides to build a new office, good guanxi helps secure a good location and a lower price than otherwise. Guanxi with a client speeds up the deal at the best possible price. In business, guanxi is a form of social capital owned by the businessperson and associated with his/her organization. (Chen 2001).

9.6.1 How can guanxi and patronage be differentiated?

There are grounds for arguing that guanxi and patronage are essentially the same, and grounds for arguing that they are distinct. Guanxi and patronage relationships are similar in that, first, both are based on interpersonal trust. Second, they join individuals in informal relationships that have no contractual basis. Third, they set a pattern of mutual obligation and provide a channel for the exchange of different resources. Fourth, they have no fixed duration. Fifth, they distinguish insiders from outsiders. Sixth, both patronage and guanxi may reflect a high cultural context – although, as we have seen, patronage arises in all national contexts.

However, in other respects patronage and guanxi have to be distinguished. Whereas patronage is based on a vertical axis, guanxi can function on either a vertical or horizontal basis. For example, classmates of equal status may be joined by guanxi obligations, without any one of them having superiority or dominance. Second, the economic motive may sometimes be far less important than the basis of loyalty and affection. Thus guanxi may be less coercive than patronage.

The interpretation made may depend on the significance of a particular instance. If the manager is interested in the extent to which informal relationships facilitate the exchange of resources, he/she might decide to treat guanxi and patronage as related and to make predictions based on this generalization. If the focus is moved to the axis of the relationship – vertical or horizontal – then it might be wiser to look for differences.

The problem that arises in using guanxi as an analytical tool is that the concept is often used imprecisely, both by Chinese and non-Chinese. Sometimes the term is employed so universally that it lacks any descriptive worth, and sometimes with so narrow a reference that the meaning is distorted.

Guanxi relationships can exist between family members, between personal friends, and between business associates who might not normally be counted as personal friends. The international manager working in an environment where guanxi loyalties influence decision making needs to take the trouble to identify precisely the ties that bind participants in a particular instance.

In all cultures, positive personal ties are based on affection and a sense of personal obligation – for instance, between family members, friends, and classmates. How can the relationship between father and child in Iraq, Guatemala, and China be significantly distinguished in practice, other than by the fact that the latter finds its justification in Confucian ethics? Iraq and Guatemala are not Confucian societies but they also have ethical systems that stress the importance of healthy parent–child relationships. Chinese commentators often argue that guanxi relationships are uniquely Chinese, but non-Chinese might decide that its practice is often hard to distinguish from similar behaviors elsewhere.

The outsider faces an additional difficulty in that when the Western media show interest in guanxi, they tend to use the term too narrowly, implying only corrupt practice. This tendency has grown stronger since the 1997 recession in Asian economies, and Western observers have developed a taste for lecturing Asians on how they might correct their business practices. For example, in 2001 a magazine article cited a Chinese-American academic who was hopeful that China's entry to the World Trade Organization:

> ... will lead to a system that relies more on rules rather than on relationships. That could reduce the importance of *guanxi*, or connections, [a Chinese form of patronage] which has long been essential to getting things done in China.... The Chinese government has already made progress in diminishing the role of *guanxi*, Li says, explaining it this way: "Banking reform is getting rid of relationship banking, the smuggling crackdown is getting rid of relationship trading, the separation of the army from business is ending relationship business."[7]

Of course it is to be hoped that business criminality is punished by the Chinese courts – just as it is in the United States, the United Kingdom, and elsewhere. However, there is little point in calling for a ban on a total cultural system that is also expressed in innocent relationships between family members and friends. In sum, the international manager needs to discriminate between malignant forms of guanxi (and patronage) that harm the organization and benign forms that help foster strong, positive relationships and organizational cultures.

9.7 Managing Informal Systems

This section deals with the management of informal systems, whether characterized as patronage or guanxi.

It might appear that business patronage/guanxi is in decline. The growing dependence on information technology seems to be leading to a greater standardization of work structures. Since the Asian economic recession in 1997, companies with multinational commitments have become less tolerant of local anomalies, and Anglo notions of "transparency" in business behavior are increasingly treated as an ideal.

But these informal systems are unlikely to be easily banned – except perhaps in those manifestations of outright criminality, as the discussion above suggests. They are not limited to serving narrow economic ends; they express broad social functions within their cultural environments. And because they reflect deeper values associated with communication within high-power contexts, and power distances and collectivism, legislation is unlikely to achieve much.

As society changes, the cultural underpinnings try to adapt. One example of the adaptability of the urge to interact in patronage relationships is given by a Hong Kong manager in her twenties who noticed that members of the new middle class were deliberately creating and extending their guanxi networks in order to achieve social legitimacy by adhering to traditional standards.

9.7.1 Informal systems in a formal structure

Efforts to build a modern organization are hindered when the loyalty of members is divided between their informal systems and the formal structures established by management. (The differences were summarized in section 9.3.5.) Individuals relate to each other in both arrangements. The organizational superior and subordinate may be linked in a patronage network, but not always. When formal and patronage roles do correspond, the reporting and controlling functions of the formal structure are reinforced.

When the formal superior and the patron of a network of clients are different persons, and when these two persons are in conflict, the loyalties of subordinates are divided. The greater the disparity in patronage network and formal structure, the greater the danger to the organization.

The contradictions between patronage and impersonal criteria for recruitment and promotion are most acute in countries that have not yet fully developed their modern bureaucracies. In Pakistan, patronage or *Sifarish* is basic to social and political life. As a rule, political leaders are tribal or clan leaders and when they achieve power are expected to find employment for their clansmen – who helped them win their positions. During Miss Benazir Bhutto's first tenure as Prime Minister a Placement Bureau was given the function of securing positions for clients of her elite. The Bureau placed 26,000 people.

> *Sifarish* did the government little harm among the voters, but the scale of it was a big reason for Miss Bhutto's sacking. . . . Neither the civil service nor the army likes to see newcomers, often incompetent, jumping on to the promotional ladder; and both were infuriated by Miss Bhutto's casual attitude to the systems and procedures that govern their worlds.[8]

Miss Bhutto's first administration collapsed in 1989. Her second collapsed in 1996, for similar reasons.

> The army and the bureaucracy were antagonised by the rampant corruption of her government and the favouritism and patronage showered on loyalists while competent administrators were sidelined.[9]

9.7.2 *The risk to bureaucracies in less-developed societies*

The international manager may have to work or negotiate with state bureaucracies in patronage societies. He/she needs to understand the pressures that constrain the professional bureaucrats. Often, they are caught by the contradictions between traditional and bureaucratic values.

The patronage network advances the needs of its members and excludes non-members. The modern organization has rational ends (profit in the private sector, efficient administration in the public sector) and serves the entire organization and its backers (stock holders, "public interest"). These aims need not be in conflict – when efficiency in their limited sphere of activities secures rewards for network members. However when there *is* conflict, the patronage network is in essence parasitical.

The logic of bureaucracy dictates that *all* recruitments and promotions are determined by impersonal criteria. The notion of bureaucracy means that relationships between superior and subordinate are defined in terms of their different responsibilities. The individual's responsibilities reflect his/her qualifications and are formalized in his/her job description, which can be formally compared to the responsibilities of other individuals.

When unqualified clients are appointed, the bureaucracy suffers in two ways. First, the client placeholders are not competent to perform their jobs, and this reflects on their bureaucratic superiors rather than on their patrons. The Pakistani case above gives an example. Second, the professional reputations of all other members are devalued and undermined.

When bureaucratic structures meet the needs of members and the wider community more effectively than does patronage, patronage loses its grip. Bureaucracy gains in influence when:

- it is strong and impartial;
- bureaucrats observe their own rules and corrupt officials are punished;
- officials are freely accessible;
- welfare services are effective;
- opportunities for social and physical mobility are present;
- public resources are channeled equitably.

9.7.3 *The "outsider" manager and informal systems*

The cross-cultural manager trained in a culture relatively free of patronage may find it difficult to adjust to a culture and organization where informal power arrangements are normal.

The Anglo manager is conditioned not to "see" informal systems within the organization. He/she may either overlook patronage/guanxi or stereotype it as inherently corrupt. But ethnocentric responses should be avoided. The outsider first needs to understand how the system works within the organization and how it affects task and communication relationships among members. Second, he/see needs to understand why the informal system might be preferred – that is, why it seems to promise greater rewards than does the formal structure. An ethical response might then be appropriate, but only when the dynamics of the system have been examined.

By their nature, patronage and guanxi systems are not transparent, and outsiders face a particular problem in understanding if they do not have a working knowledge of the language used by the participants. But insiders are well aware how the system operates, who is involved, and what resources are exchanged.

If the outsider has legitimate power to ban the system, he/she might be tempted to attempt it. But overt compliance with a ban does not necessarily signify a fundamental change in the organizational culture. Attempts to directly eliminate patronage or guanxi have to be weighed against possible short-term loss of morale and weakened vertical linkages.

The international manager might be more successful in modifying the conditions that make the informal system a preferred alternative to formal structures. This means improving formal structures, and making them more rewarding and more accessible.

Formal structures attract members when:

- the bureaucratic rules are accepted;
- implementation of the rules is accepted as fair (e.g. rewards and punishments are fair);
- rules governing relationships between peers, superiors and subordinates are accepted;
- task specifications are accepted.

9.8 Implications for the Manager

Compare how important the informal and patronage relationships are within an organization *in your own culture* and another organization *in some other culture*.

1 What cultural features explain the significance and functions of patronage relationships within each organization? Take into account such cultural, social, and economic features as:
   - typical power distances;
   - typical individualism/collectivism;
   - typical needs to avoid uncertainty and fears of outsiders;
   - high-/low-context features;
   - the authority exercised by national political and administrative institutions;
   - the quality of public officials;
   - the existence of welfare services and public resources;
   - degrees of private poverty/wealth;
   - opportunities for social and physical mobility.
2 Within each organization, identify the patronage networks.
   - Who are involved as patron and as client(s)?
   - What resources are exchanged between patron and clients?

- In what respects does the organization as a whole benefit from the activities of this network? (Consider factors including motivation, loyalty, and speed of communication.)
- In what respects does the organization suffer?

3 Compare your answers for the two organizations. How do you explain differences?

9.9 SUMMARY

This chapter has examined informal systems. The emphasis has been placed on understanding patronage and guanxi as systems that meet participants' needs and respond to factors in their cultural, social, and economic contexts. The responsible manager who makes this analysis is capable of evaluating how they contribute to the culture and productivity of the organization.

Section 9.2 discussed INFORMAL RELATIONSHIPS. Formal and informal relationships were distinguished. The latter include patronage, friendship, and guanxi systems. Section 9.3 examined PATRONAGE relationships in greater detail, and saw that they express mutual obligations between patron and client(s) and may distribute a stream of resources on a reciprocal basis over a lengthy period of time. Outsiders to the network are excluded. Section 9.4 examined how far SOCIAL and CULTURAL conditions influence the growth and decline of patronage relationships. Section 9.5 focused on patronage relationships between persons in GOVERNMENT and BUSINESS sectors.

Section 9.6 examined GUANXI relationships, and asked how far guanxi should be regarded as a local Chinese variety of patronage and how far as a distinct phenomenon. It discussed the problems that can arise when the concept is used imprecisely.

Section 9.7 dealt with the problems of MANAGING members of a formal structure when they are also participating in INFORMAL SYSTEMS. The outsider cannot take for granted that informal and formal structures match, and that the organizational chart accurately maps lines of real influence.

9.10 EXERCISE

1 What relationships are exemplified between the participants in each of the situations (a)–(g) given below? Decide between:
- friendship;
- formal;
- family;
- patronage;
- guanxi;
- any other.

For each, give your reasons.

2 Which of these relationships do you think are unethical? Why?

(a) In Asian Country B, Charnvit has worked in his company for 7 years. All this time Sanet has been his boss. Khun Sanet is a good-hearted man, who regularly asks Charnvit for news of his family. He passes on his best wishes to Charnvit's wife and children, whom he once met at a New Year party arranged by the company.

(b) In Latin American Country Y, Paulo is illiterate, but nevertheless was appointed to his present position of clerk in the provincial government. He reports directly to the Governor, who is his wife's cousin, and who hired him. He is responsible for turning out the vote in his village. He is always proud to attend family celebrations hosted by the Governor.

(c) In African Country K, Tamba and Musa are distant cousins, and were in the same class at school together. Since then Tamba has secured a safe job in a local government department. Musa has a small company producing low-cost stationery products. He has a history of illness and the business has not been a success. Tamba tries to help by recommending his low-cost products to the purchasing manager of his department. He sometimes has to lie in order to give his friend an attractive reference. The purchasing manager has to choose between competing stationery companies, but in order to oblige his friend and colleague Tamba, sometimes buys from Musa.

(d) In Central European Country H, Sandor and his long-term girlfriend Rosa have been close for many years. Rosa has a good job in the buildings department of their local district government office. Sandor has a business importing and selling low-cost building materials. He has a history of fighting with his ex-wife, who still owns a share of the company, and this has distracted him from giving the company his full attention. Recently the company has been operating with low profit margins. Rosa is trying to help by recommending Sandor's products to her boss, the buildings manager. She never lies about the quality of the products. The building manager is new to this job and this town. His chief responsibility is providing cheap but adequate housing for the many war refugees in the district. He does not yet know Rosa well, but has been told by others that she is trustworthy, and so he is increasingly happy to act on her recommendations. This simplifies his time-consuming chore of selecting between the many competing suppliers and means that he can devote a greater share of his energies to rehousing the refugees.

(e) In Taiwan, Mr. Leung and Mr. Wang were students in the same class and have been business associates for many years. They do each other favors when the opportunity arises. Last week Mr. Leung asked Mr. Wang to help him find a job for his son, Leung Qi. By chance, Mr. Wang is looking for someone with Qi's qualifications to work in his company, and he was able to oblige.

(f) In New York, Mr. Smith and Mr. Brown were students in the same class and have been business associates for many years. They do each other favors when the opportunity arises. Last week Mr. Smith asked Mr. Brown to help him find a job for his son, Peter Smith. By chance, Mr. Brown is looking for someone with Peter's qualifications to work in his company, and he was happy to oblige.

(g) In African Country X, traffic policemen have a habit of demanding bribes from motorists stopping at lights. Every demand is justified by claims that the motorist has been seen driving dangerously, or that the vehicle is not roadworthy. Motorists who refuse are taken to the police court where they waste considerable time waiting for their cases to be heard, and in the end they are usually found guilty and fined.

Notes

1 Jonathan Sumption, "Magnificent despots," *The Sunday Telegraph*, November 9, book review of Strathem, 2003.

2 Editorial: "The fall of the House of Lords," *The Daily Telegraph*, November 8, 2001.

3 Anthony Daniels, "A continent doomed to anarchy," *The Sunday Telegraph*, July 24, 1994.

4 Donna Bryson, AP, "A mother's agony: sons trapped in gangs," *Bangkok Post*, May 31, 1995.

5 "Bombay's Riotous Mobsters," *AsiaWeek*, November 22, 1991.

6 I am grateful to Shi Yu-lin for introducing me to the literature on guanxi, to Zhang Ning for his suggestions, and to Anny Wang Yen-chuan for her useful comments on an early draft of this section.

7 Bruce Einhorn, "Trading despotism for democracy," *Business Week Online*, October 16, 2001.

8 "Between the dock and the hustings," *The Economist*, September 8, 1990.

9 Ahmed Rashid, "The Oxford graduate who failed in history," *The Daily Telegraph*, November 6, 1996.

CHAPTER TEN
Planning Change

10.1 Introduction

Chapter 8 saw that the organization uses structures to control how members perform tasks and communicate. This chapter deals with organizational planning as an attempt to CONTROL activities in the future. In both respects, controls are exerted in order to increase the likelihood of achieving company goals.

In general, organizations don't invest much in planning when the situation is stable and there seems no need to break with routine. But when serious threats or extraordinary opportunities appear, either in the organization or in the external environment, extensive and radical planning may be needed.

Here is an example of planning, on a national level. By the end of the 1990s, Japanese society was suffering unusual tensions. The economy was in decline. Levels of bankruptcies, company closures and unemployment were hitting record levels. Juvenile crime and suicide rates were rising. The "Prime Minister's Commission on Japan's Goals in the Twenty-first Century" was established in order to propose radical solutions. In January 2000, the Commission reported on its ideas of how to create a new Japanese culture.

The report broke openly with conservative tradition. It stressed the need for "individual empowerment" as a change from the traditions of social homogeneity and conformity. It pointed to the inadequacies of the old values of loyalty, patience, and hard work, and the reward of lifetime employment. It proposed a shift away from egalitarianism towards reward systems designed to reward excellence. It criticized habits of seeking consensus when this covered over significant disagreement and competition, and argued for a break with the cultural insularity that characterized Japan's relations with the rest of the world.

In response to opponents who feared that Japanese identity may be lost Mr Hayao Kawai, the chairperson of the Commission, commented that:

> "real identity is what you have to establish in the future. In order to find our identity in the 21st century, we have to be open to the world."
>
> Mr Kawai said Japanese have to accept more foreigners and cultures from abroad and not simply stick to "the identity of the past."[1]

In its broad outlines this report resembles a classic plan produced by an Anglo organization. It first analyses the problems, and advocates a change in the culture – just as an Anglo plan might suggest changes in the organizational culture. Conservative opposition is expected – just as some members of an organization can be expected to resist a change. The needs for good communication and discussion are stressed, and a champion must be found:

> [a member of the Commission] said he hoped the new report would spark debate and be supported by the prime minister.[2]

However, the comparison to organizational planning cannot be stretched too far. The process of a cultural change on the national level is difficult to manage and the results unpredictable. Implementation processes cannot be predicted or controlled in detail. Other countries that have consciously tried to redefine their cultures have met with only partial success at best; Turkey's attempt to become a European power, first proposed by Mustafa Kemal Ataturk in the 1920s, has still not reached fruition. More recently Mexico has aimed to become North American, and Australia an Asian power. (See Huntington, 1998, pp. 144–54.) It is still too early to judge whether the report prepared by the Japanese Commission has caused changes in Japanese society or whether it functioned only to reflect changes that were already under progress – such as the death of lifetime employment.

This chapter deals broadly with questions of planning. It focuses on planning as a reflection to environmental disturbance, and as a political event within the organization.

10.2 The Meaning of Planning

We don't plan the past. I can't plan what to eat for breakfast yesterday. All planning deals with events in the *future*. In this sense, planning is a symbolic activity. In present time, events in the future are not known, cannot be predicted with absolute accuracy, and cannot be entirely controlled. This means that planning is also an OPTIMISTIC activity but it implies that planning can influence the future.

When do people invest time, work, and resources in planning? First, they plan when there seems to be a reasonable likelihood that this can help secure a desired objective or give protection against an unwanted threat. Second, people do not plan when the outcome appears certain; the sun will certainly rise in the east tomorrow, and so there is no point in my planning for a western rising. Third, the investment made in planning is influenced both by the likelihood of success and the importance attached to the outcome. When it is very important that the outcome is achieved, the investment is greater. When the outcome is not important, the investment is less. When there is a 1 percent chance that the company will fail, resources may be used in different activities than in planning against failure. When there is a 50 percent chance, this becomes a much more important item on the planning agenda.

The term "planning" is used with many different meanings which reflect different assumptions about the relationship between the planner and possible future events. The purpose of this chapter is to examine these assumptions and to distinguish different types of planning. This chapter is primarily concerned with planning for radical change. But before we move into that main topic, other types of planning are briefly discussed.

This section deals with:

- planning as forecasting;
- scenario planning;
- routine planning.

Subsequent sections focus on planning for change.

10.2.1 *Planning as forecasting*

At one extreme planning makes predictions about the future; weather forecasting is one example. This describes possible future events and leaves individuals free as to how they might respond. Whether or not they wish to change their behavior in response to the prediction is up to them to choose.

Planning as forecasting includes:

■ CONTINGENCY PLANNING. This explores the impact of a single hypothetical event on a given situation.
■ SENSITIVITY ANALYSIS. This examines the impact of a change in one variable when all other variables do not change. The planner tests for a series of variables in succession.
■ COMPUTER SIMULATIONS. These make objective simulations when a range of variables are manipulated.

SCENARIO PLANNING may be counted as a form of forecasting, but is increasingly perceived as a response to the problems of planning in an unstable environment, and so is dealt with in section 10.5.2.

10.2.2   *Routine planning*

Routine planning occurs when an operation is performed regularly, but needs to be slightly reorganized each time in order to take account of slight changes in the context and the participants. For instance, the human resources department organizes the annual training program for new sales staff. Although the basic model is unaltered, no one year's program is entirely like that of the previous year. The number of trainees and the syllabus vary; new trainers are hired; new topics may be introduced; facilities may need to be changed (a new hotel, more teaching rooms) and budgets adjusted.

This planning is routine and does not enjoy high priority. It is conducted by relatively junior managers and experienced senior management may be involved only in overseeing and monitoring roles.

10.3   Planning for Change

Attitudes towards planning are influenced by a range of factors. These include:

▮ PERSONALITY: optimists and pessimists plan towards different goals.
▮ INDUSTRY: banking and advertising, for example, have different needs to avoid and take risks in the future.
▮ ORGANIZATIONAL CULTURE: an entrepreneurial company looking for new opportunities and an established, conservative company needing to protect itself against new competitors will plan for different futures.
▮ NATIONAL CULTURE: for example, in cultures where needs to avoid uncertainty are high, members may invest in planning to protect themselves against, say, unemployment, and give less emphasis to planning how to optimize their salaries (Japan being an example). Where needs to avoid uncertainty are lower, as in the United States, members may stress planning to optimize their salaries and pay less attention to planning long-term employment.
▮ RELIGION and PHILOSOPHY: a dislike for long-term planning may be influenced by a fundamentalist religious belief that only God can see the future, and that any attempt to do so challenges God. In Morocco, a Muslim society:

> futurity for . . . many Moroccans was not something that could or should be rigorously planned for in advance. To attempt to secure the future, the day after next, was close to being sacrilegious.   *(Finlayson, 1993, p. 224)*

In many Muslim societies, hopes and plans for the future are qualified by "Insh 'Allah" – as God wills.

Table 10.1 The classic planning model

---

1 Proposing an objective for change – what the change will achieve;
2 collecting relevant data;
3 analyzing the data and projecting past and present conditions into the future;
4 designing a set of alternative plans by which the objective can be achieved;
5 selecting the best alternative;
6 implementing the selected alternative;
7 monitoring and evaluating the implementation stage;
8 making necessary modifications, based on stage 7 output.

10.3.1 Planning in the company

The company plans new goals and procedures by which to achieve them in response to:

- alterations in its internal features;
- alterations in the environment.

These alterations present new opportunities and threats which the company cannot respond to adequately by applying routine solutions. Changes have to be planned and implemented. The classic model for planning change has eight stages (see table 10.1), 1–5 concerned with formulating the plan and 6–8 with implementing it.

This model is "ideal" in the sense that it provides a theoretical framework which is often modified in practice (and is perhaps never entirely fulfilled). For example, the proposed objective – stage 1 – may have to be revised at a later stage as the process is worked through, perhaps when the data analysis shows new opportunities or new threats which the original proposal does not encompass. Or the design of alternative plans – stage 4 – is reduced to a single alternative when the person responsible for the planning is also responsible for selecting and implementing the plan.

The model is commonly modified when:

- financial and other resources are not available to apply it (e.g. there is neither time nor money available to invest in the monitoring and modification stages);
- members of the organization see their interests threatened, and demand the plan's cancellation or modification.

This second reason brings us to an important point. Planning and its implementation affects a range of people who have their own interests, and planning succeeds only when it takes account of these. That is to say, planning is a political process which must take account of people's economic, cultural and other interests.

In any organization, members may feel threatened by plans for radical change and may resist it. They are in the habit of evaluating structures and procedures only in

Table 10.2   Conditions for implementing a change plan

---

a   There is a perception that change is needed because
   1   levels of dissatisfaction with present conditions are intolerably high; *or*
   2   a significant threat arises which cannot be tolerated; *or*
   3   a significant opportunity arises which cannot be overlooked.
b   Senior (and other influential) members of the organization believe that change is possible.
c   A specific change can be formulated.
d   The proposed change is welcomed.
e   Initial implementation procedures can be identified.
f   Resources for implementing the change are available – including change agents, training facilities and capital.
g   Persons taking part in and affected by implementation processes can be motivated.
h   Environmental forces are supportive of change, or at worst neutral.
i   The likely cost of change appears less than the cost of
   1   continuing under present conditions; *or*
   2   failing to meet the threat; *or*
   3   failing to exploit the opportunity.

---

terms of their own interests. They do not like being told to give up old routines and adapt to new systems. They react against proposals for change when these threaten their status and self-esteem (Bate, 1999). They dislike risk when this includes the possibility of learning unfamiliar skills and at worst, losing their jobs. Whereas top-management may perceive a new strategic possibility as an exciting professional challenge, middle management and below see it as dangerous.

10.3.2   The politics of planning

By describing planning as political we mean that members must be persuaded to commit themselves to the change proposed. If they will not commit themselves, the goals of even the best plan will not be achieved. The planner must show members of the organization that the plan lies in their interests. We now examine conditions under which resistance can be overcome and members agree to implementation of the proposed change. These are summarized in table 10.2.

When any one of the nine conditions in the table is *not* present, the odds are stacked against the implementation of a plan. Put another way, this means that change plans are unacceptable when the perceived cost of making the change is greater than the expected benefit.

Calls for change are also unlikely to be attractive when everybody is comfortable with the current situation; when nothing is broken, there is no point trying to fix it. But senior management has the responsibilities of looking ahead to possible changes in the business environment, and preparing to take advantage of possible opportunities and guard against possible threats. For example, consider HSBC. In 2001, the bank:

... had grown its assets by 20 percent to 25 percent annually for three decades and consistently racked up a return on equity that put it near the top of any ranking. That's the kind of performance that tends to inhibit change. [The new CEO, John] Bond needed a convincing rationale to shake things up ... wants to fix something that isn't obviously broken.

The changes that Bond initiated included investment in internet development, a new logo, and a focus on wealth management for HSBC customers. He explained:

"I keep telling my colleagues that there is no such thing as static success. To be successful, you have to be dynamic and you have to keep changing."[3]

In general, top managers often have problems "selling" radical plans to managers at middle and lower levels, who are not mainly responsible for analyzing the environment and predicting long-term business cycles.

10.3.3 Participants

Persons in the organization involved in this political process of planning include:

- The PLANNER.
- A CHAMPION is a person with authority and influence. The champion secures support at senior levels and commits the organization's resources to achieving the plan.
- SUPPORTERS among superiors, peers, and subordinates. Their support must be reinforced. NEUTRALS must be won over to support. If OPPONENTS cannot be persuaded to support you, you hope to move them to a position of neutrality.
- CHANGE AGENTS are responsible for implementing the plan and leading the change in each unit. They will also be responsible for communicating the plan.
- MANAGERS who are responsible for running the organization during implementation and after the changes have been made.
- AFFECTED PERSONS who will live with the consequences of the plan. They may feel anxiety when the change is proposed and they see their interests threatened. How can they be involved in the process?
- PERSONS IN THE ENVIRONMENT. Customers, suppliers, financial analysts, journalists, officials, and politicians may all be affected by the plan.
- OTHER STAKEHOLDERS (discussed in section 13.5.7).

10.3.4 Barriers to change

Possibilities of making decisive change are reduced when the conditions listed in table 10.2 do not apply, or are negated by opponents of change; see table 10.3.

Table 10.3 Barriers to change

a There is NO perception that change is needed;
b senior (and other influential) members of the organization do NOT believe that change is possible;
c NO specific changes can be formulated;
d proposed changes are NOT welcomed;
e initial implementation procedures can NOT be identified;
f resources for implementing the changes are NOT available;
g persons taking part CANNOT be motivated;
h environmental forces are NOT supportive of change;
i the likely cost of change appears GREATER than the cost of continuing under present conditions.

10.3.5 How opponents kill the plan

Opposition to the plan develops when:

- members perceive that it threatens their existing or future interests;
- it creates unacceptable degrees of uncertainty;
- it promises unequal benefits – some units will benefit less than others;
- it seems not to recognize the legitimate worries, ideas, and opinions of members;
- the needs for planning and implementation procedures are badly communicated and are misunderstood (see section 10.3.6 below).

Opposition may come from various quarters. Here we consider opposition shown by subsidiary staff to a plan developed in headquarters. Because they belong to the same organization, they have many interests in common, at least in theory. But headquarters managers make a mistake if they overestimate the degree of this common interest, and underestimate disparities in how they and subsidiary staff perceive the business environment. Particularly if they have been empowered in other respects, subsidiary staff wish to protect their independence. They may feel that they are doing their best in their particular circumstances, and do not see any need to change their agenda.

Here are tactics by which subsidiary management may prevent implementation of a plan introduced by headquarters managers or outside consultants acting on behalf of headquarters.[4]

▌ They DENY factors in the model (table 10.2). For example, they deny dissatisfaction with present circumstances, that change is possible, that specific changes can be formulated.
▌ They acquire a right to decide on change in certain key areas – for example, human resources. When any plan seems likely to involve changes in the human resource function, local management have the right to VETO it. In practice, they sometimes

apply this veto only late in the implementation process – which creates extreme frustration for headquarters change agents.

▋ They DELAY. Local managers know that headquarters change agents are on short-term contracts. Eventually these change agents will give up trying, or will be promoted, or sent home.

▋ They insist that every detail be discussed in committee, and TALK endlessly. They may arrange the composition of the committee so that opponents outnumber the supporters and neutrals.

▋ They cause CONFUSION by circulating misinformation and conflicting information.

▋ They WRECK the communication structures so that the plan is not effectively communicated.

▋ They insist on PREREQUISITES for change – such as training – and then make sure they don't happen. Potential trainees are discouraged or prevented from attending training.

10.3.6 A model for communicating the plan

The benefits of the plan may appear obvious to the planner but not to the other persons affected – and as we have just seen, may be invisible to staff in a subsidiary whose interests are influenced by other economic and cultural factors. They have to be persuaded. This means that the planner (or delegated persons) must efficiently communicate different aspects of the plan. This model for communicating the plan adapts the *contextual categories model* presented in section 5.2.1 and is shown in table 10.4. *The importance of communicating the plan is major.* A badly communicated plan is unlikely to succeed.

Table 10.4 Model for communicating the plan

- **To whom** should (different aspects of) the plan be communicated? These persons include the categories discussed in section 10.3.3.
- **Who** should communicate with each of these persons?
- **What** aspects of the plan should be communicated to each?
  These include
  - the REASONS for making the change;
  - the LIKELIHOOD of success;
  - DETAILS of the change process; procedures; responsibilities; resources available;
  - implications for TRAINING;
  - how forces in the ENVIRONMENT can be expected to respond;
  - the COSTS of change as opposed to the greater costs of not changing.
- **When** should the plan be communicated?
- **Where** should the plan be communicated?
- **How** should the plan be communicated? What medium and style is appropriate? The message must be adequately communicated; neither under- nor over-communicated.

This communication involves employees in planning and implementation. In theory, those who contribute derive a sense of control over the process. Those who feel ownership are more disposed to accept the plan as a contract.

The communication process is ineffective in the following circumstances.

- The need for appropriate communication is not recognized.
- Systems for communicating and implementing the plan are not in place.
- Resources for communication are not available and the planning budget does not allow for the expense.
- The communications model (table 10.4) is applied inappropriately.
- Communication is not followed up with action. Repetitions do not substitute, and the more often the plan to change is repeated and no attempt is made to implement it, the less believing grow the audience. When Japanese Prime Minister Ryutaro Hashimoto visited Washington in 1997:

> he told President Bill Clinton, and anybody else who would listen, that he was determined to remake his country's economy, its diplomacy, even its culture. . . . It was a sign of just how frustrated people in the US and Japan have grown with such proclamations by Japanese politicians that these bold-sounding remarks were treated with either derision or yawns.[5]

- Employees lack the motivation or skills to implement the plan.

10.3.7 *Appropriate timing*

Appropriate timing is essential. When a plan is introduced too slowly it becomes bogged down in bureaucratic inertia, and pockets of resistance have a chance to grow and to undermine the radical change process. By implementing the plan quickly and "routinizing" it, you may outflank your opponents before they mobilize their forces. But if you act too quickly employees are not committed. They feel insecure. They resist both your sleight of hand and the policing necessary to safeguard an unwanted change. It is important to allow time in situations where resistance will fade as more people become used to the notion of change and more understanding of how they can benefit. In such cases the manager focuses on communicating goals and allaying anxieties.

The contexts of national and organizational cultures influence the speed with which change can be made. Industry values may also be significant. For example, high-tech industries are often tolerant of change made with little lead-in time, whereas heavy industry is less so. In a context where experimentation is welcomed, your audience is more receptive, and time spent in teaching new routines is reduced.

A further problem may arise in giving members time to forget the old priorities and routines which are being replaced. If the old has become second-nature and automatic, a longer time is spent in their forgetting it and learning the new.

10.4 Planning in Different Cultures

The planning systems adopted by any particular company are heavily influenced by factors in its environment, including the industry and national culture, and by its organizational culture. These factors determine how the company answers these questions (adapted from table 5.1):

▊ WHY is planning needed?
▊ WHO plans?
▊ WHAT is planned?
▊ HOW is planning done?
▊ WHEN is planning done?
▊ HOW is planning communicated?
▊ HOW is planning implemented?

This means that systems that work well in one company may be counterproductive in some other where different environmental constraints operate; work in one country but be counterproductive in some other; work in headquarters but be counterproductive in a subsidiary. Whitley (1992, p. 85) makes the point:

> Particular ways of structuring work within firms and relations between them – and so the nature of firms as economic actors – are effective only in particular institutional contexts . . . so that, for instance, reliance on Anglo-Saxon formal planning and control systems for co-ordinating work is unlikely to be very successful in Chinese communities.

This section deals first with the influence of national culture, then turns to organizational culture.

10.4.1 The influence of national culture

National cultures vary in their perceptions of when and how planning is important. Hofstede argues that where tolerance of ambiguity is relatively high and needs to avoid uncertainty low, planning is less detailed and more long-term. Also, there is less emotional resistance to change. However, it does not follow that all proposed changes are equally welcomed any more than that, at the opposite extreme, all changes are equally feared. Where tolerance is low, planning is more detailed, and may be made the responsibility of specialist planners. Because uncertainties need to be resolved as quickly as possible, short-term feedback systems are emphasized.

For example, in Japan, planning is treated as a formal process, at least below the top level. Sullivan and Nonaka (1986) found that junior managers planned strategy by the classic model of analyzing the issue and isolating the most appropriate solution. However, top managers followed a process which was:

partial, tentative, fragmented, incremental, empirical, inductive, messy, individualistic and path-finding.

The two processes were followed simultaneously, top management feeding down guidelines which were developed and formalized below.

Comparisons between Japanese and Hong Kong planning show that the former demanded more detailed information. The Japanese and Chinese managers all gave subordinates the responsibility for developing alternative plans. But the Chinese kept more information to him/herself, and was more likely to take the final decision in a process that was less collectivist – in this respect more like an Anglo top manager.

The classic Western planning model depends upon "hard" financial data and computer predictions of market change. Elsewhere as much emphasis may be placed on shared understanding of the environment, historical precedent, "best guesses," and superstition. In Hong Kong when starting a venture, business people may gamble heavily on the lucky number eight, which in Cantonese translation sounds like *faat*, or "prosperity."

10.4.2   National culture and the champion

Culture influences perceptions of who has rights to champion plans for change. Where power distances are relatively wide, subordinates are not trusted to make effective plans and planning is left to the superior – which, in a family company in Latin America or Southeast Asia, means the owner and perhaps his/her close family members. A subordinate who pushes too strenuously to implement his/her personal agenda is perceived to be challenging their rights to control. Rigorous monitoring of the implementation process is unlikely if this threatens the owner's face.

Where power distances are narrower, lower levels do have opportunities to provide the vision – in theory. In practice only exceptional companies actively encourage "intrapreneurial" initiatives below the level of departmental heads.

10.4.3   National culture and the communication of planning

Cultural factors influence norms for communicating planning. In low-context cultures, where written text is treated as more reliable than speech, greater reliance may be made on written documentation which provides input to meetings where the plan is then discussed. In high-context cultures the order might be reversed and documentation is prepared only after a spoken agreement has been reached by the interested persons.

Culture also influences what STYLE is most appropriate. Where power distances are narrow and the organizational structure is relatively flat, plans are communicated so that they build a broad consensus. This means inviting suggestions and comments, even from persons whose interests are only marginally affected. Informal channels may be at least as important as formal ones. But where power distances are wide, only senior members are consulted, and subordinates are informed of change plans.

Where power distances are great, subordinates may not expect to be informed in any great detail. Decisions are then cascaded down, perhaps using both formal and informal channels.

In Anglo management theory, a participative style may secure employee commitment to the plan and so foster a common sense of ownership of the change process. This raises the odds on making the change successfully. But in some cultural contexts, where power distances are wide, the notion of employee participation may attract little interest – at least until the workforce have been trained to participate.

10.4.4 Timetabling plans in different national cultures

Trompenaars (1997) distinguished between sequential and synchronic cultures. In SEQUENTIAL cultures, time is perceived as measurable and planning is treated as an important activity. Trompenaars gave examples from the United Kingdom and the Netherlands, and discussed the influence on the conduct of business in northwestern Europe and North America. The implications for planning are that:

- an initial plan is preferred, and straight paths are made to achieve it;
- management by objectives (MBO) is popular;
- employees are motivated by schedules for achieving their plans, and by career planning.

But in SYNCHRONIC or polychronic cultures, members prefer to juggle various activities in parallel and straight-line planning has less importance. Examples include cultures across the Middle East, Latin Europe, Africa, and much of Asia. Plans are changed according to circumstances. Past experience, present circumstances, opportunities, and possibilities cross-fertilize to decide the best course of action.

This distinction is too broad to differentiate specific cultures – for example, how planning routines vary across Southeast Asia, in Thailand, Malaysia, and Indonesia. But it is useful, first, if it alerts the international manager to the possible problems of trying to impose headquarters planning models on a subsidiary where the culture has other temporal priorities. Second, it has implications for organizational structures. Sequential planning models reflect notions that the flow of information to the planners is likewise sequential. But increasingly in today's business world, this is not the case. The flow is continual, and of varying (and uncertain) reliability. Bush and Frohman (1991) argued that American companies had depended for too long upon a conceptual model of the innovation process that emphasizes the sequential involvement of groups of specialists. They propose as an alternative a CONCURRENT MODEL, in which communication between different specialists is both simultaneous and spontaneous.

The result is interactive learning that covers technology, customer needs, distribution, financial strategy – in short, all the elements needed to complete innovation. *(p. 26)*

10.4.5 Planning horizons

Preferences for short- or long-term planning are influenced both by culture and by the individual's psychological make-up. Short-term planning tends to be less comprehensive and detailed. Monitoring procedures are taken less seriously than where planning is long-term, and planning is restricted to narrower groups of managers. Long-term planning is more strategic, and makes greater use of strategic information sources, such as data banks, trade journals, reports, and conferences. Almost by definition, planning schedules adopted by top management, with strategic responsibilities, tend to be longer term than those of middle and junior levels who have different responsibilities.

Cultures vary in the emphasis they give to short-term and long-term planning. However, there is some uncertainty over which cultures can be categorized as short-term and long-term. Early research (Negandhi, 1979) suggested that time horizons were longer in the United States than in three Asian countries (India, the Philippines, and Taiwan), and that these were longer than in three Latin American countries (Argentina, Brazil, and Uruguay). On the other hand, the Hofstede (1997) concept of the "Confucian Dimension" classified the Asian cultures of China (ranked first), Hong Kong, Taiwan, and Japan as having the longer term orientations of the 23 classified, and Pakistan (ranked twenty-third), Nigeria, and the Philippines as having the shorter term orientations. The US and UK are at seventeenth and eighteenth places.

It may be the case that *all* cultures tend towards longer term planning for some activities, and shorter term planning for others, but that cultures do not correspond in what activities they consider worth longer term planning. That is, the question arises, what activities merit strategic planning? For example, Thai family businesses respond rapidly to changing market conditions and in this respect planning is short-term. But Thai managers show long-term priorities in planning their careers (Mead et al., 1997). Hampden-Turner and Trompenaars (1997) found that the Asian tiger economies are very long-term in developing knowledge and elaborating core competencies.

10.4.6 How organizational culture influences planning

The organizational culture influences attitudes towards planning styles and responsibilities. Each organization has its own culture, and hence its own attitudes towards planning, but table 10.5 gives a rough map for the four broad types:

- the entrepreneurial business;
- the family-owned business;
- the full bureaucracy;
- the old-established company.

In practice, these four types are not discrete. That is to say, the culture and planning systems in any one company may be influenced by more than one type. A family

Table 10.5 Organizational culture and planning

CULTURE	Entrepreneurial	Family-owned	Full bureaucratic	Old-established
PLANNING INTERESTS	Innovation	Owner's needs	Rule-bound; safety first	Experience
PLANNER	Innovative planning group	The owner	"Expert" planning group	Old-established seniors
ATTITUDE TO RISK	High tolerance	Fear of losing face	Low tolerance	Low tolerance
STATUS OF THE PLAN	Flexible	Determined by the owner	"Legal"	Justified by precedent
COMMUNICATION	Ideas and counter-ideas debated throughout	Only as directed by the owner; *no* counter-ideas	Formalized and rule governed	Determined by precedent

company may also be entrepreneurial and risk taking, or old-established and influenced by its history.

In the OLD-ESTABLISHED business, innovation may be disliked if this contradicts the accumulated wisdom of experience. Structures become fossilized and are unable to respond to changes in the environment. Planning becomes routine. In the ENTREPRE-NEURIAL type, structures are relatively fluid and employees feel more confident in communicating across structural boundaries than they do in, say, the bureaucratic type. Particularly if the company is new, there may be no culture of long-term thinking, and planning is made in response to immediate circumstances.

In a FAMILY business, the owner may do all planning. If planning decisions do not have to be justified to other members, he/she may find it convenient to overlook or run together the formal stages in the classic planning model (table 10.1). In the worst cases, the family business has no coherent plan at all, and at the owner's whim may even switch wildly between businesses.

At the opposite extreme, planning procedures in BUREAUCRATIC organizations are more likely to be determined by established formal procedures at each stage of the planning process. Planning is made the responsibility of a nominated group of expert planners, and other members are not normally expected to contribute. Monitoring and feedback processes may be restricted to checking that these procedures have been correctly followed. Failure is routinely blamed on circumstances outside the planners' control – for example, the actions of competitors or government. In the worst case, the culture of formal planning is too powerful; so much time is given to planning that it slows up all other systems. For example, committees are formed and no decision can be taken until they report.

10.5   Planning in an Unstable Environment

National culture, organizational culture, and industry priorities are not the only factors that decide planning style.

Planning is based on analysis of accurate INFORMATION from which projections are made. Easy access to data published on the web has reduced some barriers to sharing information. This gives companies in the developed, information-rich economies a planning advantage over companies in less-developed economies. The use of research facilities, consultants, and specialists is expensive and these facilities tend to be located in the developed economies. Haines (1988) gave an example from Nigeria, where two prominent brewing companies commissioned a report on total demand for beer in the country. Their sales turnovers amounted to well over £100 million, and they had sophisticated accounting systems. Yet the marketing function had to operate without the normal starting point of marketing analysis, namely accurate market research conducted by expert market researchers.

A young company may lack understanding of what information it needs in order to plan, and have little experience of available data sources. Although planning aims to establish areas of certainty in the unknown future, it can be based only on what *is* known – past and present conditions – and succeeds only to the extent that future events conform to projections made from past events. The inexperienced planner with no precedents from which to project may be at a disadvantage.

On the other hand, the experienced planner may be hamstrung by historical precedent and be less equipped to respond to new opportunities and threats. He/she stumbles when the unexpected occurs. Planning based on projections of existing conditions did not help governments and companies foresee the collapse of communism in the Soviet Union and Eastern Europe after 1989, and when this collapse occurred existing business and political planning had to be scrapped.

In unstable industries or when the market is in turmoil, and up-to-date information is unavailable, the classic model becomes increasingly unworkable. Chow's (1996) analysis of small enterprises in the People's Republic of China argued that they:

> do not have any long-term planning and concentrate on short- or medium-term objectives due to their worry that they would easily become conspicuous targets during political upheavals if they grew too much.   *(pp. 55–6)*

Thus environmental uncertainty influences what planning is made and how it is implemented. This point is developed below.

10.5.1   A post-modern world

Thus far we have taken the classic planning model (table 10.1) for granted. The conditions for its application are that the company has adequate financial and skill resources, and in addition:

- an organizational culture in which formal planning is valued;
- access to reliable data;
- adequate time to progress through each of the eight stages.

These conditions are often not present. Section 10.4.6 saw why formal planning may be inappropriate in the cultures of family companies. And in all types of organizations, problems of guaranteeing reliable data and adequate planning time become increasingly severe.

Events in our post-modern world are changing so fast that many organizations are no longer able to commit to planning for longer than two or three years ahead, other than in very general terms. Up-to-date information may seem easily accessible using communication technologies, but this is always liable to be updated. The speed of communications has increased to the point at which distinctions between past and present times become increasingly less significant and they have less and less impact on how we think about the future. Links between links of cause and effect seem to be breaking down. There is less and less agreement on what is important in the world, and even how we decide on importance.

Change in our environment is discontinuous and uncertain. Extraordinary events occur without warning and their repercussions cannot be planned – the events of September 11, 2001 give an example. Trust in science and scientists is declining, and new technologies are no longer seen to guarantee controlled and predictable results. The manager may be unable to make convincing predictions beyond a few months, or even weeks ahead.

In the past, organizations invested in planning so that they can respond more efficiently and quickly to changes in their internal arrangements and in the environment. The paradox is that the greater the investment made in formal planning and the greater the importance given it, the more bureaucratic and slow it becomes – and this makes the organization less able to respond. Rather than enhancing, it restricts organizational flexibility.

The classic planning model is sequential and involves investments of information and time – for example at levels 2 and 3. But in a post-modern world, yesterday's data may no longer be valid, sequence is increasingly perceived as random, and timing horizons become shorter. In other words, the conditions under which the classic planning was once useful are less likely to apply.

10.5.2 Scenario planning

SCENARIO PLANNING explores the impacts of a range of uncertainties, possibly changing at the same time. Scenarios are built on a basis of historical data and project significant trends into the future. They can include the planner's subjective interpretations, and factors such as a shift in cultural values, which cannot be formally modeled (Schoemaker, 1995).

Scenario planning tries to compensate for two common errors in planning: over-predicting, which leads to overconfidence; and under-predicting, which leads to restricting the possibilities for action too narrowly. Given a question, the planners develop a number of plausible scenarios – sometimes three, one predicting a positive outcome, one a negative outcome, and one a middle-of-the-road outcome.

An example of a scenario question might be "how will the growth of the Chinese economy effect our Southeast Asian subsidiaries in the next 10 years?" The positive scenario might find evidence for expecting growth, possibly in cooperation with Chinese producers or developing niches that they overlook. The negative scenario might develop the notion that Chinese dominance will drive the company out of the market. The third scenario finds both positive and negative expectations.

The scenario planner is a facilitator and educator who produces material that can be applied by top managers when designing strategies. Scenarios do not themselves constitute strategies, but they push managers into considering alternative futures, and how they would behave under these conditions. They express a "What if . . . ?" condition; for example, what might happen to the industry if the Chinese economy collapses? What might happen if the company is unable to hire sufficient numbers of local specialists? They aim to stretch managers' imaginations outside what is conventionally accepted as probable.

Lindgren and Bandhold (2003, p. xi) describe scenario planning as a form of responsiveness:

> A powerful tool for anticipating and managing change on an industry level or environmental level, and scenario thinking is the strategic perspective necessary in today's turbulent business environment.

This responsiveness reflects, and fosters, a "thinking and playing culture" (p. 2) within the organization.

Robson (2002) focuses on scenario planning as a communication activity. This implies that the precise forms and functions are bound to differ, each more or less appropriate to the needs of the participants. He found differences in scenario plans made by Shell in Kenya and China. In Kenya:

> native Kenyans produced the scenarios because the issues raised were close to their hearts and affected both themselves and their families at a very personal level. . . . The method of creating the scenarios leant heavily on group work and storytelling which has a strong tradition in African cultures.   *(pp. 31–2)*

But in China, severe problems occurred in translating the notion of scenario planning into the language and culture, and he found within Shell:

> scenario planning done almost exclusively by outsiders and the emphasis is on readability.
> *(p. 33)*

This raises questions about how the cultural context influences the design of scenarios and their communication. What scenarios might be developed in a foreign subsidiary where participants come from different cultures? Scenario planning undertaken by mixed groups of headquarters and local staff may have a secondary function, of developing an organizational culture in which contributions made by both groups are seen to have equal worth.

10.5.3 The learning organization

The organization is forced to respond to unpredictable shifts in the environment by making very rapid decisions. It can no longer apply complex and time-consuming systems of collecting data needed for planning how to achieve a specific goal. Data collection and analysis must be continual and general in scope. External and internal environments are continually monitored. Systems are developed for identifying the specialist knowledge and skills owned by members. Planning becomes increasingly pragmatic and incremental. It focuses on looking for gaps in the market that the company is equipped to fill more efficiently that its competitors, and that can bring enhanced profits.

The problems of planning change in a post-modern world have given rise to the notion of the learning organization. The organization learns both from its successes and failures, and becomes adept at identifying new goals, creating new solutions, and at sharing knowledge among its members (Sugarman, 2001). Planning and implementation layer over each other, and the planner learns from attempts to implement early stages of the plan as much as from data. Goals and plans are determined by the organization's capacity to learn from its environment and its own culture, and so continually modified. The resources of data and their analysis available to the organization determine the formulation of goals, rather than goals determine data analysis. This process of adapting to the environment may result in the organization adopting new structures and systems (Forte et al., 2000).

Chapter 13 deals with strategy, and looks in greater detail at the problem of making long-term decisions in a world that is constantly changing.

10.6 Implications for the Manager

1 Review the CLASSIC PLANNING MODEL (table 10.1). Use this to evaluate a change plan developed in an organization that you know well. How far does your plan match the model? What factors restrict its application? Consider these factors:
(a) national culture;
(b) organizational culture;
(c) identity of the planners, champion, change agents;
(d) size of the organization;
(e) industry factors;
(f) other factors in the environment.

2 Review the CONDITIONS FOR IMPLEMENTING A CHANGE PLAN (table 10.2). Use this to evaluate a change plan developed in an organization that you know well. How far do these conditions explain the planners' success (or lack of success) in implementing the plan?

3 Review the MODEL FOR COMMUNICATING THE PLAN (table 10.4). Apply this to an organization that you know well. Typically, how far is this model applied? What factors restrict its application?

4 Review planning priorities, procedures, and implementation in an organization that you have known over the past few years. What factors have caused changes in these priorities, procedures, and implementation? Consider the following:
   (a) technological change;
   (b) competitors and competition;
   (c) human resources and staff;
   (d) customers and change in the market.

10.7 SUMMARY

This chapter has examined the theory and practice of planning, and has taken account of cultural influences. All planning represents an attempt to control future events, and therefore has symbolic and optimistic dimensions.

Section 10.2 examined the MEANING OF PLANNING, and focused on planning as forecasting, scenario planning, and routine planning. The central theme of the chapter, PLANNING FOR CHANGE, was discussed in section 10.3. The "ideal" *classic planning model* was introduced. In practice, this may be seldom applied in full – in part because planning is a political process in which different participants have interests which may conflict and influence the process. The conditions necessary for implementing a change plan were discussed, along with the various participants in the process. The importance of communicating the plan appropriately was emphasized.

Section 10.4 dealt with the impacts of national and organizational CULTURE on how PLANNING is conducted. Section 10.5 examined the problems of PLANNING IN AN UNSTABLE or post-modern ENVIRONMENT, and saw how these lead to new priorities in data analysis, planning, and implementation. The staged classic planning model is no longer adequate to respond to an increasingly less predictable world.

10.8 EXERCISE

This exercise asks what value planning has in different contexts and what factors need to be considered.

What plans would you typically make *now* for each of the events outlined below? What other plans might you make at later times? What factors explain your different plans?

1 Next week you have to meet an important business client at the airport. You have never met him before, and have not seen his picture. He is arriving on an international flight. The precise date and time of arrival is still unspecified.

2 Tomorrow (or the next working day), you hope to go to work/study as usual, at your normal time. You expect to eat your normal food, and dress as usual.

3 In two weeks the government publishes its budget. You own a company employing 500. If business taxes rise by more than 2 percent you will be forced into bankruptcy. If the taxes are unchanged you expect a small expansion of business over the next year – provided that you do not make unnecessary financial commitments now. If taxes drop by 2 percent or more you can earn large profits provided that you rapidly increase your product range.

4 You are planning to make two presentations to major clients. These presentations are designed to elicit investments in the same research and development project. The first client comes from Culture X, whose members typically have high needs to avoid uncertainty and tolerate high power distances. The second client comes from Culture Y, whose members have low needs to avoid uncertainty and tolerate low power distances.

5 Every year, your country is afflicted by very heavy monsoon rains, which regularly wash away large quantities of farming land. You are a farmer (like your ancestors before you). The monsoon season starts next week.

6 A consultant's report predicts that your company can only survive if your 10 sales people acquire advanced new IT skills. You know that the team will resent losing time in training and would rather be out selling. They are a tightly knit group and loyal to each other – and to you. Three of them may be too old to acquire the skills, and in this case the CEO will expect you to replace them.

7 What planning is necessary in order to arrange that the sun rises in the west tomorrow? WHY?/WHY NOT?

Notes

1 "Japan's conformist culture attacked," The Japan
   Times online (http://www.japantimes.co.jp/
   cgi-bin/getarticle), p. 15.

2 Jonathan Watts, "Dare to be different, Japanese are urged," *The Guardian*, January 19,
   2000.

3 Assif Shameen, "Hold on tight," *AsiaWeek*,
   January 26, 2001.

4 This list is based on work by Ray Carter, to
   whom I am indebted.

5 Jacob M. Schlesinger, "Japan seems ready to
   scrap rusty machine," *Asian Wall Street
   Journal*, May 9–10, 1997.

Culture and Management

CASE   QUALIFICATIONS FOR THE JOB

This case examines cultural differences between Japanese and US university education

Hiroko said: "In Japan, before we go to university, we have examination hell. My parents pushed me to get good grades so that I could enter a good university. They didn't care what subject. Then in my university, students gave club membership a higher priority than getting good grades in examinations. So I chose classes at which attendance wasn't taken so that I could spend more time in club activities."

John said: "In Chicago, I worked hard in university. Sure, I joined some clubs, but my classes came first. I studied economics, and majored in banking. I got a job in the Chicago and Main Bank. They liked my grades."

Hiroko said: "Yes, I work in a bank in Tokyo. But they didn't care much about my grades. Actually I studied physics. They didn't care about the subject."

John was surprised. At the first opportunity he discussed Hiroko's case with a Japanese friend of his father's. "Do you really recruit students like her?"

Mr. Fujimoto was a company recruiter. He commented: "Yes, that sounds right. Club membership is very important to us. We often pay that most attention. If your friend was an officer in a club, she can probably harmonize a team to produce good teamwork and to work under pressure. Someone like that doesn't have to submit grades.

"Also, when I'm recruiting I go back to my university and talk to my old professors. They recommend certain students. And I always listen. I know that I can trust them."

John said: "But how can you employ someone who doesn't know anything about banking?"

"No problem. We give all new entrants three months training when they join us."

John commented: "If American universities behaved like that, they wouldn't be doing their job properly."

QUESTIONS

1 What does Hiroko's experience tell you about Japanese culture?

2 Why might John's comment be correct for the United States?

3 Why might his comment be incorrect for Japan?

DECISION

4 *You are recruiting for the Tokyo subsidiary of an American brokerage. The top management is American. What criteria do you apply?*

CHAPTER THREE **Shifts in the Culture**

CASE COMPUTERS IN THE BUSINESS SCHOOLS

This case looks at cultural differences in the use of technology

A leading Thai university collaborated with a leading American business school to introduce an MBA program. The American school contributed its syllabus and all courses were taught by visiting American faculty. The students, who were almost all Thai, were expected to reach high levels of English language competence before registering. The schools had equally well equipped computer rooms, where many students prepared their assignments. Because the same program was being taught in both schools, the assignment inputs were identical.

In the American school, each student worked alone at a computer, in silence, not talking to his or her neighbors. Any disturbance was resented.

In the Thai computer room, students gathered in groups around computers, noisily discussing the output with each other and other groups near them. There was no question of it being overcrowded. Many computers were unused.

QUESTIONS

1 How does the American behavior reflect American culture?

2 How does the Thai behavior reflect Thai culture?

3 In what respects is the new technology inducing a shift in the two cultures?

4 In what respects is it not inducing shifts in the culture?

DECISION

5 *You are Human Resource Manager in the Thai subsidiary of an American multinational company. Headquarters has decided that you should introduce new information technologies currently in use there. You have been asked to research how this might influence structural relationships in the workforce. What questions do you need to ask?*

CHAPTER FOUR **Organizational Culture**

CASE TRANSPLANTING ORGANIZATIONAL VALUES

This case looks at the difficulties of successfully transferring a culture

This illustration shows what can happen when values in headquarters organizational culture are transplanted to another culture in which they are inappropriate. It comes from a novel (Elton, 1999, pp. 48–9). The main character is sitting in a British restaurant, a branch of an American chain. His coffee arrives,

> about half of it still in the cup, the rest in the saucer, lapping around the grimy thumb of Jack's server.
>
> "One coffee", the server said. "Enjoy your meal."
>
> The fact that Jack was clearly not having a meal was of no concern to this boy, whose instructions were to say "Enjoy your meal" on delivery of every order, and that was what he did. Jack reflected on the problems of imposing a corporate culture. There was simply no point attempting to make English kids into Americans. You could put the silly hat on the British teenager, but you still had a British teenager under the silly hat. You could make them say, "Enjoy your meal,"

"Have a nice day," and "Hi, my name is Cindy, how may I help you right now?" as much as you liked, but it still always came out sounding like "Fuck off."

QUESTION

1 Which of these problems can the organization resolve?
   (a) Britons are too bad mannered to serve in restaurants;   YES / NO.
   (b) Americans are too polite to serve in restaurants;   YES / NO.
   (c) The organizational values of this British subsidiary reflect American culture rather than British national culture;
                                          YES / NO.
   (d) The organization is hiring poor-quality staff;   YES / NO.

DECISIONS

2 *If you think any of (a), (b), or (c), are problems, how should the organization solve them?*

3 *What might your solution cost?*

4 *Will it give value for money?*

CHAPTER FIVE **Culture and Communication**

CASE TEXTING THE BAD NEWS

This case shows the importance of communicating appropriately

When the British firm Accident Group went bankrupt, about 2,500 staff were thrown out of work. These staff were informed by a text message from the CEO that said:

"All staff who are being retained will be contacted today. If you have not been spoken to you are therefore being made redundant with immediate effect."

The message apologized for the nature of the call, adding: "I would have preferred to do this on a face-to-face basis. On the time scale available, this has not proved possible."

But the sacked staff were not mollified by this attempt at an apology.

Offices in Manchester, Birmingham and Liverpool were ransacked by staff, who carried off computers and other equipment.

A claims assessor with the firm commented

"I could hardly believe what I saw. There were people walking out with computers. One chap quite high up in the company had loaded his car with laptops and driven off."[1]

QUESTIONS

1 What reasons are there for saying that this message was successful?
2 What reasons are there for saying that this message was unsuccessful?
3 Could the ransacking have been avoided? If so, how?

DECISION

4 *Your company has suddenly gone bankrupt. You have employed 2,500 staff, but now you have to make them all redundant.*
   (a) What message do you send them?
   (b) What medium do you use?
   (c) Write the text of this message.
   (d) What outcome to your message do you expect?

1 Michael Peterson, "Firm sacks staff by text message," *Daily Telegraph*, May 31, 2003.

CHAPTER SIX **Needs and Incentives**

CASE   LOVING TO BUILD PIANOS

This case examines company goals vs workforce wishes

Suppose that in Ruritania, Mr. X owns a company that manufactures musical instruments. The company produces cheap instruments that serve the needs of schools, cheap nightclubs, and town bands. He then buys a second company, the Ruritania Piano Company, and plans piano production to serve the same market. He plans to produce 12 pianos a week.

The workforce are highly skilled, highly motivated, and work long hours – often in their own time. However, they are only interested in producing top-class pianos to top concert hall standard and, at this standard, can only produce two pianos a week. They are very unwilling to lower their standards to produce the cheap instruments that Mr. X plans to sell, and threaten to quit. After reviewing the situation, Mr. X realizes that he has to revise his goals. Instead of producing cheap pianos, he will start a new line in top-class instruments which he believes he can sell to concert halls in Ruritania and abroad. In this business environment, Mr. X's compromise is interpreted as good business sense.

QUESTION

1   What does this tell you about:
    (a)   the labor market in Ruritania?
    (b)   Ruritanian national culture?

Now suppose that the *same events* occur in Darana, where Mr. Y owns a company producing cheap

musical instruments. His new acquisition is the Daranese Piano Company, where the highly skilled and motivated workforce similarly object to lowering their standards.

But, after reviewing the situation, Mr. Y decides not to modify his goals. This means he has to dismiss the existing workforce and hire a new workforce. In this environment, Mr. Y's refusal to compromise is interpreted as good business sense.

QUESTIONS

2   What does this tell you about:
    (a)   the labor market in Darana?
    (b)   Daranese national culture?
3   What is the difference between a motivated workforce and a workforce motivated to achieve company goals?
4   Which is illustrated by these cases?

DECISION

5   *In your culture, suppose that you purchased the Piano Company.*
    (a)   *How would you resolve this difference between your goals and the interests of the workforce?*
    (b)   *How does this decision reflect factors in your labor market?*
    (c)   *How does this decision reflect factors in your national culture?*

CHAPTER SEVEN **Dispute Resolution and Negotiation**

CASE DISAGREEING WITH THE BOSS

This case examines the problem of misunderstanding culture

Agatha was Taiwanese and for 2 years worked in the Taipei branch of an Australian finance company. When she resigned, she explained why.

"Working in the company I was confused about the communications system. The top managers were Australian and they wanted everybody to learn Western management. I reported to a Taiwanese manager who had studied in Australia. He was loyal to our Australian bosses.

"A few times a week my department had meetings, which my manager chaired. Every time he asked us to provide our honest opinions and ask questions, but no one did. No one wanted to answer any questions or provide any suggestions. However, after meetings, every one of them would talk about what they thought and tell me why they disagreed with the manager. When I asked why they didn't say anything in the meetings, they told me the manager did not sincerely want our suggestions.

"One day I broke this tradition during meetings, and I gave an opinion which was opposite to what the manager thought. Later I was told by my colleagues that the manager thought I was very 'challenging' which did not mean positively in this company. He was angry although he did not say anything to me. After a few months I realized that I could not be promoted, and so I started to look for another job."

QUESTIONS

1 Who disagreed with whom?
2 Who agreed with whom?
3 How were the disagreements expressed?
4 How was agreement expressed?
5 How were disagreements normally settled?
6 Explain any contradictions in the manager's behavior.

DECISION

7 *You are the Australian boss. You hear Agatha's story. Is there a problem? If so, what is it, and how will you resolve it?*

CHAPTER EIGHT **Formal Structures**

CASE   RELATIONSHIPS

This case examines cultural misunderstanding for overseas students

At a time when MBA training was still relatively sparse in Japan, a small group of Japanese enrolled in a prominent MBA school in the United States. They found the first months very difficult, but told nobody about their problems until the last weeks of the 2-year program, when Yoichi, Ken, and two others attended a party with a friendly Australian, David, who was a language instructor and gave academic writing classes. After a few drinks, Yoichi unburdened himself.

"In Japan, students very seldom speak in class. Asking questions or giving your own ideas is very disrespectful, unless you are an expert and the professor asks you for a comment. But here, all the American students talk all the time. They ask questions, give opinions."

"Sometimes they argue with the professor," said a friend.

"We were shocked. At first we thought these American students must be so good that we can never compete. Then we began to listen carefully to what they said. We realized that they don't always know more than us."

"Why do you think they talk in class?" David asked.

After a pause, Ken said: "It's not the same as in Japan. Here a student makes comments because he wants to say 'I'm here, I'm contributing.' In Japan we show respect in class by listening."

"Have you talked to the professors about this?" David asked.

Yoichi looked surprised. "Not in class, of course. And we don't see them outside."

QUESTIONS
1 How do you explain the Japanese behavior?
2 How do you explain the American behavior?

DECISION
3 *You are CEO of an American-based engineering company. You have decided to establish a subsidiary in Japan. This will be staffed entirely by Japanese. How might efficient management systems differ to those you apply in the United States?*

CHAPTER NINE **Informal Systems**

CASE THE PROFESSOR'S CAR

This case looks at the informal networks common in certain cultures

In Argentina, Dr. Lalita, a professor in the local branch of an American university, had a car to sell. She asked her maid to enquire among her family and friends. Eventually the maid located a cousin, an electrician, who came to see the car. He could not afford much; nevertheless, a price was agreed. This was well below the car's value and greatly to the electrician's advantage. However, her relationship with the maid gave the professor some guarantee that the sale would not be to her disadvantage.

When Dr. Lalita wanted electrical repairs made in her old house, the maid contacted the cousin. He was very busy and hard working, but was happy to do the work for a minimal charge. Dr. Lalita was happy to recommend him to her friends – but they were expected to pay full cost for his services.

When Dr. Lalita's new car went into the garage, he lent her back the old one rent-free until it was fixed.

None of the benefits accruing from this arrangement had been promised at the time of the car sale.

QUESTIONS
1 How did Dr. Lalita benefit from this relationship?
2 How did the maid benefit?
3 How did the cousin benefit?
4 In what respects was this a patronage relationship?
5 In what respects was it not a patronage relationship?

DECISION
6 *You are the ethical consultant to the university. The authorities have learned about this arrangement, and have asked you to advise:*
   (a) In what respects is it ethical?
   (b) In what respects is it unethical?
   (c) Should the university be concerned?
   (d) If yes, how should the university respond?

CASE   PLANNING A TURNAROUND

The need to find the right changes to make

Lucia is the daughter of a successful Brazilian entrepreneur. After studying in Europe and the United States, she asked him for a job. He asked her to take responsibility for one of the family's many interests, a small company located in France. None of her very competitive siblings had shown any interest.

The company produced and sold soaps and shampoos. Earnings were down and the company was beginning to lose money. "See what you can do to turn it around," he said. "If you don't have any luck, we'll sell."

Lucia visited the factory. She found the plant in bad repair, and the roof leaked. The general manager introduced her to the 55 employees, who were obviously demoralized. The older members seemed resigned to early retirement; this was an area of high unemployment where they were unlikely to find other jobs.

On her way out of the meeting, one of the younger workers accosted her. "It doesn't have to be like this," he said. "We used to make the best soap in France and we can again. The problem is, none of the sales staff know their job. I'm not the only one who thinks so."

"Back to your station," said the General Manager, and to Lucia's surprise, the young man obeyed.

"Pierre is a hothead," the General Manager explained.

"But is he right about the sales staff?"

"They do their best," came the defensive answer. "And the real problem is our suppliers. The worse our problems, the more unreliable they grow. And the bank, of course. They say that as things are now, they can't lend us any more."

Lucia returned to her hotel in thoughtful mood. She had two options. She could return home and propose the sale. The proceeds would cover recent losses, but her reputation would suffer in the family. Or she could plan a turnaround.

QUESTION

1 What conditions for implementing a change plan are already in place?

DECISION

2 *You are Lucia. How can you improve the conditions for change?*

PART THREE
International Strategies

of the opportunities. This chapter focuses on some of the systems by which a multi-national headquarters controls its subsidiary. (Control exercised through staffing is discussed in Chapter 16.)

CHAPTER FIFTEEN **International Joint Ventures**
The international joint venture offers a range of benefits other than the possibility of making large profits. A joint venture is always bound to be risky, in part because the partners operate in different national environments, both of which may be undergoing rapid change. Success and failure factors are discussed.

CHAPTER SIXTEEN **Staffing to Control**
This chapter deals with how the company uses staffing policies to exercise the appropriate degree of control on its investments abroad – whether a subsidiary or an international joint venture. Bureaucratic and cultural control techniques are discussed. A range of factors determine the choice of local and expatriate management in the investment.

CHAPTER SEVENTEEN **Expatriate Assignments**
The concepts of expatriate success and failure are flexible, and are understood differently by different people in different circumstances. But one point on which the experts agree is that the commitment of the expatriate's dependents is vital for success. The chapter also emphasizes the importance of selection.

CHAPTER EIGHTEEN **Training and Supporting an Expatriate Assignment**
Even efficient selection from a wide pool of applicants is insufficient to guarantee the success of an expatriate assignment. A perfect match between job description and candidate is unlikely, and for various reasons job description may be incomplete. Training and support for the expatriate and dependents are therefore essential.

CHAPTER ELEVEN
Globalization and Localization

CHAPTER OUTLINE

11.1 Introduction

Chapter 1 saw how decisions made within the company are influenced by factors in the business environment. This chapter returns to the same theme on a different scale, and sees how internal and local identity is influenced by external and global factors.

The terrorist attacks on the World Trade Center and the Pentagon on September 11, 2001 involved planning in Afghanistan, Pakistan, Malaysia, Germany, Spain, United Arab Emirates, Britain, and the United States.[1] The next day, an economic journalist commented that:

> globalization, the force that has delivered a cornucopia of consumer goods, has a dark side which is a nightmare beyond the wildest imaginings of the protesters lobbying against the World Trade Organization.[2]

This chapter examines both the light and dark sides.

The organization responsible, al-Qa'eda (the network), has certainly shown itself to be global in its scope. Its members have organized operations in Sudan, Egypt, Saudi Arabia, Yemen, Somalia, Croatia, Albania, Lebanon, Argentina, Italy, the Philippines, Tajikistan, Azerbaijan, Kenya, Tanzania, India, Chechnya, Indonesia, France, Greece, and other countries (see Bergen, 2001). Between October 2002 and November 2003, major attacks were staged in Turkey, Morocco, Jordan, Kenya, Iraq, Yemen, Saudi Arabia, India, Indonesia, Afghanistan, and the Philippines.[3]

Al-Qa'eda not only matches the global capacity of companies such as McDonald's, Coca-Cola, HSBC, and Toyota, but it also, in one respect, can actually claim to be a purer global organization than these four multinational companies. Their structures are pyramid in shape and they are anchored to the country of headquarters – McDonald's and Coca-Cola in the United States, HSBC in the United Kingdom, and Toyota in Japan. Decisions reached in headquarters determine policy and operations conducted in local branches across other countries.

Unlike these companies, Al-Qa'eda does not have a single headquarters and is decentralized.

> [Despite] the erosion of the core leadership of al-Qaeda in Afghanistan and Pakistan, al-Qaeda cells in at least 98 countries are likely to learn to function wholly or partly on their own.[4]

It has recognized that hierarchical structures with a chain of command are more easily penetrated than leaderless organizations in which:

> "individuals and groups operate independently of each other, and never report to a central headquarters or single leader for direction and instruction, as would those who belong to a typical pyramid organisation." Leaders do not issue orders or pay operatives; instead, they inspire small cells or individuals to take action on their own initiative.
>
> *(Stern, 2003, p. 34[5])*

Cells are linked only by informal contacts and a shared ideology. This means that decisions reached by, say, members acting in Indonesia seem to carry as much weight as decisions made by members acting just as independently in, say, Pakistan or the United Kingdom. At the time of writing (2003) there have been no recorded instances of one part of the network disclaiming activities planned and implemented elsewhere. And so this high degree of local autonomy has had the paradoxical effect of rendering the decision-making apparatus of this terror-organization truly global.

But although al-Qa'eda might make a global impact, its appeal is relatively narrow and seems unlikely to spread beyond those already committed to its religious and ideological positions. As we shall see, American companies and other institutions have a greater reach. They reflect the core ideology of its members – American citizens – as strongly, and seem to have greater missionary appeal. Many non-Americans admire American achievements and values, and would like to emigrate there to contribute to American national life and to take American citizenship, if given the opportunity.

A "purely" globalized world economy might be hypothesized in which there is close economic interdependence between all nations in trade, investment, and cooperative commercial relationships. This implies a world in which all countries compete on an equal basis – on a horizontal basis.

For example, an Indonesian company manufactures computer technology on an international basis. The Jakarta headquarters hires Japanese technical staff. Subsidiaries in Latin America and the United States manufacture the finished items that are sold to customers in North Africa and the Middle East. It competes directly with an American company based in Chicago. But this example is obviously fictitious, and the ideal is far from being achieved in practice. The present economic realities mean that an Indonesian company marketing to North Africa is most unlikely to afford investments in Japanese design and American manufacturing, or to compete on an equal footing with an American company. In practice the only economic superpower, the United States, dominates the computer industry, and most other globalized industries. Our globalized world is structured on a vertical basis.

The term "globalization" is used with increasing frequency but with variable meanings in different contexts. These variations need not cause problems so long as they are understood. What matters more is that we recognize the structural implications of this revolution, particularly when dealing with problems of how to do strategic planning, strategic issues generally, and the development of multinational companies in response to change. These themes are discussed throughout the remainder of this book.

The chapter distinguishes between the drive towards a globalized world on the one hand and the impact on local identity on the other. Mittelman (2000) discusses the interplay between:

> . . . the thrust of globalizing market forces, sometimes propelled by the state, and a counterthrust fuelled by the needs of society. Above all, the challenge here is to discern globalization's contents – i.e. historical transformation in world order – and the resultant discontents.
>
> *(p. 3)*

This notion that globalization poses an unprecedented challenge to existing systems of national and corporate organization is developed below.

11.2   Defining Globalization

This section is about a few of the many senses in which the term "globalization" is used; it does not try to offer a single definition.

Why has the concept of GLOBALIZATION excited so much interest in the past few years? It has changed the way we think about the world. The importance of borders between different countries is reduced, and similar events and phenomena in these countries are more easily linked. The identities of cross-border structures are strengthened, and the power of organizations operating only within the nation state is weakened. Individuals who possess the necessary technical skills find it significantly easier and faster than before to implement complex interactions. To take a specific example, by pushing computer keys a banker can almost instantaneously transfer sums of money between London and New York, between New York and Bangkok, between Bangkok and Paris, and so on. The political and legal institutions of these different countries no longer present insurmountable obstacles to doing business between them.

Despite offering these commercial advantages, the set of financial and technological factors that power globalization also have negative aspects. They radically influence how we lead our lives, and it seems that the changes can be neither fully controlled nor reversed. Individuals find it impossible to plan their futures more than a few years or months ahead.

The problems of predicting the effects of globalization in part stem from uncertainties about how the notion should be defined. These uncertainties arise because the term is used in many different ways. Gowan (1999, p. 3) reflects on this ambiguity in the introduction to his text.

> The 1990s have been the decade of globalization. We see its effects everywhere: in economic, social and political life, around the world. Yet the more all-pervasive are these effects, the more elusive is the animal itself. An enormous outpouring of academic literature has failed to provide an agreed view of its physiognomy or its location and some reputable academics of Right and Left even question its very existence.

The most general sense of the term is "applying to the whole earth." For example, in March 2003 the senior London representative of the Taiwanese government complained in a newspaper letter:

> Sir – The mysterious pneumonia spreading across the globe [reference] has prompted the World Health Organization to issue a "worldwide health alert". It has sent experts to the East Asia region to investigate and yet has still to respond to three similar cases Taiwan reported this month.
>   At times like these, the isolation of those refused membership of the organisation is glaring. Legislators and many NGOs in Taiwan will lodge a strong protest against the WHO for its obvious discrimination. Not only do the Taiwanese have as much right as any other nation to the knowledge and resources the WHO can afford them, but the case demonstrates that, as killer bugs develop stronger, more virulent strains and the world becomes increasingly smaller, Taiwan's exclusion poses a serious danger to global health.[6]

Mr Yang's complaint about the WHO's political agenda (not recognizing the existence of an independent Taiwan) used the terms "globe" and "global" with an everyday sense equivalent to "worldwide" but this is not the specialist meaning carried by "globalization." In the sections below we deal with various technical uses.

11.2.1 The political meaning of globalization

In politics, the term "globalization" refers generally to increasing dependencies between national and international bodies. In practice it has taken on a more specific connotation: the development of a New World Order dominated by the United States. The United States justifies this centralization and control of the globalizing processes by needs to protect its own interests and prevent instabilities in the wake of the collapse of the Soviet system. President George Bush expressed these concerns thus:

The world is still dangerous. Surely that is now clear. Stability is not secure. American interests are far-reaching. Interdependence has increased. The consequences of regional instability can be global. This is no time to risk America's capacity to protect her vital interests.[7]

The United States has used its financial and military power to develop the leading political role in the world. Since the collapse of the Soviet Union, America is unchallenged as a superpower, and is able to exert unequaled influence on other countries. In some eyes, this gives the right to determine events across the globe.

"Is America fit to be an imperial power?" I [the interviewer, Graham Turner] asked the former head of the CIA, Admiral Stansfield Turner. I knew I was pushing my luck and the admiral, who was Director of Central Intelligence during the Carter years, was clearly irritated. "If anyone says that the United States is not fit to be an imperial power," he retorted, "the burden is on them to say why.

"I [the Admiral] believe we're fit for three reasons. One, we won the Cold War resoundingly. Two, we're both the most democratic country in the world and the best example of free enterprise – and that's the way the whole world is moving. Those who don't go that way will simply be trampled under foot.

Number three: the world needs a leader, and no one else can do it. The EU didn't stand up on Bosnia. We did. The EU couldn't stand up on Kosovo. We did. So it doesn't make much difference whether we're fit or not. We're there, and no one else is."[8]

Such an attitude may be justified, but it does not make friends.

The United States expresses its global muscle through both military means and economic means. Countries that accept American political priorities are rewarded with trade agreements and development aid.

International monetary and financial relations are always the product of both economic and above all political choices by leading states. Studies of globalization which fail to explore the political dimensions of the international monetary regime that has existed since 1973 will miss central features of the dynamics of globalization. This international monetary regime has operated both as an international "economic regime" and as a potential instrument of economic statecraft and power politics. The name given to it here is the "Dollar–Wall Street Regime."   *(Gowan, 1999, p. 4)*

Governments that do not accept American priorities are opportunities for economic growth and, in extreme cases, may be actively destabilized – opposition groups are financed, and perhaps supported with military power.

A degree of non-compliance may sometimes be allowed. In March 2003 several small countries resisted demands for a vote in the UN Security Council declaring war on Iraq, despite American threats to curtail aid or promises to increase it. France and Russia, both permanent members of the Security Council, threatened to veto any vote and eventually the United States and Britain were forced to withdraw their proposal. These opponents to the initiative were driven largely by their local electorates.

But outright rebellion is punished severely. States such as North Korea and Myanmar (Burma) that have refused to subscribe to American capitalism and remove themselves from the international economic system have been unable to secure trading subsidies and preferential agreements, and pay an enormous economic cost.

The 1962 military coup led by General Ne Win ushered in 26 years of socialist and self-imposed economic isolation from the outside world, and ties with the outside world were reduced to a minimum. The 1988 coup forced the abandonment of this "Burmese way to socialism" and brought in economic reforms designed to encourage trade with global markets. But the Myanmar economy continued to suffer isolation; now it was imposed by the United States and Europe, who objected to the country's political arrangements.

The Myanmar case indicates that the benefits of economic globalization are enjoyed only by those countries prepared to accept or at least to give lip-service to Western concepts of democracy, or to countries like China that are powerful enough to ignore calls for "universal" human rights. In practice, the concept of universal human rights has proved adaptable to circumstances. It has not been of assistance to the Burmese people, for whom:

> the onslaught of depression has been relentless. The country's people have suffered under the effects of misrule for decades, and still cannot see any light at the end of the tunnel. Especially since the mid-1970s, the lot of the average Burmese has worsened almost day by day, so that now they are at their lowest point ever.... Virtually every sector of Burmese society has been crippled by an oppressive sense of hopelessness.
>
> *(Maung Maung Oo, 2001)*

The economic damage ensuing from non-compliance with global standards has serious repercussions on the social and cultural life of the community.

11.2.2   *Global trade*

In management literature, perceptions of globalization are sometimes limited to signifying a quantitative increase in international trade – whether measured by value or volume. In 1913, merchandise exports accounted for 9 percent of world GDP; in 1990, they accounted for 13 percent.[9] Local firms are confronted with increasing numbers of foreign competitors in their home markets, and:

> more than 70 percent of all goods produced in the USA have faced direct competition from non-domestic sources. For example, consumer electronics firms based in Taiwan and South Korea sell their products in the US market.   *(Mühlbacher et al., 1999)*

But this phenomenon is not new. One effect of competition has always been to punish a loser and to drive it out of the market. In general, the firm able to produce at the same standard but at lower cost is likely to prevail. The novel factor is that when firms compete on a global basis as opposed to a local or national basis, the loser is as likely to be driven out by a competitor based in some other country as by a neighbor.

In Europe, trade has been conducted across ethnic and national barriers since before the birth of Christ. At one time or another, Phoenicia, Carthage, the Hellenic world, and Rome all stood at the center of trading networks that dominated the economic life of the region. Although each of these systems inevitably declined in importance over time, the drift has been the progressive increase in international trade, measured both in terms of volume and worth.

In Asia the regional dominance of the Chinese has extended for even longer. The Silk Roads between China and the West were garrisoned during the Han Dynasty, over a hundred years before the birth of Christ.

> Another trade route through Burma to Siam and India (long used secretly by Chinese merchants) was officially identified. And the sea route from South China across the Indian Ocean to Arabia and Africa was found to be seeded already with small Overseas Chinese merchants colonies more than two thousand years ago. *(Seagrave, 1995, p. 53)*

In sum, we cannot define the current phenomenon of globalization simply as a quantitative increase of trade, which has been a continuous process over thousands of years. We need a definition that captures the unprecedented changes that are occurring in our political and economic lives.

11.2.3 *Global capital*

Globalization theory commonly refers to the ever-increasing mobility of capital across the globe, and the impact that this has on national economies. However, it involves more than simply a quantitative increase in capital enterprise.

"Capitalism" is defined as the investment of finance in creating new productive capacity, and hence international or global capitalism means the investment of funds earned from one country in a project based elsewhere. This is not the same as global trade; the profits derived from trade only constitute capital when it is reinvested or is available for investment.

Capitalism was internationalized centuries ago. For example, the Rothschild banking family was founded in Frankfurt by Mayer Anselm (1744–1812) and his five sons established branches in Vienna, London, Paris, and Naples. The company continues to be based in Frankfurt but funds move easily between the original branches and many new branches. Also the many complexities have historical roots.

> The whole canopy of forms of capitalism – commercial, industrial, banking – was already deployed in thirteenth century Florence, in seventeenth century Amsterdam, and in London before the eighteenth century. *(Braudel, 1984, p. 621)*

Gowan (1999) points to a recent shift in modern capitalism that can be associated with globalization. He notes the difference between money-dealing capitalism and the employment of capital in the productive sector. In the first case, the capitalist aims to make profits from trading funds regardless of the sector from which these profits arise, and in the second case, the capitalist invests money in the production of goods and services which are sold at a profit and possibly contribute to social life. These two functions also have long histories. But Gowan argues that the phenomenon of globalization is characterized by a massive increase in money-dealing capitalism and a relative decline in productive capitalism.

11.2.4 Global industries

A GLOBAL INDUSTRY is commonly taken to mean an industry which is able to operate across national boundaries with a minimum of disruption. This is made possible both by a lack of government regulation and by common operating procedures and structures. That is, firms in the industry have the same or very similar priorities and do not distinguish between competitors in their own country and competitors elsewhere.

The need for dependability and trust has led the banking industry to adopt procedures that can be recognized and applied everywhere. For many years the Japanese industry stood out against accepting the global structures; however, the increasing fragility of the industry after 1970 forced it to conform to American and European norms. Developments in information technology now mean that capital transactions can be made almost instantaneously to anywhere in the world. An electronic capability also reduces needs for large investments in premises and staff.

A global identity may simplify procedures and reduce misunderstandings, but cannot eliminate all weakness. Strategic and market uncertainty, credit liquidity, and foreign exchange dealings are all factors that cause risk. In addition a report by the Electronic Banking Group of the Basel Committee for Banking Supervision (2001) also noted that some other risks were increased. These included:

- operational risks – including risks associated with the technological infrastructure, security, the integrity of the data, system availability, internal controls and auditing, and outsourcing;
- reputational risk;
- legal risk.

Transportation industries, such as air transport, also tend to be highly globalized. Very similar systems have to be followed in all countries, and the language used with certain procedures may have to be universally applicable. For example, air pilots are required to use English when communicating take-off and landing priorities with air traffic control staff everywhere. Other industries have far less need to apply the same systems: for instance, there may be no need for department stores serving local markets in Tokyo, New York, and Sao Paulo to follow common operating procedures.

11.2.5 Global/multinational companies

In general this book refers to "multinational" companies rather than to GLOBAL companies. This is to avoid confusion; companies with multinational interests relate to their investments and customers in a range of ways, and in the following chapters the term "global company" is used with a specific meaning to refer to one type of multinational relationship.

In general, multinational companies are defined as those that own and manage investments located in countries other than that of headquarters. Ownership structures vary according to a range of factors that include:

- the legal requirements of the country of headquarters;
- the legal requirements of the country of investment;
- the industry norms;
- the organizational culture;
- the organizational strategy.

Management structures may vary widely. Different companies have different needs to control relations between headquarters and foreign investments, and these needs are reflected in how control is centralized and decentralized. The design of formal structures is influenced by the factors listed above, *and also* by:

- the goods or services produced and marketed by the company;
- the relationships with customers and suppliers;
- the activities of technologies;
- sources of new technologies;
- needs to safeguard new technologies;
- needs for local expertise and knowledge;
- local labor pools;
- needs to communicate with headquarters;
- needs to communicate with the local environment;
- the age and health of the investment and its needs for control from headquarters;
- and so on.

These factors are discussed in chapters 14 and 16, where the different relationships between multinational headquarters and subsidiaries are examined in greater detail.

In sum, "multinational" (or global) companies have varying needs in their relations with the various factors in their environments, and serve those needs by creating structures that vary enormously.

11.2.6 Global products

A GLOBAL PRODUCT is developed and sold in response to common demands in different nations. When the marketing manager identifies shared customer aspirations and similar marketing infrastructure (in terms of distribution system, logistics, media and regulations) the company can develop a standardized good or service that appeals to the shared needs. A global product creates a sense of shared interest and identity among its producers and purchasers, whatever their country, and differences between national and foreign markets disappear. For example:

> Coke has successfully purchased the once civic-minded song "We are the World" on the way to "eliminating the very concept of a 'domestic' and 'international' Coca-Cola beverage business. *(Barber, 2001, p. 294)*

In practice, the list of truly global products is short. It includes certain makes of automobile, electronics, cigarettes, drinks such as Coca-Cola and some whiskies, and makes of fast food – for example, Kentucky Fried Chicken. Moreover, few products are global in all respects. In different countries, a product claimed to be the same everywhere may be produced from different materials. For instance, in Muslim countries, hamburgers might be made from lamb or chicken but never from pork, which is forbidden; the same electronic device may be produced from slightly different components, perhaps less in response to local taste than to local licensing regulations.

A product is varied in order to meet different needs in different countries. KAO soap is sold across Asia, but is differentiated by scent. The Japanese do not like soap that has a strong smell, while the Thais prefer strong-smelling soap. Fast food provides other examples.

> The success of Kentucky Fried Chicken in China, and to a lesser extent, other global fast food giants, like McDonald's, is the result of a rapid transformation of Chinese lifestyles, which are becoming more geared to speed, convenience and choice.
> "Our brand is doing very well, not just in terms of traditional food, but also with dishes we have developed totally within China," says Mr Su [the local head of operations]. A range of soups and Chinese-style chicken have been developed for the mainland market, as has the practice of opening for breakfast, something that KFC does not do in the US.[10]

Marketing managers might wish otherwise, but in practice even a global product may be purchased by different market segments, or valued for different reasons. In Chicago, fast food may be consumed by office workers as a rapid lunch at midday, perhaps in the street. In Bangkok, students may sit for hours in the fast food outlet. They value the restaurant as a symbol of youthful modernism, and they meet there in order to participate in it.

11.2.7 Recapitulation

The discussion above argues that the term "globalization" is applied differently in different contexts. However, this does not mean that it is free of any precise meaning; it certainly cannot be used as synonymous with "international" or "multinational." In each context, a precise meaning can be applied although this may not be the same as that applied in other contexts.

The following section tries to pin down the historical development of globalization and to show why it is revolutionary. Globalization has radical importance for the development of international business in the twenty-first century.

11.3   The Roots of Globalization

We have seen that globalization can be defined in many different ways. This book treats it as a set of processes that have historical and cultural roots, because this means we can locate its recent origins precisely in time – in the late 1970s. This aspect of globalization arose from:

- the internationalization of finance;
- the internationalization of production;
- the development of information technologies.

11.3.1   The internationalization of finance

In the early decades of the twentieth century, capitalist production tended to be restricted to the nation in which the headquarters was located. A capitalist might have far more in common with capitalists from his own country – whether or not they belonged to the same industry – than with capitalists from elsewhere. This affinity extended beyond culture; they depended upon and contributed to the same financial systems, which were in many ways still local.

The disasters of the First World War, the slump of the 1930s, and the Second World War eroded the autonomy of national financial systems. After 1945 the least damaged of the major belligerents, the United States, led the development of security and economic systems which would safeguard the world from further destruction. Also, Washington needed trade partners, and the economic recovery of Japan and the major European powers seemed the best way to block the progress of communism. In Europe, the United States invested in the highly successful Marshall Plan. The Bretton Woods system was designed to create financial stability. Exchange rates were fixed within 10 percent. The dollar acted as an international currency, and the value of the dollar was fixed in gold. Each country's government exercised its own exchange controls. The World Bank and IMF were established under American controls to police and stabilize this system.

It seemed that in 1972 the American guarantee of world peace, Pax Americana, was beginning to break down. The United States had overspent in financing the wars in Southeast Asia, and in response to the emergent Eurodollar. Washington stopped honoring its promise to transfer every dollar into gold and the Bretton Woods agreement collapsed. The financial game changed radically. Freed from centralized controls, foreign currencies could be traded for each other across borders like any other commodities. Speculators made the best of their opportunities and wealth was increasingly created from paper money rather than from production.

Financial markets grew at rapid rates.

> The total value of financial assets traded in global markets in 1992 was $35 trillion, twice
> the GDP of the twenty three richest industrial countries. . . . These assets have been grow-
> ing at two and a half times the rate of GDP since 1980, and estimates put their value at
> $83 trillion by the year 2000.   *(Harris, 1998, p. 23)*

In the past, a far greater proportion of wealth was derived through the creation of goods and services that served social needs. But in the era of financial globalization, wealth is increasingly derived from trading financial assets, so that this activity now offers the greater return on capital. A comment by Walter Wriston, former CEO of Citibank, indicated the secondary status of productive investment:

> "In the age of global banking, selling rapid information about money is the key to making
> money".   *(cited in Barnet and Cavanagh, 1995, p. 386)*

In the 1990s, the growing strengths of some European and Asian economies forced the United States into a greater awareness of its needs to protect its own economic superiority. The Washington Consensus developed cooperation between the Treasury and those international organizations that the United States dominated, such as the World Trade Organization and the International Monetary Fund (IMF). The IMF ideology of free-market economics and foreign direct investment was increasingly used to give American companies access to foreign markets without necessarily facilitating foreign investments in the United States. That is, the IMF was most active in pushing for those structural adjustments that best suited American interests.

The internationalization of finance means, first, that business people everywhere should be able to move capital around the world almost instantaneously and without hindrance from national governments. In practice, American influence over the inter-national regulatory authorities gives American companies a leading edge.

Second, the drive towards globalization has been led by banks, other companies in the financial industries, and other service companies. With the exception of the oil producers, most businesses that sell a manufactured product have been outstripped (see Strange, 1994, p. 77).

11.3.2 The internationalization of production

In the first half of the twentieth century, economic leadership passed from Europe to the United States. After 1945, the American economy emerged as the major international creditor, owed vast war debts by the previous leaders, the United Kingdom and France, and far more productive. American production systems became increasingly global:

> designing goods for a world market, producing in several countries at once and directing
> their financial and marketing strategies to the world economy and not just to the national
> economy of the United States.   *(Strange, 1994, p. 73)*

But it was still the case that in any one production centre, all aspects of the production process were centralized under one roof; raw materials were fed into one end of the factory and the completed automobile emerged from the other.

This philosophy dominated manufacturing systems until the 1970s when Toyota and other Japanese manufacturers began to experiment with the internationalization of production. The principle of this new post-Fordian system was that the manufacture of a complex good could be diversified to different locations. Each manufacturing centre depends upon good relationships with local suppliers and good communication with up- and down-stream centres. The different parts of the good are then assembled at a location conveniently close to the sales outlet. This means that different aspects of manufacture and assembly can be located outside the home country – just as Toyota cars targeted at Southeast Asian markets were assembled from engines, gearboxes, chassis, and so on, produced in different countries across the region.

The Japanese automobile and electronics industries were the first to develop this international division of labor. Manufacturing plant in each country specialized in producing those parts for which the local resources of talent, materials, and capital investment best suited it. This globalization of production meant that Japanese companies could produce and sell almost anything anywhere. Their success in pioneering the techniques meant that by the 1980s Japan seemed to be the only economic giant set on a course of continuous expansion. The United States was facing a crisis of archaic manufacturing plant. Having rebuilt its industrial base since the Second World War, European countries apparently enjoyed an advantage, but were hobbled by continuing fuel shortages.

The globalization of production was facilitated by the globalization of finance. The breakdown of localized exchange controls meant that capital could be moved across national borders to purchase new plant and materials, hire a new workforce, or acquire a competitor. Both aspects of globalization did more than make adjustments to the prevailing economic system; they introduced major structural changes. They were made possible by a third factor, the development of information technologies.

11.3.3 The development of information technologies

In the 1970s, readjustments in the US manufacturing sector caused a shift in economic power from the traditional heavy industries to the development of new industries associated with information technologies. In geographical terms, this meant a shift from towns like Detroit and Chicago to Silicon Valley. America's competitive edge in the development of the microchip technology helped rebuild the US economy. Developments in IT enabled the United States to restructure industry and organizations and to take advantage of its leading role in the financial sector. Capital is easily transferred around the world by pressing a few computer keys. The United States was quickly followed in exploiting the technology by its principal competitors, and increasingly, by middle-ranking economies that had previously played little part in international business other than by hosting multinational subsidiaries.

At a time when developed national markets were saturated and the structural limits on real wage increases reached, this technological revolution has allowed capitalists to escape national restrictions. Mittelman (2000, p. 38) comments that:

> with new technologies, especially space-shrinking systems of transport and communications, the sites of manufacturing are increasingly independent of geographical distance. Capital now not only searches for fresh markets, but also seeks to incorporate new groups into the labor force.

IT not only frees production's geographical dependence on headquarters, but also gives the company greater facility in transferring production from one location to another. The implications for local labor forces and cultures are explored below.

11.4 Global–Local Contradictions

Globalization has contributed to growth in many countries, but not in all, and has the effect of creating a new division of labor. African countries are economically furthest removed from the main globalizing powers and have benefited least.

> Africa's share of world trade has declined steadily over time, increasing its isolation from the global economy and its detachment from growing world prosperity. Over the past decade, sub-Saharan Africa's trade has grown 39 percent, while world trade has increased 85 percent. In the same period, African GDP grew less than 8.5 percent, against a global figure of more than 44 percent.[11]

The institutions most likely to lose from globalization include national governments and their agencies. They lose responsibility for and control over local decision-making. The experience for individuals is that the locus of power has been shifted even further from their control. They become powerless. There is no point in an Indonesian bank official complaining to his manager about their marketing strategy if the bank has been bought by an American bank and all strategy is decided in New York. There is no point in a British fisherman complaining to his Member of Parliament about regulations governing the fishing industry, because fishing policy in regard to British waters is no longer decided by the British Parliament but by officials in the European Union.

This section develops three interrelated themes: the effects of globalization on labor markets, the emigration and immigration of labor, and the cultural impact.

11.4.1 Globalization and human resources

When the necessary resources are available in different locations, the company is able to move production from the higher-cost location to the lower-cost. When the technologies and skills are also available, the company is not restrained by the difficulties of moving its workforce. It relocates, and hires a new, local workforce.

The cost of labor is a major factor determining production cost. This means that if the cost of labor in one country is less than in some other, global employers have an incentive to locate their production in the less expensive location. In effect, the jobs are moved from the first country to the second. Those first-country employees who are unable or unwilling to move with their jobs lose them. Even if they do move with the job, they are likely to be paid at a lower rate in the second country.

Suppose that a global company GlobCo is paying its American-based computer analysts £1,000 a week. Then it learns that in India an available pool of computer analysts *offering the same skills* is prepared to perform the same work for only £300 a week. It is now in GlobCo's interests that it moves that part of its production to India and makes savings by hiring the cheaper Indian labor and laying off its American workforce. The output – computer data – can be easily moved around the world using information technology, and the fact that GlobCo subsidiaries based in the United States, France, and Japan all require the data does not inhibit plans to make the move.

Here are real-life examples.

In 2000 the Bank of America needed IT talent so badly it had to outbid rivals. But ... [in 2002–3, the bank] slashed 3,700 of its 25,000 tech and back office jobs. An additional 1,000 will go by March.[12]

These jobs had not left North Carolina because business was failing. Rather, up to 1,000 were outsourced to companies in India where work was costing only $20 an hour, as compared to $100 in the United States. The Indian labor might be relatively cheap, but it was also expert. Indian suppliers recruit staff from the massive numbers of knowledge graduates trained by local technology universities.

Similarly, in 2003 HSBC – the world's second largest bank – moved 4,000 British jobs to India, China, and Malaysia in the biggest single export of finance positions to Asia. The jobs involved mainly processing work and telephone enquiries. At this time the bank employed 55,000 people in the United Kingdom. Meanwhile:

some forecasts say as many as 3.3m jobs in the US and 2m in western financial services will be lost as a result of the trend to move jobs to lower costs countries such as India. In the UK, 200,000 job losses have been predicted by 2008.[13]

It follows that if a new and even cheaper source of labor – again offering the same skills – is found elsewhere, say in Bangladesh, the company transfers that part of its production again. And so the Indian branch would suffer job losses equivalent to those currently affecting the American and British labor markets.

The point is that jobs are transferable under conditions that:

- production processes can be fragmented without loss – say, process A performed in a Country X location, process B in a Country Y location, and so on;
- the production output can be transferred between locations without incurring significant losses;
- the same skills are available in different locations.

And the jobs are transferred to the lowest-cost location when all other factors are equal – skills levels, other resources, and so on.

MNCs have learned from this development. So far as possible they design jobs so that they can be easily transferred. Secondly, labor forces are restructured to be as flexible as possible, disposable, and to incur the least overheads. In the US, the fastest growing type of work is part-time, temporary, and performed at home. (See Harris, 1998.)

11.4.2   The impact of migration

One implication of the collapse of national boundaries is that movement between countries is easier than in the past, and all people enjoy increasing opportunities to live and work where they want. Thus, globalization has the effect of fostering migration, and determining whether skilled or unskilled economic migrants move to wealthier countries that need their labor: "as capital goes global, so does labour" (Harris, 1998, p. 28).

With one exception, the more-developed economies have been ideologically predisposed to accepting not only skilled but also unskilled migrants on very easy terms. In general, migrants have provided them with the cheap labor force needed for continuing economic growth. The exception has been Japan, where only migrants of Japanese origin have been accepted. This, coupled with the decline in the native Japanese birth rate, and the consequent "greying" of the population, has meant a decline in the productive labor force at a time when the country is facing serious economic difficulties. It has, however, meant that Japan has been able to retain a local cultural identity to a greater extent than have its Western competitors.

In theory the movement of working populations reduces economic and cultural differences between countries. But problems arise in practice.

11.4.3   The effects of mass emigration

Large-scale migration causes problems in both the country from which the migrants come and the target countries to which they move. In their original home countries, the traditional social structures are undermined by the mass emigration of the working population when only the very old, very young, and those unable to emigrate are left to depend on earnings remitted by their relatives working abroad. The loss of working people in their prime endangers social and cultural structures. In the target countries, mass immigration inflames resentments and insecurities among those locals who feel their economic and cultural identities are at risk.

Most people prefer to emigrate to where the standard of living is highest, and the economic opportunities greatest. Location matters, and opportunities for "life, liberty, and the pursuit of happiness" depend more on where one lives than on anything else.[14] Those who have the education, skills, and connections are freest to exploit the opportunities and to pursue happiness.

The relatively free, honest, and prosperous societies attract more immigrants than do, say, Liberia and Sierra Leone, and those who make the move to these rich countries tend to be more energetic, better educated, and more skilled. Once there, they enjoy greater opportunities for further economic and professional advancement than are available in Liberia or Sierra Leone. The countries that they have left lose twice – once because their competitors have gained additional talent; twice, because they have lost whatever skills they had.

In practice then, this aspect of globalization does not spread economic opportunities equally across the world. They tend to be focused in societies that are already prosperous. The better qualified people of working age move to these nations and their productivity results in these nations growing ever more prosperous and developed. Their intellectual and artistic cultures are enriched by the influx of new ideas and values. Hence they attract yet more skilled migrants. And so the gap between more- and less-developed countries widens rather than narrows.

Perhaps the majority of emigrants are most attracted by the opportunities presented by the United States, and would settle there if selected. This gives the United States the advantage in recruiting those most likely to be productive at all levels of the economy and so to reinforce its control of global economic, political, and cultural systems.

11.4.4 The effects of mass immigration

Migrants are often not fully integrated in the welfare system and other supports designed to benefit the local population. The original immigrants may be prepared to accept the hardships they encounter, but their children, born in the receiving country, are less so. These include many who:

> ... are citizens of that country and who are less compliant than are their parents. Many of these people are marginalized in the educational system and in access to employment. Thus, Britain's young blacks and France's young Arabs feel they are treated like outsiders, even if they are nationals of the countries in which they reside.
>
> *(Mittelman, 2000, p. 71)*

In the case of Western Europe, Muslims account for one-third of all immigrants.

In the past few years most west European countries have seen the rapid growth of political parties exploiting anti-immigration sentiment. For a range of reasons these parties tend to be short-lived, but their disappearance may not mean that the underlying tensions have been resolved. In practice, attitudes take time to change, and only when both the immigrant and local populations have learned to trust each other. Laws designed to criminalize anti-immigrant resentments do not guarantee a multicultural population at peace with itself.

However, worries about the long-term effects of encouraging mass immigration are no longer restricted to political extremists. In the United Kingdom, a senior journalist with the establishment newspaper the *Times* explained (in the weekly journal *Spectator*) why traditional government policy is increasingly challenged by mainstream opinion. He listed nine ill effects:

1 Mass immigration exacerbates the housing crisis.
2 Britain is already overcrowded and does not have the infrastructure to support a further population expansion.
3 Mass immigration (as opposed to limited immigration of skilled workers) damages the employment prospects of those already here, in particular the unskilled.
4 Imposing mass immigration on a society that doesn't want it damages relations between the communities that are already here.
5 Mass immigration increases income inequalities.
6 Mass immigration is no solution to an ageing society because immigrants grow old at the same rate as non-immigrants.
7 Mass immigration of unskilled workers promotes low-skilled, low-wage industries and reduces productivity.
8 Temporary migration tends to become permanent and is largely uncontrolled.
9 White flight is ghettoizing Britain's cities and fragmenting communities.

These complaints about the effects of mass immigration add up to an argument against globalization.

11.4.5 The cultural stimulus to globalization

We have seen that globalization has been chiefly propelled by financial and technological developments made by Americans, and so reflects American political and economic priorities. At a deeper level it reflects such values as:

- a relatively high tolerance of competition and a readiness for conflict;
- a drive to make change;
- high individualism;
- a conviction that one has the right to impose one's perception of right and wrong on other cultures.

These are values particularly associated with Anglo cultures, and so the phenomenon of globalization expresses American values on both the material and cultural levels.
  This coherence in American responses to their environment helps explain why American-led globalization is so powerful an ideology. It also helps explain why the United States is the only superpower and has no obvious rival in the short term. Even Japan, which has contributed significantly to internationalizing production processes, lacks the cultural and ideological drives to impose its values across the world. Contemporary Japanese culture does not foster a spirit of empire-building on the scale practiced by the United States.

11.4.6 The globalizers: a culture group?

Globalization reflects an ideology of modernity and the assumption that a single, universal community can be established, founded on principles of reason that are accepted by

everyone. The assault on traditional value systems is spear-pointed by global organizations and, on a human level, by those who decide strategy in these organizations.

These persons responsible for taking globalizing decisions include the following:

- The owners of prominent global companies in the private sector; the large capitalists
  and shareholders. These companies include banks and IT companies.
- Senior managers of these global companies; senior managers of international
  not-for-profit organizations. These include organizations with an extra-national
  identity, such as the United Nations and the World Bank, national organizations,
  such as embassies, and international non-governmental organizations, such as Oxfam
  and Care.

How far can we say that they constitute an international "class"? This depends on your
concept of the notion "class," but they certainly have powerful common interests. They
spring from their own national bourgeoisies, but are increasingly alienated from them,
and appear to have more in common with each other than with members of their
national groups. They share broad economic and political interests and have interlocking
directorships. They communicate by using a shared global language (English). They have
shared global tastes in food, clothing, cultural pursuits, and sports. (Golf appears to be
most general.) Many have studied at the same elite universities and business schools.

Can we say that they constitute a culture group? At a superficial level, probably
they do, although in terms of Hofstede's criteria for a national culture, not. (This may,
of course, mean that Hofstede's criteria need to be revised.) Of greater practical concern
is that the number of persons capable of acting as "pure" global managers, equally
competent and disinterested in all cultures, is possibly quite small, and then only for
a short period in their careers.

11.4.7 Globalized control

The globalizers (whether or not considered a "class") do not exercise direct rule on
national governments, but through exercising influence on national governments they
have an indirect effect. They use their organizations to persuade national governments
to conform to the dictates of globalization. They exert influence through control of their
companies and other organizations, by formulating and implementing strategies for
globalization. These strategies are always likely to be antagonistic to local and particular interests, at least in the long term. In this respect, members of the globalizing class
are opposed to the democratic theory that major decisions are made by politicians
responding to the will of the national majority, and expressed through democratic
processes.

Key decision-makers have increasingly less need to reflect and respond to national
interests, and the interests of local populations. The overall effect of this drive towards
a globalized rationalism, outside the control of local politicians, is to strip away a sense
of value in local political action. Local politicians who fail to support local interests lose

local trust. Those who fail to meet the needs of the globalized class risk attack from that quarter and may be unable to hold onto power. In either case, the capacity of the politician to adequately represent his or her constituency is endangered, and so democratic institutions in general are endangered.

International organizations in the non-profit sector frequently justify imposing common practices across countries by claiming, firstly, that these will bring efficiencies of scale. In practice, these expectations are not always met. The interests of a wide range of constituents need to be satisfied before binding decisions can be made, and this means that decisions may be made much slower than by national governments who have to respond to fewer pressure groups. The European Union gives an example: Frits Bolkestein, the European Commissioner in charge of the single market:

> has warned repeatedly that the EU's failure to adopt laws quickly in the fast-moving global economy is crippling efforts to compete in frontier technologies. New laws often take so long to wend their way through the EU's labyrinthine system that they are out of date before reaching the Statute Book.[15]

In the case of the EU, the effects of structural inefficiencies are compounded by financial inefficiencies and corruption.

Second, these organizations may justify their practices by claiming that these are "inevitable." But as globalization grows in scope, public acceptance of this "inevitability" may be decreasing. For example, in 1998, 80 percent of those polled in the UK on the likelihood of the country being forced into the EU Euro system considered it "inevitable" sooner or later. By 1999, this figure had fallen to 69 percent; and by 2003, to 54 percent.[16]

In this case of the EU project, the declining enthusiasm for it across Europe, and in general a growing distrust of expert pronouncements, may reflect post-modern pessimism about plans to control the future or an increasing resistance to interference in local affairs. This threat to local identity is experienced even more acutely elsewhere in the world, and may be resisted with violence – for example, in Arab countries concerned with American influence in Palestine and the region.

11.4.8   The impact of cultural engineering

Grey (1990, p. 1) explained the underlying beliefs thus:

> [Western capitalism] will soon be accepted throughout the world. A global free market will become a reality. The manifold economic cultures and systems that the world has always contained will be redundant. They will be merged into a single free market.

This enterprise seems designed to mold values, attitudes, and behaviors. But is it practical? Chapter 4 examined the problems that management faces when trying to impose its values on a single organization culture. And Elsom (forthcoming) points out why cultural engineering conducted on a global scale is most unlikely to meet its supposed objectives. Rather than leading to a fairer world order, it increases ever greater disparities between those countries that can contribute and those that cannot.

> Eighty-two countries are currently facing famine, half of them in Africa. They cannot grow enough food for their populations nor afford to import it. What has made matters worse is that their traditional social structures, such as tribal and family loyalties, have been undermined by the poor imitations of Western management models imported with the investment and development aid.   *(Ms., p. 55)*

The impact of the collapse of national and regional boundaries has been to force economically less-developed countries to share market space with wealthy countries with whom they cannot hope to compete. An analogy is provided by a country that has a football league consisting of 24 clubs distributed in three divisions. Every year clubs A, B, C, etc., regularly dominate the first division; poorer clubs P, Q, R, etc., compete for the third division trophy. Then, one year, the football authorities decide that the divisional structure need no longer apply and all 24 clubs will play each other in one league. The result is that clubs A, B, C continue to dominate but now in the expanded league. But clubs P, Q, R no longer have any realistic expectations of emerging with a trophy.

They are doomed to be forever labeled "losers." It is no surprise if morale plummets.

The effects are not only political and economic. The state is unable to restrict the inflow of cultural artefacts imported from outside. In the case of a developed and prosperous country, this may not be important; the local culture is sufficiently vigorous to compete. But in the case of a developing country the effect can be disastrous. For example, a television station in a poor country lacks the resources to create its own programs that compete with Western news and entertainment, and so are forced into dependence on these cheaper imports. Hollywood serials may be enjoyable in the short term, but they do not reflect local political, economic, and cultural realities outside the United States (possibly outside Hollywood), and so have the long-term effect of weakening the integrity of the local culture.

The frustration felt by members of that culture may be expressed in opposition to perceived interference by the globalizing power. Hence the terrorist policies followed by al-Qa'eda and other extremist groups do not simply express fundamentalist Islam. They can be read as a measure of the powerlessness felt in the developing world by those unable to compete with the cultural stereotypes projected by the West, and this powerlessness is expressed through that aspect of the local culture that stands apart from the all-encompassing values of globalization – in this case, militant Islam. Stern (2003) discusses a number of Islamic, neo-Nazi, and White supremacist groups and argues that they:

> view the September 11 attacks as the first shot in a war against globalization, a phenomenon that they fear will exterminate national cultures.   *(p. 38)*

We can expect terrorist and revolutionary ideologies to be increasingly attractive wherever large populations feel that they have been displaced from their accustomed economic, political, and cultural systems, and have been thrust into an apparently valueless globalized world. They provide meaning to the disoriented and culturally deprived.

11.5   Implications for the Manager

How does globalization affect your organization?

Decide which of these statements apply to your organization (company, business school, or other). If necessary, check your answers with people who have worked there for longer.

(a) Ten years ago it was possible to predict major changes in product/service markets a year ahead. This is no longer the case.
APPLIES/DOES NOT APPLY.

(b) Ten years ago it was possible to identify our main competitors (competing companies/business schools/others) in the year ahead. This is no longer the case.
APPLIES/DOES NOT APPLY.

(c) Ten years ago, it was possible to keep my understanding of new technology up-to-date. Now, technologies are changing so quickly that this is no longer the case.
APPLIES/DOES NOT APPLY.

(d) Ten years ago it was possible to predict major changes in labor markets a year ahead. This is no longer the case.
APPLIES/DOES NOT APPLY.

(e) Ten years ago, how long did you expect the majority of newly appointed staff to stay with your organization:
  • more than 20 years?
  • 16–20 years?
  • 11–15 years?
  • 6–10 years?
  • 1–5 years?
  • less than 1 year?
Now, how long do you expect the majority of newly appointed staff to stay with your organization:
  • more than 20 years?
  • 16–20 years?
  • 11–15 years?
  • 6–10 years?
  • 1–5 years?
  • less than 1 year?

Where there have been changes between the experiences of your organization 10 years ago and now, explain why.

11.6 SUMMARY

This chapter has examined the phenomenon of globalization. This topic is important, and influences how far companies can plan their futures in rapidly changing business environments. It is developed throughout the remaining chapters.

Section 11.2 dealt with the problems of formulating a single precise DEFINITION OF GLOBALIZATION. The term is used differently in different contexts. But whatever emphasis is given in a particular context, it should *not* be interpreted as simply the expansion of trade and capitalism between different countries. This expansion has a long history, and is nothing new. The important point is that globalization is a new process that has developed only since the late 1970s and is eroding the influence of national institutions and borders, and is transforming international relations between countries and regions.

Section 11.3 dealt with the ROOT factors that have been responsible for the development of GLOBALIZATION. It focused on:

- the internationalization of finance;
- the internationalization of.production;
- the development of information technologies that have enabled the two internationalizations.

Section 11.4 dealt with the dynamic relationship between GLOBAL and LOCAL structures. One effect of globalization is that companies are increasingly able to move production between labor markets, transferring jobs to wherever the necessary skills are cheapest. A second effect is that lower skilled workers can migrate between countries looking for work with relative ease. Third, the cultural stimulus for and effects of globalization were considered.

11.7 EXERCISE

This exercise gives practice in researching a global product.

Select a global product that you use in your country – for example, a beverage, a fast food item, an item of leisure wear.

1 Find answers to these questions.
  A: Background research.
     (a) What company produces this product?
     (b) Where is the company headquartered?
  (c) In what countries other than your own is the product sold?
  B: Production.
     (d) In *your* country, what materials are used to make this product?
     (e) From where do these materials come?
     (f) In the *other* countries, what materials are used to make this product?

    (g) From where do these materials come?

C: Marketing.

    (h) In *your* country, which market segments are most likely to use this product? (For example, which age group, professional group, salary group?)

    (i) Why do they use the product?

    (j) How frequently do they use the product?

    (k) In the *other* countries, which market segments are most likely to use the product?

    (l) Why do they use the product?

    (m) How frequently do they use the product?

D: Sales.

    (n) In *your* country, what advertising media are used to sell the product?

    (o) Where do the purchasers purchase the product?

    (p) For whose use do they purchase the product?

    (q) How frequently do they purchase the product?

    (r) In the *other* countries, what advertising media are used to sell the product?

    (s) Where do the purchasers purchase the product?

    (t) For whose use do they purchase the product?

    (u) How frequently do they purchase the product?

2 Analysis.

    (a) Compare your answers to:
- Production: d, e; and f, g.
- Marketing: h, i, j; and k, l, m.
- Sales: n, o, p, q; and r, s, t, u.

    (b) In what respect is your product *most* globalized?
- Production, Marketing, Sales.

    (c) In what respect is your product *least* globalized?
- Production, Marketing, Sales.

Notes

1 Rohan Gunaratna, "Womaniser, joker, scuba diver: the other face of al-Queda's No 3," *The Guardian*, March 3, 2003.

2 Neil Collins, "World pays the terrible price of globalization," *The Daily Telegraph*, September 12, 2001.

3 Raymond Whitaker, "There may not be a victory. For al-Qaeda, murder is an end in itself," *The Independent on Sunday*, November 13, 2003.

4 Rohan Gunaratna, "Womaniser, joker, scuba diver: the other face of al-Queda's No 3," *The Guardian*, March 3, 2003.

5 Stern quotes Louis Beam of Aryan Nations.

6 Waili Yang, "Taiwan's warning," Letters to the Editor, *The Daily Telegraph*, March 20, 2003.

7 G. Bush, 1990. President Bush's Address to Congress on the Persian Gulf Situation, *Washington File*, Washington DC, Department of State. This part cited in Ashcar, 2002, p. 9.

8 Graham Turner, "An American Odyssey" (part one), *The Daily Telegraph*, June 16, 2003.

9 Niall Ferguson, "The anarchists are wrong, but they ask the right questions," *The Daily Telegraph*, May 2, 2001.

10 Richard McGregor, "KFC adds fast food to fast life in China," *Financial Times*, January 20, 2003.

11 Tom Nevin, "2003 gains offset 2002 pains," *African Business*, July 2003, pp. 37–8.

12 Pete Engardio, Aaron Bernstein, and Manjeet Kripalani, "The new global job shift," *Business Week*, February 3, 2003.

13 Jane Croft, "HSBC to cut 4,000 jobs in switch to Asia," *Financial Times*, October 17, 2003.

14 "Location, location, location equals the wealth of nations," *Financial Times*, September 25, 2002. See also Sala-I-Martin, 2002.

15 Evans-Pritchard, A. and Sparrow, A. "Britain leads Europe – in red tape stakes," *The Daily Telegraph*, November 20, 2001.

16 Figures researched by Resistance (New Alliance, www.newalliance.org.uk), June 2003.

CHAPTER TWELVE
Family Companies

CHAPTER OUTLINE

Introduction

The Anglo Model: Environment, Culture, and Management

The Chinese Model: Environment and Culture

The Chinese Model: Management

Changes in the Chinese Model

Implications for the Manager

Summary

Exercise

Notes

12.1   Introduction

In 2000 the international communications mogul and CEO of News Corp. Rupert Murdoch appointed his son James to head his television company Star in Hong Kong. Before taking the job, James had almost no experience of TV or Asia.

> But Rupert Murdoch wasn't looking for an expert: he wanted a trusted emissary who would look after his interests with the unswerving dedication of, well, family. In Asia, where family connections carry tremendous weight, someone with the Murdoch pedigree makes an ideal ambassador. Besides, Rupert already had somebody who knew about TV and Asia: himself.[1]

This story shows an Anglo family company behaving like a family company in the Chinese business world – which is where James Murdoch is operating. The owner and original entrepreneur prefers to appoint his son, who can be expected to show loyalty, rather than find an outsider who may be far more qualified.

In 2003, James emerged as heir apparent. A newspaper commented on succession issues in the family. Rupert Murdoch had:

... made it pretty clear that his empire is a family company. One day, one of his offspring will take over, as the third generation of the dynasty, and he has organised things so he controls enough votes to enforce his will.

He has plenty of offspring to choose from, and may not have finished yet. Of the six, James currently looks the most promising...

James is said to have many of his father's talents, including ruthlessness, and he has made a fair fist of running Star TV in Asia, but his older brother Lachlan can hardly be pleased at the latest turn of events. Rupert's third wife Wendy has two children (and counting).... As students of the dynamics of dynasties will tell you, succession is the point at which a family's grip on power is most vulnerable.[2]

A few days later the same newspaper commented:

In China, they call it *guanxi*. Loosely translated, it means "connections", or the network of personal ties that grease the wheels of business. Here in Britain, we'd probably call it nepotism.

Either way, it helps explain how a 30-year-old college drop-out with only a few years' broadcasting experience in Asia seems set to become the youngest-ever head of a FTSE 100 company.

For James Murdoch has the kind of *guanxi* that most aspiring chief executives can only dream about.[3]

This degree of family control might now be unusual in an Anglo culture. But it is common in Hong Kong, which:

... has one of the largest concentration of family firms, with 290,000 operations owned and run on family lines. Family firms account for 98 percent of SAR [special administrative region] companies.[4]

A family company is defined as a company started by an individual, and ownership and financial control is held by members of the family. When the owner leaves the company, ownership may be passed on to other members of the family. Family members may also work for the company.

Small business can be found wherever they are permitted by law. Klingel (2002) cites figures that family companies comprise 67.2 percent of all in Malaysia, 66 percent in Hong Kong, and 66.9 percent in Germany. But despite the popularity of this form of enterprise, small and medium sized companies face serious difficulties surviving and prospering in modern economies dominated by large global corporations. A strategy that many pursue is to internationalize their interests and operations. This strategy forces the company to make decisions about how far to internationalize its style and culture, and how far it benefits from developing its local characteristics.

Bjerke (2000) argues that our understanding of family companies is largely based on Western scholarship, and in particular on US thinking. In fact, much of this American literature is prescriptive, proposing how family companies might be established and managed with optimal efficiency. There is a considerable literature on Chinese family companies, but this is largely descriptive and analytical.

It is sometimes assumed that the American model is appropriate elsewhere as a guide to efficient practice (see Carney 1998). But this may not necessarily be the case. For example, Anglo experts perceive danger in familial relationships when members work together in management. Bork's (1986) text, *Family Business, Risky Business*, argues that family and company roles should be separated so that the danger of owner-managers personalizing their professional relationships with other family members is reduced. But, as we see below, in other cultures this overlap may be precisely the reason why family members, who can be expected to show greater loyalty to the shared enterprise, are preferred to outsiders.

The chapter deals with the issue of how far family companies from different cultures can be modeled the same, and how far they should be differentiated. It focuses on two types: those typical of the Anglo cultures, in particular of the United States, and traditional companies in Southeast Asia, where Chinese values predominate. These illustrate the two extremes. In one, the company is protected against the perceived dangers of family commitments and emotions by bureaucratic rules and regulations. In the other, these commitments and emotions are employed as a means of building loyalty to the joint exercise.

Neither guarantees survival. In the United States and Singapore, failure rates are similar, and in both places less than 20 percent of family companies survive three generations. This chapter does not argue that either is superior. Just as systems that prove productive in Southeast Asia may not necessarily be appropriate in the United States, systems that work in the United States may not always be suited to Southeast Asia. The chapter also examines how traditional Chinese companies are adapting to the business environment since 1997.

12.2   The Anglo Model: Environment, Culture, and Management

The ownership of Anglo companies may be majority held by the family but ownership is less concentrated than elsewhere – say in Southeast Asia and Germany (Klingel, 2002).

12.2.1   The Anglo model within its environment

Relations with the environment tend to be calculating and unemotional, being determined by impersonal and economic criteria rather than by family and clan emotions.

Institutions in the business environment, such as the legal system, the banking and financial systems, and government agencies, are given greater trust than in other cultures. The family company joins trade associations with similar firms, attends conferences, and shares information on market opportunities and threats.

12.2.2   Cultural influences on the Anglo model

The attitudes held by Anglo firms towards the employment of family members and outsiders, succession issues, and the environment, and sources of finance, can be in part explained by cultural factors.

Hofstede (1997) finds that where needs to avoid uncertainty are weak, "citizens are positive towards institutions" (p. 134) – which include government and bureaucracies, such as banks. This is expressed in a willingness to seek loans and investments from outsiders who require financial information relating to the firm's core interests. Conflicts and competition – for example between board members and different levels of the hierarchy – are expected, and are tolerated for so long as they are perceived to be productive.

In individualist and low-power contexts, the entrepreneur derives much authority from his/her function or expert power rather than from family status. Of course, family status still counts for more than it could in a public non-family Anglo enterprise, but far less than in a Chinese family company. The entrepreneur cannot expect that his/her position in the family and company offers protection against criticism and challenges from other members of the family.

In an individualist culture "laws and rights are supposed to be the same for all" (p. 73). This means, firstly, that group interests, including family interests, are unlikely to be given automatic priority; and secondly that family connections may be less efficient than institutions in securing economic resources. Individuals are assessed on the basis of their skills and experience. Family membership does not automatically qualify the individual for employment, and competent outsiders are readily recruited.

Where collectivism is relatively low, notions of family loyalty are weak. Compared to members of a Chinese family company, family members may not feel driven to hang together in response to outside threats. Because family membership does not guarantee a shared body of experience and opinion, communications may be no faster or more reliable than in a public company managed by unrelated outsiders. Communications are bureaucratized and perhaps expressed by text and e-mails that have legal status, rather than by word of mouth.

12.2.3   Employing family members in the Anglo model

Anglo family companies are very conscious of the threat posed by conflict between relatives. A London Business School report warned in 2003 that in the United Kingdom:

> ... family tensions will remain the key threat to these enterprises and anyone ignoring the issue could end up out of business.
> "The trouble is that you can't put the family behind you unless you cease to be a family firm ..." [the author commented].[5]

The standard advice made by Anglo consultants to family companies is that you avoid this threat by *not* employing family members if possible, and, if you have to, employ *only* when this person has the appropriate work experience and qualifications needed for the position. If hired, the family member should:

- be paid a fair market salary;
- be promoted, rewarded, and if necessary terminated, on the basis of job performance;
- *not* participate in the hiring of other family members;
- *not* directly supervise other family members.

In sum, impersonal job-related factors determine employment policies. The fact that Joe is your son-in-law or even your son is no reason to hire him unless he is qualified. Rather, your relationship is a reason for *not* hiring him.

This case from the United Kingdom shows bureaucratic values applied within the family company. A married couple built up a business and on his death she passed it on to their two sons. She continued working until her sons sacked her. She appealed to an industrial tribunal that her sons had dismissed her unfairly, and accused them of trying to alter the terms and conditions of her job as wages clerk to:

> ... stop her speaking at creditors' meetings. [Her eldest son answered that]: "Mrs Medley was the only one to refuse to sign an employment contract. She was usually a stubborn person who abused the mother–son relationship."
>
> He agreed that she was not sent a formal redundancy letter but said: "We don't believe she was made redundant. She walked out because of family bickering.
>
> "There have been many family rows. When she realised the money she invested in the company would not have to be repaid by her two sons she became upset."[6]

Mrs. Medley won compensation – but for the bureaucratic reason that she had been dismissed unfairly, and not in respect of the family relationship. This reflects a business culture in which impersonal and rational criteria decide employment conditions.

12.2.4 *Employing outsiders in the Anglo model*

The alternative to employing family members is employing outsiders with particular skills. Anglo business history provides many examples where this has saved the firm. Many of today's old family companies:

> ... have been given a new lease of life at some point in their history by injecting fresh talent from outside: at the turn of the century Samuel Courtauld transformed his family mourning-crêpe business into a synthetics empire after bringing in two outsiders who developed viscose rayon.[7]

Experts are recruited to fill particular functions, and are hired on the basis of their professional qualifications and experience.

Anglo management scholars recommend that the board of directors includes professionals recruited from outside the family. Outside directors may be defined as directors who are *not*:

- members or close associates of the controlling family;
- present or retired employees of the company.

The function of these outsiders is to give impartial advice which is not influenced by personal relationships, and to bring in new expertise. Gersick et al. (1997) argue that perhaps only two or three family members are needed on a good working board. In practice, no precise number can be specified, and factors such as the business environment, history of the company, competences available and in demand, influence board recruitment.

12.2.5 Succession issues in the Anglo model

In the United States, only about 10 percent of family companies plan succession more than a few months in advance of the owner's departure. If the owner married more than once and succession is in doubt, these questions arise:

- Who succeeds as controlling owner?
- What is the status of minority family owners?
- What rights and obligations does the new controlling owner have to his/her predecessor's management policies?
- What rights does the previous controlling owner, for as long as alive, have to interfere in day-to-day operations?

Commonly, legal advice is taken and a court may be asked to rule on these questions. However, resolution by legal means is expensive and may only deepen the conflict. A company that adopts bureaucratic management principles and that gives board positions to non-family members has gone some way to ensuring that these disputes do not arise.

12.2.6 Financing the Anglo model

Family businesses in the Anglo world typically raise "start-up" seed capital from a range of sources. These include personal and family savings. In addition the entrepreneur might try to secure venture capital, a bank loan or government loan.

12.2.7 Principles and practice

Sections 12.2.1 and 12.2.2 described the business and cultural environments within which the Anglo family company operates. Sections 12.2.3–12.2.6 have dealt with the management principles appropriate for separating family and business responsibilities, and these preferences can be explained in part by cultural analysis. However, practice in Anglo family companies does not always fit these principles, as the introductory case of the Murdoch family makes clear. And despite the experts' many warnings against employing family members, research conducted in the United Kingdom found that, in

2003, 39 percent of their survey companies consisted solely of family members, and a further 38 percent had no more than two non-family members.[8] Here are further examples that show a discrepancy between principle and practice.

The United Kingdom glass manufacturers, Pilkington, set down criteria for family employment. A family member must show that he/she is better qualified than an outsider; but when they are equally qualified, the family member is preferred. In the Bahamas-based conglomerate, Jardine Matheson, the Keswick family retains control through minority ownership. The majority non-family holdings are widely dissipated.

In the United Kingdom, prejudice against employing outsiders is thought to be one of the main causes of failure, and why only 24 percent of family businesses reach a second generation and a mere 14 percent survive to the third:

> sons take over even though outside expertise may be needed; and then they stay for too long.[9]

But there must be other reasons to explain failure in family companies. Similar failure rates are racked up in Southeast Asia, where the mass employment of family members has, at least until recently, been the general rule.

12.3   The Chinese Model: Environment and Culture

In history, many societies have contributed towards the Southeast Asian reputation for family entrepreneurialism. There have been the Arabs, Sikhs, and Gujaratis; the Sumatrans from Padang and the Buginese from Sulawesi; the Malays of Penang; Filipinos operating in the United States and Australia; and colonialists, such as the British and the Japanese.

Are there significant features that distinguish the Chinese family company from family companies typical of these other entrepreneurial groups, and from family companies in the Anglo world and elsewhere? Lim (1996) found only minor differences between overseas Chinese and indigenous businesses in Southeast Asia, and the

> ... considerable similarities are based on adaptation to similar environmental conditions, particularly the abundant opportunities for entrepreneurship, the utility of networks and relationships, and the natural evolution of family-based enterprise ...   *(p. 67)*

Nevertheless, the Chinese have set the model. This is despite their being a small minority throughout the South East Asian region (about 6 percent) and less than 50 percent in all of those countries except Singapore, where they make up about 75 percent.

Companies in the region have benefited from a range of factors, including:

- investment by Western and Japanese multinationals – and competition with them;
- transference of hard and soft technologies from investors;
- tariff and tax reductions, and economic liberalization;
- political liberalization and democratization;

- well-educated workforces and improving educational systems;
- flexible labor markets and weak labor unions;
- strong female participation in the labor market;
- developing infrastructures.

Not all of these factors are present in all countries in the region. But they are widespread, and often give local companies competitive advantages over their competitors abroad.

12.3.1 The immigrant status of Chinese business in Southeast Asia

The Chinese communities in Southeast Asia share characteristics which are common to immigrant groups. They have a history of struggling to make themselves secure economically and to retain their cultural identities in non-Chinese environments. They often show a distrust of government – which at times has been justified – and of those outside the family and community.

Although they share these attitudes, they do not constitute a monolithic group. Chinese communities settled across the region at different times and have different histories in their relations with the indigenous peoples. Local governments follow different policies in regard to the Chinese and their business. In Thailand, ethnic Chinese make up between 8 and 10 percent of the population; intermarriage with Thais has been extensive. In Malaysia they make up about 35 percent and intermarriage between Malays (who are Muslim) and Chinese (non-Muslim) is rare. Government policies discriminate in favor of Malays in education, employment, and investment, although Chinese businesses make up the majority. In Singapore they make up 80 percent and in the Philippines 2 percent.

In Indonesia the ethnic Chinese constitute 4 percent of the population, but control approximately 73 percent of listed firms by market capitalization. In times of crisis in the past, they have provided a convenient scapegoat for the problems experienced by the Muslim majority and have frequently been accused of a lack of commitment to national goals. In 1995, President Soeharto's brother-in-law criticized those big Chinese businessmen who controlled:

> ... an estimated 85 percent of the country's economic activities ... [but] have no interest in developing the country's cooperatives as stipulated in the constitution. "They are not willing to spend a small part of the wealth they have made in the country to help the business activities of indigenous people, like those in Malaysia," he said.[10]

Not surprisingly, Chinese business communities in some of these countries harbor suspicions of impersonal official agencies – in particular those reporting to taxation authorities. Family businesses tend not to join government-sponsored trade associations, and instead rely on personal patronage and guanxi relationships within the bureaucracy. These attitudes reinforce an even longer history of distrust. Until recently mainland China has lacked a recent history of impartial government and a strong legal system. (But it should be noted that trade associations are successful elsewhere in Asia – in Japan and Korea for example.)

These factors help explain why, to varying degrees, the Southeast Asian Chinese have found it difficult to trust the local authorities and have looked to their families and clans for support and protection. This has implications for:

- the selection of industries in which Chinese family companies typically invest;
- how Chinese family companies structure their companies;
- who they employ;
- how they raise finance.

12.3.2 Building an international identity

The successful Chinese family company or group of companies may be spread over a range of countries and continents. (In this respect it differs from Italian or Indian companies, which – with some important exceptions – tend to be restricted to their region and country.) Wherever there are family members to participate in managing subsidiaries and related companies, the company looks for opportunities to establish itself.

A Chinese family company builds an international identity by developing its cross-border family and clan connections. First, this offers financial advantages. The wider the network, the easier it is to move capital to the points of greatest safety and of highest profit. Second, this arrangement offers production and marketing advantages. Suppose that an entrepreneur employs his eldest son in the family shop in Hong Kong. He trades gems with his uncle and cousins in Los Angeles and Singapore and buys property from a clan member in Thailand. He sends his younger sons to study in the United Kingdom, Canada, and Australia, where they seek residence. A daughter works for a cousin in Amsterdam. Eventually, these children return to work for the flagship company or to establish their own companies.

However, an international identity does not guarantee success. In the Anglo cultures local businesspeople do not recognize the meaning of guanxi, and the Chinese company cannot depend on its traditional tactics of relying on networks to arrange financing and reduce transaction costs. Fewer market niches can be accessed through connections because information is distributed more evenly than in Southeast Asia. A company faces difficulties if it tries to set up abroad by immediately creating a production subsidiary rather than going through the preliminary stages that a strategically driven Western firm might choose (Van den Bulcke and Zhang, 1995):

- exporting directly;
- then, securing a local agent;
- then, setting up a sales subsidiary;
- only then, going into production.

Those Chinese companies that *do* succeed abroad develop business skills and relationships appropriate to the non-Chinese environments in which they hope to operate.

Pananond (2001) sees how four multinational Thai companies have used selective networking to off-set their lack of financial and technological assets. Yeung (2000) shows that Chinese companies headquartered in Hong Kong often give their foreign affiliates considerable autonomy in running their own affairs, and exercise control and coordination through informal networks. That is, control is less centralized than in non-international Hong Kong companies.

12.3.3 Chinese business interests reflect characteristics of the Chinese model

One analysis of the top 500 ethnic Chinese-controlled public companies in Asia showed the greatest number in land and property development (in total 119). Other popular industries were (in descending order) banking, hotels, engineering and construction, textiles and fibres, finance, computers and semi-conductors, and food (East Asia Analytical Unit, 1995, p. 149). Chinese families are not usually involved in long-term heavy industrial projects.

In many of these industries, the entrepreneur needs to respond rapidly to changes in government policy and market position, and develop well-placed connections in these areas. Relationships are formed with both Chinese and non-Chinese government and business leaders who can offer business deals, protection, and privileged information. Strong informal links are made with suppliers, subcontractors, and customers.

Management must exercise skills in correctly estimating price, place, and time, and in responding rapidly to competitive opportunities and threats. It is accessible on a short-term basis and entry and exit may be rapid. Participation does not depend on investing in a large permanent workforce or costly technologies – as is the case with heavy industrial projects.

In sum, traditional Chinese family companies can be highly efficient in moving into niche markets and in acquiring labor through guanxi relationships. They are less efficient in accessing new resources of capital and in securing labor using bureaucratic structures.

12.3.4 Cultural influences on the Chinese model

The policies traditionally followed in Chinese family firms in respect of employment of family members and outsiders, succession issues, raising finances, and interacting with the environment are partly explained by factors in the cultures.

Hofstede's model (1997) shows most of these cultures located in or near the PERSON-NEL BUREAUCRACY quadrant; needs to avoid uncertainty, collectivism, and power distances are in most (but not all) cases greater than in the Anglo cultures.

Where there is a greater need to avoid uncertainty, "citizens are negative towards institutions" (p. 134). An antipathy towards outsiders strengthens dependence on members of the group. And where values are collectivist, "collective interests prevail over individual interests" and "opinions are predetermined by group membership" (p. 73). Collectivist loyalty is expected between family members. Because they share a view of the world, family members communicate efficiently in routine situations – but in a crisis, shared perceptions of the world may not be sufficient.

Where power distances are large, the entrepreneur derives his authority from his/her position rather than from function or expert power. He can take decisions quickly and without fear of a challenge. His/her authority is decisive in all situations, whether or not he has greater knowledge of the problem, or whether some other family member is better qualified.

Children try to avoid challenges and conflicts which seem likely to disrupt family and company harmony. When the entrepreneur is absent, the senior child temporarily assumes his/her authority.

Wong (1986, p. 311) explains the entrepreneurial drive of Hong Kong by the cultural values associated with running one's own business.

> The norm on self-employment was vividly expressed by a small Hong Kong industrialist who reportedly said that "a Shanghainese at 40 who has not yet made himself owner of a firm is a failure, a good-for-nothing." ... Such a preference is not confined to the small industrialists. ... Nearly two thirds of those I interviewed chose the option of becoming the owner-manager of a small firm rather than the senior executive of a large corporation if both alternatives were available to them early in their career.

Since Wong wrote this, international companies have been increasingly active in the region. They offer new opportunities for well-paid and prestigious employment. It would not be surprising if the drive towards self-ownership and management had diminished. However, even ten years later, research conducted in Thailand found that more than 50 percent of the MBA-student informants planned to start and manage their own businesses (Mead et al., 1997).

12.3.5 *Confucianism and the Chinese model*

How Chinese companies deal with the external environment and with their internal arrangements is often explained by reference to Confucianism. There can be no doubt that this ethical system has had a major influence on Chinese culture. However, a danger lies in overstating its importance and ignoring other factors that have also influenced the development of the Chinese family business.

The culture of Southeast Asia is *not* homogeneous. National and sub-cultural differences are significant. Fukuyama (1995) points out that "there is no unified Confucian challenge to the West" (p. 97). Confucianism in Taiwan is expressed by a multiplicity of small family companies and a relatively weak central government. In Singapore it is applied as a state ideology by a powerful government, and a 1989 White Paper defined the "shared values" of Singaporeans as (Huntington, 1998, p. 319):

> Nation before [ethnic] community and society above self;
> Family as the basic unit of society;

Regard and community support for the individual;
Consensus instead of contention;
Racial and religious harmony.

Thais of Chinese descent seem to have little explicit knowledge of Confucian teachings, yet in the workplace express them continually in their attitudes towards superiors and subordinates and the organization as a family-like structure.

The qualities that Hofstede associates with Confucianism have appeared elsewhere. In Europe, Protestant capitalism in the eighteenth and nineteenth centuries was also based upon the success of family companies, in which the family unit was tightly knit; the authority of the family head often went unquestioned; virtue resided in working hard to acquire relevant skills and education, and in practicing thrift. Perhaps the present-day success of Asian economies should be explained less by Confucianism than by the operations of closed family hierarchies in particular economic contexts.

McVey (1992) makes a fourth point. In the nineteenth century Max Weber and other sociologists used Confucianism to explain why Asian economies seemed unlikely to catch up with the West. The "Confucian culture" argument has had a curious career:

> for it began not in its present role of explaining why capitalist development in East Asia has been such a success but rather of suggesting why the Chinese were unlikely to make good capitalists.
>
> *(p. 9)*

Only after 1945 when Asian economies began to grow, but not in accordance with Western models, did scholars advance the Confucian argument in order to explain their distinctive successes. Then, after 1997, the notion of Confucianism (referred to as Asian values) was used by other scholars to explain the economic slump in the region. In sum, then, the concept of Confucianism has been used at different times to explain both Asian stagnation and Asian boom; and the more loosely it is employed, the less its analytical value.

Confucianism (and culture in general) alone does not explain the development of Chinese family companies. They owe their success to the interplay of cultural factors and factors in the business and economic environments, and not to *only* the one or the other. Confucianism does contribute to developments in the Southeast Asian economies *when other factors are present.*

12.3.6 The dangers of overemphasizing the importance of culture

As with all cultural analysis, there are dangers of overemphasizing the importance of culture as an influence on Chinese family companies, and overlooking:

- the extent to which non-Chinese companies are influenced by similar factors;
- the influence on Chinese family companies of non-cultural factors.

For example, Huang (1999) finds these differences (among others) between how succession issues are handled in Chinese and Anglo companies:

- In Chinese companies, the process of succession is governed by top-down decision making.
- Mutual trust is built around guanxi. The importance of personal relationships means that close relatives are usually chosen to succeed to general management positions.

But, to take the first point, succession issues are also decided by top management in Anglo companies. Although the opinions of lower levels may be taken into account, juniors do not make the final decision. And the second point: family business people in Anglo cultures may not articulate the principles of guanxi, but they too are far more likely to choose the new CEO from the controlling family. Garcao et al. (1997) calculated that perhaps only 12 percent of American family companies had non-family CEOs.

In practice, application of comparative cultural analysis is most appropriate when differences are expressed in terms of comparisons. A statement that "Chinese companies are more likely to do X than are Anglo companies" may be more convincing than "Chinese companies do X whereas Anglo companies do Y."

In any society, a successful company responds to a range of factors in the environment of which culture is only one, and at least ostensibly its response is largely influenced by economic factors.

12.4 The Chinese Model: Management

The traditional Chinese company has a simple structure, either as management "spokes" around a powerful founder, or as a management structure on two levels. The East Asia Analytical Unit (1995) noted that:

> one survey of over 150 ethnic Chinese entrepreneurs found that 70 percent still operated around one of these two simple structures. *(p. 141)*

Figure 12.1 shows a hypothetical company. The entrepreneur has staffed all management posts with close relatives. The company is organized on a strongly vertical basis below top management levels, and very little information is communicated between functions; perhaps Wong, Chung, and Oi scarcely know each other.

At the level of functional management – and assuming that family relationships are good – information is communicated relatively quickly. John Tan and Lee Tan are unmarried and live in their father's house; L. K. Tan and his wife, and Amy and her husband Henry Siew, occupy houses in the same compound. And it is usual that all members of the family eat their dinner together. Hence Mr. Tan is able to collect information and to relay his decisions quickly, and any decisions for which he invites participation are efficiently made.

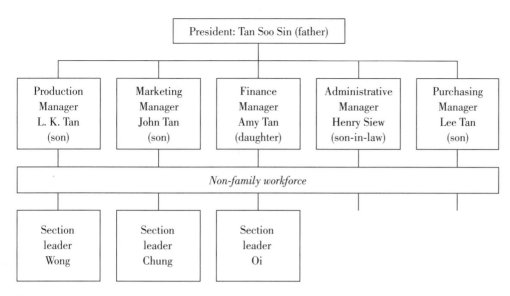

Figure 12.1

12.4.1 Employing family and clan members in the Chinese model

Family business owners in both the Anglo and Chinese environments face the problems that arise from overlapping family membership and management. We have examined a common Anglo response: professional and bureaucratic relationships and standards are emphasized in the hope that they will restrict opportunities for family discord. The traditional Chinese response is the reverse. As a qualification for membership and promotion, loyalty is valued over professional and bureaucratic status.

Most loyalty can be demanded from immediate family members; greatest demand is placed on their loyalty, and they are the most trusted. The bureaucratic controls exerted in an Anglo company may be absent – so that, in extreme cases, no regular salary is paid. A young Hong Kong Chinese commented:

> "I used to work in the family business. But my brother didn't pay me. I complained to my Mum and she said you should be doing it as a favor."

It was taken for granted that a member of the family would be willing to work from a sense of loyalty and be contented with just a room and food. In their terms, the family was properly respecting her family membership, and so it was not appropriate to introduce the criterion of meanness. But, in common with others of her generation, she had been exposed to Anglo work values and preferred the impersonal concept of being paid a fair rate for the job, whatever the identity of her employer.

The concept of nepotism (defined by the dictionary as giving employment and other favors by a person in authority to his relatives) often carries negative connotations in the Anglo management literature but does not in Chinese business. But this is to stereotype. Within the local context, family employment may be both positive and productive.

Immediate family members are the most trusted. Members of the extended family (for example, cousins) may be the next most, then clan members next most. But patterns of family recruitment differ in different clans and Chinese societies. Anecdotal evidence suggests that a Cantonese family company may still be restricted to only members of the immediate family; a Shanghainese company may recruit from wider in the clan.

Non-Chinese often take for granted that the Chinese community is homogeneous. But there are many clans who have histories of varying relationships with each other. In Hong Kong and Taiwan, they speak different languages (Cantonese and Mandarin) and may have to resort to English in order to understand each other. The Chinese in Malaysia include these language groups: Hokkien (about 34 percent), Hakka and Cantonese (both around 20 percent), Teochew (12 percent), Hainanese (5 percent), Kwongsai, Hockchiu, Henghua, Hockchia, and others (2 percent or less).

In the past very few Chinese family companies have employed outside directors, although this situation is now slowly changing and needs to acquire new skills are driving some in this direction. Craig (2002) suggested that in future we may see a move towards Anglo practice in the use of outside directors, but even in the Anglo cultures this is a slow process.

12.4.2 Employing outsiders in the Chinese model

The maintenance of family harmony is of crucial importance, and on occasion this may override needs for efficiency. This is apparent when an unqualified family member is appointed in preference to a qualified outsider, perhaps from a different clan, from whom the same levels of loyalty cannot be expected. The traditional company fears that a non-family member might:

- leave to set up business on his/her own, and compete;
- be poached by a competitor;
- supply confidential data (e.g., accounting and financial data, customer and supplier lists, process secrets) to a competitor;
- supply confidential information to the authorities.

These fears are particularly acute if the outside employee acquires skills that are valued in the labor market. The company may be unwilling to train a non-family member – and so the repertoire of skills available is restricted to those held by family members.

Given these worries, outsiders can expect to be closely supervised. Their formal obedience is expected and enforced. Communication is mostly one-way and top-down. But once an outsider is trusted, he/she may be bound closer to the company by a process of family-ization, in which he/she is patronized more generously, as though a family member.

However, these generalizations about traditional recruitment practices cannot always be taken for granted in the fast-changing economies of modern Asia. Employment decisions are increasingly complex and may involve permutations of family relationship, emotional ties, education, skills, market competition, and the stage of company development. In some circumstances, a childhood friend from another family, or a total outsider, may be more trusted than even one's own children.

A small-scale research project conducted in Taiwan by Wang (1998) suggested the following:

- The main criteria are that the recruit should be trustworthy and sufficiently skilled.
- The desirability of professional skills varies across functions, being very high in finance and relatively lower in human resource management.
- A total outsider is trusted most in production and sales, then in finance, then in personnel management, and least in general management.
- Although the first choice of managerial recruit is a member of the close family, the second choice is a complete outsider (who is Chinese).
- Managers educated in the West are more willing to accept outsiders into management.
- Patterns may differ across Chinese societies; societies which have developed most recently are least likely to accept outsiders. On the basis of very limited data Wang hypothesizes that Hong Kong companies may be more willing to accept outsiders, particularly in the early stages of growth.

These findings are tentative, and do not take account of the differences between those managers who have experience of employing outsiders and those considering the move. But they are sufficient to suggest areas for further research.

12.4.3 Succession issues in the Chinese model

A Chinese proverb reports that "Wealth doesn't last more than three generations." In this respect, Anglo and Chinese companies are similar. One reason that Chinese companies:

> ...tend to become unstable by the second or third generation is that "the legitimacy of the power structure breaks down," says the University of Hong Kong's Mr Redding. It's no longer clear who the owner is and who the father figure is, he adds. "You go to cousins and brothers and uncles and nephews and God knows who. And the glue breaks down."[11]

One Thai businessman refers to this stage of family-business development as:

> a "cousin's confederation" where the third generation operates by mutual cooperation even though they may operate different companies which may be outside the group.[12]

In the past, social conditions made it easier to form a "cousin's confederation." The entire extended family collected together for traditional festivals such as Chinese New Year and the Moon festival. But the erosion of collectivist values and greater mobility means that nuclear families celebrate festivals on their own. Hence, relationships between different households in the extended family become more distant.

Anecdotes collected from Saudi Arabian businessmen suggest that, in that environment, succession is almost bound to modify the organizational culture. In the first generation, the company is owned and top-managed by the original founder. He controls his subordinate managers – typically sons – by parental diktat and his word may go unchallenged. He may be succeeded by his eldest son, but the new CEO is in a different relationship with the other managers – his brothers – and is forced to negotiate his authority. If this eldest brother is perceived to have charisma and intelligence, the new arrangement works well enough. But if an ambitious younger brother is obviously better suited, management may be divided.

The problems of maintaining loyalty in both Chinese and Saudi families are complicated in cases of:

■ MULTIPLE FAMILIES. When the owner takes a number of wives, either in sequence or at the same time, and each produces children, conflicts arise over succession rights.
■ GENERATIONAL CONFLICTS. At one time father and children shared experience and expectations. Of late the younger generation is better educated – often abroad – and those with management qualifications are less willing to accept policies based on experience.

How does the Chinese entrepreneur guard the company against the effects of family conflict? One answer is to separate areas of responsibility so that no family member develops a full understanding of the company interests and strategy. But while this may secure the company during his/her tenure, it can lead to greater confusion in the event that he/she suddenly passes away. A second answer is to diversify family interests across a group of companies so that the group suffers minimally should one company fail. Each child might be given a controlling interest in one company and a minority interest in others. Hence the group's activities benefit from good sibling relationships while no one need suffer if one child fails. Indonesia offers striking examples of linked cross-holdings. The Salim group includes hundreds of companies spread across a wide range of markets in many countries.

12.4.4 Financing the Chinese model

Many traditional businesses are undercapitalized and never achieve their potential growth. Where the banking system is inefficient, banks take the safer option of lending to state enterprises. In China, a manufacturer of paper cups:

> . . . wanted to boost production to ride a trend of restaurants serving tea in paper cups with colourful plastic holders. Although he had plenty of collateral in the form of sales contracts, machinery and inventory, lenders wouldn't grant him even a small line of credit to maintain a steady supply of paper. To raise funds, Mao sold his house and moved into a

space above his office.... "The government sees state enterprises as its sons, so it helps them," Mao says dejectedly. "I get nothing, so someone else will drink up my market."[13]

The opposite may also be true; the traditional business feels uncomfortable with the idea of outsiders examining the company books and financial statements – particularly if they might have links with competitors or the tax authorities. For this reason they may be reluctant to borrow from banks and other bureaucratic institutions, or to make a public share offering. The traditional solution is to raise capital from:

- personal savings;
- family savings;
- successful business deals and accumulated profits;
- if these sources are inadequate, from the wider clan.

As a result, many traditional companies remain undercapitalized and can never achieve the growth they are capable of.

This dependence on family is not unique to Chinese or even Asian companies. Klingel (2002) finds that German companies also prefer to rely on internal financing if possible.

12.5   Changes in the Chinese Model

The sections above have focused on models of traditional Anglo and Chinese family companies. Both these models are now in a state of flux. Scholars are beginning to doubt the wisdom of entirely bureaucratizing the Anglo model. It is beginning to be recognized that, after all, effective family relationships can contribute to building loyalty and motivation. Chinese companies are also changing.

Like family companies everywhere, many Chinese companies fail, often for reasons that are not culture-specific. In all countries some companies are badly managed. Management may misread the market and overlook opportunities. The founding owner may become set in a conservative management style, and refuse to restructure in response to a changing environment. His/her management style may be too autocratic. For example, the Chinese entrepreneur born in an age when communication styles were typically top-down may resist two-way communications with his children who have acquired greater technical expertise than his.

12.5.1   *Problems arising from the context*

Other reasons for failure may be specific to the cultural context. For example, Chinese cultural conservatism might adversely influence structural, managerial, and technological priorities. We have seen that a refusal to hire outsiders limits the size of the company to the size of the family. Similarly a dependence on family-based capital starves the company of investment. Family members aware of the services offered by modern banking systems are alienated by persistent requests for financing. One Hong Kong manager reported:

> "I lent money to my brother but he didn't pay me back till God knows when, and he didn't pay me interest. Family members don't pay interest. But banks expect it."

Traditional reward structures may also inhibit development. In the past, profits were shared within the company. Over the past decades, new problems have arisen in deciding whether to pay family members the market rate and how to assess their work.

If the extended family breaks up under pressure from modern life-styles, the loyalty of members can no longer be taken for granted. Junior members see alternative opportunities in the wider job market and rail against being exploited as cheap labor. In the worst case, talented and qualified members leave and the company is forced to depend on those less-qualified who have no alternatives for employment.

12.5.2 Solving the problems

The economic uncertainties resulting from the 1997 crisis have undoubtedly damaged many Southeast Asian family companies. But it is a mistake to assume that the crisis has led to an irrevocable decline in the fortunes of the small- and medium-business sectors. Many Chinese family companies have used the crisis as an opportunity to rethink their strategies. For example, they are hiring more professional managers at senior levels. In 1997 the Hong Kong branch of headhunters Korn/Ferry International reported an increasing trend in Asian family companies in Hong Kong, Singapore, Malaysia, and Indonesia to hire outsiders as CEOs or chief financial officers.[14]

Chiu and Siu (2001) examine different right-sizing strategies adopted by small- and medium-sized companies in Hong Kong after 1997. These strategies aimed to achieve staffing levels that enabled the companies both to retrench after the crisis and to prepare for the economic upsurge that promised to follow.

According to one Chinese manager studying in the United States the lessons learned there by his Asian colleagues and taken home include:

- separating ownership from management in the Anglo style – once a Singaporean cooked in his own restaurant; now he buys a string of restaurants, hires a cook for each and supervises all;
- instituting fair systems for employee evaluation;
- decentralizing top management;
- instituting proper accounting systems;
- hiring outside professionals.

Given that these are common practices in Anglo companies (see section 14.3) they are not radical in a global context. But they mark considerable steps forward for the traditional Chinese company.

12.5.3 The MBA solution

The manager mentioned above was studying for an MBA degree in a top American business school. The decision made by many Chinese entrepreneurs to invest in Anglo MBA training for their children shows an attempt to modernize. However, so far as the traditional company is concerned, MBA training is a double-edged sword.

The company gains a range of valuable technical skills, particularly in finance. However, some aspects of MBA training are less relevant to Southeast Asia. Much of what Anglo MBA schools teach in many marketing courses and most human resource management courses is not relevant to business conditions in, say, Bangkok or Jakarta.

Anglo MBA schools have the central mission of training managers to operate in bureaucratic companies based in mature economies where annual growth seldom exceeds 4 percent. These conditions do not apply in Southeast Asia, where growth rates may fluctuate wildly and entrepreneurial skills may be more critical. Also, the Chinese entrepreneur may hope to keep his/her children within the family business, but MBA students are trained to manage across a range of industries and to move between industries.

These points do not argue against MBA programs as such; the best teach essential skills. But when offered outside the Anglo economies whose needs they are primarily intended to serve, they do demonstrate a paradox of management training. The traditional company decides to upgrade in order to compete more effectively, and invests in a type of training which can have the effect of transforming the company to the point that it no longer represents its former self, may no longer fit with its business environment, and may lose its function.

12.5.4 Westernizing the Chinese family company

The East Asia Analytical Unit (1995, p. 144) proposed that the Chinese family company was best served by Westernizing. The stages by which this could be achieved are, in summary:

- draw in expertise from outside the family but still within the clan;
- bring in outsider middle managers to balance control by family members;
- raise capital from banks;
- restructure and streamline;
- list the firm on the local stock exchange and raise capital from international bond markets;
- sell down family stock to a bare majority holding.

Chinese family companies are beginning to make far greater use of the web as a means of communicating with the business environment. But a Taiwanese manager reports that they are still very conservative about supplying financial data.

Since the crisis, the degree to which Anglo experts have tended to measure Chinese family companies in terms of how far they correspond to Anglo models seems to have escalated. Certainly these companies can learn from the West. But given the successes achieved by Asian economies over the past decades (1997 aside) the Chinese entrepreneur might wonder whether these models are necessarily superior in all respects. And the introductory case suggests that Anglo companies can sometimes learn useful lessons from their equivalents elsewhere in the world.

12.6 Implications for the Manager

How does national culture influence strategy within family companies that you know? Make comparisons between:

- a small family company typical of *your own culture*;
- a small family company typical of *some other culture* that you know.

1 In each of the two companies:
   - are family members employed?
     (a) if you answer *yes*, in what positions are they employed?
     (b) what criteria are used in appointing them?
   - in what positions are non-family members employed?
   - how quickly and efficiently do members communicate?
   - what disputes arise between family and non-family members?
2 Compare your analyses of *your-own-culture* company and *the-other-culture* company:
   - what significant differences do you observe?
   - how do you explain these differences?
   - how far can these differences be explained by
     (a) the national cultures?
     (b) the business environments?
     (c) family memberships?
     (d) other factors?
   - which of (a)–(d) do you think is most important in explaining the differences?
3 What lessons might each of the two apply from the models discussed above of the:
   - Anglo family company?
   - Chinese family company?
4 Successful Chinese companies benefit from:
   - close interaction with the environment;
   - use of informal networks;
   - highly centralized decision making;
   - focusing on low margin and high volume in order to penetrate markets.
   Can these lessons be applied by the Anglo family company?

12.7 SUMMARY

This chapter asked how the development of a family company is influenced by its environment. It focused on two extremes: the company typical of an Anglo culture, and the Chinese family company in Southeast Asia.

Section 12.2 examined ENVIRONMENT, CULTURE, AND MANAGEMENT style of THE ANGLO MODEL. Relationships within the company are bureaucratized, to the point that outsiders may be preferred to equally qualified insiders. In environments where market information is easily accessible, informal contacts count for less. Section 12.3 examined the BUSINESS AND CULTURAL ENVIRONMENTS within which the Southeast Asian CHINESE company functions. The impact of Confucianism was examined; this gives only a partial explanation for the success of the company and the Southeast Asian economies. MANAGEMENT ISSUES were discussed in section 12.4. This dealt with the structure, employment policies, succession issues, and financing of the CHINESE MODEL. But the CHINESE MODEL is CHANGING. Section 12.5 saw how Southeast Asian family companies have responded to the 1997 crisis and the need to compete in global market places.

12.8 EXERCISE

This exercise shows how industrial and cultural factors affect the systems implemented in the family company.

1 *Family company A* makes paper cups for the fast-food industry. The cups are cut from sheets of pre-printed card and glued. When this company is based in (a) the United States and (b) Hong Kong, what are the implications for:

- recruitment policies?
- training policies?
- control in the workplace?
- relations with the environment?

2 *Family company B* makes laser technology, used in space research. When this company is based in (a) the United States and (b) Hong Kong, what are the implications for the same issues listed in question 1?

Notes

1 Michelle Levander, "Making of a mogul," *Time Asia*, December 17, 2001.

2 City Comment, "Heirs apparent, heirs presumptive and Rupert Murdoch's greying hair," *Daily Telegraph*, September 17, 2003.

3 Matt Born, "Sky job looms for the Murdoch college boy who kept learning," *Daily Telegraph*, September 26, 2003.

4 Denise Tsang, "Survey aims to help family firms clear hurdles," *South China Morning Post*, November 21, 2001.

5 A report by London Business School, cited by Richard Tyler, "Family firms run risk of tensions," *Daily Telegraph*, September 22, 2003.

6 "Sons must pay their mother for unfair sacking," *Daily Telegraph*, September 21, 1995.

7 "Splits, and survival," *The Economist*, October 31, 1992.

8 A report by London Business School, cited by Richard Tyler, "Family firms run risk of tensions," *Daily Telegraph*, September 22, 2003.

9 "Splits, and survival," *The Economist*, October 31, 1992.

10 "Local businessmen of foreign descent are less nationalistic," *The Jakarta Post*, July 25, 1995.

11 Dan Biers and Jeremy Mark, "Succession battles shake Asia's family businesses," *Asian Wall Street Journal*, June 1, 1995.

12 K. I. Woo, "Family businesses remain the backbone of the country's economy," *The Nation* (Bangkok), April 15, 1996.

13 Matthew Forney, "Betting on the wrong horse," *Time Asia*, February 17, 2003.

14 Erik Guyot, "Headhunters in Asia try to help companies owned by families," *Wall Street Journal*, February 24, 1997.

CHAPTER THIRTEEN

Designing and Implementing Strategy

13.1 Introduction

By the end of the twentieth century the Japanese fertility rate was among the lowest in the world, and so the demand for baby-food was plummeting. At the other end of the age range, Japanese adults were living longer. One in five Japanese was aged 65 or older, and it was estimated that by 2014 one in four would be.

Japanese baby-food executives needed to reconsider their strategies in order to save their companies from a very uncertain future. Hard thinking was needed. Then someone in the industry realized that they weren't simply in the business of selling food to babies. The soft, small morsels with low salt that could be easily prepared were also attractive to the elderly.[1] They were in the business of selling to people who could not digest rich food and didn't have teeth.

The decline in the baby-food market constituted a threat; the growth in the elderly food market presented opportunities. The companies were able to maintain their core product lines while readjusting their perceptions of their industry and their marketing strategies. One of the themes developed in this chapter is the importance to a company of reappraising its resources and the business environment when managing its strategy.

13.2   Formal Strategy Planning

The activity of strategic planning is generally confined to top management. In some cultures and some companies, members at lower levels expect to be consulted and asked for suggestions, but the final responsibility for making decisions on design and implementation stays at the top.

Although the notion of strategy has been applied to business only in the past 60 years, it has developed into a complex system of theories and practices. The range of different models includes Chandler's (1962) strategy and structure model, Andrews's (1971) design school, Ansoff's (1985) planning school model, Mintzberg's (1985) model of intended and emergent strategies, and Porter's (1990) competitive strategy model. The definition assumed or articulated by a company is influenced both by these scholarly contributions and by its relationship with the market and industry, and the specific problems it faces in adjusting to a changing environment. Adjustment problems were discussed at the end of chapter 10. The company needs to take long-term decisions in regard to customer demand, the development of markets, how they distinguish themselves from competitors, relationships with suppliers, staffing, and so on, at a time when the internal world of the company and its environment are changing at an unprecedented rate.

This chapter deals with a range of different approaches.

(a)   A formal plan of action. A deliberate response to changing opportunities and threats in the environment (see sections 13.2.1–3). This category may include a formal plan made as a matter of routine (see section 13.2.4) and a formal plan associated with a decisive event in the organization – say, the arrival of a new CEO (see section 13.2.5);

(b)   A plan of action that focuses on applying resources (see section 13.3).

(c)   A plan of action that focuses on positioning the organization in relation to the competition (see section 13.4).

(d)   An emergent plan; an incremental process of change made in response to the environment (see section 13.6). The stream of small changes may or may not be justified to stakeholders in documentation (see section 13.6.1).

Approach (a) reflects a process of formal long-term strategic planning, and (d), at the other end of the continuum, an emergent stream of small changes. These approaches represent different emphases rather than alternatives that can be strictly demarcated. No plan should be designed without some consideration of the practical problems that may arise in implementing it, and each in a stream of pragmatic decisions is selected in the hope that this can help achieve a long-term aim – even if this is not fully articulated.

13.2.1   The formal plan of action

In the past, Anglo companies tended to focus on the traditional approach represented by (a), above. For example, David (1993) defines strategy as:

... the art and science of formulating, implementing, and evaluating cross-functional decisions that enable an organization to achieve its objectives.   *(p. 5)*

This traditional definition expresses the notion of strategy making as a deliberate activity. Management takes a conscious decision to make a radical change with its past. The organization is no longer able to achieve its goals by the existing strategy, or a new goal has to be formulated. David makes clear that all units of the organization might be involved in this change process, which means that there have to be cross-organizational linkages in place to coordinate their different inputs of the different units. Different departments may design their own strategies, but these have the function of deepening and developing aspects of the overall strategy and are not alternatives.

13.2.2   Stages in the formal plan

Designing the strategic plan is a formal process; papers are written, analyses and projections made, formal meetings attended. The plan is expressed in documentation. Principal activities of the planners are:

▌ DEFINING goals;
▌ ANALYZING data;
▌ DESIGNING the strategy;
▌ IMPLEMENTING the strategy.

These simple categories can be used to generate more complex models. That presented in table 13.1 is still very simple, but shows how formal strategic planning can be mapped onto the *classic planning model* given in table 10.1.

In general the stages are ordered as in table 13.1 – but this is not inflexible and (bi) and (bii) are obviously interchangeable. Planning at any one stage forces the planner to review decisions taken at an earlier stage and to predict later stages. Identifying goals is the first formal step in planning, but also presupposes previous thinking about the organization's resources and its relationships with the market.

13.2.3   Goals

Goals are the objectives or outcomes that an organization seeks to achieve, and the formal strategic plan has the function of mapping the most efficient route to achieving them. Strategic goals are simple and long-term.

Every organization has the minimal goal of survival. Usually this is not articulated, although here is an example when the urge to survive was made clear.

> Liang Xinjun, a director of the Fosun Group, one of China's largest private steelmakers, says the company's aim is not to make money yet – it is simply to survive.

Table 13.1   Strategic planning mapped onto the classic planning model

Classic planning model		*Strategic planning*	
1	proposing a change	a	DEFINING goals (see section 13.2.2)
2	collecting relevant information	bi	ANALYZING internal resources (see section 13.3)
3	analyzing the information and projecting past and present conditions into the future	bii	ANALYZING competitive advantage (see section 13.4)
4	designing a set of alternative plans for making the change	c	DESIGNING the strategy
5	selecting the best plan		
6	implementing the selected plan	d	IMPLEMENTING the strategy (see section 13.5)
7	monitoring and reviewing the implementation stage		
8	making necessary modifications, based on stage 7 output		

> But given Fosun's rapid growth, from a standing start with its first steel investment in the late 1990s ... it may be the survival of the group's rivals that is more on line.[2]

Strategic planning and management is more usually concerned with explicit goals and plans. The tactical details are hidden from outsiders, but the broad direction of change may be well publicized. The explicit goals must be clearly understood by a range of stakeholders, which means they must be clearly stated and unambiguous.

Different types of goals may be specified. These include:

- FINANCIAL GOALS. The main financial goal is always the maximization of value to the shareholders. Other financial goals contribute to this.
- MARKET GOALS (e.g. to win or maintain a position as market leader).
- POLITICAL GOALS (e.g. to win cooperation from other bodies within the environment).
- ETHICAL GOALS (e.g. to contribute to society, to achieve social and humanitarian goals).
- CULTURAL GOALS (e.g. to build a positive organizational culture).
- Others may be identified.

In any company, the FINANCIAL GOALS are most important. However successful it is in achieving the subordinate goals, the company goes out of business if it fails to make sufficient profit. Subordinate goals are designed to help achieve the financial goals, at least in the long term. For example, only those marketing goals are selected that promise to make more money. The company aims to build a culture that improves productivity so that it can make more money. And a keen sense of ethical purpose improves morale and gives the company a strong image in society, even if in the short term this involves investment.

The achievement of profit may not usually be explicitly prioritized in non-profit-making organizations: these include charities (such as Amnesty International and Médecins Sans Frontières), international organizations (such as the United Nations), and government organizations including ministries and embassies. Nevertheless they also need to balance their books and are in danger of closure if expenditure regularly exceeds income.

The goals directly influence the strategies selected; financial strategies are directed to meeting financial goals, marketing strategies to marketing goals, and so on.

A company strategy can only succeed when planning at all levels of the company is coherent and integrated. This means that plans made by all component units of the company are directed to achieving the superordinate goals. That is, detailed operations in the marketing department are planned and implemented by its own departmental strategy which is integrated with all other departmental strategies; those in the production department by the production strategy, those in the R&D department by the R&D strategy, and so on.

13.2.4 The routine plan

Formal planning is sometimes made a matter of bureaucratic routine. For example, the organization assumes that at regular intervals corrections to the existing strategy will be needed in order to respond to the expected stream of change in the environment.

During the growth years of the 1950s and 1960s, many companies produced five-year plans, and some governments still do. Making strategic planning a routine process may be efficient, but it carries the risk of restricting the scope of possible goals and of underestimating the importance of novel factors that do not fit the planning model. Routine planning needs to be continually reviewed and modified so that it keeps up to date with the company's circumstances and position in the environment.

When the company has to respond to unpredictable change occurring at a rapid rate, a routine model does not provide sufficient flexibility. In the United Kingdom, the Chancellor of the Exchequer presents a budget to Parliament for approval every April. In recent years it has become practice that the Chancellor also submits "mini-budgets" at other times during the year, in order to make adjustments to the annual plan that may become out-of-date within a few months.

13.2.5 Strategy marking internal change

In any culture, the appointment of a new CEO constitutes a major internal change in the company. In Anglo cultures, where higher levels of individualism are tolerated, the CEO is often expected to signal his/her arrival by embarking on strategic planning.

In these contexts a new CEO might be very uncomfortable if asked to continue his/her predecessor's policies in the long term. The new strategy sends messages to both insiders and outsiders that one chapter in the life of the organization has closed and another begun, and as such has symbolic value. The appointment of the new CEO may have been made *because* the board sees the need for a new strategy – although this is not the only reason for CEO change.

13.3   Analyzing Resources and the Competition

The strategic process always involves analysis of two sets of factors:

1   those internal to the organization, *and*
2   those in the business environment.

Any strategic decision-making process must pay some attention to these two areas of analysis. In some companies, greater attention is paid to the first, in others to the second. The precise balance in any one case depends on how far the company is looking for a strategy by which to apply its internal capabilities more effectively within its industry, or is reconsidering its position within the industry, or a move to a new industry in which it can earn a higher rate of return than do its competitors.

13.3.1   Analyzing resources

This strategic approach is based on the notion that the company is essentially a bundle of resources and capabilities, and these determine how it can manage a long-term strategy most effectively. An audit of the resources available helps the company to decide whether it is using its resources efficiently and whether they might not be better applied in developing new products or even in a new industry. It exploits them to develop advantages over competitors and develop core competences.

Different types of resources may be audited:

▮   TANGIBLE resources (finance, materials, location, plant, technology-as-artifact (see section 4.3.7), etc.) The analysis of the financial status of the company is always essential. This means:
   (a)   appraising all financial data relating to current performance;
   (b)   on the basis of this appraisal, predicting the financial potential of continuing the present strategy into the future, and predicting the financial potentials of new strategic alternatives;
   (c)   then selecting the optimal financial strategy;
   (d)   finally, setting financial targets for those whose task it is to implement the strategy.

■ INTANGIBLE resources. These include:

- CAPACITY (reputation, patents, research capacity);
- SKILLS (intangible technology, human resource skills, knowledge, commitment of employees);
- SYSTEMS. This component includes the internal arrangements discussed in earlier chapters; the organizational culture, management communication, structure, systems to motivate, systems to resolve dispute, informal relationships, planning systems.

Grant (2002) argues that for most companies:

> Intangible resources contribute much more than do tangible resources to total asset value. Yet, in relation to company financial statements, intangible resources remain largely invisible ... *(p. 141)*

The reason is that intangible resources cannot be easily costed. For example, how can the value of "knowledge" be reliably estimated?

Analysis of intangible resources contributes to the analysis of competitive advantage – in that it explains why you have an advantage or how you can achieve one – and to implementation processes. Many companies emphasize their structures and culture as critical ingredients in planning and implementing strategy. For example, human relations policies are designed to help attain goals. A strategy calling for innovation may mean recruiting persons willing to take initiatives and then rewarding them for entrepreneurial behavior – whether or not these are initially successful. A strategy of cost reduction means establishing narrowly defined and measured job specifications.

The audit of resources already under its control helps the company calculate those further resources needed in order to achieve the strategic goals. For example, the decision to widen its product range may mean acquiring new materials, new technologies, and new skills.

13.3.2 Knowledge resources

In cases where the company deliberately builds a learning culture, systems designed to develop and apply knowledge have strategic importance (see section 4.3.8). Companies become increasingly aware that the "hidden" knowledge possessed by their employees represents a strategic resource, if only it can be applied.[3] For example, a company posted a manager to its international joint venture in Brazil. After 2 years, he returned to headquarters. A few months later, the Brazilian government changed and his opposite number in the partner company emerged as an important minister. Thus the company acquired a friendly contact in the Brazilian government, and this influenced decisions about the scope of its investment in the country.

However, identifying and exploiting knowledge is problematic. In theory it might sound a simple process but, in practice, a company usually only recognizes and absorbs its members' experiences when these relate to what it already knows. This means that a company is most likely to reject radical experiences when these might offer the best opportunities of developing in very new directions.

13.3.3 *Organizational capabilities and competitive advantage*

The point above, that knowledge is only useful when ways are found to exploit it in a productive way to the advantage of the company, applies generally to all analysis of resources. A company identifies its ORGANIZATIONAL CAPABILITIES and develops systems to apply them.

Capabilities consist of capacities to produce, and the concept is relative; the company is more or less capable of producing X in comparison to competitors who also produce X. That is, the company focuses on developing and exploiting those internal resources that will give it a competitive edge.

A company gains COMPETITIVE ADVANTAGE when the customer favorably distinguishes the company and its product from some other organization and its competing product. That is, the company's strengths and weaknesses are defined either *relative to the competition* or *relative to the alternative investments* that the company might make.

Three points arise. First, competitive advantage is never absolute and always relative. It does not mean that the product meets any absolute criteria of quality, only that it is best in the eyes of the customer, who prefers it to competing products.

Second, the factors giving this advantage must be apparent to the consumer so that they influence his/her purchasing decision. A competitive advantage is based on such values as quality, price, breadth of product line, reliability, performance, after-sales service, styling and image, and regular deliveries (see section 14.3.2 for an example). Comparatively high quality at a comparatively low price gives competitive advantage. Different products express different values; a book is sold on the basis of quality and appearance, not of after-sales service. On the other hand, if I am aiming to purchase a dish-washer, the after-sales service offered by the manufacturer may be an important factor in swaying my decision.

The company may have goals of promoting other factors, such as an effective human resources policy, but this, in itself, does not constitute competitive advantage because the consumer does not base his/her decision to purchase on it. My human resources policy may support my advantage if it enables me to get my high-quality product onto the market at low price. This support is essential – as is my R&D policy, use of funds and physical assets, and all internal arrangements. Without them I would be unable to produce at all. These COMPLEMENTARY ASSETS help me develop competitive advantage but are not factors that directly sway the consumer's purchasing decision.

Third, because the company wishes to protect and improve its competitive advantage it has to protect and improve the essential supports. Hence, strategy design means not simply identifying strengths and weaknesses in the internal resources that provide support. The company must go further and plan how to enhance its resources of skills and knowledge.

13.4   Positioning the Company

This approach focuses on the importance of gaining market share. The company seeks to become a market leader within an industry which offers the best opportunities for profitability. This means analyzing the factors that influence the development of those industries in which it aims to participate. The strategist uses current and projected figures to assess their present and future profitability, market growth rate, and the opportunities for product differentiation.

Porter (1990, p. 35) provided an important model that can be used to analyze the business environment. The dimensions of the five-forces model are:

- rivalry among competitors;
- bargaining power of buyers;
- bargaining power of suppliers;
- threat of new entrants;
- threat of substitute products and services.

This assumes that the business environment is a battlefield in which the company is constantly at war with others, and defines strategy in terms of how it can secure an advantage in competition with them.

A full analysis of factors in the external environment – recall the list given in section 1.2 – includes markets. To what market segments will the product be sold? In addition, a company planning to invest in a country where it has not previously worked may need to ask questions about such factors as:

- the degree of government interference;
- corruption;
- official grants;
- preferences given to local competitors;
- political personalities.

13.4.1   Resources and environment

However exhaustive the analysis of the environment, this approach has limited value unless the strategist also takes into account those resources which the company can exploit when interacting within the environment and establishing itself in the industry. That is, resource analysis and competitive analysis must proceed together.

Collis and Montgomery (1995, p.124) point out that the value of resources derives from how effectively they are being used, given the environment:

> the greatest mistake managers make when evaluating their resources is failing to assess them relative to competitors.

The writers drive home the point that analysis of resources must be made with a sharp eye on the changing market environment within which they are deployed. Specifically, the planner asks:

- How easily can the resource be imitated? The easier to imitate, the less is the value.
- How quickly will the resource depreciate?
- Who captures the value that the resource creates? Many of the profits from a resource flow to distributors, suppliers, customers, employees.
- Can a unique resource be trumped by a substitute?
- Whose resource is *really* better – yours or the competitor's?

A resource-based approach and a competitive approach are not strict alternatives. They give different emphases to the same strategic question; how can the company match its capabilities to the changing business environment? We now deal with two analytical systems which take into account both approaches.

13.4.2 Scope

A company is bound to take competitive considerations into account when appraising the resources available and those needed, and appraises its resources when planning how to secure and defend a market niche against competitors. This point is illustrated by the notion of SCOPE.

The identification of scope tells the company in what business(es) it already participates and in which new businesses it should aim to participate. If the scope is not clearly defined, the selected strategy is in danger of focusing on the wrong product, misusing internal resources, and misreading the market and competitive factors. Faults in defining the scope occur when it is delineated either too broadly or too narrowly. In the former case, the company is likely to scatter its resources too finely across a range of products and markets. In the latter case, it is blinded to alternative uses that its products can serve and hence to new markets.

This shows the importance of keeping an open mind on scope. If you define the question "What business are we in?" too rigidly, you are in danger of overlooking changes in markets and the environment. A wider question is "What business could we be in?" This means asking what new capabilities does the company need to take advantage of changing conditions. This has implications for examining the firm's resources in relation to its environment. The introductory case gives an example of a firm which readjusted its scope by rethinking how to market and sell its products.

13.4.3 Strengths, weaknesses, opportunities, and threats

In theory, a correct analysis of its present strengths and weaknesses tells the company what it *could* do in the future; and of opportunities and threats – what it *might* do. This notion still has general value, but for several reasons strategic planners no longer give it the emphasis that they once did. First, planners increasingly recognize that within an unstable environment a single factor might quickly change from being, say, a strength to being a weakness, or an opportunity to a threat. Second, individuals might classify factors differently; an optimistic personality finding a strength where a pessimist sees a threat. Third, these subjective impressions are influenced by national culture; for example, headquarters managers with relatively low needs to avoid uncertainty perceive opportunity whereas managers in a subsidiary, where even low levels of uncertainty are poorly tolerated, sense a threat.

13.5 Implementation

In the past, management theorists and consultants placed greater emphasis on design and less on implementation. Revenaugh (1994, p. 38) complained that:

> ... in strategic planning, literature abounds on how to develop a plan, but there is comparatively little said about how to implement a strategic plan once it is developed.

Modern theorists have moved towards redressing the balance. Grant (2002, pp. 11–12) discusses examples of successful strategies, and derives four common elements;

1 goals that are simple, consistent, and long term;
2 profound understanding of the competitive environment;
3 objective appraisal of resources;
4 effective implementation.

Several factors explain this change of emphasis. First, there is a growing awareness that in our unstable post-modern world, the impact of long-term strategic planning cannot be predicted with any accuracy. Increasingly an initial stage in strategic development consists of experimenting with alternative solutions to problems that may still be only vaguely articulated (see section 10.5). That is, early implementation contributes towards planning, and the two stages are run together. Second, in rapidly changing organizations, attention has to be paid to the political aspects of persuading members to accept the design and implementation. This means that developing a constituency favoring change and communicating with the various interested groups, or stakeholders, becomes a priority.

Both Percy Barnevik (once voted top executive in Europe) and Jack Welch (described in *Business Week* as the top US executive) agree that success depends on the company not only designing appropriate strategies but also by implementing them appropriately. They agreed that the implementation phase should take at least 90 percent of the total effort necessary to carry out a change program adequately. Barnevik says that the challenge to get people to support and then to accomplish the strategy is 95 percent execution and that the differences in execution are what differentiate the successful companies from the less successful. (See Flood et al., 2000, p. 31.)

13.5.1   Implementation systems

The term IMPLEMENTATION SYSTEMS refers to the systems that management applies in order to achieve its strategic goals. At one level, they include structures such as:

- Subsidiaries. Aspects of foreign subsidiary management are discussed in chapters 14, 16, and subsequently.
- International joint ventures, discussed in chapters 15, 16, and subsequently.
- Mergers, licensing contracts, agency agreements, turnkey agreements, etc., discussed in section 14.2.

They also include systems designed to revolutionize the structure, such as re-engineering, and to reform processes such as quality circles. These are both discussed below.

All these are operated as means to achieving the strategic goal; *they are not strategies in themselves*. Management forms a joint venture in order to improve its financial position, to increase market share, to develop knowledge and skills that can be applied to achieving subordinate goals, *not* simply for the excitement of participating in a joint venture. Management does not re-engineer for its own sake and will not do so unless there is a clear perception of what can be achieved in that context.

13.5.2   Re-engineering

Hammer and Champy's (1993) concept of RE-ENGINEERING was designed to achieve strategic goals by re-engineering those processes that drive the organization. It suggested how companies might redesign their business processes and so achieve dramatic improvements in critical measures of performance (cost, quality, capital, service, speed). It aimed to make radical changes:

> not by enhancing existing processes, but by discarding them and replacing them within entirely new ones.   *(p. 49)*

A business process (defined as a collection of jobs contributing towards production) was redefined when related jobs were combined and performed in a more natural order – which might mean they were performed simultaneously. When a series of related jobs could be combined and performed in a continuous rather than interrupted process, needs for checks and controls were reduced. This reduced the importance of boundaries between departments, and of middle managers responsible for overseeing departmental activities. A second function of middle management, supplying expert information, was relocated to information technology. Decision making and planning now became the responsibilities of anyone with access to a database and skills in using modeling software.

Information technology enabled production workers to communicate as widely as they needed. Because communication was open and easy, information could be communicated more broadly on a horizontal basis. It no longer needed to be communicated upwards and downwards between workforce and supervisors. The intended effects of this re-engineering were that:

- people who once did as they were instructed would now make choices and decisions on their own;
- assembly line work would be simplified;
- functional specialization would become less important, and specialist departments lose their reason for being;
- fewer middle managers would be required to command and control.

In practice, re-engineering proved to be an extremely painful process, and by one estimate entirely succeeded in only 30 percent of the cases in which it was tried in the United States. (Ronen, 1995, discusses reasons for failures.) An effect of reducing middle management was to remove the level of the company in which the values of the organizational culture were most entrenched, and thus to weaken the culture. Subsequent writings by Hammer and Champy have backed off from the greater radicalism of the original program. Hammer (1996, p. 67) emphasizes the human advantages and costs. Although the program offers freedom at work, this "involves ambiguity, and for some people the payoff isn't worth it." He is talking about individual psychology but the point might apply to culture groups with relatively low tolerances of ambiguity.

13.5.3 Quality circles

Whereas re-engineering aimed to overhaul management systems, the concept of the QUALITY CIRCLE had more modest aims: to make existing systems more efficient. The quality circle contributes to achieving strategic goals of producing more efficiently and maximizing profit margins. It was invented by an American, W. Edwards Deming, and was adopted by Japanese firms in the 1950s. A small group of employees, usually in a manufacturing unit, took responsibility for analyzing and recommending improvements to their technologies and processes. They typically met after regular working hours and did not expect overtime payment. The circles made a major contribution to Japanese production between the 1950s and the early 1990s.

13.5.4 The problems of implementation

Implementation may always be traumatic. For example, the new strategy calls for the termination of outdated brands and the development of new. This means that some staff are dismissed and new staff hired, new skills learned and old skills forgotten. The design of new tasks and relationships has structural implications. In order to coordinate and monitor developments new committees, task forces, liaison and integrating roles are established.

The problems of implementation are multiplied when a strategy is designed in one branch of the company to be implemented elsewhere. For example, a headquarters strategy is exported for implementation in a subsidiary located in a different culture. For instance, an exported strategy may be undermined by non-cultural factors. In Czechoslovakia, the 1990 Joint Venture Act offered attractive conditions to foreign companies wishing to invest in the country (Ferris, Joshi, and Makhija, 1995). By the middle of 1991, over 2,500 joint ventures with foreigners had been approved, but only 10 percent had commenced activities. A major deterrent to investment was the problem that the foreign partner faced in evaluating the stake offered by its Czech partner. The application of traditional firm valuation procedures to state-owned enterprises in the former Soviet bloc countries was not possible. Socialist-styled financial statements lacked capital market prices and any useful managerial data.

13.5.5 Cultural factors influence how strategy is formulated and implemented

This section examines how culture influences attitudes towards how strategy is formulated and implemented. It asks how far strategic thinking is molded by Anglo culture, and what are the implications for formulating and implementing strategy elsewhere when the persons involved belong to other cultures. (But culture may not always be the most important factor, as the sections before make clear.)

The references in the sections above make clear that Anglo writers dominate current thinking on strategy. Mintzberg (1994, p. 415) cited evidence of planning being most common and:

> most formalized in the United States, followed closely by England, Canada, and Australia, with Japan and Italy at the other end of the scale.... Thus the propensity seems to be not just American but Anglo-Saxon, although the Americans have certainly been in the lead.

This might be interpreted to mean any of the following:

- companies in other cultures do not perform strategic planning;
- companies in other cultures do perform strategic planning but do not write about it;
- companies in other cultures perform other, non-Anglo, forms of strategic planning.

The third interpretation is adopted here.

Aspects of formal strategic planning in Anglo companies reflect the culture in a number of other ways.

▋ Formal strategy planning is a DELIBERATE PROCESS, derived from conscious analysis of specified data and directed to meeting rational criteria. Dean and Sharfman (1996) conducted a longitudinal study of American companies to discover a positive correlation between decision success and rational decision-making processes. Rationality was defined in terms of how extensively the planners looked for information, analyzed this information, and negotiated the decision among group members.

But other cultures place greater reliance on knowledge of the situation derived from personal relationships and intuitions. These are informal sources that often cannot be justified as rational.

■ Formal strategy planning has a high tolerance of explicit COMPETITION and CONFLICT. Porter (1990), for example, sees the market as a battlefield and describes relations between companies in terms of "conflict," "forces," "threats," "power." The typical Anglo company uses strategy as a means of differentiating itself, by performing different activities from named rivals, or similar activities in different ways.

But other cultures are less tolerant of OPEN EXPRESSIONS of conflict – for instance, where needs to avoid uncertainty are higher. This does not mean that their strategies are not competitive, but rather that this aspect is covert. A 1995 company report by the Japanese company, Otsuka Pharmaceuticals, starts:

> Otsuka, people creating new products for better health worldwide. The prime goal of Otsuka is to create products which promote health around the world. The innovativeness of Otsuka's products is assured by its satellite research network system which allows individual researchers to give full play to their creativity.

This is typical in that it communicates the company's goals in terms of a universal mission and not of conflict with rivals. Porter (1996, p. 63) argued that Japanese companies (with some exceptions) do not openly compete; "rather, they imitate and emulate one another."

■ Planning is LONG TERM in designing strategy.

But other cultures may be more flexible in responding to changes in the environment, even though retaining long-term interests. Porter comments that Southeast Asian companies:

> ... do deals. They respond to opportunities. They are widely diversified because their opportunistic mode of operation drives them."[4]

■ Planning involves a relatively BUREAUCRATIC company structure. Established impersonal control systems are applied to designing and implementing the strategy.

In any culture, planning in a small company is always likely to be more flexible and less bureaucratic than in a large one. But given companies of an equivalent size, companies in *other*, non-Anglo, *cultures* may give less importance to bureaucratic priorities. Chapter 12 shows that Chinese family businesses in Southeast Asia tend to be hierarchical, and strategic decisions are made by the owner, often without consulting other family members.

■ Planning involves a tolerance of revolutionary and RADICAL CHANGE, and a belief that this can be organized. Hammer and Champy (1993) title their most famous book *Reengineering the Corporation: A Manifesto for Business Revolution*. And Taylor (1995, p. 71) writes that:

> Strategic management, or more accurately strategic leadership, is about managing radical change to achieve a dramatic improvement in performance.

But in other cultures, where tolerances of uncertainty are lower, radical change is not welcomed. Members prefer to make small incremental changes. Lasserre and Putti (1990, p. 23) write that the major characteristics of the business environment:

> ... indicate that corporate strategy formulation and implementation in Southeast Asia would be better served by the adoption of an incremental adjustment approach rather than by analytical strategic planning.

In sum, it is argued here that that the assumptions underlying formal planning in Anglo companies are not universal. The implication is that a strategy designed in an Anglo headquarters may not be automatically understood in a subsidiary set in some other cultural setting. Where the values are significantly different, strategic thinking has to be mediated before it can be effectively transplanted.

13.5.6 Transplanting strategic systems between cultures

This section deals with the problems of transplanting strategic management from one culture to another, and illustrates it with examples of implementation systems.

Strategic systems are commonly transplanted in

- international joint ventures;
- multinational companies owning foreign subsidiaries;
- deliberate borrowings from a foreign management system in order to resolve local management problems.

In these three circumstances cultural factors influence how easily the transplant can be made. When an implementation system is transplanted between widely varying cultural contexts inefficiencies are inevitable. Here are two examples.

TRANSPLANTING RE-ENGINEERING

Hammer and Champy's (1993) model of re-engineering reflected values in their American culture:

- *Low needs to avoid uncertainty.* It calls for ambiguity in job responsibilities, tolerance of change and restructuring processes, conflict and dismissals. It is highly stressful.
- *High individualism and low collectivism.* It calls for the erosion of departmental boundaries and demands individual initiative and decision making.
- *Low power distances.* It calls for reductions in middle management and management authority, and a flattening of the hierarchy.

Although the writers subsequently softened their hard-line position (for example, see Hammer, 1996), the relationship between the company and employees is contractual rather than ethical, and the company had no moral obligation to continue to keep redundant employees.

In sum, the principles of re-engineering reflect mainstream American business culture. The question is how far they can be transplanted to contexts with a different culture.

In 1995 Colin Jones and the present author conducted a small research project investigating the attitudes of Thai managers to re-engineering. It was hypothesized that cultural differences might prove to be a barrier to the adoption of re-engineering in Thai companies. Relative to American culture, Thai culture has:

- high needs to avoid uncertainty;
- low individualism and high collectivism;
- high power distances (Hofstede, 2001).

The relationship between the company and employees has an ethical dimension, and managers are expected (by employees and generally by society) to consider the interests of their workforce.

Some of the 42 managers interviewed had thought about the topic only superficially: "I am interested because it is a new idea in management, particularly in globalization." But the great majority were investigating the implications for their companies or were already involved in re-engineering. None expected it to be easy. The relationship between Thai manager and employee has a moral dimension which poses problems for restructuring: "Culture is a factor. If a worker has been with you for 20 years can you fire him without emotion in your mind? You have to find him another job, perhaps in another one of your companies." A dislike for radically changing work routines and organizational structure was expressed frequently: "When you re-engineer a lot of people suffer. They don't want to learn the computer [but] they feel they will not have a job;" "People see change and get scared. They think they will lose their jobs." The general problems of building teams across unit boundaries, even in un-engineered companies, were noted by a few. One said "we [already] have a problem with different experts. The mineral engineers, geologists, metallurgists, so on, they all think they are right and do not want to talk to each other."

The informants were most concerned about the implications for hierarchical control. "People get used to what they have done before. They get used to power, they get used to layers [of hierarchy] and get used to lots of people to serve them;" "In Thai culture people are used to looking up and waiting to be told what to do. That makes re-engineering difficult."

As for the general implications: "Sometimes the culture of the foreigner cannot be adapted and Thai people cannot accept it. Some parts of re-engineering can be used for Thai culture but I don't believe all of them." Informants were undecided over the degree of adaptation needed; in general, serious difficulties were thought more likely in a family company than in the subsidiary of a Western multinational. As to who should lead the re-engineering process, managers shared a suspicion of teams exclusively composed of foreigners, who "don't know Thai culture;" teams must include Thais.

In this cultural context, incremental change is preferred to the ambiguities of radical change in the structure: "It takes time in Thai culture. You can't re-engineer all sections together." Some informants doubted whether this gradual approach could, strictly speaking, be labeled re-engineering at all: "Maybe it cannot work in a Thai company because it should change the structure and the people, and most Thai people follow the old [strategy] of preferring to make small, small improvements but re-engineering means change everything." The ambiguities involved in making a change can be offset by appropriately communicating needs for the strategic transplant, advantages of the change, and new responsibilities; "In Thai culture you have to convince people."

These interviews seemed to support the hypothesis, and McKenna's (1995, p. 16) conclusion – based on other data – that:

> the message of business re-engineering is inappropriate in certain environments and cultures at present, although it may indeed be the message necessary in the future.

The general point is to raise the question of how strategic systems can be applied from one culture to another.

TRANSPLANTING THE QUALITY CIRCLE

When Japanese companies first began to transplant the quality circle from the United States, they prepared at length. They analyzed the cultural implications of the technique and the conditions under which it could be grafted on to their existing structures and within the cultural context. In transplanting, they adapted.

In the 1970s, American companies were slipping back in the race against Japanese competition. In an attempt to emulate their rivals they began "re-importing" the quality circle, but usually without attempting to re-adapt it and most failed. This was in spite of warnings. Schein (1981), for instance, argued against solutions that did not sufficiently recognize the differences in the environments in which Japanese and American companies operated. Japanese cultural practices could not be transplanted to an American setting as though they were rice seedlings.

When an implementation system is borrowed inappropriately and no attempt is made to adapt it to the new context, one of three things happen:

- the system is rejected;
- the system functions as planned, but its operation transfers the problem elsewhere in the total system – as when a new road designed to alleviate traffic pressure creates new pressure points elsewhere;
- the process functions as planned, but its operation causes new problems.

Japanese success in adopting the American concept of quality circles demonstrates that systems *can* be successfully transplanted. But every system reflects the cultural priorities of its original context, and adaptation may be necessary before it can be transplanted.

13.5.7 Communicating the strategy to stakeholders

One aspect of strategic management is communicating planning to those who need to know. These persons are often referred to as the STAKEHOLDERS. The concept is imprecise. For example, David (1993, p. 98) defines them as the individuals and groups of persons who have a special stake or claim on the company. Stakeholders include employees, managers, stockholders, boards of directors, customers, suppliers, distributors, creditors, governments (local, state, federal, and foreign), unions, competitors, environmental groups, and the general public.

But these categories cover almost everyone; if everyone is to be treated as equally "special," no one is special. David recognizes that:

> all stakeholders' claims on an organization cannot be pursued with equal emphasis. A good mission statement indicates the relative attention that an organization will devote to meeting the claims of various stakeholders. *(p. 98)*

Given the strategic interests of his/her particular company, the manager first needs to decide what aspects of the strategy should be communicated to each group; and second, which groups of stakeholders deserve priority treatment in implementing the strategy. These are the groups in whose interests the company is being run. The decision made at this point entails deciding which groups of stakeholders need *not* be given priority treatment.

In practice, this often means weighing the interests of shareholders against those of employees. Yoshimori (1995, p. 33) notes that in the United States and United Kingdom a "monistic" outlook is dominant; the firm is perceived as the private property of its shareholders. Germany and to some extent France hold a "dualistic" outlook; a premium is placed on shareholder interests, but the interests of employees are also taken into account. Japan takes a "pluralistic" approach. This:

> assumes that the firm belongs to all the stakeholders, with the employees' interests taking precedence. This ... manifests itself in the form of long-term employment for employees and long-term trading relations among various other stakeholders (the main bank, major suppliers, subcontractors, distributors), loosely called keiretsu.

In dealing with corporate governance in newly emerging Asian economies, Phan (2001, p. 131) examines the relationship between owners, managers, and other stakeholders. The point to emerge is that precise definition may be less significant than the identification of the relationships existing between stakeholders, and how these relationships are expressed.

13.6 Emergent Strategy

Thus far we have focused on strategy as an attempt to control future activities. Anglo organizations, in particular, have traditionally shown a need for linear planning, in which the strategic exercise consists of a series of stages, so far as possible distinct from each other. For example, data collection precedes planning, which precedes implementation. But this presumes a business environment in which investment in these stages is justified.

But the new environment is increasingly unpredictable. Change has become discontinuous in the sense that the unexpected is now ordinary, and our reservoir of experience is no longer adequate to deal with it (Andrews, 2005). For example, we have recently been faced with the September 11 crisis, the war in Iraq, SARS. Michaud and Thoenig (2003, p. 14) eloquently describe the implications of turbulence for the business world:

> Protection against competition has been reduced. Time horizons have shortened. The economic battlefield has changed radically. Financial death is now more sudden and more certain for anyone who does not know how to state and restate strategies and actions, a daily position and a future.

The rate of environmental change means that getting goods to market as fast as possible becomes increasingly the one priority. In order to satisfy local markets as quickly as possible, decision making has to be localized and the functions of centralized control are eroded (Allee, 2003, pp. 29–30). The planning function is among those weakened.

13.6.1 *An emerging response to change*

Industries adapt to this crisis differently. Petroleum companies make massive long-term investments in prospecting, drilling, extracting, and refining, and still often have planning horizons of 25 years. Newpaper companies manufacture a new product once or even several times a day, and show very little interest in any strategic planning.

When the company is forced to modify its perceptions of itself on a regular basis in response to changes over which it has no control, the STRATEGIC DIRECTION EMERGES from small steps made in response to change in the wider environment. Instead of depending on time-consuming processes of data collection and analysis, managers apply simple rules-of-thumb telling them how to exploit opportunities and to guard against threats.

For example, a retailing company, Apex, has a policy of starting a branch in every town with a population of more than 100,000 where no more than three of its main competitors also have branches. When six or more competitors are represented in a location where Apex operates, Apex sells its interests and reinvests elsewhere. Similar rules determine the range of brands offered on the market. Thus the coherent development of Apex does not result from deliberate, long-term and formal planning, but emerges over time.

Emergent strategy occurs as a rational response to an increasingly chaotic environment in some cultures; elsewhere, it may always have been preferred. In cultural contexts where the insecurities of long-term planning are not readily accepted, planning may naturally be fluid, and the ordering of planning stages is naturally plastic. Hampden-Turner and Trompenaars (1997, p. 145) gave the example of the Japanese use of the quality circle:

ACTION PRECEDES PLANNING. In other words, you – or your competitor – act first and this leads you to plan, implement and check. The circle exemplifies action-learning, not the hypothesis and deduction of traditional inner-directed science.

The son of a business family in the Philippines said: "We never write a strategy. We make decisions every evening at the family dinner." When this was reported to a group of businessmen from Saudi Arabia, they commented: "Here it is entirely different. We make our business decisions over breakfast and review them when we eat in the evening." In practice, of course, the differences were slight. In both cultures the businesspeople were managing their future directions on a strictly incremental basis. Data were collected from observations of the markets, meetings with customers and suppliers, reactions to the media. The sum of recognizing and understanding the opportunities and threats was continually being modified. Action was taken on a day-by-day basis, in response to principles and this learned knowledge.

This pragmatic approach to doing business may be confusing to outsiders. The absence of "hard" data sources that are generally available is sometimes perceived as an "informational void." Haley and Tan (1996) contrast the availability of strategic journals in the United States and Southeast Asia, and argue that the information necessary for sound strategic decision-making is absent from the latter region. However, the rapid development of Asian economies over the past few decades suggests that this lack does not necessarily betoken strategic impotence. And even a wealth of data does not guarantee good decision making – as the fate of even major corporations such as Enron shows. In the new economic realities, the development of "secret" knowledge may be as effective as the conventional treatment of structured information.

13.6.2   Recording the emergent strategy

Emergent strategy is recorded when the manager needs *post hoc* justification for the steps taken. The strategic direction is made clear for the benefit of stakeholders, including investors who need to be assured that they will benefit, and managers who need a clear picture of the point from which they have traveled and the possible destinations ahead. An accurate record raises morale.

On the other hand, if the management and investment teams are small, possibly comprising family members, only a modest record may be considered necessary. The strategic direction of the company is manifested in its activities, the financial records, lists of customers and suppliers.

13.7   Implications for the Manager

Apply this model in a multinational company that you know. Use it to propose how a strategic system might be transplanted from headquarters to a target subsidiary.

MODEL FOR TRANSPLANTING A STRATEGIC SYSTEM

1   (a) *Define your strategic goals.*
    (b) *Define your aim in transplanting the system.* How might the system help you achieve your goals?
2   *Collect information about the system.*
3   *Analyze the system.* How does it reflect the cultural and non-cultural characteristics of its home context? (Take into account factors associated with the economy, industry, market, national culture, and organizational culture.) What is the system expected to achieve within its home context?
4   *Analyze the target context.* How closely does the system reflect the target context? What are the relevant cultural and non-cultural characteristics of the target context that will affect implementation?
5   (a) *Design plans for adapting the system* so that it can achieve your goals (stage 1) and be appropriate to the target context (stage 4).
    (b) *Design plans for communicating the adapted system* within the organization in the target context and to appropriate parties in its environment.
    (c) *Design plans for any necessary training.*
6   *Implement the adapted system* (implement stage 5).
7   *Monitor the implementation* (stage 6).
8   *Modify as necessary* (depending on the stage 7 output).

13.8 SUMMARY

This chapter has discussed a range of approaches in designing and implementing strategy. At one extreme, a strategic plan is designed in a formal process; at the other, strategy emerges from an incremental process of small changes. The factors which influence the approach taken include the emphasis given to resources held within the company as a means of securing advantage, its need to position itself within the competitive environment of its industry, cultural factors and the perception of how far ahead the company can plan in response to change.

Section 13.2 dealt with the notion of FORMAL STRATEGY PLANNING. The financial goals always have prime importance, first in determining the subordinate goals and then the priorities expressed in the plan. RESOURCE priorities were examined in section 13.3. These included members' knowledge which can be used to give competitive advantage. Section 13.4 focused on how the company gains market share by analyzing the industry and wider business environments, and POSITIONING THE COMPANY to take advantage of them. In practice, resource analysis and environmental analysis go hand in hand, and whatever emphasis is taken, the other cannot be ignored.

The success of any strategic plan depends strongly on how it is IMPLEMENTED. Section 13.5 focused on issues of how strategy designed in one context can be implemented in another. The problems of transplanting an implementation system were examined. Section 13.6 dealt with EMERGENT STRATEGY.

13.9 EXERCISE

Read this short case and answer the questions.

Mr Charnvit was a Thai manager working for a Bangkok reinsurance company. He was generally reckoned to be an expert in his field, and the best in the country. He was growing old, and close to retirement, but every time the CEO suggested that it was now time that he passed on his specialized skills and understanding of client needs to other managers, he hesitated. He prided himself on this knowledge and the reputation that it gave him, and did not wish to share it.

Top management became increasingly concerned. If Mr Charnvit could be persuaded to pass on his secrets, the company would benefit greatly. On the other hand, if he became incapacitated or died before training his successors, the company would have lost a prized asset. Many of his clients would move their business to other firms and the company would lose its competitive position as market leader.

QUESTIONS

(a) Why might Mr Charnvit's knowledge be included as a company asset?

(b) Why might Mr Charnvit's knowledge *not* be included as a company asset?

(c) Applying your answers to (a) and (b), write a definition of company knowledge: "Company knowledge is defined as......................................"

(d) Is Mr Charnvit's knowledge:
- A strength?
- A weakness?
- An opportunity?
- A threat?

Notes

1   Chester Dawson, "No kidding – a new market for baby food," *Business Week*, January 27, 2003.

2   Richard McGregor, "Surviving drives the strategy at Fosun," *Financial Times*, September 22, 2003.

3   Tom Lester, "Accounting for knowledge assets," *Financial Times*, February 21, 1996.

4   Michael Porter, "It's time to grow up," *Far Eastern Economic Review*, March 14, 1996.

CHAPTER FOURTEEN
Headquarters and Subsidiary

14.1   Introduction

Two short cases illustrate different relationships between headquarters and the subsidiary. First, a locally owned steel company in Korea established a guesthouse for the use of its business visitors. The guesthouse manager had once worked in the top hotel in Seoul and he took care in selecting and training an expert staff. The guesthouse was an immense success. The company decided to expand it and open it to the general public.

The management team in the new hotel were local and perfectly understood the local market, and they made increasing profits. But unhappily, the managers of the steel business had failed to update their technology and the company went into decline. Eventually it was purchased by an American steel company, Minnesota-Blandings, and the purchase included the hotel. But after a few years, the new owners began to think that the local management problems were insuperable, and the expense involved in expatriating headquarters staff unjustified. They then sold on the steel works but kept the highly profitable hotel, which had again expanded its facilities.

Minnesota-Blandings was now the proud owner of one of the best hotels outside Seoul. But top management decided that there was no point incurring the cost of expatriating anyone from headquarters to manage it. First, their people knew the culture of the United States, not Korea. Second, they understood steel, not the hospitality industry. Third, the Korean managers were so successful that they did not need advice from outside. So the American owners decided that little direct control was needed, and so long as the hotel continued to meet the financial goals negotiated every year, the Koreans were empowered to run their business as they thought best.

The second case involves an American soft drinks company, Berry Cola Inc. Berry Cola was the company's main product, produced throughout the world according to the same recipe. The brand message was that when drinking Berry Cola customers shared in a global culture and lifestyle. They were members of a single community. Hence the company was determined that there should be no local variations in the product, and for many years ensured this by managing all their international subsidiaries with managers expatriated from the Wisconsin headquarters.

Over time, local staff in the Southeast Asian subsidiaries began to agitate for the appointment of local managers to top positions. Reluctantly, the board agreed, and a Thai marketing manager was appointed in the Thai subsidiary. Everyone agreed that Khun Charnvit was an excellent choice to be a pioneer. He was young, highly intelligent, ambitious, and an excellent manager.

But within a few months, it became clear that Khun Charnvit was exceeding his job description. He had started a new advertising campaign that appealed entirely to local tastes and interests, and was rumored to be developing his own products. Top management decided that these initiatives were not compatible with company policy, and reluctantly they asked for his resignation. He was succeeded by an American marketing manager posted from headquarters.

These two cases show very different control styles. The Minnesota-Blandings hotel attracted a local Korean clientele and was expertly managed. Headquarters realized that the appointment of an expatriate manager would not add value, and would not justify the cost. They did not need to invest in overseeing day-to-day operations, and as a result they adopted an appropriately light control style. On the other hand, the relationship that Berry Cola Inc. had with their customers worldwide meant that headquarters had to guarantee that all aspects of production and marketing met global standards, and for these commercial reasons applied centralized controls. When factors such as the product, the market and competition, and rights to technology enforce that headquarters keep full control of all operations, highly centralized control can be more efficient and justify the expense.

Both headquarters were American, and so in this case national cultural difference was not an issue in deciding why the two companies should adopt such different management styles.

This chapter deals with RISK and CONTROL of factors likely to cause risk. It first examines the relationship between the company and the local environment, then between headquarters and subsidiary. It examines different multinational structures, and examines the factors that influence the choice of structure and how the headquarters chooses to control its foreign investments.

14.2   Risk for the Multinational

When the company decides that investment abroad provides a tool for securing its strategic goals, it chooses from a range of alternative structures, the last three of which in the list below (international joint venture – discussed in the next chapter – merger, and subsidiary) involve the company in making investments abroad – that is, developing as a multinational company (MNC):

- various agreements – for example, a licensing contract with a local company; a partnership; franchise; agreements for R&D, product development, servicing and manufacturing;
- a turnkey agreement – that is, contracting to construct and/or deliver a "ready to operate" system, plant, etc.;
- an agency or representation;
- an international joint venture (IJV) formed with a local partner (discussed in the next chapter;
- merging with a local company (this is attractive to companies within a highly competitive market because by pooling resources they increase their prospects of survival – for instance, banks must invest massively in computer systems in order to save on labor costs: they need an international network in order to attract an international clientele and a merger makes this possible);
- a subsidiary, either from scratch or from an ongoing company that has been acquired.

A company may apply different structures in different countries, for different reasons. For example, Acme Company based in the United Kingdom decides to sell its products in Country A, where it has no previous experience. It first contracts sales to a local company under licence, and plans that when headquarters managers have learned something about local market conditions, to make an investment that will be more rewarding. The company also wishes to develop a new product in Country B. Managers have experience of the country and realize that needs for local knowledge and contacts with the government are essential; therefore they negotiate an R&D/production joint venture with a local partner that has the necessary expertise. The company has considerable experience of working in Country C and has no concerns about operating in that environment. The preferred option is to establish a 100 percent owned subsidiary – but first it needs local plant, and so a turnkey agreement is contracted with a local property developer to build the factory.

MNCs were defined in section 11.2.5 as companies that own and manage investments located in a country or countries other than that of headquarters. Any investment made in some other country that conforms to different political, economic, legal, and cultural structures incurs some risk, even if the level is low. An inappropriate investment raises the level of risk. In the example above, when Acme Company moves into Country A, it selects a licencing agreement, because this provides an opportunity to learn about the environment, and thus reduce the level of risk in future dealings. Given the company's lack of experience in Country A, the immediate establishment of a subsidiary might be counted risky. Whether or not the degree of risk is justified depends on the expected earnings.

When selecting the location for a new investment, the company looks for basic infrastructure and a potential for economic development. It chooses *not* to invest in a country which:

■ lacks an attractive investment climate;
■ lacks skilled human resources at attractive prices;
■ is perceived as unacceptably RISKY.

Such conditions can be found in many areas of the world. Representatives of the developing world argue that they arise because of the greed and short-sightedness of the developed countries. For example, the collapse of the September 2003 talks to liberalize trade and reform agriculture worldwide was blamed on the Europeans' refusal to cut state subsidies to their farmers, and the Americans' insistence that developing nations abolish or reduce tariffs protecting their markets from the dumping of heavily subsidized American exports.

14.2.1 Environmental risks

The environment is a major source of risk. Knight and Pretty (2003) calculate that risks from the business environment account for 46 percent of all risk (other risks arise from: transactions, 17 percent; operations, 14 percent; finance, 14 percent; investor relations, 9 percent). Environmental risks may stem from the competition, economic context, and political context.

COMPETITIVE RISK arises where:

• competitive structures are unstable;
• local and international new entrants threaten to break into the market;
• new and substitute products threaten;
• new technologies threaten;
• changes arise in structures of supply and demand.

ECONOMIC RISK is perceived where:

• public resources suffer waste, corruption, and mismanagement;
• economic and financial conditions are unsatisfactory;
• potential markets and their proximity are poor;
• natural resources are not locally available, and are expensive;
• infrastructure systems are poor;
• local labor is inadequately skilled and educational standards are low;
• inducements offered to invest are poor;
• taxation is discriminatory;

- tariffs, import and export controls are punitive;
- payments cannot be enforced;
- unfair local competition is protected by local officials;
- repatriation of earnings is restricted.

POLITICAL RISK is perceived where:

- industrial and legal disputes are given official support;
- war, revolution, and terrorist attacks occur or threaten;
- the subsidiary's assets are confiscated. Forced divestment is termed expropriation when one (or a few) firms are affected, and nationalization when all firms in an industry (or industries) are affected.

The concept of risk is difficult to objectify: Borner, Brunetti, and Weder (1995) attempted this by quantifying political credibility on a scale of 1 to 6 – with 1 indicating a government that is completely trustworthy and predictable. However, Thawley (1996) argued that the political performance ratings are not correlated with actual private investment and economic growth, and that they overlook expectations of future growth. And an apparently risky location, that frightens away its competitors, may offer commercial advantages to an entrepreneurial company that has a relatively higher tolerance of risk. For example, a company gambles on maintaining its investment in a risk spot because it hopes that this gesture will win government support and favored treatment in the future.

14.2.2 *The government's perception of risk*

A government usually welcomes multinational investment, in particular when it leads to the transfer of technology and the growth of labor skills. The larger investors, who demonstrate a greater commitment to local development and are less likely to suddenly quit or go out of business leaving debts, may be given preferential treatment. However, under some circumstances it may feel itself at risk from the activities of an MNC. This occurs when the activities of the subsidiary are perceived to:

- threaten the country's growth or defence;
- develop a monopoly position that stifles local competition;
- attack a powerful local monopoly;
- improperly repatriate profits;
- hire talented locals away from local companies;
- exert unfair influence in local politics and legislation;
- exert a negative influence on local culture.

Finally, trust breaks down when the subsidiary fails to meet its contracted conditions for the transfer of technology.

The government and company need to communicate their interests, and to try to understand the other side. In a rapidly changing world their interests are sure to change. These shifts may result from internal factors over which they have some control (a new financial policy, new strategic priorities) or from factors over which they have little control – for example, the development of competing technologies, changes in the marketplace. When interests diverge significantly, the company is no longer welcome.

14.2.3 The company reassures the local community

When the company establishes a new subsidiary, it tries to overcome basic environmental risks by reassuring the local community of its intentions to act as a good corporate citizen.

When Bayer, the German pharmaceutical company, first proposed establishing a chemical plant in Taichung harbor, Taiwan, the official response was cautious. A similar plan by du Pont, to build a factory in Lukang, had led to unprecedented demonstrations by local people concerned by the threat to their environment. Taichung was a small and traditional town, and the government wanted to avoid a repeat performance.

Bayer decided to form good relations with the community. Senior officials visited influential Taichung leaders, and the aged and respected. They showed respect to the chairman of the representative committee. At the traditional Moon Cake festival, the company spent $10,000 on cakes, purchased from the town's best-known shop. When they visited the townspeople to distribute the cakes company representatives explained the plan, the expected impact on the environment, and how the local community might benefit economically.

Such an approach is intended to gain initial acceptance and in time to develop a lasting partnership. It provides a model for other companies moving into an unfamiliar cultural environment. However, this alone cannot guarantee a risk-free future.

14.2.4 How the company recognizes and responds to risk

Measures of risk are always influenced by personality and culture. Suppose that a contract to invest in a country in the throes of civil war is offered to two companies. Company A rejects the offer on the basis that the dangers are too great, but Company B calculates the possible earnings when the strife has been resolved and accepts – cheered by the fact that its competitor has withdrawn.

The company tries to protect itself by controlling those factors in which it perceives greater risk. The headquarters sees the subsidiary at greater risk when:

- it is young, and newly established, rather than acquired;
- it is under-performing;
- it is operating in an unstable environment, where the environmental risk factors listed in section 14.2.1 are significant.

In any of these instances, it might decide to fill senior posts in the subsidiary with its own expatriated managers. Further factors are discussed below.

14.2.5   *Risk in technology*

The following areas of technology were distinguished in section 4.3.7:

(a)   product technology, including patents;
(b)   the processes and technical knowledge needed to operate the product technology;
(c)   managerial techniques and systems;
(d)   experiential or tacit knowledge (see section 13.3).

Here we are concerned with perceptions of risk in the development of (a), product technology, and in the use of (b), the related process technologies.

Headquarters feels needs to safeguard its product technologies and control their use when there is a possibility that the technology will be stolen. Headquarters also wants to be confident that the product technology is being properly operated and that skilled technicians are on hand to repair it efficiently if it should break down.

An international food company operating in Indonesia expatriated only production staff and engineers. Indonesians staffed all other posts – the general manager, finance manager, marketing manager, and so on. Headquarters had prioritized this function because it realized the importance of maintaining continuous production. If production was interrupted and the schedule of weekly or even daily deliveries to its many outlets across the country broke down, the company would lose its competitive advantage over other food producers who were not able to promise regular deliveries. Hence it was essential that the plant be properly operated and kept in good condition. Headquarters did not necessarily doubt the qualifications of its local production staff, but the expatriates were bound to the company for their continuing careers and pensions, and so were highly motivated to maintain standards.

14.2.6   *Risk in the culture*

Headquarters is more likely to perceive the national culture expressed in the foreign subsidiary as a source of risk when its own national culture has high needs to avoid uncertainty and the cultural distance is perceived to be wide.

Hofstede's (2001) model showed that when the national culture of the headquarters has high needs to avoid uncertainty, the greater is headquarters' insecurity over subsidiary independence and the greater the tendency to centralize subsidiary structures under headquarters control. This helps explain the greater expatriate staffing of Japanese subsidiaries than of either European or United States subsidiaries.

Rosenzweig and Singh (1991) assumed the notion of cultural distance and developed a number of hypotheses based on an earlier version of Hofstede's model: for instance, that:

- the cultural similarity of a multinational subsidiary to other firms in the host country is positively related to the tolerance for uncertainty in the headquarters country culture;
- reliance on formal mechanisms of control is positively related to the distance between the national cultures of headquarters and subsidiary.

The implication is that when members of the headquarters country are tolerant of ambiguity, headquarters permits the subsidiary greater autonomy. When the subsidiary exercises its freedom to respond to local conditions, it develops management and market systems that express local priorities rather than headquarters-culture priorities. It responds in much the same way as do locally owned companies. But when the headquarters culture reflects high needs to avoid uncertainty, higher levels of control are imposed.

14.2.7 Risk in the industry

Some industries are more exposed to risk. High-risk industries include banking, securities and commodity brokers, and highly technical industries such as telecommunications. Any breach of security is bound to be more expensive than a breach in a relatively low-tech industry such as rubber production or textile manufacture. When the perception of risk is high, headquarters expatriates more staff to control procedures and protect company interests. Thus the number of expatriates gives one (not the only) indication of how seriously the headquarters perceives the risks of doing business in that environment.

Harzing (2001) looked at numbers of headquarters nationals expatriated to top management posts in subsidiaries around the world. Her results reflected Hofstede's rankings for uncertainty avoidance. The Scandinavian countries, which have high toleration of uncertainty, had the lowest numbers of expatriates and the Far East and Middle East the highest. With regards to service industry, the lowest numbers were found in business and management services (12.7 percent) and the highest in banking (76.1 percent) and securities and commodity brokers (84.8 percent). In manufacturing industry, she found the lowest expatriate staffing levels in commodity-based and usually low technology industries such as rubber (20 percent) and stone, clay and glass products (23.6 percent). The highest were in the relatively higher technology industries of telecommunications equipment (53.2 percent) and motor vehicles and parts (62.2 percent).

In sum, headquarters expatriates were more common in a subsidiary whose headquarters was in a country with relatively high needs to avoid uncertainty; in a large MNC; and where there is perceived to be a wide cultural distance between the national cultures of headquarters and subsidiary.

14.2.8 Risk in transferring competitive advantage

Competitive advantage secured in headquarters or in one subsidiary cannot be automatically transferred to another subsidiary. What has advantage in the first market may have less in another if customers there prefer a competing product. Sustained investment is needed to secure that advantage in the new market. The company may be forced to invest heavily in developing the complementary assets that help secure the advantage – including staffing the subsidiary, training new employees, and transferring technologies.

Beugré and Offodile (2001) use data collected in sub-Saharan Africa to argue that an organization's policies can lose their effectiveness when transferred to a new cultural environment. They develop a culture-fit model that makes a synthesis between modern management techniques and local cultures.

14.3   Control

Control costs money; insufficient control can result in a loss of profits and over-control costs in terms of expatriation. How does the firm find the appropriate balance? The company control style may have to be modified for each overseas investment. Each exists in a different environment, and has different resourcing and staffing capacities.

Decisions have to be made about:

- what sort of control is needed;
- how the appropriate control is enforced.

The instruments for control from which the company selects include:

- the structural relationship;
- organizational culture;
- budgets and other financial instruments;
- technology;
- staffing policy (examples have already been noted above and chapter 16 deals with the topic in detail).

14.3.1   Controlling through the structural relationship

Bartlett and Ghoshal (1989) classified four models of companies operating foreign interests: global, multinational, international, and transnational companies. Each of these expresses a different structural relationship between headquarters and subsidiary. The particular relationship in any one company is determined by such factors as the industry, product type, and market forces.

▌ The GLOBAL company centralizes its key functions – including marketing and finance. Headquarters produces the new technology and disseminates it to subsidiaries. Cost advantages are achieved through economies of scale and global-scale operations. The need for efficiency and economies of scale means that products are developed that exploit needs felt across the range of countries. Specific local needs tend to be ignored. The fictionalized Berry Cola in the introductory case illustrates this model.

■ The headquarters of the MULTINATIONAL company decides financial policy but otherwise permits subsidiaries considerable autonomy in determining management style and responding to local product needs and markets.

■ The headquarters of the INTERNATIONAL company retains considerable control over the subsidiary's management systems and marketing policy, but less so than in the global company. Products and technologies are developed for the home market, extended to other countries with similar market characteristics, then diffused elsewhere. The developmental sequence is decided on the basis of managing the product life-cycle as efficiently and flexibly as possible.

■ The TRANSNATIONAL company evolved in the 1980s in response to environmental forces and simultaneous demands for global efficiency, national responsiveness, and worldwide learning. The transnational model combines features of multinational, global, and international models. A product is designed to be globally competitive, and is differentiated and adapted by local subsidiaries to meet local market demands. Whereas the international company originates the product in the headquarters country and then transfers it to the subsidiary, the transnational might reverse this process. Resources, including technology and managerial talent, might be distributed among subsidiaries and integrated between them through strong interdependencies.

Griffin and Pustay (1999) distinguished three types, the multidomestic, global, and transnational.

■ The MULTIDOMESTIC company views all country markets as different. It encourages the independence of its subsidiaries in marketing and operations.

■ The GLOBAL company views the world as a single marketplace. It standardizes all marketing and production facilities.

■ The TRANSNATIONAL company is structured so that its operating units can operate independently. It tries to combine the benefits of global scale with the benefits of local responsiveness. Complex organizational structures are established to coordinate two-way communications between parent and subsidiaries. What happens in practice is that the headquarters takes decisions for some functions such as production and R&D, whereas functions such as marketing and human resource management are adapted to its local culture by the subsidiary.

14.3.2   *The transnational and its environment*

The TRANSNATIONAL evolves in response to constant change in the environment. For example, management recognizes that in a particular culture, customers greatly value their person-to-person relationships with members of the sales and marketing teams, and that local staff are far better equipped to develop these relationships than are expatriates.

Andrews et al. (2003) discuss this point in the context of Southeast Asia, and argue that many Western-based companies rely overmuch on systems and strategies developed at headquarters. For example, Castrol modeled its Equipment Services Division in Thailand on a parallel unit that had been highly successful in the United Kingdom and in Malaysia. But the Thai team rejected it, partly because local market segmentations differed significantly, and partly because:

> the working processes assumed by the ESD unit were held by the vast majority of interviewees to be culturally misaligned. The formality, professional and official nature of the ESD setup – deemed in the West to be its strong point – was branded "useless," "unsuitable," and "damaging" in an environment where customers were gained and held almost purely on the basis of personal relationships.   *(p. 211)*

The transnational aims to develop subsidiaries that are *both* highly flexible in their own locations *and* also closely integrated with other subsidiaries. Blumen (2002) says that in this new "age of connective leadership" managers "learn to integrate interdependence and diversity" (p. 90). He/she learns from its environment and then makes the acquired knowledge accessible throughout the company; and so is also responsible for applying the lessons learned by others. They share not only flows of parts, finished goods, and capital, but also locally acquired skills and knowledge. A manager who succeeds in one branch is likely to be posted to some other.

14.3.3   The structural models have to be flexible

In its ideal form the transnational is able to respond and adapt to its environment as though it were an organism. In Allee's (2003, p. 34) words, nowadays:

> we are fascinated with networks, systems and complexity. We are beginning to view organizations as living systems.

But the Bartlett/Ghoshal and Griffin/Pustay frameworks are ideal, and very few companies fit precisely into any one category. The Swedish telecommunications giant Ericsson is frequently cited as an example of a transnational. Ericsson learned from the Australian telecommunications market, transferred the knowledge back home, then applied it worldwide. The company developed:

- an interdependence of resources and responsibilities among organizational units;
- a set of strong cross-unit integrating devices;
- a strong corporate identification and a worldwide management perspective.

However, Ericsson does not entirely fit the transnational model. The majority of local managers are Swedes, appointed from their pool of career international managers based in Stockholm. It is true that their products are varied for different regional markets but these variations are dictated by local production and licensing requirements rather than by taste.

14.3.4 The case of Coca-Cola

Every successful company evolves over time in response to commercial and competitive pressures, and may move between categories. For many years, Coca-Cola was highly globalized. The main product sold everywhere, and all aspects of marketing and production are still controlled from Atlanta. For example, the Middle East and North Africa division was headquartered far outside the region, in the United Kingdom.

However, at the end of 1999, Coca-Cola profits were falling.

> Along with its dismal earnings news last month, the company disclosed that bottlers in some key markets had too much soft-drink concentrate on hand, suggesting to some analysts that Coke had stuffed the pipeline to meet its own volume targets.
>
> The bleak performance left Coca-Cola looking more vulnerable as its once impeccable public image was stained by crises – from the biggest product recall in company history to a racial discrimination lawsuit filed by a group of its black employees.
>
> The company has run afoul of regulators in Europe, Mexico and Australia over its plan to acquire the Cadbury Schweppes brands and over marketing practices like giving incentives to retailers to sell Coke instead of rival products.[1]

The company responded to these problems by appointing a new CEO, Douglas Daft, and he naturally started by introducing a new strategy. He had plans:

> to eliminate 6,000 jobs, or about one fifth of its workforce, as part of a major restructuring.... The cuts affect 2,500 positions at the company's Atlanta headquarters, 2,700 outside the US, and 800 jobs elsewhere in the US.... [Mr Daft] was trying to decentralize Coca-Cola's operations so the company can react more quickly to local conditions.[2]

An immediate example of this decentralization was that the Middle East and north Africa headquarters was moved from London to Manama in Bahrain. This transfer was part of the

> "strategic alignment of the company in terms of becoming more local and driving the business closer to the markets," [the divisional president] said.
>
> "We kind of lost our way for a while, we weren't connected with consumers, with our customers, with our bottlers," he said. "This is really saying we are local, it's still one product but it's got to be connected locally."[3]

This shows a company needing to respond to local markets more immediately, and so modifying the structural relationship between headquarters and subsidiary. Coca-Cola no longer exemplifies the systems category of the global company as precisely as it had done in 1999. In terms of the Bartlett and Ghoshal framework, it has moved towards the international model, and of the Griffin and Pustay framework, a modified global-multidomestic model.

14.3.5   Strategic human resources in the transnational

Human resource management contributes to strategy when it influences what corporate goals are planned and implemented.

The human resource manager advises top management on the skills and knowledge that the company has at its disposal and can expect to acquire in the future. At a time when the importance of knowledge creation is recognized the old question asked the human resource manager, "where can we find the labor to perform operation X?" gives way to questions "what strategic advantages do our labor resources give us?" and "what operations should we be planning in order to apply them most effectively?" This reflects the resource-based theory of the firm, which perceives the MNC as a network of resources transacted among subsidiaries. In practice, the "strategy will determine how these resource transactions are structured among the various subunits" (Taylor et al., 1996, p. 967).

The transnational has to learn from its different environments and the experience of its various other branches in order to become effective. It needs managers capable of this learning, and this places a responsibility on the HR department to select and train managers capable of creating and using knowledge. These managers must be flexible. They will be keen to take part in planning their careers across the range of units.

In practice, an awareness of the importance of developing capabilities and new areas of knowledge should subfuse all management activities, not merely formal activities associated with the HR department. And the logic of strategic HR is that the entire company becomes HR-oriented, so that questions of defining strategic goals in reference to likely future capabilities become the concern of all units. All managers acquire international interests, and those bound for expatriate postings should be capable of taking assignments wherever the company decides to use them.

How far is this practical? Forster (2000) makes the point that although business operations may be increasingly international, this doesn't mean that managers are. The notion of the "pure" international manager is vague. The individual has his/her preferences for culture and may not operate at the same level of efficiency everywhere. He/she has personal interests and plans, and may have limited tolerance to the dislocation and upheaval that accompanies continually relocating to new assignments. Perhaps many managers are capable of maintaining this routine for a few years, but very few throughout a career.

The staffing implications are discussed at greater length in chapter 16.

14.3.6   Loosening control by empowering the subsidiary

The theory of organizational empowerment means giving the subsidiary greater control over its own affairs. Supporters argue that benefits accrue from decentralizing the company and encouraging the subsidiary to make decisions that previously belonged to headquarters. It assumes that local staff are sufficiently expert to take over from expatriates, or will soon become expert. Empowerment motivates staff, releases energy, builds commitment, and develops new skills. They feel a far greater sense of ownership over operations and the outcomes. Capable local managers emerge, and can be further developed at headquarters. Stewart (1995, p. 65) argues that:

> people must be given freedom and space, encouraged to work to visions and objectives they help create. They must have quick feedback of the results of their efforts.

The move to self-management benefits the individual, the subsidiary, and the company. When an empowered subsidiary is making decisions, it builds closer links with the local environment and can respond more quickly to local needs.

Malone (1997) claims that empowerment is not simply another management fad but a response to fundamental changes in the economics of decision-making. The ability to respond quickly to changes in the market is essential, and even a global company must increasingly recognize local needs – as the Coca-Cola case (section 14.3.4) shows. In the knowledge-based economy that is emerging, globally connected, the company needs decentralized management structures to make local decisions. The development of information technologies and falling communication costs enable the company both to decentralize and to maintain a strong corporate identification. A policy of empowerment moves the company towards transnationalism.

Empowerment describes a localization of control, and does not necessarily indicate that all staffing is local. Expatriates might serve in an empowered subsidiary reporting only to subsidiary managers. On the other hand, a unit that is entirely staffed by locals might be controlled by strategies, policies and systems made in headquarters. However, there must be a tendency for empowered subsidiaries to depend on only locally recruited staff.

Before top management decides whether or not to empower a subsidiary, it finds answers to these questions:

- Do subsidiary staff have the necessary skills, and if not, can they acquire them?
- Do subsidiary staff have the information needed? If not, where can this be acquired?
- Do headquarters staff trust subsidiary staff?
- Are subsidiary staff likely to be more or less motivated by the opportunities presented by empowerment?
- What might be the economic benefits and costs of empowering the subsidiary?
- What might be the economic benefits and costs of *not* empowering the subsidiary?

Empowerment may not always be the answer. The subsidiary can never be entirely autonomous and headquarters always holds some autonomous control – it needs to retain control of financial operations. Other units may be given different degrees of empowerment – for example, sales might be entirely localized while headquarters retains some influence on marketing. These differences create internal tensions. Successful local managers are likely to be in greater demand on the local labor market, and so the company has to pay more to keep their services. Problems arise if the environment changes and headquarters claws back control over operations that seem in particular difficulty; disempowered local managers are demoralized.

Finally, empowerment assumes a tolerance of uncertainty among headquarters staff. Stewart (1995, p. 69) quotes the CEO of a Canadian subsidiary:

> "The problem is that decentralized, empowering relationships demand an enormous level of self-confidence on the part of the home management and a certain mindset. Empowerment is not a style of management – it's a philosophy."

Where this self-confidence is lacking, empowerment is not feasible.

14.3.7 *Loosening control through the technology policy*

The greater the importance of technology in the subsidiary, the greater the influence of control exerted through the technology policy. When control of technology is decentralized and local technologists are empowered, decentralizations occur throughout the subsidiary.

It used to be the case that in highly global companies, new technologies were developed at headquarters, adapted for local consumption, and disseminated to the subsidiary. The company aimed to gain maximum protection against the theft and misuse of technology by centralizing control over it.

Now the situation is changing. In industries where streams of competitors are entering and leaving the market and fast responses are essential, the subsidiary cannot afford to wait for headquarters to approve every decision. Increasing numbers of MNCs are setting up foreign units with a main responsibility to produce research, and these function as technology-focused profit centers. The subsidiary evaluates local demand and responds more rapidly than headquarters could. For example, European and Japanese telecommunications companies have located their units for software development and engineering as near as possible to their major customers in the USA. Thus the companies save the expense of time lost in adaptation.

Theft is now less of a concern. Technology life cycles have now shortened so much that the potential value of the new technology may be less and hence the potential cost of its theft is less. This cost may be less than the cost of not delivering the technology to the market at the earliest possible time. Thus market pressures drive decentralization.

Decentralizing the production of technology has the effect of empowering the subsidiary to decide on its own policies, possibly up to the level of strategic planning, and so decentralizes organizational structures. Kuemmerle (1997) distinguishes two headquarters-subsidiary structures based on technology creation:

- the subsidiary produces original technology which feeds back to headquarters;
- the subsidiary produces technology based on information flows from headquarters.

The creation of technology depends, first, on finding an appropriate site – perhaps clustering with other technology producers near a university campus; and second, finding a pool of technologists or persons who can be trained to the necessary standards. Where there are insufficient numbers of skilled persons, the development of subsidiary-based technology is fraught with difficulty. However, where there is an abundance of locally skilled persons – or persons with sufficient educational grounding to be trained further – a policy of decentralization provides work and experience. When the subsidiary is located in a less-developed economy, this gives a powerful stimulus to the growth of local talent.

14.3.8   Controlling through budget

The more dependent the subsidiary on headquarters' budgetary policy, the more immediate the control that headquarters exerts. But when decisions over expenditure are relaxed, control is pushed down to subsidiary management. For example, if headquarters demands that the subsidiary explain and seek permission for all expenditure over $100,000 control is centralized within headquarters. But if headquarters allows the subsidiary total discretion for all expenditure up to the limit of $10 million, control is looser.

14.3.9   Controlling through the organizational culture

This topic is discussed throughout chapter 16. There, organization cultures are conceived in terms of needs for more bureaucratic or more trust-based relationships between management and employees. The balance selected has implications for the use made of expatriate and local managers, and how management exercises appropriate control.

14.4   Implications for the Manager

Analyze your own MNC or some other to which you have access. Analyze relations between headquarters and three units abroad.

1   Which of these arrangements apply in headquarters' control of these units abroad?
 (a)   licencing agreement;
 (b)   agency agreement;
 (c)   turnkey agreement;
 (d)   IJV;
 (e)   subsidiary.
 In each case, what factors influence this choice of arrangement?
2   Why are headquarters controls needed in each unit?
 • In each, what risks are perceived?
3   In what respects is your MNC a global company?
 • In what respects is it a transnational company?
 • Is it more global or more transnational?

4 How does headquarters control each unit?
   • By using the structural relationship?
   • By using budgets and other financial instruments?
   • By using its technology policy?
   • By using organizational culture?
5 In each unit, how far does headquarters apply:
   • bureaucratic controls?
   • cultural controls?

14.5 SUMMARY

Section 14.2 discussed factors that place the MULTINATIONAL at RISK, and examined the types of control by which headquarters can reduce risk in its subsidiary. Tight control is expensive and is not necessarily an advantage. The company imposes controls on its subsidiary in order to ensure that strategic goals are met and risks guarded against.

Section 14.3 examined options for imposing CONTROL. It dealt with structural relationships and focused on two extremes, global and transnational structures. The advantages and disadvantages of empowering the subsidiary were examined. The section saw why some companies are decentralizing the production of technology. It noted that budgetary mechanisms are controlling. Controls imposed by means of organizational culture and staffing are discussed at length in chapter 16.

14.6 EXERCISE

You are CEO of Croyden Forest Foods USA. You have subsidiaries in seven different countries. In Ruritania, your subsidiary harvests and crushes different seeds and nuts, from which it extracts valuable oils. Fifty percent of your earnings come from sales of analonin oil.

Your company owns the technology of the crushing plant, which is programmed by your patented software. A computer programmer expatriated from headquarters writes the software at post. The crushing process imposes great pressures on the hardware that is continually breaking down. At present, a further two production engineers have been expatriated to operate and maintain it. Your board are worried about the security implications of withdrawing all expatriates from posts involving valuable technology. All other staff, including the general manager, are Ruritanian.

Over the past 3 years costs have grown and profits have fallen. Last year this subsidiary earned profits of R$3 million, but you expect a decline of 15 percent per annum in the next 2 years. Given the ENVIRONMENTAL FACTORS below, you now have to consider the future direction of the subsidiary.

Environmental factors

1 The industry is experiencing a period of great turbulence.

2 No foreign MNC has ever won a case against a local company in Ruritanian courts.

3 Your software is protected, and cannot be easily copied.

4 You have been invited to form a joint venture with a French company planning to harvest forest foods in Indonesia. If you enter this venture, your technologies will make a major contribution.

5 A Japanese company is manufacturing similar hardware, for sale on the open market.

6 A powerful local company has recently announced plans to enter the seed-and-nut crushing industry.

7 Rumors are circulating that a Taiwanese competitor, TPF Products, has patented a synthetic substitute for analonin oil. TPF Products is not competing in Ruritania.

8 Weather conditions in Ruritania have been excellent this year, and you expect a bumper crop of seeds and nuts at low prices.

9 World demand for analonin oil has been in decline over the past 5 years, but you expect a major increase over the next 3 years. Further than that you cannot predict.

Given the limited data available, which of the options below seem sensible? What further data do you need before making your final decision?

Options

(a) Continue as at present.

(b) Withdraw from Ruritania immediately; sell the subsidiary.

(c) Withdraw all expatriates, and turn over their jobs to Ruritanian staff.

(d) Withdraw only your computer programmer, and licence the production of software to a local firm.

(e) Withdraw only your production engineers, and employ local staff to operate and maintain your hardware.

(f) Sell your hardware patents, but maintain your software patents. Maintain all expatriates as at present.

(g) Withdraw the present expatriate staff, sack the Ruritanian general manager, and expatriate a general manager from headquarters.

(h) Purchase a stake in TPF Products.

(i) Reduce your investment. Empower your Ruritanian subsidiary with responsibilities to decide on expatriation and technology policies.

(j) Centralize your control. Sack the Ruritanian general manager and all functional managers; replace them with headquarters expatriates.

(k) Impose tighter budgetary controls.

(l) Any other options. Please add:
....

Notes

1 Constance L. Hays, "Daft shakes up Coke, pushing local decisions," *International Herald Tribune*, February 7, 2000.

2 "Coca-Cola to cut 21% of its work force," *Asian Wall Street Journal*, January 27, 2000.

3 "The real thing," *Gulf Daily News*, February 23, 2000.

CHAPTER FIFTEEN
International Joint Ventures

15.1 Introduction

An American engineering company recognized that its best and perhaps only hope for long-term survival was to form a strategic alliance in the People's Republic of China. A search team was sent to find a partner.

International joint ventures with most of the possible partners were not practicable because their interests differed too sharply. The Americans wanted to build a long-term position for growth within the region whereas most of the Chinese were looking for a rapid transfer of technology from which they could benefit immediately before searching out a new partner able to supply the next technology. The Chinese would not commit to a 10 year deal.

Incidentally, these different interests contradicted stereotypes of the two cultures. Americans are usually thought of as short-term in their orientation but in this case had good commercial reasons for planning years ahead. Chinese culture is stereotyped as long-term but the first 43 companies approached had equally good cause for aiming at a short alliance only. This case provides further support for a point argued throughout this book, that culture may not always be the most significant factor in determining behavior.

The search team spent 18 months visiting potential partners before agreeing on terms with the forty-fourth company they pursued. Negotiations then took a relatively modest 6 months, and work started on the day that the contract was signed.

This case demonstrates the importance of investing in finding the best possible partner for a joint venture; the greater the need for a successful joint venture, the greater the investment that has to be made. It also shows the importance of recognizing where fundamental interests coincide and differ.

The chapter deals with two main topics: reasons for investing in an international joint venture (IJV), and the practical problems of reconciling cultural and other differences, and making the project work.

15.2 Why Form an IJV?

Section 13.5.1 indicated the range of structures and systems used to implement the company's strategic goals. When the company adopts an international profile in positioning itself in relation to its competitors, it may select the option of forming an alliance with a foreign partner or partners. Different forms of alliance involve varying degrees of control, commitment, risk, and organizational complexity. The choice of alliance is influenced by external factors, and also by internal factors such as the firm's resources and experience.

One such alliance is the international joint venture. It has limited but tightly defined aims. It expresses an alliance with another company that also needs to satisfy strategic goals, and the alliance may be discontinued when one partner feels that it no longer helps achieve their goals. When it revises its strategic goals, an existing alliance may be less (or more) welcome than before.

Here is a definition adapted from Shenkar and Zeira (1987).

- The IJV is created by the investments of two or more parent companies.
- The IJV is a separate legal organizational entity, and belongs entirely to neither/none of its parents.
- It is jointly controlled by its parents.
- These parents are legally independent of each other.
- The headquarters of at least one parent is located outside the country in which the IJV operates.

Some IJVs are formed on an equity basis. More flexible arrangements may depend on contracted cooperation without involving the legal commitments of equity. Some IJVs may have more than two parents. In general, the more parents, the greater the administrative complexities and the greater problems of managing the project. Sometimes, both (or all) parents are located outside the IJV country. Coca-Cola (Vietnam) was started as an IJV between Coca-Cola (USA) and a Singaporean bottler; originally it did not employ any Vietnamese managers.

A multinational company is defined as one that has one or more investments located abroad – in countries other than that of its headquarters.

- These investments include wholly owned subsidiaries, partly owned subsidiaries, or joint venture projects in which ownership is shared with at least one other partner.
- These investments might be concerned with production, marketing, R&D, etc., or more than one of these functions.

The IJV was not always the preferred vehicle for implementing a strategy of foreign growth. Up until the 1970s, United States businesses lacked confidence in local management, and preferred to centralize control; hence they chose the wholly owned subsidiary. IBM's policy of 100 percent ownership led to conflict with the governments of Nigeria and India. The company would not agree to equity participation, and in 1977 pulled out of India. General Motors owned 100 percent of equity in its six overseas subsidiaries. But the mood changed, and by 1975, six of its 40 subsidiaries were jointly owned, and 12 out of GM's new foreign subsidiaries had been IJVs. By the early 1990s, the IJV had replaced the wholly owned subsidiary as the most widespread form of foreign investment by American companies.

Governments increasingly recognize the benefits of IJVs, and many less-developed countries have jettisoned centralized regulations restricting foreign ownership. Decision making may be decentralized. For example, the post-Suharto regime in Indonesia saw a change in strategy towards foreign oil companies, and the tendency now is to grant local provinces far greater control over their natural resources, so that:

> foreign oil and mining companies will no longer be able to count on automatic renewals of contracts and will probably need to accommodate provincial political and economic interests if they hope to maintain natural resource concessions.[1]

Fukuyama (1991, pp. 102–3) argued that the less-developed countries have been persuaded to liberalize their legislation concerning foreign control of equity by the examples of the Asian economies, whose dynamic growth confounded dependency theory and neo-Marxist arguments for protectionism against the developed world. Asia's boom has apparently demonstrated that economic liberalism is a path to economic development – although globalization may not be an entirely painless experience. The advantages and disadvantages of globalization were discussed in chapter 11.

15.2.1   IJV profitability

A company enters an IJV partnership in order to satisfy its strategic goals. However, IJVs are not always immediately profitable, and profitability is sometimes difficult to prove. Figures for market share and sales levels may be interpreted differently by the parents and the IJV management and have to be treated with caution, and these "objective" measures may be no more reliable than were subjective assessments of long-term advantage. In the short term, alternative forms of foreign investment often bring greater profits. Kent's (1991) longitudinal analysis of deals made by the seven major oil companies (British, Dutch, and five American) showed that joint ventures produced significantly lower gross yields than did non-joint ventures.

There can be no doubt that many IJVs appear to fail, often because they fail to meet their financial targets. Park and Ungson (1997) review the research and suggest a figure as high as 50 percent. Given that many companies would prefer to hide a failure that might frighten off some other prospective partner, the real figure might be much higher.

Failure might be most obviously signaled by early termination. The parents dissolve the project prematurely, or one withdraws. One early study of 1,100 projects found that 84 were dissolved, 48 changed control, and 182 became wholly owned subsidiaries of the American parent (Franko, 1971). However, early termination or withdrawal does not necessarily mean failure. An IJV might be terminated because it has achieved its aims ahead of schedule – that is, it has been an unexpected success. Or perhaps one parent sees advantage in acquiring the project as a wholly owned subsidiary and the other in selling out.

Given these difficulties in measuring the success or failure of IJVs and problems in predicting and measuring their profitability, why do so many companies persist in entering them?

15.2.2 *Reasons for forming an IJV*

The partners may have shared interests in forming an IJV that gives them both opportunities to:

- create greater market power by combining resources;
- reduce risk by sharing risk (i.e. the costs of investment and production are shared);
- reap economies of scale;
- cooperate in order to avoid expensive competing (i.e. the IJV is an alliance that restricts your own capacity for independent action, but also restricts that of your partner, who might otherwise be a dangerous competitor).

Here are other examples of interests which may not correspond for the two partners.

- The IJV offers, for the less technological partner, opportunities to benefit from the transference of technology.
- The IJV offers, for the less well-managed partner, opportunities to acquire new management systems. Ford learned management lessons from Mazda, which had five times fewer finance and control managers.
- The IJV offers, for a failing company, opportunities to regain a competitive edge. Rover linked up with Honda, and Chrysler with Mitsubishi in order to win back market share.
- The IJV offers, for either partner, symbolic benefits. A project formed with a high-status partner from a more developed economy may give increased local standing to a company from a less-developed country. An Indonesian manager explained:

"when your company forms an alliance with other companies from other countries, the image that they bring to your company is that [it is] going international. When the local company P T Bimanta na Telecomunication formed an IJV with AT&T, they suddenly gained the trust of the government. [It seemed] reliable to take projects because of the big name of AT&T."

- The IJV offers, for either partner, opportunities to acquire experience as the first stage to taking the project over and re-establishing it as a subsidiary. This reflects a strategy of centralization.

The IJV offers the foreign partner:

- the opportunity to meet the host government's requirements for doing business in the country – for instance, a foreign company is only permitted to operate in the country if ownership is shared with a local company;
- opportunities to learn about local marketing conditions and to develop customer networks;
- opportunities to gain access to local resources, including production facilities, labor, and materials.

The IJV offers the local partner:

- opportunities to generate up-stream and down-stream industries. For instance, the development of an IJV pulp mill encourages local entrepreneurs to increase logging facilities and to invest in paper manufacture.

The IJV offers the local government:

- opportunities to encourage foreign investment – the foreign partner may be allowed to take only minority ownership, and must fulfill conditions regarding local employment, technology transfer, purchase of local materials, etc.

15.2.3 How partners contribute

Sections 15.2.1 and 15.2.2 show how a company can benefit from participating in an IJV. In many respects, the foreign partner and local partner benefit differently. The same point applies to the contributions that they make. It is in the nature of the arrangement that the foreign partner contributes international inputs and the local partner makes local inputs. More specifically, the foreign partner contributes:

- international know-how and access to international connections;
- international reputation;
- access to international product markets;
- access to international labor markets;

- access to international finance;
- access to international technologies;
- access to other international resources;
- international distribution.

The local partner contributes:

- access to local connections, including government contacts;
- local reputation;
- knowledge of government regulations;
- knowledge of local culture;
- access to local product services;
- access to local labor markets;
- access to other local resources;
- local distribution.

15.2.4 Reasons for not entering an IJV

Your company may decide not to form an IJV in a given country or with a given company when:

- you do not expect to receive the benefits listed in sections 15.2.1 and 15.2.2.
- you are not prepared to make the contributions listed in section 15.2.3.
- you perceive the risks to be unacceptable – for example, the business environment is too volatile and government guarantees are not acceptable. (The risk factors influencing the decision to invest in a subsidiary, listed in section 14.2.1, also apply in the case of IJVs.)

Other reasons for your NOT entering an IJV – either in a particular country, or with a particular partner – include the following:

- You lack experience and knowledge of the country of operations. An expatriate manager based in Ho Chi Minh City advises:

    Vietnam's market has vast potential, but it takes time and effort to find solid local partners to form a joint venture, obtain and vet information, negotiate agreements and secure government approval. . . . There is a common saying among the barflies about doing business in Vietnam: "The government interprets the law for its friends, and applies the law to strangers." Vietnam is no place for strangers to do business. The foreign investment law is tailored to approve investments based on the government's view of how a company and its projects will further certain economic and social objectives.[2]

- You do not wish to share profits.
- You do not wish to share control of essential resources – for example, technology.

- You expect an alternative arrangement to be more profitable – for instance, operating through a wholly owned subsidiary.
- The company is already market leader and its primary need is to exploit an existing competitive advantage. In this situation, establishing a wholly owned subsidiary is the better alternative.
- You cannot afford to make the necessary investments.

Cultural factors influence the decision. Where trust is low and foreign influence feared, an offer from a foreign company may be perceived as a threat. An Indonesian manager commented:

> "We think that they will take away our jobs and positions. I have an example from my own company. One of my managers . . . had to leave to take a position in the new IJV [formed with an American partner]. When I first suggest that to him, he is so shocked that he thinks I do not like him anymore. Actually by going to the IJV company he gains my trust and a big responsibility, and more authority is waiting for him. After I explain to him, he understands. We see in this that we are more emotional to change."

15.3   The Compatible Partner

The case in the introduction showed that choosing a partner may not be straightforward. Searching for the best possible may be expensive and demands careful research. Section 7.5 listed the factors that need to be researched – including those associated with the national context and with the specific company.

Partner selection is a crucial process, and determines the mix of resources that are available. The company is looking for a partner with whom it has STRATEGIC FIT. This means that:

- their different strategic interests are not in conflict;
- both need the IJV in order to achieve these different strategic goals;
- their strategic goals for the IJV are compatible;
- each can supply necessary resources.

Here is an example of how partners can work together in achieving the same limited goal because it helps each meet his broader goal. I aim to make cakes and use orange peel but not the juice, and you aim to make soft drinks and need orange juice but not the peel. These strategic goals are not in conflict. We both need oranges in order to achieve our different goals. So together we purchase and process oranges, each extracting that part of the oranges which suits our needs without conflicting with the other's need.

15.3.1   Compatibility in business interests

The concept of strategic fit does not mean that both partners should be in the same industry – in fact, often it is better that they are not.

Suppose that you refine petroleum and plan to set up an IJV to develop industrial paints, which of these possible partners might best suit your needs:

- a travel agent?
- a bank?
- a construction company?
- a petroleum refiner?

The travel agent is in an entirely different business, and can probably offer nothing relevant to the development of paint. The bank can provide financing, but no relevant expertise. The construction company belongs in a complementary industry and can offer skills, knowledge, markets and business contacts that you lack. When both partners contribute and learn from the other, fruitful cooperation is possible.

There is little point in joining with a competitor who has precisely the same interests and brings the same resources to the table. The petroleum refiner may not offer any technology or business contacts that you cannot supply. But companies in the same industry do form alliances when they hope to benefit from discrepancies in technology, systems, and markets. IJVs formed by the Swiss food firm, Nestlé, include alliances with Coca-Cola, General Mills, and two companies in the People's Republic of China (a coffee and creamer plant, and an infant formula and milk powder plant).[3]

A partnership in the same industry might be valued if it offers opportunities that arise from its different environment. Such an IJV gives the foreign partner access to a local market, and the local partner access to the international market. In 1997 two securities companies, the Premier Group of Thailand and SBC Warburg, formed a joint venture designed to provide Warburg with local expertise and Premier with international access.

15.3.2 *Resource complementarity*

Partners must not only share goals; they must also be able and willing to achieve these goals. Each demonstrates its commitment to the project by contributing the organizational and financial resources decided by the agreement. The efforts made by each should complement and not duplicate those efforts made by the other. The application of resources must be complementary. In addition, both must be prepared to invest their reputation and important business contacts.

A project is unlikely to succeed when the supply of resources is not complementary; for example, when both insist on supplying staff but neither is willing to commit the necessary technology.

15.3.3 *Compatibility in size*

The parents may be more likely to trust each other when they are of similar size. Difference in size is destructive if one uses its greater resources to dominate the IJV in its own interests alone. Problems arise if managers from the large secure company are unwilling to participate and adapt, and will not share information with the partner and the IJV.

However, the development of business by internet and other electronic media means that businesses can expand and contract in a very short time, and the size of staffing complements and physical resources is no longer so accurate a guide to a firm's financial and knowledge power as once it was. In companies that are technology intensive, the numbers on the payroll may be irrelevant. The main point is that staff on both sides should have the will to succeed and be conscious of the cost of a failed project.

Questionnaire research into foreign direct investment in the People's Republic of China discovered that the attitude taken by the Chinese bureaucracy was influenced by such factors as the investor's care for its relationship with the government, the profitability of the IJV, the foreign parent's commitment, timing and location, and technology transfer issues, but that "the size of the investor does not seem to matter much" (Thawley, 1996, p. 9). The investors were divided over whether size was an issue.

15.3.4   *Compatibility in time-scales*

The parents need to share a time-scale. Suppose that Parents A and B are both prepared to invest 5 years' development costs. The project is set fair. But contradictions arise when Parent A aims at reinvesting profits made during the initial period whereas Parent B wants a quick return from its investments.

The introduction provides an example of a company experiencing difficulties in locating a partner that needed a long-term venture. In that case, the problems arose from needs for technology transfer.

15.3.5   *Trust*

The most important factor in choosing a partner is that you feel able to trust them and they trust you. Trusting them means that you understand their needs and interests and feel competent to predict their behavior in routine circumstances. It does not necessarily involve emotional commitment. Trust is developed when the partners:

- have compatible interests – as above;
- have compatible sizes – as above;
- share time-scales – as above;
- apply the same priorities in planning IJV goals and strategy, and in implementing the strategy;
- agree contractual details;
- agree on development stages;
- agree on the design of management style, structure, and systems;
- agree on systems for communicating between the parents, the IJV and parents, within the IJV, and with the environment;
- agree on criteria for evaluating IJV development and success.

15.4   Explaining Success and Failure

As mentioned above, the IJV is more likely to succeed when each partner trusts the other. This means trusting that the partner is genuinely committed to the project and will do its best to abide by all agreements between them.

15.4.1   Trust and mistrust between partners

When the points listed in 15.3.5 apply, trust develops and the odds on success improve. A previous history between the partners also helps to stabilize the relationship, and an atmosphere of reciprocity and good-will prolongs it. But when these conditions do not apply, trust is harder to achieve. Opportunism and short-term gamesmanship can destroy the relationship, and the IJV parents act less as partners and more as rivals.

Mistrust arises for a range of reasons. For example, perhaps one partner has failed to prepare sufficiently, and has underestimated the commitment that must be made. Perhaps the foreign partner has negotiated on the basis of occasional visits, with little real understanding of the local environment. It could also be that the negotiations and contractual documents are confused and fail to spell out the IJV goals and each side's rights and obligations, and as a result misunderstandings occur. The partners then fall into conflict over their interpretations of strategic goals, commitments to resourcing, sharing of costs and benefits. A study made of Canadian high-technology alliances emphasized that the first year of operations is particularly fraught with difficulties, particularly those associated with partner selection, communication, and reconciliation (Kelly et al., 2002). The implication is that first-year operations demand the wholehearted attention of headquarters, who must be prepared to renegotiate aspects of the agreement. The Fedor/ Werther model (discussed in section 15.5) provides a tool for uncovering areas of compatibility and incompatibility.

It is a mistake to assume that the IJV negotiations end when the contract has been signed. In many non-Western cultures, the implementation process is the point at which the practical bargaining starts. Unfortunately, it is then that many Western headquarters assume that all the serious problems have been resolved and that they can safely turn over responsibilities for the IJV to a new hire or junior staff member who lacks commitment, knowledge, or competence. The problems that arise can be avoided if a senior manager involved in the original negotiation continues his/her involvement.

Another problem is when one partner has learned faster from the IJV and so is able to dominate the relationship and no longer needs the other. Also, cultural differences can lead to poor communication and misunderstandings. Cultural differences may be more severe between some countries than others. Lasserre (1999) found that Western companies expressed greatest satisfaction with IJVs in Japan; then in Indonesia and Malaysia; then China and Vietnam; then Korea and Thailand, where levels of dissatisfaction were high.

If one partner reduces its interests in the IJV because of internal changes in its own situation, this can also cause mistrust and failure. For example, it appoints a new CEO with new strategic goals or the IJV champion is replaced in his/her post. The partner develops new priorities and downgrades the IJV. The same problems arise when one partner reduces its interests in the IJV because of changes in its environment. This point is developed below.

15.4.2 Why change in the environment influences trust

Change in the environment may force the partner to alter its perception of the IJV's strategic goals or to modify its commitment. New opportunities in new markets, new competition, new technologies, new economic and political constraints imposed by the government may all explain why a partner loses interest in the IJV. It may have negotiated the IJV in good faith, fully intending to commit all contracted resources, but for reasons beyond its control, corporate priorities have changed. It no longer needs the venture to succeed in order to achieve its strategic goals, or can no longer afford to invest in it, or no longer values a long-term relationship with its partner.

Both partners operate in volatile environments, and it is in the nature of an IJV that they operate in different environments. Their local markets and competition differ. They are subject to different local political, social, and economic pressures. These environmental differences make any alliance inherently unstable.

Suppose that the taxation system in your partner's country is suddenly revised; and that they are now under pressure to make a profit from the venture in the next 2 years rather than only after 5, as was originally agreed. They begin to hold back resources, or request a renegotiation. At worst, they decide to withdraw.

This factor of environmental uncertainty explains why many companies increasingly prefer short-term alliances with highly specific goals. The partners might use an initial limited alliance in order to test the possibilities for a greater commitment and to build trust.

15.4.3 Trust and mistrust within the IJV

The success of the IJV hangs not only on relationships between the partners but also on trust and mistrust within the IJV, between staff posted to the IJV and their headquarters, and between the IJV and its environment.

An IJV succeeds when project staff trust each other and when persons posted from the two parents develop productive relationships. Before project operations start, a shared project culture is fostered by mixing staff from the parents in groups, where they work together on project planning. They exchange non-critical technological and business data.

Mistrust within the IJV arises when

- staff from the two partners interpret the goals of the IJV differently;
- staff join the IJV ignorant of the needs and interests of their colleagues from the other partner;
- local staff feel threatened by a stronger foreign parent;

- differences in the partners' national cultures lead to misunderstandings;
- differences in the partners' organizational cultures, structures, and systems lead to misunderstandings.
- conflicts arise from human resource and technology transfer policies – staff from one partner cannot supply the skills and other resources to which they are committed.

15.4.4 Trust and mistrust between staff posted to the IJV and their headquarters

An IJV is more likely to succeed when staff posted to it feel confident of the support of their headquarters. Mistrust arises when:

- support promised by headquarters fails to materialize;
- staff feel that their long-term career prospects with headquarters are in jeopardy;
- staff are not adequately compensated for taking part in the IJV;
- the partner fails to communicate its goals effectively within headquarters;
- subordinate levels responsible for servicing the IJV perceive it as a drain on their resources, and give it a minimum of attention.

15.4.5 Trust between the IJV and its local environment

The IJV needs to secure trusting relationships with a range of organizations in the local environment. They include:

- professional associations and trade unions;
- consumers and consumer associations;
- stockholders;
- environmental agencies;
- suppliers, distributors, agents;
- analysts and the media;
- religious groups;
- the government and bureaucracy at national, provincial, and municipal levels.

15.4.6 Fit between national cultures

Jolly's (2002) study of Sino-foreign IJVs found that cultural differences and language differences constituted the two most significant barriers to knowledge transfer between the partners. Perceptions of cultural distance can be fatal, particularly when the partners have different first languages.

On the other hand, an IJV is more likely to succeed when the partners perceive a fit between their cultures. CULTURAL FIT occurs when barriers to knowledge flows are low and communication is accurate. In such circumstances, trust increases and technologies are transferred efficiently with a minimum of misunderstanding.

Your culture influences how willing you are to trust a possible joint venture partner. Shane (1993) studied perceptions of transaction costs in American affiliates across 38 countries. He found evidence that members of low power distance cultures are more likely to trust in joint venture partnerships. But where power distances are high and trust is low, people need greater control, fear paying greater transaction costs, and prefer sole ownership.

Your culture also influences your perception of whether your business interests and IJV goals are compatible, whether differences in size are important, and what time-scale should apply. In theory, you and your partner are more likely to agree on these points when your cultures are close. That is, a venture formed by parents of similar cultures stands a greater chance of succeeding than does one between dissimilar cultures. However, this cannot be taken for granted, for two reasons. First, Park and Ungson (1997) find that American–American IJVs (that is, alliances within the same culture) are *more* likely to fail than those between American and Japanese partners.

How can this be explained? It seems that Japanese companies actively seek stability in their alliances in order to enhance their reputations in anticipation of dealing with other firms in the future (p. 302). Also, they may enter the alliance only after fully researching their partner, and are more frightened of losing face should the alliance fail. This implies that the company's strategic needs and the investment it makes in ensuring a stable fit and a willingness to adapt to the partner's needs may be a more significant influence than the degree of cultural similarity.

The thrust of Park and Ungson's study is supported by Salk and Brannen (2000), who investigated a successful German–Japanese IJV and found that national culture was not a statistically significant influence on performance.

> Our data suggest that differences themselves do not cause problems; rather it is how a team's context and individual team members' orientations to local (team) norms channel these differences.
> *(p. 200)*

That is, the efficiency of structures and individual influences is of greater significance than culture in determining success or failure. One implication of this study is that companies of very distant cultures should not allow this difference to inhibit plans for an IJV, so long as they can agree on inputs of expertise and structures for communicating.

Second, the concept of cultural fit is subjective, and difficult to substantiate by objective criteria. No two cultures correspond at all points. Cultures which are similar in some respects may vary widely in others – as Hofstede's (2001) data show. The cultures of Finland and Switzerland have similar needs to avoid uncertainty (ranked 31/32 and 33 respectively) and similar power distances (46 and 45) but Finland is far the less masculine (47 compared with Switzerland at 4/5).

Hofstede (1985) hypothesized that synergy between organizations took place when cultures were balanced around the masculine and feminine mean and were close on the "organizational" dimensions of power distance and uncertainty avoidance (pp. 355–6). He cited the examples of British and Dutch cultures (more masculine, more feminine; otherwise similar). Most problems would be experienced by cultures that differed on the organizational dimensions. Hence, a typical company in a full-bureaucracy culture (for instance France or Belgium) could expect greater problems cooperating with a company in a personnel-bureaucracy culture (Denmark, New Zealand, United Kingdom) than with a company from, say, Korea or El Salvador. These two cultures are very close to France and Belgium in terms of both power distance and needs to avoid uncertainty, although in other respects are far apart.

15.4.7 *Fit between organizational cultures*

When talks designed to lead to a strategic alliance between Mitsubishi of Japan and Daimler-Benz of Germany broke down:

> analysts say the match has been strained from the beginning because the companies have fundamentally different structures.
>
> Daimler-Benz, a much smaller company than Mitsubishi, has traditionally had a close-knit management structure that has tended to set out clear strategic goals and forge ahead. Mitsubishi, an amorphous conglomerate of several large companies, has moved much more cautiously with internal factions often disagreeing over broader policy, analysts said.[4]

The companies were unable to overcome differences in their strategies, structures and organizational cultures.

Staff posted to the project from the two parents are more likely to work well together when their organizational cultures are similar. This does not mean that they should be identical – an impossible condition. Rather, there must be a sense of comfort about how the other does business, a willingness to work together and learn, and a need for shared solutions. There must be a willingness to communicate and to avoid misunderstandings.

Staff posted by their headquarters are more likely to feel loyalty to their parent company – which is responsible for their long-term career development and may eventually pay their pensions – than to the IJV, to which they are seconded for a short time. People with different cultures, career goals, and compensation structures are being asked to start working harmoniously together. Unless they have been prepared to work together and cooperate in developing a new culture, problems arise (see Cascio and Serapio, 1998). These are discussed in the next chapter.

15.4.8 *The IJV organizational culture is inherently unstable*

Most IJVs are inherently unstable arrangements, for a number of reasons. First, it is because their parents exist in different, rapidly changing environments. Second, the partners need control and the IJV needs independence. Third, the partners join together (partly) in order to learn from each other and this learning reduces the level of mutual need between them, thus reducing the need for cooperation – which may have been one reason for their establishing the IJV in the first place. Fourth, there is an inherent structural weakness: not one but three different management hierarchies (in the partners, and the IJV) are involved in decision making. The overlaps in authority are always likely to cause misunderstandings and give rise to factionalism. Fifth, as partners learn to work with each other, differences in their national and organizational cultures may become less important. These factors mean that the influence of the partner's cultures is mutable and their fit is continually changing.

15.5 Sharing Control

Fedor and Werther (1996, pp. 48–51) proposed eight stages for developing a "culturally responsive alliance" by which they meant an alliance:

> . . . that takes advantage of the partners' complementary strengths to exploit the opportunities available in its operating environment.   *(p. 46)*

Thus the IJV draws on the strengths of its two parents to create a new culture.
  The eight stages are as follows:

1 Each partner identifies its own cultural profile.
2 Negotiating teams compare profiles and identify areas of cultural compatibility and incompatibility.
3 Teams develop a joint business purpose. This ensures that both partners uncover areas in which partners converge or diverge in their plans for the IJV.
4 The teams plan the degree of operational independence permitted the IJV by the partners.
5 The formal structure of the IJV is agreed.
6 The management systems of the IJV are planned to reflect those functions and structures in which it is dependent on its parents and those in which it is independent.
7 The selection of the managing director and key staff is agreed. This agreement reflects the writer's belief that these leaders are "both the creators and carriers of the culture" (p. 50).
8 In those IJVs that continue to depend on the parents for critical services, the demands of the IJV may require changes in the inputs they make. These are assessed.

This model is powerful. It links problems of building an organizational culture, the design of structures between headquarters and subsidiary and within the subsidiary, to the selection of senior staff. What it does not do is show how the partners balance their control over the IJV and manage senior staffing in order to achieve this balance.

15.5.1 Who manages the IJV?

Each partner hopes to exercise as much control as is necessary to protect its interests and achieve its goals. The trick is to achieve the necessary level of control while still maintaining as light a touch as possible over operations.

Partners agree on a balance of management responsibilities. Each takes responsibility for those functions in which it is the stronger. For instance, an American manager working in a Swiss–US joint venture reported that his IJV had:

"... been fortunate that [the Swiss parent] ... has assumed a subordinate role and that [the American parent] has been willing and capable of fulfilling the dominant role. The effect on [the IJV] is that all ordering, invoicing, inventory, distribution, tax obligations, and financial reporting is done through [the American parent] systems. The [Swiss parent] influence comes mainly from product-oriented issues."

Which partner contributes top management? The partner who contributes most resources has a prime claim on the post of CEO. Factors determining allocation of other senior positions include:

- the availability of MANAGEMENT TALENT in the partners and in external labour markets;
- the GOALS of the IJV – an IJV dedicated to marketing is headed by a marketer, one dedicated to production by an engineer;
- needs to safeguard proprietary TECHNOLOGY – a partner that makes significant technological inputs may demand control in order to protect itself against theft and guarantee efficient operations and maintenance;
- needs to safeguard MARKETING expertise – for example, the local parent balances the technological parent's inputs with knowledge of local markets and customers.

These allocations, made at the early stages of IJV planning, may all seed later conflict. For example, the non-technological partner begins to claim that the inputs made by its partner are out of date or overvalued, and do not justify the scope of control which the technological partner had initially claimed. Or, over time, the foreign parent develops its own knowledge of markets and customers, establishes its own data base, and so weakens the local monopoly.

15.5.2 Balancing ownership and control

Kumar and Seth (1998, p. 580) summarize proposals for:

- integrative mechanisms creating direct contact between executives of the partners and the IJV management;
- the participation of IJV board members in the IJV's strategic planning and performance-monitoring processes;
- the socialization of managers in training sessions, meetings, seminars with parents;
- systems to motivate IJV managers to align their interests with those of the partners;
- staffing top management of the IJV with parents' representatives;
- developing an IJV board of directors who participate in strategic planning and performance monitoring.

These systems should bring the various parties together and help build trust between them. They provide structure that enables the partners to express their needs for control and the IJV to express its needs for independence. In practice, the balance between these forces is being continually renegotiated, and the mechanisms provide opportunities for the parties to communicate and resolve problems. They express an understanding that negotiations between the partners are not completed merely by signing contracts, but continue throughout the implementation of the project.

15.5.3 Communicating between the parents and the IJV

The sections above argue that good relationships between the partners and other parties involved are important in order to improve the odds on success. The integrative mechanisms listed above are augmented by systems designed to prevent misunderstandings occurring in communications. Communications need to be managed:

- between the parents;
- between each parent and the IJV;
- within the IJV;
- between the parents or IJV and audiences within the environment.

Communication is always most efficient when it is selective. This means, first, that the parties concerned must:

- avoid under-communication;
- avoid over-communication.

IJV development is set back when vital information is not communicated. Trust between partners is damaged when one of them fails to communicate technical data for the project through fear that these will give the other parent an advantage. (In practice, any company is unlikely to employ its most up-to-date technology and best scientists on an IJV.)

Problems also arise when the various parties over-communicate, and communications are not prioritized. In many projects, the quantity of information flow is achieved at the expense of quality. The greater the quantity of unimportant messages that flow in, the less easily can the manager identify and act decisively upon those that matter – particularly if the communication is not in his/her native language. And the process is expensive; both direct and indirect (time, energy) communication costs are incurred.

15.5.4 A communications plan

A COMMUNICATIONS PLAN defines relations between the partners and IJV management, and decides communications responsibilities. Here are four parameters adapted from the contextual communication model shown in table 5.1:

- WHO (in each partner, and the IJV) should be responsible for communicating, given a particular topic?
- TO WHOM (in each partner, and the IJV) should different messages be communicated?
- WHAT topics should be communicated?
- HOW should messages be communicated? The plan indicates the appropriate style and medium. These may change at different stages of the project. Bartmess and Cerny (1993, pp. 94–5) point out that:

> in reality, electronic mail, facsimile, and telephone communications work well only after initial relationships have been established. Even then they cannot support the rich, constant nature of the communication required [in developing trusting relationships].

An Austrian–Vietnamese IJV planned to announce a new development to the Asian media. The CEO of the Austrian partner traveled to Saigon to join in the celebrations. He arrived at the IJV to discover that his opposite number in the Vietnamese partner and the IJV CEO had pre-empted him and had made the announcement a day early, thus taking all the credit for themselves. He was so angry that he withdrew his company from the project.

An effective communications plan should try to ensure that such problems do not occur. It clarifies relations between the partners and IJV management with the different parties in the environment, including the media. The above categories must be spelled out. It must be clear who should be responsible for communicating with the environment, given a particular topic. The alternatives include persons in one or both partners, the IJV, or an agent or external party (for example, an agent or public relations consultant). It must also be clear to whom in the environment the different messages should be communicated and what topics should be communicated to the environment, and how.

15.5.5 How the IJV affects the organizational cultures of the partners

Parenting an IJV project influences the culture of the partner headquarters by fostering a culture of internationalism.

This is ADVANTAGEOUS when the headquarters benefit from an inflow of new ideas and technologies, and develop new knowledge. It is DISADVANTAGEOUS when the outflow of staff to the IJV (and inflow of replacements) impairs internal cohesion. A positive culture is weakened when staff feel pressured by responsibilities for which they have no training and experience. Supporters of the project are isolated.

In order to respond to problems and opportunities arising from parenting the project, headquarters streamlines and reorganizes its structures. Siddall et al.'s (1992) case study of British Petroleum shows that headquarters responded to its international commitments by

- reducing paperwork;
- adopting new matrix structures;
- flattening hierarchies;
- breaking down boundaries between units;
- rethinking roles, and relationships between headquarters and units abroad.

Its international commitments forced the company to decentralize and develop structures in which ease of access to units and individuals with knowledge was treated as an organizational priority. Staff positions were reduced and structural interdependencies simplified.

15.6 Implications for the Manager

In your experience, how far do you think cultural values influence the planning and implementation of an IJV? How much importance do they have, compared to other factors? Base your answers on any knowledge you may have of a current or terminated IJV project.

1 Why did the parents decide to establish the IJV in partnership?
- What advantages and disadvantages did the IJV partnership offer the local parent?
- What advantages and disadvantages did the IJV partnership offer the foreign parent?
2 Why did the IJV project succeed, or fail?
- What factors influenced the success or failure of the IJV, from the local partner's point of view?
- What factors influenced the success or failure of the IJV, from the foreign partner's point of view?
- If you think the IJV failed, what factors might have prevented this? Consider these:
  (a) preparation;
  (b) choice of partner;
  (c) trust between the partners;
  (d) trust within the IJV;
  (e) the contract and other documentation;
  (f) fit between national cultures;
  (g) fit between organizational cultures;
  (h) planning for control;
  (i) how control was exercised.
3 Describe communications:
  (a) between the partners;
  (b) within the project;
  (c) between the partners and the project;
  (d) with the environment.
- In what ways did communications influence success or failure?

15.6 SUMMARY

This chapter has examined factors that influence partner selection, and the planning and implementation of an IJV.

Section 15.2 defined the IJV and examined reasons WHY companies are often eager to FORM AN IJV – despite the uncertainties over immediate profitability. It looked at the benefits that each partner can hope for and the contributions that it must expect to make. Reasons why a company might decide against entering an IJV were discussed.

The problems associated with SELECTING A COMPATIBLE PARTNER are dealt with in section 15.3.

Section 15.4 examined factors EXPLAINING SUCCESS AND FAILURE. The importance of trust between the partners is supreme. This can be badly damaged when changes in either's business environment leads to a revision of interests and a new attitude towards the IJV. Outcomes are also influenced by trust within the project, between staff posted to the IJV and their headquarters, and between the project and the local environment. The section also dealt with the fit between the national cultures and organizational cultures of the two partners.

Section 15.5 dealt with the problems that partners face in SHARING CONTROL. Questions as to which partner provides the CEO and senior managers are usually decided by the investments made and interests in particular functions. Integrative structures, including a communications plan, are established in order to build trust between partners and the IJV, and provide channels for communication.

15.7 EXERCISE

This exercise gives practice in preparing a communications plan.

1 Review your answers to the exercise in chapter 7 (the negotiation between the business college and Acme Hotels). Assume that the IJV is implemented as you have planned it.

2 What are the implications for communicating:

- within the project?
- between the parents?
- between the project and each parent?
- with the environment?

What communication needs might each party have? What problems can you foresee?

3 Prepare a communications plan that can resolve the problems that you predict.

Notes

1 Timothy Mapes, "Indonesia signs landmark oil accord," *Wall Street Journal* (Europe), January 9, 2002.

2 Michael J. Scown, "Manager's journal: barstool advice for the Vietnam investor," *Asian Wall Street Journal*, July 15, 1993.

3 John Templeman et al., "Nestlé: a giant in a hurry," *Business Week*, March 22, 1993.

4 Richard E Smith, "Daimler-Mitsubishi Divorce?" *International Herald Tribune*, March 7, 1991.

CHAPTER SIXTEEN

Staffing to Control

16.1 Introduction

Chapter 14 examined a range of techniques by which headquarters applies appropriate controls to the subsidiary. Control may be exerted through:

- structural relationships (sections 14.3.1–14.3.6);
- technology policy (section 14.3.7);
- budget (section 14.3.8).

This chapter focuses on the use of staffing to provide the appropriate levels of head-quarters control, both in the subsidiary and the IJV. This story illustrates some of the strengths and weaknesses of expatriate staffing.

Peter, a Briton, was about to complete his assignment as Managing Director of the Manila branch of an American bank. Over a long lunch, he reminisced with a non-banking friend.

> "Before this I was in Thailand for two years. I've been here in the Philippines for two years. After a break, they'll post me again for a further 2 years, probably to Indonesia. It's policy: always have a headquarters manager in the top jobs. That gives headquarters more confidence.

There's one thing I've learnt, though. We fly in, settle for a limited period and think we run the bank. On paper, yes we do.

"In practice, though, we don't have time to learn enough. We usually don't speak the language. We often can't communicate with junior staff. And it takes months to learn local practice and recognize who matters in politics and the local markets. And even then our control is often superficial."

"So who does run things?"

"The top local managers. They speak good English and most of them have spent some time with us in New York. They know what we want. On the other hand they speak the local language and know their own community. They have their own power structures in the bank. We expatriates think we run things, but in fact our control is often symbolic."

Headquarters policy designed to regulate work relationships between expatriate and local managers may not correspond to how the persons concerned actually interact in the workplace, and planning how control *should* be exercised and how control is exercised *in practice* may differ widely. This chapter examines why the traditional answer to problems of controlling the MNC subsidiary – headquarters staffing – is often less productive than using local management. The next two sections deal with staffing the subsidiary, and then section 16.4 examines staffing an IJV.

16.2   Bureaucratic and Cultural Control

What options does headquarters have when deciding how to manage its human resources in a foreign operation? At one extreme it might depend heavily on rules and regulations. This emphasis reflects the notion that the relationship between company and employee is based on a legal contract and can be measured in job performance. At the opposite extreme, control is negotiated through mutual respect, loyalty, and trust and the relationship is perceived to be based on a psychological contract – which is continually renegotiated. Jackson (2003, p. 26) comments that

> there appears to be a tradition within Western studies of HRM and organizations to under-emphasise the value of "trust" while simultaneously over-emphasising the value of "control."

And by implication, companies based elsewhere may expect more from trust than from bureaucratic controls.

Jaeger (1983) described these two approaches in terms of:

- bureaucratic control of the subsidiary;
- cultural control of the subsidiary.

Each of these is expressed in a philosophy of how managerial staff can be used most efficiently.

16.2.1 Staffing for bureaucratic control

In Jaeger's (1983) model the aim of BUREAUCRATIC CONTROL is that the subsidiary should develop a culture of impersonal and bureaucratic efficiency. Headquarters encourages these values by enforcing impersonal rules that govern selection, recruitment, training, rewards, and that regulate the individual's behavior and output (see section 8.3).

∎ The CONTROL OF BEHAVIOR focuses on the monitoring and evaluation of activities. This control is exercised by headquarters staff, headquarters expatriates, or local managers, using regulations, rules, text and electronic instructions, manuals, and reports. Training focuses on developing specific technical competences.

∎ OUTPUT CONTROL means developing reporting and monitoring systems by which the subsidiary reports on its activities to the headquarters, and assessing subsidiary performance on the basis of data submitted.

When bureaucratic control succeeds, the subsidiary grows into an efficient operating unit that can build its own culture. The expenses involved may be light. The weakness is that loyalties to headquarters are weak. Relationships conducted through e-mails do not win loyalty when the subsidiary is in a collectivist culture, where personal relationships between superior and subordinates are all-important. Headquarters may be unaware of organizational developments that could threaten company interests.

16.2.2 Controlling through the organizational culture: cultural control

The aim of CULTURAL CONTROL is to develop loyalty to the company and to headquarters managers, so that the subsidiary culture eventually replicates headquarters culture. Cultural control is created through implicit norms that persuade members to make a moral commitment to the company. Manuals are used as training tools, but at least as much emphasis is laid on developing an awareness of the organization's norms and values and integrating a newcomer into the shared culture by structuring his/her personal interactions with established members of staff.

Cultural control companies aim to induce headquarters' values at a much deeper cultural and psychological level than do bureaucratic control companies. Techniques used to induce cultural control are most intense in the subsidiary's early years, and include:

- staffing with large numbers of expatriates who act as role-models;
- employee socialization programs;
- frequent visits between the subsidiary and headquarters – for example, headquarters staff make consultancy and advisory visits, and subsidiary staff are given training visits to headquarters;

- company seminars;
- social events, which include activities such as dining and drinking together, picnics, group travel, and group sports.

The strengths of cultural control are that it can develop powerful commitments between headquarters and subsidiary. However, the costs of maintaining high expatriate levels and constant visiting between headquarters and subsidiary are bound to be high. In addition, it can alienate local staff when the headquarters holds values that do not fit with the local culture – or when locals suspect that it does.

> In 2001, McDonald's faced furious protests in India over allegations, which it denied, that it had laced its French fries with beef fat. The Indian Mutiny of 1857 was sparked in part when Indian soldiers employed by the British East India Company heard rumors that their cartridges had been greased with animal fat. Few companies learn from history.[1]

Any conflict between the interests of the headquarters and of local society may cause low morale among local employees, whose loyalties are divided. Bureaucratic control does not place their employees under this psychological constraint.

16.2.3   National culture and the choice of control style

Bureaucratic control reflects a tolerance of ambiguity by headquarters staff. The organizational culture of the subsidiary is allowed to develop its own characteristics, which are bound to reflect values in the local national culture. On the other hand, controlling through the growth of a positive organizational culture reflects relatively high needs to avoid uncertainty. Bureaucratic structures are applied but are considered insufficient to generate the trust needed between management – which may be largely expatriate – and local workforce when the subsidiary is abroad, and located in a foreign culture. And so trust must also be developed on a personal level through personal relationships.

The extremes of bureaucratic control are more likely when the national culture of headquarters has relatively low needs to avoid uncertainty and an expectation of individualist decision-making – in the Anglo and Scandinavian cultures, for example. Cultural control occurs in collectivist cultures where ambiguities needs are high – in Japan and Korea, for example.

The two models of bureaucratic and cultural controls are "ideal" – there may be no companies that entirely fit either one. In practice, all companies fit at various points on a continuum between the extremes, and may move between them depending on circumstances in the company and the wider environment. For example, when the subsidiary is new, headquarters might invest in more cultural control; and when local managers have shown their competence, the headquarters withdraws expatriates and moves towards bureaucratic techniques. When the business environment is stable, headquarters might reduce personal controls, but when new competitors enter the market and conditions become uncertain, the company might decide that personal interventions are necessary in order to develop the sense of common purpose and identity.

Anglo companies are more likely to exercise bureaucratic controls over their sub-sidiaries abroad, and Japanese and Korean companies use cultural control *all other things being equal.* But all other things are often not equal. There may always be special factors that lead an Anglo company into adopting a more cultural style, or, say, a Japanese company into applying cultural controls.

For example, an Anglo company worries about the security of its technology, and decides to invest in motivating personal loyalties between local subsidiary technologists and their counterparts in headquarters. Alternatively, a Japanese company buys a foreign business for its investment value only, decides that headquarters staff are not needed to control the use of technology or are less competent to do so than are local managers, and that bureaucratic structures are sufficient to guarantee the stream of profits.

When headquarters controls the technology and expertise, resources are needed to guarantee effective use and protect its intellectual rights. The relationship between control of technology and culture is demonstrated by its negative – a case in which Japanese companies did *not* have the technical know-how and so were unable to exercise culture control. In 1989 and 1990 Sony and Matsushita took over two Hollywood film producers, Columbia Pictures and MCA. Sony sent only one Japanese manager to Columbia and Matsushita left MCA's management team in place, sending only a few Japanese staff and these not to the studio. Both Japanese MNCs' policies:

> . . . towards the entertainment business [are] being driven by the same simple point: the parent company's obvious ignorance. When Japanese firms operate factories abroad, they act as teachers, bringing in their superior manufacturing methods. In the entertainment business it is different. The Americans are teachers and the Japanese are the students. . . . Sony and Matsushita have concluded that, if they are to stay in entertainment, they have to do things the American way. That means no penny pinching, and giving the American managers a free hand. . . . It is an uncomfortable formula for Japanese bosses accustomed to being in control.[2]

The location of the subsidiary and the availability of local staff also influence the decision as to what style of control is needed. Japanese companies tend to rely more on cultural controls in Asia than in Europe. Delios and Björkman (2000) found that Japanese companies used expatriates with a control function in their Chinese sub-sidiaries to a greater degree than in their US subsidiaries.

Harzing (1999) re-examines Jaeger's categories. She distinguishes:

- bureaucratic formalized control;
- personalized centralized control;
- control by socialization and networks;
- output control.

Bureaucratic controls exploit the use of artifacts, and are more direct, formalized, and explicit. Personalized controls are based on culture and social interactions and networks, and tend to be indirect and implicit.

16.3   Expatriate or Local Management?

This section deals with the question of who should occupy senior posts in the subsidiary (at levels of CEO, Managing Director, functional managers, senior technicians). The claims of two groups are discussed:

▮ EXPATRIATE managers, who belong on the headquarters staff and are posted from there to the subsidiary;
▮ LOCAL managers, who are on the staff of the subsidiary.

A number of sub-categories are discussed in section 16.4, in the context of staffing the IJV. These include third-country nationals and persons hired by the IJV or by a partner on its behalf, with no contractual obligations beyond the life of the IJV.

By expatriating its managers, headquarters is apparently able to exert greater control, but at a cost. There may be greater advantages associated with local management. For any one company, the appropriate balance between expatriate and local staffing depends on its circumstances; the particular opportunities and threats, strengths and weaknesses that influence its decision making.

16.3.1   The advantages and disadvantages of expatriate staffing

What are the advantages and disadvantages of employing a HEADQUARTERS MANAGER to run your foreign subsidiary? The ADVANTAGES include the following. (These points apply whether headquarters is based in New York, Berlin, Tokyo, Taipei, or anywhere.)

* Headquarters control is greater.
* Headquarters organizational culture is more easily spread to the subsidiary.
* Headquarters staff gain experience abroad. Managers gain understanding of international business through expatriate assignments, and the organizational culture of headquarters becomes internationalized.
* Headquarters becomes more sensitized to subsidiary needs.
* Headquarters is more able to control local managerial and technical skill levels.
* Headquarters is better able to protect proprietary technology, and operating and maintenance standards.
* Headquarters and the manager share a common national culture, and at this level, cultural differences and misunderstandings do not arise.
* Communications between headquarters and subsidiary are stronger.
* Headquarters is better able to influence operations at critical times – for example, when the subsidiary market grows unstable; when the subsidiary is ailing; in a start-up.
* Closer links are made with other subsidiaries that are managed by headquarters staff.

Expatriate headquarters management also carries DISADVANTAGES. These include the following.

- Local staff get fewer opportunities to manage.
- Political risk is increased when the expatriate does not understand the local political situation.
- The expatriate takes time to develop local connections.
- The expatriate has less sensitivity to local market demands.
- The expatriate may not know the local language.
- The expatriate has less experience of managing local staff.
- Training for the expatriate assignment has to be provided (see chapter 18).
- Expatriation costs are incurred.
- The expatriate may cost more to reward.
- Disparities in rewards between the expatriate and local staff create ill-feeling among local staff.

16.3.2 *The advantages and disadvantages of local staffing*

The advantages and disadvantages of employing local managers to run the subsidiary mirror the disadvantages and advantages of expatriation. The ADVANTAGES include the following.

- The multinational is "internationalized," particularly if subsidiary managers are rotated back to headquarters.
- The subsidiary can be empowered.
- The local manager is developed and given opportunities to manage.
- The local manager is better connected in local markets and has a keener sense of local needs.
- Political risk is reduced when the local manager deals with government officials.
- The local manager has more experience of managing local staff.
- There is no demand for expatriate training.
- Expatriation costs are avoided.
- The local may cost less to reward.
- Ill-feeling arising from disparities in expatriate and local rewards is avoided.

Among the possible DISADVANTAGES are the following.

- Headquarters control is weakened.
- The subsidiary is more likely to develop an organizational culture at variance to that of headquarters.
- Headquarters staff do not have opportunities to work abroad. The organizational culture is in danger of growing parochial.
- Headquarters is less sensitized to subsidiary needs.

- Headquarters is less able to control local managerial and technical skill levels.
- Headquarters is less able to protect its proprietary technology, and operating and maintenance standards.
- Headquarters and the manager do not share a common culture, and their cultural differences can give rise to misunderstandings.
- Communication between subsidiaries (each managed by a local manager) may be harder to maintain.
- Communication between headquarters and subsidiary is weaker. Local managers may have less understanding of the worldwide organization and identify less with its strategic goals.
- Headquarters is less able to influence operations at critical times.

16.3.3   When is expatriate or local staffing better?

When should the company post a headquarters manager to run its foreign subsidiary, and when should it invest in a local manager? There is no answer that holds true for every situation. The lists of advantages and disadvantages above make clear that the decision must depend on factors particular to the company. For example, if the headquarters of Company A, marketing a global fast-food product, sets a high priority on uniform, centralized control, has staff available and can afford the costs, expatriate postings are a priority. If headquarters needs close control, it must be prepared to invest more. On the other hand, if headquarters wishes to decentralize control and focus on meeting local demand, it may decide not to incur the costs of an expatriate appointment and instead appoint a local manager.

In a rapidly developing economy, expatriate employment frustrates the more ambitious local staff who do not perceive that the expatriates are any better qualified than themselves. Writing about this problem in East Asia, Hailey (1996, p. 32) cites anecdotal evidence showing how this depresses local morale. Only

> a minority of expatriates have the necessary skills or experience to operate independently in the local environment. Another local manager said it was "frustrating when I seem to know more than the expatriate, and I am the person the expatriate has to lean on."

When expatriates depend on locals, the latter transfer their skills to headquarters. To add insult to injury, expatriate managers from developed economies working in less-developed economies are usually paid far more than local managers, especially when travel and relocation allowances have to be paid. Selmer (2001, p. 153) cites evidence that expatriate managers in China often require an 80 percent higher compensation than local managers doing the same job. But this is *not always* the case. Sometimes a highly qualified local manager who speaks several languages, has experience in a range of countries, and has political and business connections, may command a higher salary than an expatriate.

When technological skills at the required level are not available at the right price in the local labor market, a company may find it cheaper to import expatriate experts.

In 1996 Singapore Technologies advertised in the *Irish Times* for Irish engineers and managers to start a semiconductor factory in Southeast Asia.[3] The cost of labor has to be weighed against the value of productivity. More expensive labor may be more productive.

16.3.4 How culture influences the decision

A range of factors influences how the advantages and disadvantages of expatriate and local management are interpreted, and the national culture of headquarters is highly significant. In her analysis of staffing in a range of regions (Africa, Canada, Eastern Europe, Far East, Latin/South America, Middle/Near East, United States, Western Europe), Tung (1982) found that Japanese MNCs were more likely to staff senior levels in their foreign subsidiaries with Japanese, or headquarters-country nationals than were European firms (with Europeans) or American firms (with Americans).

Japanese culture has relatively high needs to avoid uncertainty, and, in such cultures, headquarters is cautious about appointing local managers to the top position, and more willing to assign trusted headquarters staff. That is, the Japanese place great store on the advantages offered by an expatriate appointment (recall section 16.3.1). These include:

- ease of control by headquarters;
- ease of spreading headquarters organizational culture in the subsidiary – this implies the development of cultural control (discussed in section 14.3);
- greater control of local managerial and technical skills levels;
- greater protection of technology;
- headquarters and the subsidiary manager share a common national culture and language, thus facilitating communication.

It also means that they discount the disadvantages, which include:

- local staff lacking opportunities to manage;
- greater political risk;
- ignorance of the local language (in some cases);
- expatriation costs.

Some of the disadvantages listed in section 16.3.1 are also overcome by keeping top managers in post far longer than is feasible in many American and European companies (see section 17.3.6), and then organizing extended handing-over periods between the outgoing manager and his replacement. For example, these opportunities to create and pass on knowledge of the local environment help overcome a foreigner's lack of local connections and insensitivity to market demands. On the other hand, the relatively low needs to avoid uncertainty in Anglo cultures means that Anglo companies have fewer inhibitions about appointing local managers, and this is reflected in Tung's findings.

16.3.5   *How other factors influence the decision*

These other factors influence the decision to appoint an expatriate or local manager.

▌ INDUSTRY FACTORS. An industry that depends on legal precision and reliability demands has greater needs for headquarters controls, and this often means an expatriate top management. In addition, the rapid movement of capital and resources on a global basis needs global experience. For instance, banking procedures are highly standardized and experience acquired in one branch can be applied elsewhere. On the other hand, retail trade practices are localized and experience of managing a department store in Dallas is of limited value in Seoul.

▌ STRATEGIC factors. If the subsidiary serves local markets a local appointment may be appropriate. If it serves international markets and is integrated with other subsidiaries, a headquarters manager may be suited. A decentralizing strategy points to appointing a local; a centralizing strategy, to expatriating a headquarters manager. A transnational alternative is to select from a third-country subsidiary.

▌ TECHNOLOGY. When headquarters has strong needs to safeguard headquarters technology, it expatriates technical staff. Needs for reliable operations and maintenance may also sway the issue.

▌ AGE AND CONDITION. A subsidiary may require control from headquarters when:
  • in a start-up phase;
  • ailing;
  • the environment is unstable.
When operations improve, production improves, and local managers take over from the expatriates.

▌ HEADQUARTERS AVAILABILITY. Is there a headquarters manager qualified to take the post? And, if so, is there another manager qualified to replace him/her at headquarters? A company may be inhibited from investing abroad by a lack of managers willing to work expatriate. A 1995 survey of 200 Singaporean multinationals showed that they needed to boost the number of expatriate Singaporean managers and professionals by 130 percent. The firms were sending abroad fewer than 900 key personnel and were looking to send 1,165 more over the next 3 years.[4]

▌ Local NATIONAL POLICIES on staffing levels in foreign-based multinationals. Many countries operate visa restrictions, for example by rationing the numbers of expatriate work permits issued to an MNC branch on the basis of the size of the investment that it is making in the local economy.

▌ LOCAL AVAILABILITY. Is there a local manager qualified to take the post, and can the company benefit from his/her appointment? Qualifications may include an ability to speak the headquarters language.

▌ Criteria for HEADQUARTERS PROMOTION. If expatriate postings are necessary for internal promotion, the headquarters manager welcomes the opportunity.

▌ Local DEMAND FOR MANAGEMENT SKILLS. Headquarters may be deterred from promoting a local manager who is then poached by a local competitor. In some countries, multinationals constantly lose local staff who use their term of employment as training preparatory to joining local companies or setting up on their own.

▪ EMPLOYEE PREFERENCES. It is usually assumed that employees prefer a local manager, with whom they can more easily communicate. This is not always the case. Selmer's (1996) study of subordinate preferences in Hong Kong discovered that "the leadership style of expatriates was preferred over local bosses'" (p. 172). The style of American bosses was most appreciated among the expatriate nationalities studied, followed by that of British managers; then Japanese and other Western managers; and least preferred, other Asian managers. But it must be said that subordinate preference for a particular management style does not necessarily mean that those managers are more effective and more productive.

▪ LOCATION. The closer that headquarters and subsidiary are, the easier it is to move staff between them for visits and training.

▪ COMMUNICATION. How complex or routine is communication between headquarters and the subsidiary?

These factors are interlinked. For instance, cost and labor market factors are closely linked with questions of availability and promotions policy, which reflect strategic decisions and industry factors. The decision is complex, and there is no absolutely right or wrong answer that fits all situations.

16.3.6　Differentiated fits

In practice, a headquarters may not have the same relationship with all its subsidiaries, and a staffing policy that bears fruit in one situation may be quite inappropriate elsewhere. In the case of any one subsidiary, the relationship is influenced by factors in its own unique situation. These factors include the subsidiary strategy, products, labor force, and environmental factors such as markets and customers, competitors, national culture. These different fits mean that staffing decisions also vary. For example, the subsidiary in Country A is well-established, selling a mature product line designed to suit the needs of local customers, and control is happily entrusted to an entirely local management team. But the subsidiary in Country B is new, producing technology according to headquarters specifications in a highly competitive market; the top managers are expatriated from the R&D department in headquarters. These different managements express different needs for control.

In time these relationships might change. The subsidiary in Country A is hit by a succession of difficulties and headquarters decides to introduce an expatriate at the top level. The subsidiary in Country B matures and develops self-confidence, and a decision is made to empower it by handing over all management to local staff. The next two chapters deal in greater detail with expatriate managers and with priorities in selecting, training, and supporting them for assignments abroad.

16.4   Local Managers

The case in the introduction makes clear that senior local managers can exert enormous influence within a subsidiary. This influence is in part formal. They understand

- headquarters perceptions of goals, internal resources, external environment, strategic priorities;
- subsidiary perceptions of goals, internal resources, external environment, strategic priorities.

And they communicate these between subsidiary and headquarters.

They also have access to informal networks to which the expatriate may never belong. They often work under great stress, balancing loyalties that at times are bound to be in conflict. In many developing countries, the local culture may have expectations of working relationships and structures that do not conform to those held by managers expatriated from developed economies, and the success of the subsidiary depends heavily upon these managers' skills in interpreting between the cultures of their fellow locals and expatriate top management. It is important that their interests should be recognized and their loyalties retained.

The section focuses on senior local managers reporting to expatriate top managers, but the same general points apply when the top manager is local and reports directly to headquarters.

16.4.1   *The recruitment of local managers*

The MNC hopes to promote top local managers who not only have technical and managerial expertise, but also have these cross-cultural skills. But it has problems in securing managers with this potential if it uses inappropriate criteria and techniques when recruiting them at entry-level.

This means, first, not depending solely on techniques that are appropriate in the home national culture of the headquarters but are inappropriate in the local culture. For instance, it:

- searches inappropriate labor pools;
- applies inappropriate search techniques (newspaper advertising is not effective in all contexts);
- applies inappropriate selection techniques (a personality test designed for one culture may be inaccurate elsewhere: a Chinese manager considered "aggressive" in his Taiwanese company was assessed as "passive" by a psychometric test administered in a British business school);
- applies incomplete criteria (priority is given to behavior that fits a headquarters profile only);
- offers salaries and other rewards that are not competitive with those offered by local firms.

16.4.2   *Female recruits in Japan*

Second, the company should be careful not to depend solely on recruitment criteria usual in the local labor market, particularly when these discriminate against women and minorities who may provide a pool of underutilized talent.

For many years in Japan (Hofstede's most masculine culture), prejudice barred women from employment in managerial positions. The situation is changing, but custom still makes it difficult for women to compete on equal terms. Jackson and Tomioka (2004) cite examples of this prejudice: female applicants may be sent less information on the company than are male applicants, and even that information which they do receive may be male-oriented. The authors refer to one instance and wonder

> What was the company thinking about? They send a recruitment mail-shot trying to attract a talented woman recruit, but in their prospectus they only show upwardly mobile men. Did they choose to ignore the obvious irony? Or did they not even realize it?
>
> *(p. 104)*

According to Renshaw (1999), Japanese women are Japan Inc.'s "hidden assets." An underemployed pool of well-educated women eager for a challenge presents excellent opportunities for non-Japanese companies wishing to recruit a motivated workforce.

They should also beware of slavishly following criteria commonly applied in the headquarters country, which may not apply in the country of the subsidiary. For example, Anglo universities train relatively few women engineers, and these countries tend to favor male engineers. But other countries do not differentiate, and the Anglo firm working in China, for example, cannot assume that a female applicant for an engineering post is in any way less qualified and less experienced than her male competitors.

16.4.3   *Retaining the loyalty of local managers*

Tensions set in between expatriate and local staff when the local staff perceive that expatriate staff are rewarded at higher rates for the same work, or – worse still – lower performance. Morale plummets, production suffers and expatriates become isolated from their local colleagues.

Headquarters retains the loyalty of local managers in the following ways.

- Showing that it trusts their judgment, particularly about local conditions. Subsidiary managers (whether or not local nationals) are more likely to be satisfied with global decision-making when headquarters listens to their views.
- Appraising and promoting them by criteria that recognize both their contributions to the global organization and their local expertise.
- Giving them responsibilities appropriate to their level in the MNC.
- Compensating them at rates that are fair, if not equivalent to expatriate rates, and providing appropriate benefits.

- Providing them with opportunities to rotate to headquarters and other subsidiaries.
- Having personnel officers devote equivalent time to both locals and expatriates when planning their careers.
- Providing appropriate training. Giving equivalent consideration to both locals and expatriates when training budgets are designed.

16.4.4   *Training local managers*

The increased globalization of management means that training courses and workshops given to managers in the Western developed countries become increasingly popular and useful in the wealthier developing economies. Popular topics include:

- leadership/motivation/communication;
- general management;
- human resource management;
- organizational change and development;
- strategy development;
- negotiation skills.

However, it cannot be assumed that any one topic can be usefully presented in the same style everywhere. Previous chapters have shown how values in the culture modify ideals of leadership, motivation, and communication. A style of leadership appropriate in Country A may not be appropriate in Country B. Concepts of strategic planning and implementation are also influenced by culture.

Economic, cultural, and labor market factors all influence the interpretation to be placed on the concept of human resource management. In a less-developed economy geared towards quantity manufacturing using cheap labor and where cheap labor is plentiful, low-level skills in personnel management are sufficient. But in a developed economy where companies compete for limited supplies of skills and knowledge, greater attention is given to making the most productive use of these resources.

Human resource structures differ in Anglo countries where management–union conflict is expected and in other societies where unions have less power and are less aggressive.

When there are significant developmental differences between the countries, the problems of transferring management know-how may be complex. Yavas (1992) discusses the variables that inhibit the process of transplanting management skills to less-developed countries. He notes that:

> traditional concepts of exclusive authority which lead to an unwillingness to share managerial power and information still characterise many organisations in Africa.   *(pp. 23–4)*

In these societies, power and information is hoarded. The person having information is respected, and is only likely to share it out when absolutely necessary, and perhaps at the last possible moment. This implies that training materials reflecting traditional

Anglo concepts of informational flexibility are unlikely to be immediately accepted, and the materials need greater explanation and exploitation than is necessary in an Anglo culture.

The implication is that programs designed to train local managers must take into account the local conditions and needs, and that headquarters priorities may be insufficient.

16.4.5 Teaching headquarters culture to local managers

Local managers who choose to work for the subsidiary are predisposed to the headquarters values that it reflects. (Those who are not so predisposed, and cannot make the adjustment, soon quit.) In the event that the headquarters wishes to indoctrinate them with its own values – and so adopt a style of cultural control, it has two options:

- expatriate headquarters managers to the subsidiary;
- send subsidiary managers for visits to headquarters.

The second alternative – short-term attachments at headquarters – serves instrumental functions of:

- developing local managers' international experience;
- exposing them to other aspects of the company's work;
- further deepening their commitment to the company culture;
- rewarding them, when an invitation to headquarters brings status in their professional and social contexts.

However, this acculturalization process has to be carefully handled. Intensive training of local managers in headquarters values carries the risk that they over-identify with headquarters and lose their commitment to local values and hence their local power bases. As long ago as 1974, Perlmutter and Heenan warned that the MNC should not set out to turn local managers into headquarters clones. They discuss the case of local European managers rotated to headquarters in the United States.

> This kind of ethnocentrism produces a tendency for U.S. companies to accept those who will acculturate and become "more American than the Americans." A most surprising development is to see a non-American come to headquarters with the reputation of knowing Europe, become alienated from Europe, and accept proposals that reflect the ethnocentric orientation of headquarters. *(p. 126)*

In effect the local manager becomes more efficient at communicating headquarters ideas and experience to the subsidiary than vice versa.

This inhibition against expressing local priorities (dubbed "Affiliate's Disease" by Professor F. Gerard Adams) has four ill effects. First, it implies uncritical acceptance of every message and strategy emanating from headquarters. Second, it has the effect of centralizing headquarters control – whether or not headquarters wishes this. Third, the clone loses his/her capacity to interpret between headquarters and local cultures. And, fourth, it alienates subordinate locals who need effective representation. That is, it creates a morale problem in the local organizational culture.

This implies that the company should place a priority on recruiting and training those local managers that have the personality and skills to interpret effectively between the two organizations; and should avoid the temptations of over-indoctrinating local managers to the point that they become clones.

16.5 Staffing the IJV

Three parties have interests in exercising control within the IJV; the two partners, and the IJV management. In the event that they all choose to exercise control through staffing, project staff are likely to be a highly heterogeneous group, which poses problems for management.

16.5.1 *The project staff are heterogeneous*

IJV staff may be selected from a number of labor pools. Figure 16.1 gives an illustration. The foreign Partner X is based in Country P; the local Partner Y, and the IJV project, are based in Country Q. Staff may also be recruited from third-country Country R and other third-countries. Assume that the project has a planned life-span of 5 years.

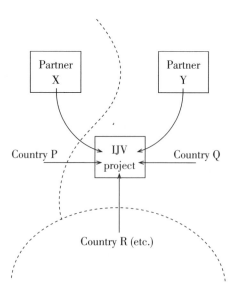

Figure 16.1 Staffing the international joint venture

IJV staff are recruited from these labor pools:

1 Partner X. When the project ends in 5 years' time, these project staff return to Partner X.
2 Partner Y. When the project ends in 5 years' time, these project staff return to Partner Y.
3 Country P. These project staff are recruited either by the project or by Partner X. They are contracted for the life of the project only.
4 Country Q. These project staff are recruited either by the project or by Partner Y. They are contracted for the life of the project only.
5 Country R and other third-countries. These project staff are recruited either by the project or by Partner X or by Partner Y. They are contracted for the life of the project only. (These staff are discussed further in section 16.5.3 below.)

The wider the range of labor pools, the more diverse the workforce and the wider should be the possibilities for creative synergy. On the other hand, the wider are the possibilities for misunderstandings and dispute.

16.5.2 *When loyalties clash*

Staff from a range of labor pools have different interests. Their different organizational and cultural loyalties can lead to misunderstanding and conflict.

For example, if there should be a dispute between the partners, or between, say, Partner X and the IJV management, staff posted from Partner X are naturally inclined to place its interests above those of the project. They hope to return to Partner X when the project ends, and depend on it for continued employment and promotion and, possibly, pension rights. They have the experience of its organizational culture, and assuming that they are nationals of Country P, Country P culture. Similarly, staff on temporary secondment from Partner Y take their company's side.

In the event of partner–project dispute, staff posted by the partner may start operating informal matrix structures, reporting to managers in both the IJV and their partner. This informal dual-reporting undermines the authority of the project CEO and complicates problems of control.

Staff recruited directly to the IJV from Countries P, Q, and R depend on the IJV during its life and have no loyalties to either partner (unless they hope to be recruited by one). Their performance is heavily influenced by their career needs, their national culture, and the evolving culture of the IJV.

The different interests of these groups may be creative when managed appropriately but dispute always threatens. Their different organizational loyalties are complicated by professional, hierarchical, and cultural factors. Competing organizational and cultural loyalties are reflected in

- relations with each other and with IJV management;
- competing interpretations of IJV goals;

- competing expectations of IJV outcomes;
- competing perceptions of appropriate structure, management systems and style, work norms, organizational culture.

IJV staff also belong to different professional groups. If one profession is associated with one cultural group, competition between professions might be interpreted as a clash between cultures.

16.5.3   *The third-country national*

Why might the IJV employ a third-country national from Country R, who is not employed by either partner? Possibly neither, nor their country labor markets, can supply the skills needed at an economic price. Björkman and Schaap (1994) noted that Scandinavian companies were more likely than North Americans to employ third-country nationals in the People's Republic of China, perhaps "because they had a smaller pool of experienced international managers" (p. 150). Against this economy must be set the additional costs of search and recruitment.

Third-country nationals who are knowledgeable of the cultures of both parents play a useful role in bridging the cultural divide and in acting as informal mediators.

The IJV that values its third-country nationals (and non-partner hires) must be prepared to invest in motivating and rewarding them. Employees from these categories show low levels of loyalty if they perceive that the allocation of rewards discriminates in favor of staff transferred from the partners. Any indication that they are regarded as second-class citizens in the project is bound to be demoralizing.

16.5.4   *The one-culture solution*

The danger of conflict is reduced when all IJV staff are drawn from a single labor pool. When *all* are transferred from the local partner, or *all* are transferred from the foreign partner, their cultural values and experiences correspond.

This solution may attract a partner that cannot spare staff from its routine operations. However, this forgoes opportunities to learn from cooperation, and means that the absent partner has to exert its share of control through some other means; for example, when its inputs of finance or technology are sufficient to dominate. It also implies considerable trust. This may only be realistic in the case of two partners who have built up trust from a history of cooperating on similar projects.

16.5.5   *Balance in project staffing*

Section 15.5 discussed the problems of sharing control in an IJV. A balance in staffing does *not* mean that a marketing manager posted from Partner X has to be balanced by a marketing manager from Partner Y. Instead, it might mean that the appointment of a Parent X marketing manager (reflecting a concern to safeguard its marketing expertise) is balanced by a technology manager posted from Partner Y (which reflects Parent Y's interest in developing marketing expertise).

Balanced recruitment meeting the needs of partners, IJV, and IJV staff is sometimes difficult to achieve. Here are situations in which a failure to provide balance can create disputes between partners and within the IJV:

- One partner tries to dominate by placing its own staff in all key positions.
- One partner withholds its best staff and throws on to the other partner the responsibility for contributing expertise.
- One partner uses the project to rid itself of "deadwood" and trouble-makers, or to secure posts for technically unqualified persons. For instance, the CEO of the partner appoints his unqualified son-in-law to a senior post.
- One partner is unable to fulfill its contracted obligations to supply certain skills, either because of internal deficiencies or because of differences in the technical and economic developments of the two countries of the partners. This factor inhibited early links between Western companies and enterprises in the Central Asian Republics – which until 1991 were tied to the Soviet Union (Pomfret, 1996). The republics lacked experienced managers competent in basic marketing and accounting – skills routinely taught in the West but not in the centrally planned economies.

Imbalances in skill levels can often be corrected by transferring skills technologies. Staff from the less-developed partner may be employed in the IJV as trainees or "shadows" of their experienced colleagues from the stronger partner. Over time, the staff-in-training play increasingly proactive roles. This arrangement works well, so long as all parties (the partners, the IJV management, and the staff concerned):

- adequately plan how the technology transfer and training activities should be implemented;
- are satisfied with the implementation process;
- are motivated to participate (questions of motivation are discussed below).

16.5.6 Motivating staff to work for the IJV

Staff may be unwilling to leave the security of their regular work and their work groups at headquarters to move to the IJV. This is a problem in collectivist cultures, where members may interpret the move as punishment and "exile" – even when the IJV is in the same country – rather than as promotion.

Staff transferred from a parent to work in the project are motivated when:

- They are given a free choice of whether or not to join the IJV;
- They recognize that working for the IJV is in their career and professional interests;
- They are adequately compensated. Resentment over inequalities in pay is damaging. Tretiak and Holzmann (1993) wrote that in the People's Republic of China:

it is a matter of pride for local authorities that local managers receive salaries equivalent to expatriate managers for similar positions. Chinese partners sometimes find it hard to understand why generous packages have to be paid to attract experienced expatriates.

(p. 13)

- They propose two solutions: negotiating for expatriates to be paid on a separate basis, which avoids putting them on the IJV payroll; or having the IJV pay their salaries and the foreign parent pay their benefits and bonuses.
- They benefit from special arrangements. Before the collapse of the Soviet Union, IJV employment offered the Soviet citizen an opportunity to travel abroad and earn foreign currency – otherwise very difficult to come by (Rosten, 1991).
- They are trained. But training can be a sensitive issue. Staff from the weaker parent are *not* motivated if trainee status is perceived to diminish their status, and if they have no professional reasons for making the commitment. For instance, staff transferred from a public sector organization, whose jobs are guaranteed and protected from competitive forces, may have no need to upgrade their skills. In this situation, skills are not transferred. Training and support issues are discussed generally in chapter 18.

16.6   Implications for the Manager

Analyze how staffing is used to control your subsidiary, IJV, or some other organization to which you have access.

How important is staffing in controlling the company's foreign investments? Make a survey of each investment, and compare them.

1   What policy does your MNC apply when staffing senior positions in its subsidiaries?
   (a)   In what respects is staffing policy uniform across all subsidiaries?
   (b)   In what respects does staffing policy take account of differences between subsidiaries, their local business/economic contexts and markets?
   (c)   In what respects does the national culture of headquarters influence staffing policy?
   (d)   In what respects do the national cultures of the subsidiaries influence the staffing policy?
   (e)   In what respects do organizational cultures in headquarters and subsidiaries influence the staffing policy?
2   In each subsidiary, is top management expatriate or local?
   (a)   In each case, why?
   (b)   In each case, how does this satisfy headquarters needs for control?
   (c)   In each case, what control does top management apply?
   (d)   In each case, how does the subsidiary benefit from this staffing decision?
   (e)   In each case, how does the subsidiary lose from this staffing decision?
3   In each subsidiary function/department, is management expatriate or local?
   (a)   In each case, why?
   (b)   In each case, what control does the manager apply?

(c) In each case, how does the function/department benefit from this staffing decision?

(d) In each case, how does the subsidiary lose from this staffing decision?

4 In each subsidiary, how are local managers recruited? What training are they given? Why is this training given?

5 In each subsidiary:

(a) Has the number of expatriate managers increased or decreased over the past ten years (relative to the number of subsidiary managers)?

(b) What factors explain any change in staffing levels?

6 In each IJV, describe staffing:

(a) staff transferred from the foreign partner;

(b) staff transferred from the local partner;

(c) staff recruited from the country of the foreign partner;

(d) staff recruited from the country of the local partner;

(e) staff recruited from third-countries.

7 What advantages arise from this staffing mix?

8 What disadvantages arise from this staffing mix?

9 What disputes arise between these groups? What factors cause these disputes? How are they typically resolved?

16.7 SUMMARY

This chapter has examined how control is enforced by staffing policy.

Section 16.2 examined two notions of the relationship between company and employee, one primarily enforced through rules and the other accentuating trust. Models of BUREAUCRATIC control and CULTURAL control were discussed. Both have implications for staffing policy. Section 16.3 dealt with reasons for choosing either an EXPATRIATE OR LOCAL top manager. Each offers advantages and disadvantages, and a range of factors determine which advantages sway the decision. Cultural factors, including headquarters tolerances of uncertainty, may be of major importance.

The headquarters may have different needs for control in different subsidiaries, and so makes different staffing decisions in each. Section 16.4 dealt with LOCAL MANAGEMENT and stressed the difficulties that senior local managers face in interpreting between expatriate top management and local staff. The importance of developing managers who can play this role means that great care has to be taken in recruitment, retaining local loyalties, and training. MNCs should consider exploiting the pools of labor that may be overlooked by local employers. The advantages and disadvantages of providing experience of headquarters operations were discussed.

Section 16.5 turned to problems of STAFFING THE IJV. In part because three parties (the two partners and IJV management) all have needs to exercise control, staff are recruited from a range of labor pools. Their different interests and loyalties can generate positive synergies but may also lead to control problems if not properly managed. Third-country nationals bring benefits when they mediate between the other groups. A one-culture solution is usually not practical. The needs to balance staff contributions and to motivate staff were examined.

16.8 EXERCISE

This exercise asks you to decide whether to employ expatriate or local managers in a subsidiary. Students can work on this on their own or in pairs.

Upanattem Universal (UU) is a multinational company headquartered in Ruritania. It develops and manufactures children's products ranging from baby food to toys and clothing. The subsidiary in Darana, Upanattem Darana (UD), employs 500 people and management is structured as shown in figure 16.2. (R indicates that the post is currently held by a Ruritanian expatriate and D by a Daranese. Numbers indicate how many years that person has been in post.)

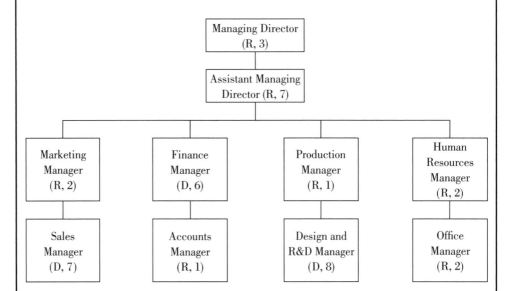

Figure 16.2 Management structure at Upanattem Darana

The costs involved in maintaining current expatriate staffing levels are increasing and some board members have queried human resource policies followed in UD. You have been hired as an external consultant to advise on the HR implications of the following sets of factors.

1 Each of (a)–(d) below lists four factors. Decide which factors affect the decision to employ expatriates or locals, then for the set, decide on who should be repatriated, promoted, or continued, and on criteria for recruitment for posts left empty.

2 Decide which factors can be ignored. Why can each of these be ignored?

3 No one need suffer! Assume that all staff have been performing satisfactorily. Any expatriates recalled to headquarters will be promoted. Any local staff that are replaced will be moved to a new, highly prestigious, joint venture project.

(a) i   Members of Ruritanian culture have low needs to avoid uncertainty.

ii UD has recently introduced a new baby food product, produced by the Design and R&D department.

iii Local market conditions are stable. UD dominates the local market, and has no significant competitors.

iv The Daranese economy is underdeveloped. Trained managerial and technical staff are in short supply.

(b) i   Members of Ruritanian culture have high needs to avoid uncertainty.

ii Local market conditions are very changeable. Until now, UD has dominated the local market, but now a major foreign MNC is competing for market share.

iii The Human Resources Manager has recently proposed a new HR strategy, designed to recruit and train the next generation of Daranese managers.

iv UU will benefit from greater communication and transfer of resources between UD and subsidiaries in other countries.

(c) i   Relations between expatriate and local staff members are unfriendly, and communication within UD is bad.

ii Communication between UD and headquarters is good.

iii The Daranese economy is developed. There is no shortage of trained managerial and technical staff.

iv Back in UU headquarters, a new CEO has been appointed. He proposes that all managerial promotions take the number of expatriate years into account. A manager who has no expatriate experience cannot hope for fast-track promotion.

(d) i   The Daranese government has recently relaxed its restrictions on expatriate visas.

ii UU headquarters staff consider that the current UU policies do not significantly reward headquarters staff who take expatriate assignments.

iii New Daranese laws offer tax incentives to multinationals that employ nationals in management positions; if UD replaces one of its current expatriates with a national, it will receive a 10 percent tax break, if two, a 20 percent tax break, and so on.

iv Members of Ruritanian culture have high needs to avoid uncertainty.

Notes

1 Michael Skapinder, "Empires of ignorance: companies should look to history for lessons in how to operate in foreign cultures," *Financial Times*, January 15, 2003. This reviews Litvin, 2003.

2 "Hooked by Hollywood," *The Economist*, September 21, 1991.

3 John Murray Brown, "'Paddy network' wires up world's computers," *Financial Times*, February 27, 1996.

4 Cherian George, "Firms 'need to double number of Singapore expats'," *The Straits Times Weekly Edition*, November 11, 1995.

CHAPTER SEVENTEEN
Expatriate Assignments

17.1   Introduction

The Italian fashion house, Po, is a global company that has achieved its great success by innovating in design, building highly centralized management structures, and developing a standard uniform image. The company projects the same image in its many branches worldwide.

The company employs a team of highly skilled shop fitters that are sent off to create the environment of every new shop. All designs are prepared in the Milan headquarters and discussed in detail with the shop fitters before they leave. Usually though, these discussions are brief. The company attempts to project the same brand image everywhere, and the basic designs never change. In all, the same color paint is used, as well as the same furniture designs and if possible the same layout.

At the foreign branch, the premises are ready prepared. No local materials are used. Everything needed is flown out by headquarters. The shop fitters complete the assignment as soon as possible and then return to Milan. They have minimal contacts with the local population. The job has been determined entirely by headquarters and they have not needed any expatriate training to do their jobs. Hence their success or failure on a particular assignment is not dependent on an ability to adjust to the foreign culture.

The company succeeds because it emphasizes Italian sophistication, and deliberately does not make any concessions to local values. But this is an extreme example.

Most companies need to take local tastes into consideration. Expatriate staff usually work with local staff, and perhaps negotiate their job descriptions with local managers. In such cases expatriates need to adjust to local conditions.

This chapter deals with the opportunities and difficulties faced by expatriates when working abroad for their companies. It examines notions of success and failure, and in particular focuses on why notions of failure are influenced by who is making the evaluation and in what cultural context. It sees how the company increases the likelihood of success by improving its selection procedures. The topic is of importance to:

- the expatriate manager and dependents;
- headquarters human resource staff and others, responsible for posting and supporting the manager and dependents;
- subsidiary and joint venture managers, responsible for hosting and supporting the manager and dependents.

17.2 Expatriate Functions

In 1930, one Anglo oil company employed 60 expatriates in Taiwan. By 2000, this number had fallen to a single individual. This decline is not unusual. Established multinationals that once sent dozens of managers to a prominent foreign posting may now depend entirely on local staff. A number of reasons can explain policies intended to reduce expatriations. These include:

- Expense. The cost of expatriations is increasingly prohibitive.
- New information technologies, which have reduced the need for the physical presence of headquarters staff.
- An increased supply of well-trained and experienced local staff.
- An increased need to empower local operations.
- Policies by the local government to reduce expatriate levels and encourage the development of local managerial talent.

On the last point, for example, in Mexico:

> the extensive use of expatriates is not a viable staffing alternative because Mexican labour law requires that no more than 10 per cent of a firm may be non-Mexican.
>
> *(Luthans et al., 2001, p. 95)*

Elsewhere, governments impose visa controls limiting a multinational to an expatriate workforce in proportion to its headquarters investment. For example, the subsidiary is only permitted one expatriate visa for every $300,000 invested.

However, this does not necessarily mean that worldwide, or in any one country, the *total* number of expatriates is in decline. More companies are involved in international business than ever, and more appear to be making expatriate assignments, even if these are only short term. A 1997 survey suggested that the total number of individuals working abroad for part of their careers may be on the rise:

> 90% of MNCs surveyed has predicted that numbers of expatriates will increase over the next years.[1]

Young managers entering the workforce now must expect to work expatriate at some time in their careers.

This book uses the term "expatriate" broadly, to refer to anybody representing their company abroad, although it will become clear that many of the points discussed below apply more to those working long assignments than to those away for only a week or two. We focus here on expatriate managers and technical staff.

17.2.1 What expatriates do

In what functions are expatriates employed by their companies? Björkman and Schaap (1994, p. 149) listed the management positions held by Western expatriates in 36 China-based international joint ventures in China. Of the 84 positions (including two part-timers) 29 were general manager, and in order thereafter, production manager (19), financial controller (10), quality control manager (7), marketing manager (5), deputy marketing manager (4), sales manager (2), others (9).

These priorities reflect traditional expatriate functions associated with needs for CONTROL when international managers were assigned with long-term responsibilities for managing subsidiaries, ventures, and departments. The managers in the Björkman and Schaap sample are apparently in this mold, serving long-term contracts lasting several years. But such postings may no longer be typical.

There are four main reasons for changes in the expatriate job market. The first is economic. Many companies can no longer afford the expenses involved in long-term expatriation. In an increasingly uncertain world, the benefits cannot be predicted, and the rewards may be insufficient to justify the risk. The second is related; branches in rapidly developing societies can hire competent local managers whose educational and professional standards at least match those of the expatriates they replace. Third, the host government may be under political pressure to develop its own management elite and so to reduce the numbers of long-term expatriates. However, short-term expatriates may be welcomed if they are able to transfer valued technologies and techniques.

Fourth, the pace of change means that short consultancy visits may have to be made in order to continually update processes in the branch. In the most rapidly developing countries, expatriate functions are changing. Now, increasing numbers of managers work abroad on highly focused, short-term projects, which perhaps last only a few weeks or months. These are designed to transfer headquarters KNOWLEDGE to the subsidiary, or to learn from the subsidiary. These functions include:

- conducting an internal consultancy;
- establishing a new system;

- mentoring;
- recruiting and training;
- explaining headquarters strategy;
- research;
- inspection;
- evaluation.

In practice, many expatriates may have dual functions associated with both control and knowledge.

This does not mean that long-term assignments are a thing of a past. Many companies still staff some foreign positions with staff prepared to accept the challenge for a number of years. What it does mean is that the range of expatriate assignments is broadening.

The advantages of short assignments are that objectives are precisely defined and activities can be more controlled. The disadvantages are that the expatriate has fewer opportunities to experiment, and to increase his sum of knowledge; that is, the long-term advantages to the company may be less.

17.3   Expatriate Success and Failure

There is little agreement on what constitutes success and failure in an expatriate appointment. The variances are wide, and reflect differences in:

- how to measure success and failure (see section 17.3.1);
- how to explain failure (see section 17.3.2);
- who makes the evaluation (see section 17.3.3);
- perceptions of cultural difference (see section 17.3.4).

In addition, cultural factors influence the conditions for success and failure. These are discussed in sections 17.3.5 and 17.3.6.

17.3.1   Measuring success and failure

Performance in expatriate assignments is measured by very different criteria. Here are some common benchmarks.

- Success is measured relative to the expatriate's performance back home. He/she is performing at least as successfully, and possibly more so.
- Success is measured relative to the job description. The expatriate is at least fulfilling the specifications of the post, and possibly exceeding them.
- Success is measured relative to the circumstances. In very difficult circumstances the expatriate is performing better than could be expected.

Failure may be signaled by the expatriate's recall to headquarters, possibly accompanied by dismissal. Or he/she is moved to another post considered less demanding. Or he/she quits.

Of course, these events do not necessarily signal failure, and may even indicate success. For example, the manager is recalled in order to take a senior post at headquarters. Eschbach et al. (2001) cite data indicating that between 10–50 percent of American expatriates curtail their assignments early. And the manager who performs below expectations may still be continued at post, perhaps to avoid embarrassing those responsible for his/her posting or because no one is available to substitute.

Failure might be measured:

- relative to his/her performance back home (e.g. the expatriate is performing worse);
- relative to the job description (e.g. the expatriate is failing to meet the specification of the post);
- relative to the circumstances (e.g. in easy circumstances the expatriate is performing worse than could be expected).

The criteria used to assess success and failure vary widely, and this is reflected in the calculations of failures: for Americans, most are within the 15–40 percent range. However, there is a range of reasons why all figures and explanations have to be treated with suspicion and demand further questions; and many of these reasons are explored in this chapter. An immediate point is that published expatriate failure rates seldom compare these to failure rates in the home country. To take a hypothetical example: a company suffering a 20 percent expatriate failure rate and a 30 percent failure rate in headquarters among persons of equivalent tenure and responsibilities should be worrying more about the organizational culture of headquarters than about that of its subsidiary.

Of course, the majority of expatriate assignments succeed – the figures above suggest between 60 and 85 percent. Nevertheless, managements and scholars are more concerned with explaining failure and correcting the conditions under which it occurs. This is not surprising, given that the cost to the organization may be heavy. Taking into account the expenses involved in transportation, rent, family moving expenses, schooling and other allowances, salary and other rewards, hiring replacement labor at headquarters, a failed foreign placement costs the company a significant sum: Eschbach et al. (2001) suggest a figure of up to $500,000 in the case of American repatriates, and some estimates are far higher.

In addition, there are intangible expenses such as the loss of goodwill among those at post who have come into contact with the failed expatriate. He/she also suffers: perhaps the loss of self-esteem, the loss of a career, ill health, and domestic disruption.

However, notions of failure are plastic and subjective, and the remaining sections of the chapter deal with the difficulty of precisely defining failure, and explaining it. For example, a comparison to performance back home is unrealistic if the expatriate is working in new and unfamiliar surroundings, particularly during the first few months of culture shock. A failure to fulfill the job description begs the question, who wrote it?

A headquarters job description may be out of date and is less likely to reflect the realities of a rapidly changing local environment than a job description written by local management. On the other hand a job description concocted by the subsidiary may not correspond to headquarters strategic needs, or to the post details originally issued to the expatriate.

17.3.2 *How to explain failure*

Why do some expatriates fail? Tung (1987) ranked causes of expatriate failure in American MNCs, in descending order of importance:

1 Inability of the manager's spouse to adjust to a different physical or cultural environment;
2 The manager's inability to adjust to a different physical or cultural environment;
3 Other family-related problems;
4 The manager's personality or emotional immaturity;
5 The manager's inability to cope with the responsibilities posed by work abroad;
6 The manager's lack of technical competence;
7 The manager's lack of motivation to work abroad.

This analysis of failure (in common with most others) shows that managerial and technical incompetence is not a major factor. Less than one-third of premature returns arise from work-specific reasons. Problems of cultural adjustment are the most important determinants of success or failure.

Tung's (1987) data show that the inability of the spouse or partner and dependents to adjust to the new culture has most influence upon the manager's own adjustment and performance. (Dependents are defined as persons at post with the manager who would not be there if he had not been appointed to the post and are at least partly dependent on his earnings.) Similarly, Forster (2000, p. 127) found that:

> employees whose partners were reporting more difficulties were also more likely to report higher stress levels and greater dissatisfaction with their job.

Black and Stephens (1989) researched the perceptions of expatriate American managers and their spouses. They based their study on data from Japan, Korea, Taiwan, and Hong Kong. These countries all have cultures that differ widely from American culture on Hofstede's dimensions of power distance and individualism–collectivism. They discovered that:

- the spouse's adjustment is highly correlated to that of her husband, the expatriate manager;
- the spouse is more likely to adjust when she feels positive about the overseas assignment.

What factors influence how far the spouse feels positive about the assignment? Two important factors are:

- whether the spouse is involved in planning the arrangement at an early stage;
- whether the spouse has been given training before departure.

But how often are these conditions likely to apply? The evidence provided by Black and Stephens (1989, p. 541) suggested that they applied only seldom:

> . . . only 30 percent of the firms sought the spouse's opinion concerning the international assignment. Also, over 90 percent of the firms in this study offered no predeparture training for spouses. Over 90 percent of the firms did not offer job finding assistance for spouses even though approximately 50 percent of the spouses worked prior to the international assignment.

Although this is an old study, there is no reason to think that the situation has changed dramatically. The dependent spouse who has a career in the home country and has to break this in order to accompany the manager to the posting is most likely to be frustrated. Harvey (1998) found that a dual-career couple face a strong likelihood of dissatisfaction and failure in a foreign assignment.

The factors that improve conditions for dependents include:

- Cross-cultural and language TRAINING.
- Opportunities to WORK (or study) for those who want to. Some countries make it easy for expatriate dependents to work. Elsewhere the interests of the local workforce are protected – for example, by reserving particular sectors to them. In some countries cultural factors mean that expatriate female employment is not normally acceptable – for example, in some Middle Eastern countries.
- The SIZE of the expatriate national community, which affects opportunities for cultural and social support.
- RELATIONS between the local and expatriate communities.
- The ECONOMIC DISTANCE between the local and expatriate communities and problems of adjusting to new economic realities.
- Perceptions of CULTURAL DISTANCE between the cultures. (This point is developed below.)

17.3.3 Who makes the evaluation

Explanations for success and failure vary according to who makes the assessment.

The categories used in Tung's (1987) ranking (examined in section 17.3.2) suggest that she collected her data from company human resource departments. It must be remembered, on the one hand, that the manager is unlikely to admit to his own "personality or emotional immaturity," his "inability to cope with the responsibilities posed by overseas work," or his "lack of technical competence." On the other hand, the HR manager needs to defend his/her own record in making the posting – although one might ask why the companies were sending abroad people who lacked maturity and motivation.

Hamill's (1989, p. 24) study of problems faced by British expatriates listed the following key factors:

- family-related problems, including an inability of dependents to adjust;
- inadequate selection/recruitment criteria;
- having technical skills rather than cultural empathy;
- inadequate pre-post briefing;
- poorly designed compensation packages;
- lack of advanced planning for re-entry;
- remoteness from headquarters and loss of status, and ensuing lack of status.

These problems were most probably *not* reported by company human resource departments. Given that it is their responsibility to organize selection, briefing, and compensation, they are unlikely to explain expatriate failure by "inadequate selection/recruitment criteria," "inadequate pre-post briefing," "poorly designed compensation packages." Rather, these sound like the complaints of unhappy expatriated staff who feel that they have been badly treated by headquarters.

Explanations given for failure depend on who is explaining. Many different persons and units have interests in the expatriate's performance. They include:

- managers to whom he/she reports at headquarters;
- managers to whom he/she reports in the joint venture or subsidiary;
- colleagues;
- subordinates;
- the expatriate him/herself.

They may all make formal or informal evaluations, and apply different criteria.

17.3.4 *Perceptions of cultural distance*

It is sometimes argued that some cultures are intrinsically harder for managers and their dependents. Bonvillain and Nowlin (1994, p. 44) focus on:

> ... the location, as studies have shown that although 18 percent of those sent to London will fail, this increases to 36 percent in Tokyo and 68 percent in Saudi Arabia.

However, intrinsic difficulty cannot be measured. What the authors do not make clear is their American bias: that is, 18 percent of *Americans* sent to London, 36 percent of *Americans* sent to Tokyo, and 68 percent of *Americans* sent to Saudi Arabia fail, not 18, 36, and 68 percent of *all* expatriates. But Arabs, for example, may have different perceptions of cultural distance, and Arab managers might find it easier to adjust to working and living in Saudi Arabia than do Americans.

In practice, cultural distance is hard to measure. Hofstede's data show that although some cultures are close on all dimensions – for example, the United States and Australia – others may be close on some and far apart on others. Greece ranks highest in *needs to avoid uncertainty* and Hong Kong is found at the other end of the scale, in 49/50 position. But in terms of *masculinity/femininity*, Greece and Hong Kong are found together in 18/19 position. So, by these different criteria, these cultures can be interpreted as both culturally distant and very close.

What may matter more is the PERCEPTION of cultural distance – and most people do distinguish other cultures as more or less "distant" and "close" to their own. Perceptions of cultural distance between his/her headquarters culture and the target culture may inhibit the manager from applying for the expatriate assignment. And should he/she apply and be selected, cultural worries are likely to inhibit performance. Selmer's (2001) study of American, French, German, Australian, and United Kingdom managers in China indicated that:

> psychological barriers to adjustment, such as their perceived inability and unwillingness to adjust, could affect how they try to cope with life and work in China.   *(p. 151)*

Those who feel that they are incapable of adjusting are less likely to explore problem-solving strategies by which they might ease their problems and develop positive relationships within the host culture.

This implies that those selecting for an expatriate assignment should be looking for a candidate who by temperament or training is least troubled by perceptions of cultural distance between his/her own and the target culture, and most likely to develop strategies for overcoming such problems as do arise.

17.3.5 *Cultural influences on the conditions for success and failure*

This leads to a wider discussion of how far cultural factors influence the conditions for success and failure. The importance of the manager's cultural background is illustrated by a list of (unranked) factors which caused stress to Japanese managers working in the United States. They include:

- insecurities resulting from being cut off from their *dou-ki-kai*, or fraternity of co-workers;
- concern over their wives' social isolation;
- concern over their children's educational opportunities on return home;
- lack of support from relatives and friends;
- cultural dislocation;
- frustration with their United States subordinates.[2]

Certain items on this list reflect aspects of Japanese culture which do not correspond to American culture. The *dou-ki-kai* consists of persons joining the Japanese company in the same recruiting season. The importance given to it reflects the importance of the work group and of long-term employment in the same company. At the time of this research (that is, before the Japanese recession which began in the early 1990s) lifetime employment was a reality for about a third of the workforce, and those who enjoyed it might expect professional links with members of their *dou-ki-kai* until they reached retirement age together.

An American manager commented on the *dou-ki-kai*:

> "There's nothing like this in the United States. I just don't know who joined the company at the same time as I did. And as for keeping in touch, that's not possible. People move around so much that you don't keep friends from work."

This institution is particular to Japan. Its influence on Japanese expatriate experience shows that factors in the home culture as much as in the local culture help explain success and failure.

The Japanese manager's concern over his children's educational opportunities on return home reflected the importance given to the school as a means of transmitting Japanese culture. At this time, Japanese educated outside the Japanese educational system were placed at a major disadvantage when looking for employment. American managers did not feel corresponding pressures.

The last factor on the Japanese list reflects the differences in communication styles typical of the two cultures. The section on high- and low-context cultures showed that a high-context Japanese manager can expect Japanese subordinates to work on deducing his priorities without his needing to articulate them. But in low-context American culture, less is taken for granted as shared and the manager has to make his directions explicit. A *Newsweek* story reported that:

> Americans, a Japanese boss [managing a US branch] often feels, need more supervision than their Japanese counterparts, who try to intuit their superior's desire.[3]

Studies of other national groups make clear that culture influences perceptions of expatriate work. A 1995 survey of 200 Singaporean managers in multinationals showed that:

> family considerations, especially children's schooling, were the top concern of employees going overseas. They were also worried that being away from home base would hurt their careers.[4]

The concern reflects an aspect of the culture: a Confucian emphasis on education.

17.3.6 *Cultural comparisons: Japanese and American expatriates*

How far does the culture of the manager influence the likelihood of his success? Tung's (1987) survey of United States, west European, and Japanese multinationals found that over 50 percent of the United States companies had failure rates of 10–20 percent, and 7 percent had failure rates of 30 percent. Failure rates among European and Japanese companies were lower: 59 percent of the Europeans recalled 5 percent of their expatriate employees and only 3 percent recalled 11–15 percent; 76 percent of the Japanese had failure rates of below 5 percent.

At first sight, this suggests that Japanese managers are naturally better equipped to endure the difficulties of expatriation than are Americans. However, a number of factors have to be taken into account.

At the time this research was conducted, Japanese expatriate assignments were far longer. In 1982 when the Japanese economy was booming, foreign postings made by Japanese MNCs averaged 4 years and 7 months, whereas corresponding postings by American MNCs averaged 1 year and 11 months. The difference reflected a range of factors, of which failure rates were only one.

On the other hand, American companies understand that they cannot hope to retain the services of their best managers by insisting that they take long postings. In general, American employees have never expected or wanted guarantees of lifetime employment and have always been more mobile. American managers are prepared to gamble on success, even in the short term, and seldom feel constrained to accept long postings abroad. Given the greater fluidity of the managerial job market and the greater likelihood of finding new employment in the event of an expatriate failure or an early move, the costs of failure were relatively less than for the Japanese manager, who may feel he has no alternative to staying with the company for the long term, and hence must accept an assignment, however long.

The Japanese employee's acceptance of this economic commitment reflects his sense of loyalty to the company. Like other Asians, he perceives his relationship with the company in terms of an ethical bond that commits both sides, whereas the American employee and employer are more conscious of the contractual arrangements. It values lifetime employment both as an expression of loyalty and as protection against life's uncertainties. Writing at the depth of the depression, Watanabe (2000) shows that:

> The major trade unions' top priority remains job security and longer working lives, for which they are prepared to accept wage cuts, if necessary. The government is also urging firms to continue employment up to age 65. *(p. 183)*

The expatriations of Americans and Japanese also differ in terms of when they are evaluated. The American may also be placed under considerable pressure by being evaluated at regular intervals in the first year. For much of this time he/she may be suffering from culture shock – particularly when he/she perceives a distance between American culture and the local culture. The Japanese, expecting to be in post for much longer, is given longer to learn the job before his/her first evaluation.

In general, the Japanese attitude towards its expatriate investments reflects a sense of relationship between employer and employee, and needs for loyalty on both sides. The Anglo attitude is more utilitarian, and the Anglo who does express a desire to stay in post may be suspected of "going native" and placing local interests before those of the company.

17.3.7   *When should the expatriate be evaluated?*

A major Japanese pharmaceuticals firm had a policy of not evaluating its expatriates for their first 6 months at post. The performance of the manager's unit during this period was attributed to his predecessor. This had the effects that:

- the old managers maintained their performance levels up to the end of their posting (they did not dare relax in the last few months);
- the old managers fully briefed their successors and eased their entry into the unit;
- the new managers had many months in which to learn the job without worrying unduly about evaluation.

During these first 6 months the new manager was visited twice or more by his headquarters mentor. Each visit may last up to a week and the mentor gave advice, answered queries, and tried to resolve problems – but did not evaluate.

How far has the prolonged Japanese recession, the end to lifetime employment, and the restructuring of industry affected Japanese attitudes towards expatriate assignments? Given that attitudes towards the company, the boss, and to colleagues are heavily influenced by culture, the changes are unlikely to be revolutionary in the short term.

Whether or not cultural factors can generate an aptitude for expatriate work, they certainly seem to influence attitudes towards expatriation and the relationship between the headquarters and expatriate. Hence, culture also appears to influence how expatriate work is evaluated.

17.4   Selecting for Success

Wise companies invest in improving the conditions for success and protecting themselves against failure. However, simple economics indicates that no company should invest more in an expatriate assignment than it can reasonably expect to get back in return. How can it improve the odds on success while holding the costs involved at an economic level? Here we ask how companies can select their expatriates efficiently. Training and support techniques are discussed throughout the next chapter.

Conditions for success may in part be inferred from analyses of failure. To apply Tung's (1987) findings in section 17.3.2, the expatriate is most likely to succeed when:

1 His/her spouse/partner is able to adjust to the different physical or cultural environment;
2 The manager is able to adjust to the different physical or cultural environment;
3 There are no significant family-related problems;
4 The manager has a good personality and emotional maturity;
5 The manager is able to cope with the responsibilities posed by work abroad;
6 The manager has full technical competence;
7 The manager is motivated to work abroad.

This provides a guide to selection criteria, and how to train and support.

17.4.1 Selection

The company hopes to select the candidate most likely to succeed and least likely to fail when:

- working in the local culture;
- living in the local culture.

Both functions are important. It is usually not sufficient that the expatriate be a good worker if he/she is a social incompetent and a cultural chauvinist. The local population perceive the expatriate as a representative of his/her company and nation, and the company is unwise to send the individual who is incapable of recognizing these responsibilities. An ethnocentric attitude in the workplace and in social situations gives rise to antagonisms that may damage the profitability of the company.

From its knowledge of a particular post and the local culture, the company decides whether it has any preferences in selecting:

(a) A male, accompanied by a spouse/partner and, possibly, other dependents;
(b) A male, unaccompanied;
(c) A female, accompanied by a spouse/partner and, possibly, other dependents;
(d) A female, unaccompanied.

A range of attitudes influence the decision, and these tend to change over time.

The great majority of expatriates are male. The bias against females is sometimes explained by industry factors. In the Anglo cultures, still only a relatively few women graduate in engineering or technology, and so, it is claimed, few are qualified for management positions, whether at home or abroad. There may be a cultural bias against promoting women into management positions, and so, again, relatively few are available to represent the company abroad.

A *Wall Street Journal* report on a consultants' survey reported of the American companies polled:

80 percent said there were disadvantages to sending women overseas.

"Clients refuse to do business with female representatives," one company [said]. Another explained: "The desired expatriate is a thirtyish married man with pre-school age children. This is to project our image as a conservative institution with good moral fiber.... Many of our potential expatriates are single, and a swinging single is not the right image."[5]

There is a paucity of data showing the relative success rates of male and female expatriation rates, and that female singles are more inclined to "swing" than male marrieds. We also lack support for other commonplaces, voiced not just in the United States (for example that foreigners' prejudices against women expatriates renders them ineffective, and that women do not want to be international managers). In fact, research demonstrates the opposite: if given the choice, women are neither less nor more enthusiastic about expatriate work than are their male equivalents, and neither less nor more capable.

Some companies make a practice of selecting family males on the assumption that this gives greater stability. If the relationship is successful and the female partner adjusts well to the experience, this is justified. But Tung's (1987) findings also suggest that, in the event of a weak relationship and a partner who finds it hard to adjust to a role of dependency, domestic pressures have a damaging effect on how the manager performs his functions.

Attitudes have changed and it is now increasingly acceptable to expatriate single males. The company may assume that a policy of expatriating a single person avoids the complications that arise from sending someone in a long-term relationship. HSBC recruits for expatriate careers on the basis that you will be single and accept being moved to a new post every 4 years. Single postings are more flexible, cost much less, and reduce the administrative load. However, factors associated with the supply and demand of labor may force the opposite decision. If the posting is considered economically essential and the only, or best, person available insists on taking a "trailing spouse" the company has no alternative to taking on this cost. American companies have even been faced with instances of "trailing parents" – the only person available for a posting that promises to earn unusual profit makes it a condition that he/she takes one or both parents.

The company decision on who to send may also be influenced by considerations of age and previous experience. Young expatriates have the advantage of greater energy and perhaps fewer domestic complications. On the other hand, they lack professional and social experience and are not necessarily more able to learn. Persons who have not previously worked abroad lack cross-cultural experience but may see problems with new eyes and find new solutions. The grizzled old-timer who has worked in a hundred different countries and by this time can never remember whether he's in Iraq or Vietnam – and has little interest in discovering which – may be adequate only for performing mechanical tasks. In practice, the company may have to decide on the basis of the individual's personal characteristics rather than on the basis of blanket generalizations.

A small company has few options. A large company has more options when its potential expatriates feel motivated to apply and a headquarters replacement can be found to take over the responsibilities of whoever is assigned from its existing pool.

If a company cannot select from its internal pool, it may need to hire from the external labor market.

The company has a range of tools that can be used in selecting, including interviews, role-plays, workshops, psychometric testing, management reports, and references.

17.4.2 Specifications

The job description specifies the tasks which the expatriate is expected to perform in the assignment, sets the standards of performance, and clarifies to whom he/she reports. A tight specification is more likely to ensure good performance – so long as it accurately reflects conditions in the foreign post and its environment. This implies that local management makes a contribution to it in order to guarantee its accuracy.

The balance between headquarters and local expectations of the post and contributions to the job description must be made clear. The expatriate and his/her immediate managers are confused and frustrated when the balance in interests is ambiguous and reporting responsibilities unclear. The various parties involved need to agree all aspects of the specification, taking into account the strategic interests of headquarters and subsidiary.

In addition, the criteria for evaluation are made clear. These spell out:

▌ WHAT activities are evaluated and expected standards;
▌ WHEN evaluation is made (e.g. at set stages in the assignment and at the end);
▌ WHO evaluates, including managers at headquarters and/or the posting;
▌ HOW evaluation is made.

17.4.3 Criteria for selection

The manager needs the necessary technical and managerial skills. But these alone are not enough. Technical incompetence is seldom the major reason for failure, and he/she also needs a range of personal qualities and aptitudes.

Successful expatriates and their dependents have positive expectations about living in the host culture. Those who expect adjustment problems and are unwilling to adjust are less likely to develop productive relationships with local nationals, or to cope with life and work in the foreign setting.

Successful expatriates are also more geocentric – that is, able to think in world terms and excited by the opportunities offered by cultural difference. The company cannot expect to find a manager equally capable in all cultures; but it does aim to appoint a person with interests in the host culture and does not appoint the obvious ethnocentric who evaluates all situations in terms of home values, tries to apply home values abroad and perceives only threats in cultural difference.

The expatriate needs to:

▌ ADAPT his/her technical and managerial skills to new business environments in order to deal with new opportunities and threats;

■ NEGOTIATE effectively;
■ recognize and SOLVE problems when working in the new culture;
■ COMMUNICATE well with people from the new cultures and form new friendships;
■ have the emotional MATURITY to tolerate uncertainty and stress in the new situation;
■ LEARN from experience and be adaptable to change;
■ INTEGRATE with others;
■ be MOTIVATED to work and live in the new culture (see sections 17.4.5 and 17.4.6).

The relationship between headquarters and the foreign unit decides what balance of skills is needed. In a highly global company, the expatriate may be reporting primarily to headquarters and his/her needs to interact with the local environment are less. In a joint venture, skills of communicating with local managers and others in the local environment are of paramount importance. In a highly unstable environment, the manager needs a high tolerance of uncertainty and stress. Particularly when the posting is new, the expatriate contributes by learning about the new environment, and building up a bank of knowledge accessible to headquarters. In transnational operations the expatriate must be capable of applying professional skills from one branch to another. He/she must be flexible, and able to reconcile the needs for a strong corporate identity with decentralization. The high-flying transnational manager can expect to be rotated regularly, work in several languages, and make decisions in very different situations. Whether or not he/she adjusts depends in large part on:

• his/her capacities to adjust to the new setting;
• the capacities of any dependents to adjust;
• the role novelty (the difference between the new role and previous roles that he/she has undertaken) – the greater the novelty, the longer is the adjustment time needed;
• the duration of the assignment.

17.4.4   Overcoming perceptions of a culture gap: the criterion of ethnic affinity

Section 17.3.4 saw that perceptions of cultural distance are sometimes used to explain expatriate problems. An apparent solution to the problem is to appoint a person who has ethnic affinities with the local unit. For example, an American company appoints a Latino American to manage its operations in Brazil, a Chinese American to China, an Afro-American to Nigeria. This policy promises to overcome the suspicions of local staff and to win their commitment. In a study of 36 joint ventures in the People's Republic of China, Björkman and Schaap (1994) found that 13 employed at least one expatriate of Chinese ethnicity.

This practice sometimes succeeds in bridging the cultural differences, but sometimes leads to misunderstandings. Locals may measure the co-ethnic expatriate by different standards than foreign expatriates. They assume that he/she shares their cultural loyalty and expect him/her to support their interests in any dispute with headquarters. These expectations are disappointed if the expatriate is committed to the country of migration and determined to prove his/her identity as a member of its culture. In sum, selecting on the basis of ethnic affinity does not guarantee a successful assignment.

17.4.5　*Motivating through the organization culture*

The successful expatriate perceives the experience of living and working in the host culture to be intrinsically interesting and essential for career growth. Selmer (2001) argues that companies should hire and select those persons who show a sense of mission and enthusiasm for overseas work and life, and should beware of persons primarily motivated by personal retirement strategies, career survival concerns, and financial greed. Those who are unexcited by challenges of working abroad are least likely to adjust. But the company cannot depend entirely on the manager's enthusiasm for an international career.

The human resources department has a wider pool to select from when more members apply. If the organizational culture actively supports expatriation, more are attracted by the opportunities of a posting abroad. The conditions are that the expatriate is guaranteed:

- fair compensation;
- adequate time to prepare for the expatriate posting – and preparation includes any necessary training;
- support at post and on return;
- training and support for dependents;
- career planning, and continued employment on return;
- enhanced promotion prospects.

Support and training are discussed in the next chapter.

It is not sufficient that these benefits are simply promised at the selection interview. All aspects of a positive organizational culture should reflect a spirit of internationalism. It matters that top management is known to support expatriation programs and to take an interest in the careers of those who take the option.

The culture is not supportive when these conditions are not present – that is, when top management is indifferent, the strains of adjusting to the new context are not rewarded, training and support is inadequate, and prospects for employment on return to headquarters are uncertain. In these circumstances few apply. The applicant pool is depleted and international operations suffer.

For example, the Dean of a successful British business school was highly entrepreneurial and took every opportunity to sign joint-venture deals with business schools and businesses abroad. Typical deals might involve a member of faculty being posted abroad for a few weeks or months, and a group of foreign students enrolling for courses in the British school and possibly an exchange arrangement by which British students traveled out. He communicated his plans to his deputy but usually no further, and long-term planning was slight. Faculty were under no obligation to make the foreign trips, but were irritated by the assumption that they could only expect promotion if they agreed to them. They were similarly angered by the sudden fluctuations in their class enrollments. The administrative staff did not appreciate their increased workloads. Unfortunately the Dean was not able to compensate staff adequately, and had no direct control over salary structures, which were administered by the central administration of the university. Eventually the faculty refused to make any further trips without adequate warning and planning, and the outcome of the ensuing conflict was that the Dean lost his job.

17.4.6   Recruiting for expatriate work

One solution to this question of how to build an organizational culture favorable to expatriate assignments is to hire staff with an initial predisposition to working abroad. Applicants at entry level are left in no doubt that they can expect to be asked to work abroad for part of their careers, and will be rewarded for doing so. On the other hand, those without cross-cultural interests and with no enthusiasm for working in new and challenging situations should seek employment elsewhere.

The company that recruits persons with least worries about cultural distances faces fewer problems when selecting for an expatriate assignment.

17.4.7   Motivating dependents

Dependents are not required to exercise the manager's technical skills in the workplace. But they do have strong needs for emotional maturity, and the abilities to communicate and make friends, learn, integrate, and be motivated by the life around them. Successful dependents are stimulated by opportunities to communicate, make friendships, and learn about the new culture.

Management hopes to motivate dependents by providing:

- early involvement in the proposal to relocate to the expatriate post, and in compensation and pension issues;
- training in how to live in the culture;
- opportunities to work in the new culture;
- support at post and on return.

17.5   Implications for the Manager

Review the policies followed by your organization in making expatriate postings, and their outcomes.

1   How does the organization measure success and failure?
- who decides whether an expatriate has succeeded or failed?
- how important is headquarters in evaluating performance?

- how important is the joint venture/subsidiary in evaluating performance?
- what criteria are used to evaluate performance?
- when is performance evaluated?

2 How far does the organization distinguish between different settings when setting criteria to measure success or failure?

3 What opportunities does the expatriate have to explain his/her success or failure?

4 How is failure typically explained:
- by headquarters?
- by the joint venture/subsidiary?
- by the expatriate?

5 How far can expatriate failure be explained by problems experienced by his/her spouse and other dependents?

6 How are expatriates selected?

7 What techniques and testing instruments are used?

8 How does the organization involve dependents in the decision to take the assignment?

9 How does the organizational culture motivate members to apply for expatriate assignments?

10 How might the selection process be improved in order to increase the odds on success and minimize possibilities of failure?

17.6 SUMMARY

This chapter has examined expatriate assignments.

Section 17.2 dealt with EXPATRIATE FUNCTIONS, and noted some of the factors that are leading to changes in the expatriate labor market. Section 17.3 dealt with notions of EXPATRIATE SUCCESS AND FAILURE. Factors influencing whether an expatriate has succeeded or failed in his/her assignment vary enormously. The spouse's adjustment is one important factor, and this may depend on whether he/she has been forced to give up a career in order to accompany the manager to the post.

They depend partly on who is making the evaluation and in what interest. Failure is sometimes explained by "cultural distance" but this is a subjective criterion. The literature suggests that Americans are far more prone to failure than are Japanese expatriates, but they are likely to be evaluated by different criteria.

Section 17.4 argued that the best protection against failure is to invest in the selection of expatriates – SELECT FOR SUCCESS. The process should aim at finding the best person to not only work but also live in the new environment. Particularly in posts where the expatriate needs to interact with a wide range of people in the local environment, technical and managerial skills may be less important than communication skills. The company facilitates the process of selecting successful expatriates by fostering an organizational culture that is favorable to work abroad, and policies for recruitment at entry level are one factor that can contribute.

17.7 EXERCISE

Read this case and answer the questions below.

Ralph was CEO of a medium-sized Canadian engineering company. The company was experiencing difficult market conditions. He had been overworking recently and he needed a rest. When the opportunity arose to take a vacation, he decided to visit friends in Indonesia.

One evening in the hotel bar he was introduced to the President of a local wood-pulp producer. As it happened, the Jakarta-based company was looking for a Canadian partner. The vacation became a business trip and within a further 2 weeks Ralph had signed an agreement committing his company to an R&D joint venture with the Indonesians. One condition was that the Canadians should expatriate a senior engineer on a 1-year consultancy.

When Ralph arrived back at his headquarters, his staff were aghast. "We don't know anything about Indonesia" complained his production manager.

"Then we'd better start learning. Business here is so bad that we have to get an international profile. And I mean now. Jobs are on the line."

An appeal was made for internal applicants; sadly, only one person responded.

Keil was a long-serving manager who was generally agreed to be a brilliant engineer. But he had no hope of further promotion. He was known to be a bad communicator, self-opinionated, and rude, and had few friends in the company.

He was tested for cultural aptitude, and achieved the lowest score that the human resource department had ever recorded. Nevertheless, the company decided that it could not afford to admit that no appointment was possible, and so Keil was posted.

Three months later the Indonesian partner demanded that Keil be recalled. He had refused to cooperate with local management and had treated his colleagues as though they were assistants. He drank excessively and showed no respect for local cultural values. The Indonesians decided to cancel the project. The posting had been a costly failure.

QUESTIONS

In this case:

(a) What skills do you think were most needed by the expatriate appointed?

(b) What skills were less important?

(c) What does this tell you about the company's international strategy?

(d) What does this tell you about the selection process used?

(e) What does this tell you about the organizational culture?

Notes

1 Cited in "Expatriation assignments on the rise," *Relocation Journal and Real Estate News*, vol. 11, June 1997.

2 John Schwartz, Jeanne Gordon, and Mark Veverka, "The 'Salaryman' Blues," *Newsweek*, May 9, 1988; and Brian O'Reilly, "Japan's Uneasy U.S. Managers," *Fortune*, 25 April, 1988.

3 John Schwartz, Jeanne Gordon, and Mark Veverka, "The 'Salaryman' Blues," *Newsweek*, May 9, 1988.

4 Cherian George, "Firms 'need to double number of Singapore expats'," *The Straits Times Weekly Edition*, November 11, 1995.

5 Jolie Solomon, "Women, Minorities and Foreign Postings," *The Wall Street Journal*, June 2, 1989.

CHAPTER EIGHTEEN

Training and Supporting an Expatriate Assignment

CHAPTER OUTLINE

Introduction	Implications for the Manager
Training	Summary
Support	Exercise
The Shock of Return	Notes

18.1 Introduction

Ed, an American, was prepared by his company headquarters to take up a posting in Taiwan. Because he needed to network locally, Chinese language training was included. The human resource department arranged for him to be given intensive classes in the Cantonese dialect. On arrival in Taipei he realized that the official language was Mandarin Chinese and that the great majority of his new contacts spoke only Mandarin and knew no Cantonese.

This story shows a company investing in language training, but inadequately assessing needs. Resources were wasted, and Ed's sense of confidence in the human resource department supporting his expatriate assignment was lessened. So a well-intentioned mistake had negative effects and Ed's assignment was less productive than it might have been. Cross-cultural training must be appropriate if it is to be useful.

In a world where the selection processes operated perfectly, and the company could select from an unlimited number of candidates, training and support might not be needed. In practice, of course, neither of these conditions apply. The company uses imprecise instruments to select the best of the few candidates available. Added to this, the business environment is changing with increasing speed and unpredictability. This means that the initial job description may be very quickly outdated. The expatriate who seems to offer precisely the right qualities at the time of selection may be increasingly less fitted over time, and need further training at post. However much is invested in selection, there are bound to be some surprise failures.

However, the opposite situation, in which the minimum investment is made in selection and the available resources are channeled into training and support, may be equally unsatisfactory. The company looks for the optimal balance in its selection, training, and support investments.

This chapter deals with training and support, to work and live in the new country, before leaving headquarters and at post, for the manager and his/her spouse and dependents. The type and degree of training and support is bound to be influenced by the identity of the expatriate selected, and hence by the selection process.

18.2 Training

Training takes place before and during the expatriate assignment, and serves general functions of preparing the expatriate to both:

- work in the local culture;
- live in the local culture (see section 17.4.1).

Training is given both to the manager and to spouse and other dependents, although the contents of their training programs differ.

Preparation before includes both teaching the skills needed and developing the trainee's expectations of the job and living in the culture. Research by Caligiuri et al. (2001) shows that the more tailored and relevant the pre-departure cross-cultural training, the more expectations were met or positively exceeded. Expatriates who have no idea of what to expect are more likely to be frustrated.

18.2.1 Needs analysis

When the selected expatriate needs a great deal of training in order to perform his/her assignment, and the assignment is considered vital, the company invests more in training. When the expatriate has few needs for training in order to perform the assignment or the assignment is not vital, the company invests less.

In either case, some needs analysis may be necessary. A formal needs analysis specifies the target behavior of the trainees (the manager and dependents). The first step is to specify skills, roles and areas of knowledge that must be mastered in order to operate successfully. Roles include both:

▪ PRESCRIPTIVE skills (that the trainee should perform) and
▪ DESCRIPTIVE skills (that the trainee actually performs).

Here is an example of these norms in apparent contradiction. The expatriate is posted as consultant to a joint venture, with a role to advise and train – a prescriptive norm.

In practice, the lack of local staff means that he has to manage certain points of the production process. This management role is not included in the job description and is covert; local concerns to maintain authority mean that foreign control cannot be admitted. Two descriptive norms apply; the consultant-as-manager, and the consultant-as-diplomat – handling the difficult issues arising from the role confusion. A training program that teaches only the prescriptive skills is inadequate. Descriptive skills also need to be developed. For example, the introductory case in section 16.1 showed that the realities of power and influence in a subsidiary do not always match official structures, and that the expatriate also needs skills to apply the informal relationships of power and control.

This raises a question; how are these descriptive needs recognized? Much can be learned from debriefing expatriates returning from work in the same situation; debriefings are discussed in section 18.4.1.

The second step is to distinguish those skills that the manager and dependents can already perform from those that must be acquired. This avoids re-teaching what is already known. A needs analysis provides the data on which the training syllabus is based. A simple model might ask the following questions:

NEEDS ANALYSIS

(a) What skills, roles, and areas of knowledge will the manager need when:
  • working in the new culture?
  • living in the new culture?
(b) What skills, etc. will the spouse/dependents need when living in the new culture?
(c) What skills, etc. are already known?
(d) What *new* skills, etc. are needed?
(e) At what standards are new skills, etc. needed?
(f) What outcomes are expected from the trainees learning and using the new skills, etc.?

Training may be needed in the four content areas below.

1 technical training (section 18.2.3);
2 management training (section 18.2.4);
3 cross-cultural training (section 18.2.5);
4 language training (section 18.2.6).

The agenda above can be applied to each of the four content categories. For example, in the case of (a):

(a1) What TECHNICAL skills, etc. will the manager need when working in the new culture?
(a2) What MANAGEMENT skills, etc. will the manager need when working in the new culture?

(a3) What CULTURAL skills, etc. will the manager need when both working and living in the new culture?

(a4) What LANGUAGE skills, etc. will the manager need when both working and living in the new culture?

18.2.2 Training alternatives

Training may be given at headquarters, before the expatriate and dependents leave, *and/or* at post. Training is given by company trainers, *and/or* external trainers. So far as possible the syllabus and training materials are tailored to the specific needs of the trainees, and may be produced by company trainers or selected from published and other sources.

The expatriate may need further training at the end of the assignment to prepare him/her for return to headquarters.

18.2.3 Technical training

The manager is given training on:

- technologies used by the subsidiary or venture with which he/she is unfamiliar, including alternative technologies;
- opportunities for technology transfer and innovation;
- constraints on the local implementation of new technology.

18.2.4 Management training

Management training is specific to the post and the local joint venture or subsidiary. The manager is trained in:

▌ the administrative RESPONSIBILITIES of the post;
▌ company STRATEGY and subsidiary (or venture) STRATEGY;
▌ its ORGANIZATIONAL STRUCTURE and systems: strategies and opportunities for change; systems for control and communication; systems for planning, motivating, and resolving conflicts; organizational culture; informal systems;
▌ investment and TREASURY factors, including accounting and auditing procedures, financial sources, investment commitments, protection of assets;
▌ relations with HEADQUARTERS: systems for control, communications;
▌ relations with OTHER SUBSIDIARIES;
▌ the local BUSINESS ENVIRONMENT;
▌ local RISK factors;
▌ HUMAN RESOURCE ISSUES: labor markets and recruitment; labor relations and policies; relations with unions; salary and reward structures; training resources and policies;
▌ ETHICAL policies.

The headquarters functional manager assigned to a general management role abroad needs a greater understanding of a range of headquarters units than he/she normally acquires within a functional specialism.

18.2.5   Cross-cultural training

Cross-cultural training aims to teach the following.

(a) ABOUT the other culture. The training teaches:
  • what values are important within the other culture;
  • how the culture is reflected in significant historical, political, and economic data;
  • how cultural values are expressed in behavior.
(b) HOW TO LIVE AND WORK effectively in the other culture. It teaches how to recognize the influence of culture on:
  • social relationships;
  • management styles, structures, and systems;
  • strategic planning and management;
  • technology innovation, implementation, transfer;
  • the business environment.
(c) HOW TO APPLY these lessons in appropriate behavior.

18.2.6   Language training

A language training syllabus varies depending on whether it aims to teach:

  • at beginner's level, at intermediate level, at advanced level;
  • reading and/or writing and/or listening and/or speaking;
  • social varieties, business/work varieties, any other varieties;
  • up to near-native speaker fluency, polite openers (good morning, how are you? my name is X, etc.), all levels between.

The mix of these categories determines the syllabus in terms of:

  • content: grammar, vocabulary, communicative discourse;
  • teaching techniques;
  • materials needed.

18.2.7   Training needs determined by organizational structure

The organizational structure determines the relationship between headquarters and the joint venture or subsidiary, and this influences what new skills are needed.

At one extreme, consider the example of the subsidiary of a global company that is highly centralized and structured so that all strategies are determined by headquarters, and structures and systems replicate those in headquarters. The expatriate reports to a headquarters manager, and works alongside fellow expatriates. All communications with subordinate staff are funneled through local managers and assistants who trained in headquarters. The expatriate needs no new skills in order to work in the subsidiary.

An example at the opposite extreme is an expatriate working in a decentralized, transnational subsidiary. He is the only headquarters manager at post and is responsible for designing and implementing strategy that responds immediately to local needs, markets, and competition.

Training is always more likely to meet its goals when it attracts the active support of top management. Particularly in transnational companies, the development of inter-national managers has strategic implications, and the human resources director works with strategic planners to develop training programs that aim to meet company goals. Support at this level gives some guarantee that:

- training meets identified needs;
- adequate resources, including finance, are committed;
- training is considered to be part of the trainee's regular duties, and is conducted during office hours;
- the trainee is rewarded for taking training (unmotivated trainees learn little);
- training sessions are undisturbed;
- adequate time is devoted to training;
- standards are maintained (the organization is committed to providing training that is thorough and rigorous).

18.2.8 Training dependents

How far the manager's spouse and other dependents adjust to living in the new culture is a major influence on the success or failure of his/her performance (see section 17.3.2). An increasingly popular solution to problems of dependents' difficulty in adjusting is that they be trained in the culture and language of the new situation. Garsten's (2001) small research project found that many companies were investing in externally run cross-cultural briefing because they felt:

> it helped manage spouse and expatriate expectations. They felt that if a spouse was happy, the assignment was likely to "fly", and that if he/she was not there would be "mega problems". This emphasis on the spouse has developed over the past decade, organisations now commonly including spouse attendance in the cross-cultural briefings – one even providing it for the spouse if the expatriate did not wish to attend. Some organisations felt that the family was so important that they provided specially tailored cross-cultural briefings for individual families. *(p. 87)*

In some cases, the spouse has greater needs for cross-cultural training than the manager. In a centralized global company, the manager follows routines influenced by headquarters and works primarily with other expatriates or local employees who have learned the organizational culture. The language used in the office is that of headquarters. These routines have the effect of channeling and restricting the manager's contacts with the local culture. On the other hand, a spouse at home, responsible for dealing with domestic servants and tradespeople, is forced into a wide range of contacts with the general culture. For these he/she may need considerable understanding of the culture and the language. Where appropriate, the manager and dependents are trained together in the culture and language; otherwise separately.

The spouse may need to understand something of the scope of operations in the joint venture or subsidiary, and the manager's general area of responsibility for this; how much is influenced by the degree of business entertainment that he/she is willing to undertake.

18.2.9   Reasons for not giving cross-cultural and language training

Most companies seem prepared to give technical training where this is necessary. At the other end of the scale, many companies still doubt the value of training their expatriates in cross-cultural skills. Some research has estimated that 65 percent of United States MNCs did not offer training to their expatriates before sending them overseas (reported in Mendenhall, Punnett, and Ricks, 1995, p. 440), although a small-scale study conducted in the United Kingdom suggests that the uptake may be improving there (Garsten, 2001).

The reasons given for NOT giving cross-cultural training include the following.

▐ Training is unnecessary because the manager is already EXPERT. It is assumed that a good domestic track record guarantees performance abroad. There may be some justification for this view in a highly centralized company where all policy is made by headquarters, and the local office is packed with expatriates; but there is very little in a decentralized, transnational company, in particular if the manager is alone in representing headquarters. In general, a good record in New York, say, is not a good predictor of achievement in Tokyo or Taipei.

▐ Training is unnecessary because the expatriate will have NO CROSS-CULTURAL responsibilities. He/she is reporting to, managing and with other expatriates and headquarters staff.

▐ TIME is insufficient. The expatriate's schedule before posting does not allow opportunities for training. The greater this time between the manager's appointment and his/her taking up the post, the greater the opportunities to give effective training. When training is given, it is typically limited to a few days' work, and may be too short to justify the investment.

▐ CONTENT cannot be identified accurately. Training is often misdirected when planned by headquarters staff who have no direct experience of the country of posting. Those responsible often underestimate the importance of language training, and do not

take advantage of consultants (in applied linguistics) able to advise on language needs in the country of the posting. (The case in the introduction gives an example.)
∎ The LENGTH of the assignment is too short. It is sometimes claimed that training should only be invested in long-term expatriates. But the responsibilities of the job rather than length of tenure is the major factor. A negotiator expecting to spend 2 weeks communicating with local managers may have far greater needs for cross-cultural skills than a technical expert working only with other headquarters expatriates for a year.
∎ The EFFECTIVENESS of cross-cultural training programs is disputed. These doubts may reflect experiences with poorly planned and delivered programs in the past.

Depending on the circumstances of the post, any one of these arguments may be convincing. Training is expensive, and is only justified if it furthers positive outcomes or prevents negative outcomes – such as when an unprepared manager and dependents are unable to adjust and have to be withdrawn.

Reasons for giving training and for not giving training boil down to the economic question; will training for a post pay dividends? This economic argument against training for a particular post is the most convincing. The company calculates the value added by training against the investment – which is complex, and includes direct costs incurred by training the manager and dependents, the loss of the manager's labor and the cost of replacement labor. If the company conducts its training on an internal basis, there are additional costs associated with needs analysis, materials production, teaching facilities, and support services.

Further indirect costs may be incurred in the labor market. The more highly a company trains its staff, the higher the price they can command on the market. In order to keep a skilled manager from moving to competitors, the company may need to better reward him/her. If he/she does move, the company has to pay search and recruitment costs in finding a replacement. Thus the company faces a decision: train staff to be more productive and necessarily pay more for their labor, or do not train and cope with less productive staff.

These factors mean that the investment can only be justified when the training is tailored to the specific demands and responsibilities of the post. This determines what skills should be taught and up to what level.

18.2.10 Training other staff categories

The sections above deal with training the expatriate and his/her spouse and other dependents. Other persons can also benefit from aspects of international and cross-cultural training. These include:

- headquarters staff with responsibilities for selecting and posting expatriates;
- headquarters staff with professional interests in the company's foreign interests (e.g., marketing staff);

- headquarters staff responsible for managing staff from another culture (an Anglo-American factory manager in Miami is taught Spanish in order to communicate with his immigrant Cuban labor force);
- staff locally employed in the joint venture or subsidiary.

Local staff benefit from cross-cultural training that helps them work more efficiently with expatriated headquarters staff, visitors, and others. For example, a company in Jakarta is taken over by a Japanese MNC; local Indonesian managers are trained in Japanese culture so that they interact effectively with their new management team. The consequences of expatriate failure are more severe when local staff do not understand the expatriate's home culture and are not prepared to make concessions.

Training local managers in the headquarters language and culture may be immediately less expensive than training headquarters staff in the local language and culture. However, it carries indirect costs. The more skilled the local managers become, the greater their value on the international job market and the wider their opportunities for finding alternative employment with competitors.

18.2.11 *Program evaluation*

Whether or not a training program achieves its goals and represents a good investment is decided by evaluation. Training evaluation tells the company whether it is using its training resources to optimal advantage and indicates areas of improvement and resolves uncertainties. It can be applied to all stages of the program.

Evaluation has functions of:

- specifying and comparing program goals and achievement;
- showing how far achievement has met program goals, given the resources available;
- assessing performance of trainers, trainees, and other persons involved;
- showing how far the program has given value for money;
- providing feedback that can be applied in selecting or developing future programs.

Evaluation is conducted by headquarters, the joint venture or subsidiary, or outside consultants. Possible internal evaluators include human resource staff, program developers and trainers, subsidiary managers, repatriates (who may have been trained by an earlier version of the program), and trainees. Accounting staff evaluate training for cost benefits.

Some evaluation can be usefully conducted at every stage of training preparation, during training, and at different times after training. Evaluation at the PREPARATION phase focuses on program goals, program development, and an inventory of resources needed and available.

Evaluation made DURING TRAINING focuses on what learning is taking place, and the factors that help and detract from learning. It reviews completed stages, checks how far the training process corresponds to the original plan, demonstrates on-going progress to trainees and trainers, and aims to motivate.

Evaluation made IMMEDIATELY AFTER TRAINING gives immediate feedback on how far achievement has met the program goals. It tells trainers and trainees what learning has taken place and what parts of the training are more or less effective. Evaluation made at PERIODIC INTERVALS AFTER IMPLEMENTATION and when the trainees are at the expatriate post, gives long-term feedback on how far achievement has met goals. It shows how much learning has been short-term and how much long-term. At each stage, the costs of training – including the costs incurred in the trainee's absence from the workplace – are assessed against expected benefits.

Evaluation is conducted by tests, surveys, interviews, observation, control group testing, and accounting and financial data.

18.3   Support

The company helps the expatriate and any dependents succeed by supporting them to:

- work in the new culture;
- live in the new culture;
- return to headquarters.

Support is given at post and when the expatriate returns to headquarters. Support schemes have to be tailored to individual needs, and are sufficiently flexible to accommodate:

- personality characteristics;
- the stage in the expatriate's career;
- the manager's job description and status, and family characteristics when the expatriate is accompanied;
- perceptions of cultural distance.

18.3.1   Support for working

The company provides support for working by supplying:

- training (see previous section);
- professional and technical support at post;
- professional and technical back-up at headquarters.

Back-up at headquarters encourages the expatriate to feel confident that his/her interests are being protected, and that the assignment contributes towards a continuing career. This means that he/she is confident of the following factors.

- The DURATION of the post. Uncertainty about the length of stay disrupts personal, domestic, and career plans, and can be a major cause of expatriate demoralization.
- CAREER SECURITY on repatriation – given in writing. The expatriate welcomes a written guarantee that on return he/she will return to an equal or better job at headquarters or in another branch after completing the posting.
- CAREER PLANNING. Before he/she takes up the post, someone at headquarters is responsible for helping the expatriate plan his/her career on repatriation. Jackson (2002) found an emphasis on career planning in cultures that stress individual achievement, tolerate high degrees of uncertainty, and accept competition and assertiveness.
- Enhanced PROMOTION PROSPECTS on repatriation.
- TRAINING and repatriation counseling for return to headquarters before or immediately after repatriation.

18.3.2 Mentoring

Some companies support their expatriates by appointing a shepherd or MENTOR. Mentors can operate at home in headquarters, and at post. The mentor is in a position to give impartial advice, and is not connected to the mentee within a management structure. (For a practical guide, see Kay and Hinds, 2002.)

The HEADQUARTERS MENTOR may be an older manager who gives advice and help based on seasoned judgment and is responsible for protecting the expatriate's professional and career interests while the expatriate is abroad. This means ensuring that all agreements reached between the expatriate and headquarters (listed in section 18.3.1) are honored, keeping him/her up to date with changes in headquarters, and reintroducing him/her to headquarters.

In practice, headquarters mentoring is difficult to achieve, not least because in a time of rapid change the expatriate cannot be confident that on his/her return, the mentor will still be working for the company.

Headquarters may also appoint an "uncle" or "aunt" to keep a check on children being educated in the home country while the expatriate is at post and to be responsible for their welfare in the event of a family emergency.

The MENTOR-AT-POST provides support and guidance, and helps the expatriate and dependents adjust to working and living in the new culture. Mentoring may be focused on both relatively young expatriates with perhaps no previous experience of working abroad, and on more experienced managers who may be aiming at new posts within the company. Feldman and Bolino (1999) discuss evidence that mentoring at post positively influences job attitudes and productivity.

18.3.3 Support for living

The joint venture or subsidiary (represented by a mentor-at-post or a human resources manager) arranges support for the expatriate and dependents in the local culture. Specifically, the post helps in:

- locating and subsidizing appropriate HOUSING;
- arranging appropriate MEDICAL FACILITIES and other social services;
- finding suitable EDUCATIONAL FACILITIES for dependent children at post with the expatriate;
- briefing on SHOPPING FACILITIES and supplies of domestic goods and services;
- briefing on CUSTOMS regulations and procedures;
- arranging appropriate INSURANCE;
- organizing SUPPORT GROUPS for newcomers;
- organizing TRAINING in the local language and culture;
- providing CULTURAL SUPPORT (e.g. helping the family keep abreast of cultural activities in the home country) – in some locations, the embassy gives this support to all its locally employed nationals;
- arranging and subsidizing regular LEAVE.
- finding part- or full-time EMPLOYMENT or STUDY for a dependent spouse.

Given the importance of spouse adjustment (see section 17.3.2) the last point is crucial. But the employment found must be significant. As one expert has pointed out:

> Giving dinner parties or cocktail receptions for visiting company executives does not count as satisfying work.
>
> Corporations should consider establishing part-time jobs and research contracts. In cases where a wife would like to upgrade her skills through local or correspondence studies, the company should foot the bill. Corporations could also emulate those governments and universities that have instituted preferential employment policies for spouses. In Beijing, this means that almost all Western embassies are staffed by embassy spouses.[1]

Support information given before arrival at post must be practical and up-to-date. The manager and dependents who arrive to discover that their briefing was inappropriate, inaccurate, or outdated are immediately demoralized. The more focused the training and support programs the better.

The company might send the manager and dependents on an information trip to the local country before they take up the assignment. This gives them opportunities to inspect the local organization and to review their needs for domestic information. Whether or not the company provides this option is decided by economic factors; the more important the assignment, the more the company invests to ensure its success.

18.3.4 *Defining culture shock*

Culture shock can be seriously unsettling. For example:

> Paris is hell for the Japanese. It gives them what one Japanese psychiatrist described as the "Paris syndrome," which includes hallucinations, depression, paranoia, and shocks to the nervous system.
>
> "French people tend to be moody," said Horoaki Ota . . . "They can be very kind one moment and very mean the next. . . . Japanese are shocked by these kinds of attitude changes as they are used to more predictable people in their native country."[2]

A bad case of culture shock during the expatriate manager's first months in post influences his/her attitudes towards the new culture, and may reduce his/her productivity. The company supports the expatriate and dependents by helping them overcome the worst symptoms.

However, the help that the company can give is limited, and some degree of culture shock may be inevitable. It is a natural response to new cultural experiences, and may be defined as a sense of psychological disorientation that most people suffer when they move into a culture that is different from their own. The expatriate cannot resort to the familiar cues in his/her home culture when developing a relationship, responding to other people's behavior, and communicating.

Compare this to your experience of first driving through a city that you have previously known from walking. Familiar landmarks now seem important, new landmarks emerge, and you see prominent features from a different perspective. Failures to recognize the landscape are disturbing.

Everyone expects culture shock when traveling to a culture that seems very distant from their own. In practice, more severe culture shock can occur when the new culture is superficially like your own. Slight differences are shocking when you expect everything to be the same.

An Indian was posted by his Chicago company to a project in Thailand. On his way from the airport he saw the crowds in the Bangkok streets, the vendors and the articles they sold, and the food stalls. Everything reminded him of Bombay and he already felt at home. On his first evening he decided to try a local restaurant. But when he walked through the door, panic overcame him. He did not know whether to find his own table or wait to be seated as in the United States. He picked up the menu and could not read a single word. He fled back to his international hotel and did not leave it for the next 2 days.

This sense of dislocation occurs when you experience behavior that does not occur in your own culture, or behaviour that occurs but with some other meaning. You may be equally shaken by the non-occurrence of expected behavior: for instance, the Anglo takes for granted that disagreement is expressed explicitly. A lack of explicit disagreement in Japan can be disconcerting.

18.3.5 The symptoms of culture shock

Culture shock is cumulative and can arise from a number of small incidents. It is usually associated with unpleasant effects:

▪ A SENSE OF TENSION AND FRUSTRATION. Your energy levels seem low and you cannot make decisions as quickly as usual.
▪ A SENSE OF ALIENATION. You feel homesickness, and antagonism towards locals and their culture. You have no desire to learn or use their language, or to meet them socially.
▪ A NEED TO BE ALONE. You resort to solitary activities, including drinking.
▪ DEPRESSION.

The culture shock cycle has at least four stages. Initially, the expatriate feels a sense of excitement and interest. This is followed by frustration and irritability when he discovers that some problems cannot be easily resolved and he cannot distinguish serious and trivial problems. In the third stage he gradually learns to overcome the minor difficulties. In the fourth stage he adjusts, and begins to communicate effectively.

Some people experience more than one cycle of culture shock when an unexpected incident leads to a new crisis of confidence, and the second cycle may be more extreme.

18.3.6   Coping with culture shock

To overcome the worst effects of culture shock the expatriate should:

- EXPECT it. It is a natural reaction to novelty among emotionally mature people. Treating culture shock as a pathology is not positive.
- UNDERSTAND why it occurs and learn the symptoms.
- BROADEN your range of business and social contacts beyond your home culture and into the local culture.
- LEARN about the new culture. Use your new friends as informants. Learn at least a little of the language.
- FIND OUT what communicative forms and behaviors are appropriate. Who should be addressed by first name? Who by title? How are invitations made, accepted, and refused? What gifts are appropriate, on what occasions, and how should they be presented? How is agreement and disagreement expressed? What do locals mean when they say "Yes, maybe"? "Tomorrow"? In what situations do these common expressions mean something else?
- CHECK your first impressions of these rules.

Experienced travelers develop their own routines for coping with the worst effects. One manager prepares by examining maps of the new city he expects to visit and spends the first days walking the streets in order to turn his theoretical understanding into practical experience.

Examine your own reactions to culture shock, and adapt the techniques above to meet your own needs.

18.4   The Shock of Return

The return to headquarters after a long-term assignment abroad can be a shock. This is sometimes known as reverse culture shock. The repatriate needs to adjust to differences from the country of the assignment. These include:

- REDUCED FINANCIAL BENEFITS. Some expatriate benefits, such as free rent and allowances, are no longer paid.
- LESS POWER and excitement. The expatriate who enjoyed seniority abroad has to fit back into a headquarters post which is more restricted and routine.
- JOB ALIENATION. A sense of being out of touch with changes at headquarters. One international manager complained "When I walked into the office the first day back, I couldn't see anyone I knew. All the old faces had gone. It was like starting out again."
- INCREASED COST-OF-LIVING EXPENSES. These occur when the expatriate posting was in a less-developed country and headquarters is in an expensive developed country.
- LESS DOMESTIC HELP. Domestic help is relatively cheap in many less-developed countries.
- A reduced SOCIAL LIFE. In countries where expatriates are few, cross-cultural managers and their families can lead intense social lives. School children leave the friends they made in their schools abroad.

For many, the most disturbing aspect of returning home is the problem of trying to communicate to colleagues, friends, and family who have problems understanding the intensity of the expatriate experience.

The company can help overcome these problems by:

- reducing the length of expatriate assignments, in particular for younger employees (although this reduces the long-term effectiveness of a posting);
- reducing expatriate allowances (although these may be necessary in order to attract managers overseas);
- mentoring and preparing the expatriate for return (see section 18.3.2), and updating the manager on changes at headquarters;
- introducing the manager and dependents to support groups of other returnees;
- before and after repatriation, briefing the manager on living conditions at home, and on his/her new post;
- debriefing the manager (see below).

18.4.1 Debriefing

The manager is debriefed by interviews with headquarters managers. DEBRIEFING serves two functions. First, it gives the returned manager and dependents an immediate function; the opportunity to discuss their experience in the country of posting assures them that this experience is valued by the company. This helps to overcome any sense of alienation and lack of purpose that he/she may have when returning to headquarters. Second, it adds to headquarters' knowledge of the country, its culture and politics, and local trading partners and competitors.

The returned expatriate is a source of expert knowledge which is informal in the sense that it may not be officially documented. He/she can report on:

- the expatriate post – opportunities and constraints;
- the joint venture, subsidiary, or trading partner – how it operates in practice;
- the business environment;
- the political and economic environments;
- the cultural context – opportunities and difficulties in living there.

A successful debriefing motivates the expatriate and provides the company with knowledge that can be applied in:

- briefing negotiators;
- analyzing the venture/subsidiary's performance, needs, and interests;
- briefing new expatriates going to that post.

Selmer (2001, p. 87) noted that although it was policy in many Swedish MNCs to rotate their managers to Singapore and elsewhere every 3 or 4 years, the expatriates were not adequately prepared.

> Swedish managers assume duties in a foreign country without systematic briefings on the local work situation by previous managers.

In sum: many companies possess potentially valuable sources of information in the form of their managers' expatriate experiences. This information can only be transmuted into useful knowledge when the repatriates are debriefed, and the output is systematized and made available within the company.

18.5 Implications for the Manager

Evaluate the TRAINING given by your organization to the following groups, when expatriated:

(a) the CEO;
(b) functional heads;
(c) managers, on long-term assignments;
(d) short-term consultants;
(e) others;
(f) dependents of the above.

1 In which of these is each group trained?
  - technical topics;
  - management topics;
  - cross-cultural topics;
  - language.

2 For each group, how successful is the training? Take into account:
   * goals;
   * expense;
   * time;
   * trainers and training facilities;
   * use made of other resources.
3 How might training for each group be improved?

Evaluate the SUPPORT given to each of the groups above.

4 How is each group supported *before* expatriation and *during* expatriation?
   * at work?
   * outside work?
5 What problems do expatriates and their spouses typically experience on return to headquarters?
6 How are expatriates and dependents debriefed on their return to headquarters? How are debriefings applied?
7 How might support for each group be improved?

18.6 SUMMARY

In order to increase the odds on him/her succeeding in the assignment, the company designs training and support packages that meet the needs of the expatriate and dependents as precisely as possible. However, economic constraints are always important. The company cannot invest more in training and support than it expects to reap in benefits.

Section 19.2 dealt with needs for TRAINING. A successful training package is based on a needs analysis that focuses on content areas of technical, management, cross-cultural, and language skills. Dependents' needs vary from the manager's, but may be no less important, particularly in regards to cross-cultural and language skills. An efficient evaluation system is needed to ensure that the training investment meets company goals.

Section 18.3 dealt with the SUPPORT given to the expatriate and dependents at post and on return to headquarters, for working and living in the new culture. Mentoring systems were discussed. The company is prepared to advise on culture shock and how to overcome the worst effects. THE SHOCK OF RETURN (section 18.4) can be as severe. Debriefing the expatriate and dependents can help resolve some of these problems, and also adds to the company's sum of knowledge about the post.

18.7 EXERCISE

This exercise practices designing a flexible support package.

Assume that you work in your own town for a subsidiary of an MNC headquartered in some foreign country. Headquarters decides to post one of its staff to manage your subsidiary for a 2-year assignment. Assume that the manager is 37 years old and male, and will be accompanied by his spouse and two children aged 13 (a boy) and 8 (a girl).

1 Decide on:
- the country of headquarters (choose from Japan, Sweden, Taiwan, Australia);
- the manager's rank and functional specialism;
- the relationship between headquarters and subsidiary (how far is the subsidiary empowered to design and implement its own strategy?)
2 Write the manager's job description, taking into account:

- needs for managerial and technical expertise;
- headquarters' needs to control the subsidiary.
3 Design a support package that will facilitate their adjustment, taking into account that:
- the manager previously worked for 2 years in a culture very different to both the headquarters country and yours;
- the spouse is an accountant, with no previous expatriate experience, and she wishes to continue working, on a part-time basis;
- the children need schooling;
- at present, no one in the family speaks your language but all are prepared to learn.
4 Now assume that the organization is headquartered in one of the other countries listed in question 1. Revise your answers to questions 2 and 3 where necessary.

Notes

1 Robin Pascoe, "Employers forsake expatriate spouses at their own peril," *Asian Wall Street Journal*, February 27, 1992.

2 "Not where *they* go when they die" (Agence France Presse), *International Herald Tribune*, October 30, 1991.

International Strategies

CHAPTER ELEVEN **Globalization and Localization**

CASE   LEVI STRAUSS

In this case, production is moved to improve profitability

Levi Strauss began producing denim jeans in the 1850s for miners heading to California in the gold rush. The company was based in San Francisco, with manufacturing plants spread across the United States and Canada. The brand expressed the tough, outdoor values of the cowboy or the rebellious motorcyclist, and for many decades was market leader. In 1996 sales hit an all-time record of $7.1 billion. But increasing numbers of new entrants were moving into the market. Gap and Diesel competed upmarket and became the designer-labels of choice. By 2002 Levi sales had slipped to $4.2 billion, and costs were rising.

By 2003 the company had been forced to close all its North American manufacturing plants. In September, the company's chief executive said that:

to cut costs the company would in future be producing none of its own jeans, contracting out the process instead.

All orders will now be produced by businesses located in countries such as China and Bangladesh and the world's most famous denim company will no longer make jeans, just design and market them.[1]

In the United States minimum wages are fixed by law, and even workers earning at the minimum level are unable to compete with labor in other countries.

QUESTIONS

1   Why has Levi Strauss decided to extend its global reach?
2   In the United States, who benefits from this case of globalized development? Who loses?

DECISION

3   *You are a textile manufacturer based in Bangladesh. You would like to expand your business. What can you learn from this story?*

1   Oliver Poole, "The all-American Levi's jeans ride into the sunset," *The Daily Telegraph*, September 27, 2003.

CHAPTER TWELVE **Family Companies**

CASE SUCCESSION PLANNING

This case highlights a succession problem for the family company

Mr. Sun lives in Hong Kong. He is a longstanding friend of yours. He runs a small but profitable business manufacturing costume jewelery. His designers and craftsmen have worked with him faithfully for many years, and the standards of craftsmanship are high. His customers, many of whom he has come to know personally, are middle aged or elderly. They value the quality of his products and are happy to pay his prices.

The business makes a comfortable living for Mr. Sun and his only child, a daughter, Mei-ling. You are sure that if Mr. Sun invested in exporting to the United States and Europe he could do even better. But he claims not be interested in making a fortune, and says that in any case he does not understand Western tastes. You suspect he prefers to deal only in the local market because he speaks only Chinese languages, and for a successful man is surprisingly shy and confused when mixing with foreigners.

Mr. Sun is very keen that Mei-ling should take over the business when he retires in, perhaps, 10 years' time. Mei-ling is very smart, and has been offered a place at a leading Australian MBA school. Mr. Sun is unsure whether he should encourage her to take up the place, or ask her to stay with him.

You have had the opportunity to talk to Mei-ling about her plans. She loves her father and is interested in the jewelery business. She is determined to study for an MBA somewhere, and if her father objects to her studying abroad will find a program in Hong Kong. She is uncertain whether she will wish to return to the family company when she completes her studies. She says:

"I would really like to develop an international career. I can see that my father is very conservative and even now he makes mistakes, which annoy me, then I feel guilty. He wants to go on running the business for the rest of his life. I don't want to spend the next 30 years frustrated. So perhaps I'll work for a Western multinational in some other industry."

QUESTIONS

1   What are the advantages and disadvantages of Mei-ling not studying?

2   What are the advantages and disadvantages of her studying in Australia?

3   What are the advantages and disadvantages of her studying in Hong Kong?

DECISIONS

4   *Advise Mr. Sun, taking into account his personal needs and the future of the company.*

5   *Advise Mei-ling.*

CHAPTER THIRTEEN **Designing and Implementing Strategy**

CASE MERGING ORGANIZATION CULTURES

This case asks how different cultures can be harmonized

In Japan in 2001, two insurance companies opened negotiations to merge. The economic situation was critical, and unless they could resolve their differences quickly and make a strong merger, both might be forced into bankruptcy. Already, both are being forced to plan redundancies.

The First Company had for many years been owned and managed by a French company, and its organization culture showed liberal French influences. The Second Company had been under Japanese ownership since its establishment in 1947. Working practices strongly reflected Japanese values.

The merger talks went well until the companies started planning their human resource structures. The First Company has practices that reflect its more Westernized history. Women could hope for promotion many steps up the management ladder, although the senior posts were all reserved for their more experienced male colleagues. Females earned up to three-quarters as much as males of equivalent rank. But the Second Company had always adopted a traditional Japanese approach: no females were appointed to management posts and females in all other posts in which males worked could not hope to earn salaries of more than half those paid to their male equivalents.

Mr. Yakimoto, the Second Company CEO, explained: "Our experience has been that in this company most female staff leave before the age of 25. That's a respected part of Japanese culture and doesn't surprise us. So, in the past we have felt that any investments made in appointing and training female managers are wasted. Females with other ideas tend not to apply to join us.

"We in top management would like to change this culture, and employ females on the same basis as the First Company do. Eventually we might employ them at all levels, with equivalent salaries. But, you understand that I'm talking only for top management. If we're going to compete on an international level, we know that we have to adopt global practices. Unfortunately, management at lower levels don't share our understanding. They are very conservative and set against any change. They're making it very difficult for us to merge with the First Company."

QUESTIONS

1 Why has it been traditional practice for many Japanese women to leave employment before the age of 25?

2 Why do the attitudes of top management and lower levels in the Second Company differ?

3 Why are the attitudes of the lower levels endangering the merger?

DECISION

4 *Design a strategy by which the First Company and Second Company can merge successfully.*

CHAPTER FOURTEEN **Headquarters and Subsidiary**

CASE CONSTRUCTING THE WORLD

This case looks at the link between culture and attitudes to moving

In the 1950s, Oskar and Petersen (O&P) was a Danish construction company based in Copenhagen. It designed and built roads and bridges in all the Scandinavian countries. But by the 1970s, the Scandinavian work had dried up and most of its projects were based elsewhere in Europe. It built an airport in England, major port facilities in Dublin, and a ring-road around Marseilles. In 1970 it was decided to de-register as a Danish company, and register in the United Kingdom. A new headquarters was established in London.

Many of the middle-ranking Copenhagen staff were offered, and accepted, the opportunity to relocate. Those who did not were replaced with British staff.

Then, just at the time that the European order book began to contract, the company was invited to tender for projects in Southeast Asia: a shopping complex in Singapore, a road in Thailand, and an airport in Vietnam. In 1982 after some consideration, the company decided that expenses might be reduced and profits optimized by making another move. O&P de-registered in London and became a Thai company, with headquarters in Ploenchit Road, Bangkok. This time, fewer of the headquarters staff agreed to make the move. Many young Thai managers and engineers found a generous employer. Thai business people were surprised and bewildered by this move.

QUESTIONS

1 Characterize the management structure of O&P. How far is it global? How far transnational?

2 How far does Danish culture explain the decisions made by top management?

3 How far does Thai culture explain the Thai response?

DECISIONS

4 *You are a consultant contracted to advise O&P. What are the advantages and disadvantages of this management structure?*

5 *The company is now being offered work in China. How should it respond?*

CHAPTER FIFTEEN   **International Joint Ventures**

CASE   RESEARCH AND DEVELOPMENT IN JORDAN (PART 1)

This case probes potential problems when the management team changes

A British educational charity started a development project with a Jordanian university. The 1-year project aimed to research English language needs in the Jordanian professions, and then design and write materials for teaching English to graduate medical students.

In the early negotiations, the charity was represented by Tim, an Assistant Director, and a junior assistant. He introduced his proposal: "This is a research and development project."

His idealism and enthusiasm convinced the Jordanian team to contribute 15 qualified teachers and an assistant project director. The partners agreed that the charity team expatriated to the project should consist of Peter, a staff member who would act as project director, and five researchers contracted from British universities.

The charity was also running projects elsewhere in the region, and before the contract was finalized, Tim was called away to resolve a problem in Cyprus. Fortunately his London deputy, Cynthia, was free to fly out and replace him. She and the assistant assured the Jordanians that the charity was giving the project its highest priority, and that Tim would continue as the manager responsible for overseeing headquarters' interests. The contract was very quickly signed in a mood of great optimism.

A few months later, Peter arrived to start the organizational planning. He met the Jordanian staff and was impressed by their energy and skills. Then the British team arrived. Everyone was looking forward to the first project staff meeting. Peter asked them to introduce themselves, then they broke into small groups to discuss how they might best participate, and structure their work. Then Peter received a phone call.

It was Cynthia, very excited: "Haven't you heard yet? Tim's been promoted. The board really liked his work in setting up your project. He's been sent to Brazil as Director of the office there. So I'm taking over from him in London. I've got some ideas for projects of my own. Training nurses in Botswana; and agronomists in Indonesia. I'm going to be busy . . ."

"But what about us?"

Cynthia laughed. "Peter, I'm sure I don't need worry about your research project . . ."

"Research and development," he corrected her.

"Yes, and development. Now that you're running it."

Peter felt a sinking feeling.

QUESTIONS

1 What mistakes were made?
2 Who was responsible for these mistakes?
3 Why did Peter feel a sinking feeling?

DECISION

4 How can the problems be resolved?

CHAPTER SIXTEEN **Staffing to Control**

CASE RESEARCH AND DEVELOPMENT IN JORDAN (PART 2)

Management has to maintain a shared vision of objectives

After the call from Cynthia, Peter started to think seriously about the management problems that might face him.

For a few weeks he continued the weekly project meetings. But the two teams seemed unable to agree on a unified plan of action or to understand each other's point of view, and each team seemed increasingly less willing to explore ideas presented by the other. Meetings dragged on for several hours.

Then Peter announced that the full team should meet only once a month.

"We need to use our time more profitably," he explained. "And we need to develop specialist skills."

"Do you mean that we don't have an opportunity to share ideas?" Rashid, one of the teachers, asked.

"I'm not saying that. Each group will have a meeting once a week and I'll attend both. And I'm sure you'll be meeting informally all the time."

In practice there was very little informal inter-action between the two teams. Peter increasingly acted as a conduit between them, explaining the research findings to the teachers, and carrying back their theoretical problems to the researchers.

Then unexpectedly, both groups attended the next meeting of the teachers and announced that they had decided to stop work.

"Why?" Peter asked.

"Because you've been lying to us," said John, one of the researchers. "We Brits were hired on the understanding that this was a research project, and that research would always have precedence over materials writing and teaching."

"Maybe we should review the materials written to date," said Peter. "The university has asked for changes . . ."

"But we see it differently," Rashid interrupted. "We Jordanians joined the project because we were told that this was a development project, and that materials were most important. And you've been telling us the same thing every week. So now we're very confused."

Both teams then announced that they would not return to work until Peter had decided on the project priorities.

QUESTIONS
1 How did Peter try to maintain control?
2 What management problems did he face?
3 How might the problems have been avoided?

DECISIONS
4 *Are there any other ways by which Peter might have resolved his problems? If yes, what?*
5 *You are a researcher hired by the charity to ensure that the problems you have identified in this and the previous case do not arise in future projects. Summarize your recommendations.*

CHAPTER SEVENTEEN **Expatriate Assignments**

CASE   OVERLOOKING THE SPOUSE

This case highlights the importance of catering for dependents' needs

Mary is an American engineer married to John. They have two children, a girl aged nine and a boy aged four.

John works in the Chicago headquarters of AcmeCo. His work is highly regarded, and when the expatriate general manager in the Yemeni subsidiary resigns following a painful divorce, John is selected to take his place. This is a promotion, and he accepts.

"Where?" Mary asks. John explains. Mary decides that the children need their father at this crucial stage of their growing-up. She agrees that they should all accompany him, although this means giving up her job. She looks forward to finding a part-time job with an engineering company when they arrive.

On their arrival she discovers that she is not permitted to work other than as a secretary within John's firm. She refuses this option. She stays at home, takes the children to school, and manages the domestic help. Her boredom and frustration is acute and she vents her fury on John. Their relationship deteriorates and so does his work. She takes the children back to the United States, and divorces John. He resigns from the company.

This ban on the dependent spouse working applies equally to Aiesha, whose husband Latif works in the same subsidiary. Aiesha and Latif come from a region of Pakistan where women are given few opportunities to make a career. Hence the ban gives her no concern. She and Latif adjust happily.

When John resigns, Latif is promoted to his job.

QUESTIONS

1   What mistakes were made? Who by?

2   How might these mistakes have been averted?

DECISION

3   You work for AcmeCo. Design a policy that will protect the company against such problems in the future.

Training and Supporting an Expatriate Assignment

CASE   CROSS-CULTURAL TRAINING NEEDS

The company's negative attitude to training is a recipe for failure

When Peter, a Marketing Manager, was appointed to reopen his company's branch in Baghdad after the 2003 war, he met with the headquarters International Human Resources Manager to request cross-cultural training.

"Baghdad, Baghdad," said the IHR Manager, looking at a map on his wall. "Now where is that?"

"Not Bangladesh," Peter said, and pointed to the capital of Iraq.

"Yes, well I don't know why top management think we should be going there at all. But that's their business and I take orders. You understand that the training budget is very limited. I can give you 2 days."

"Two days? That's ridiculous. I was hoping for 2 months."

"Were you really? And who's going to do your job while you play at being a student for 2 months? We can't afford anything like that."

"I need to understand the culture."

"Why? Cross-cultural training won't make you any more effective. You've got your professional skills and you'll be selling the same products there that we sell in London and Paris. One week."

"I can't learn the Arabic language in 1 week."

"You won't need it. We gave the statistics manager 6 hours' Arabic before he went to Tehran, and he never complained."

"But . . . but . . . ," Peter began, astonished.

"So 1 week it is," the IHR Manager concluded. "Please call again. My door is always open."

QUESTION

1 What is wrong with this company?

DECISIONS

2 *How should Peter try to change the company approach to cross-cultural training?*

3 *Write the headings of a proposal that Peter might make.*

MBA and other management degree programs often require students to write short dissertations and project reports. This appendix shows one way of planning the dissertation or report, from the first stages of deciding on a theme. It focuses on the management problems associated with planning a dissertation. It does not deal with technical questions – for example, how to negotiate access to informants, how to write a questionnaire, how to analyze qualitative and quantitative data. For these and other technical issues, see Saunders, Lewis, and Thornhill (2002).

Dissertation Planning Model

The model consists of questions asked on 12 levels.

Level 1: What is your research FIELD, or general topic area?
  (For example: Chinese family companies.)
Level 2: What is your research QUESTION? What are you trying to find out or to prove?
  (For example: how are non-family members employed by Chinese family companies?)
Level 3: What is your dissertation TITLE?
  (For example: "The employment of non-family members in Chinese family companies: the case in Taiwan.")
Level 4: What research DATA do you need in order to answer your research question?
  SECONDARY data (print and electronic):
  (a) What academic literature:
    • books?
    • academic journal articles?
    • academic conference reports?
  (b) What official reports:

- government reports?
- reports by international agencies?

(c) What journalism:
- newspaper and non-academic journal articles?
- television?
- film?
- transcriptions of television/film?

(d) What other secondary data:
- company reports?
- advertising?
- trade publications?
- financial data?
- other?

PRIMARY data:

(e) What interview surveys?
(f) What questionnaire surveys?
(g) What observations?
(h) What other primary data?

Level 5: Where will data be collected and analyzed?
Level 6: From whom will data be collected?
(In the case of primary data, who are your target informants?)
Level 7: Who will collect the data?
Level 8: How will the data be analyzed?
(What qualitative and quantitative methodologies will be applied?)
Level 9: When will the data be collected and analyzed?
Level 10: How will the dissertation be STRUCTURED?
(What chapters, sections, subsections do you need? How will they be titled?)
Level 11: By when must you SUBMIT the completed dissertation?
Level 12: What is your TIMETABLE for writing the dissertation?

(a) If you are using interview surveys, by when will you have completed the interviews?
(b) If you are using an original questionnaire:
- By when will you have piloted it? (Piloting is discussed in the next section.)
- By when will you have revised the questionnaire?
- By when will you run the final version of the questionnaire?
(c) If you are using observations, by when will you have completed making these?
(d) By when will you have collected all secondary and primary data?
(e) By when will you have analyzed all secondary and primary data?
(f) By when will you have completed a first draft?
(g) By when will you have completed further drafts?
(h) When do you need to consult with your supervisor?

How to Use the Model

When you have answered the question on Level 1, proceed to the question on Level 2, and so on.

Levels 1–3 focus attention on the research question to be tested. You start by deciding what general FIELD interests you, and then narrow it down so that it is sufficiently focused to research. The example is given of a very broad research field – "family companies" – from which a wide range of research questions can be derived. Levels 2 and 3 may coincide, but not necessarily.

Only when a precise QUESTION and TITLE have been formulated can specific research priorities be decided. Answers at Level 4 make decisions about what DATA are needed to answer the research QUESTION. Answers at Levels 5–9 deal with the practicalities of collecting the DATA and analyzing it. Your QUESTION determines what DATA you need. Some QUESTIONS can be satisfactorily answered using SECONDARY DATA, collected and possibly analyzed by other persons. Secondary data are available in libraries, the media, and the web, and a dissertation using this data can sometimes be planned and written at a distance from the events discussed. In general, all dissertations need to be grounded in secondary data; these show the reader how your work relates to and is built upon existing research in the FIELD. A dissertation based entirely on secondary data develops new interpretations of existing materials.

Your choice of FIELD and QUESTION may mean that you have to develop and analyze a body of original PRIMARY data – for example, when the secondary data is out of date, or deals only generally with an industry and is not specific to the country that interests you.

SECONDARY DATA sources are listed in the model before PRIMARY DATA sources because many dissertations use SECONDARY DATA in a literature survey as a means of reviewing past studies in the FIELD and introducing the PRIMARY DATA, presented and analyzed in subsequent chapters.

Tools for developing PRIMARY DATA include those listed here in Level 4 – structured interviews, structured observations, and questionnaires. The time used in identifying a pool of informants who are prepared to take part in these activities has to be added to that spent in developing the research tools.

An original QUESTIONNAIRE usually has to be PILOTED. That is, the first draft of the questionnaire is tested on a small group typical of the informant pool that you hope to use when you conduct the revised and final draft. This piloting gives you feedback needed to:

- eliminate questionnaire items that prove irrelevant to your QUESTION;
- eliminate items that are excessive to your research needs (a short focused questionnaire is usually preferable to a long, repetitive questionnaire that takes a long time to answer);
- revise items that are ambiguous;
- add new items that fill gaps in your research agenda.

Some new questionnaires benefit from being piloted more than once. Informants used in piloting should not be used again to complete the final version.

Answers at Levels 10–12 deal with the practicalities of STUCTURING the dissertation and TIMETABLING the DATA collection and writing-up phases. If you decide to pilot a new questionnaire to collect DATA, the time involved in this, and rewriting has to be planned.

The Model is Recursive

The model is RECURSIVE, which means that you can move up levels as well as down. If you can't decide on an answer at one level, try returning to the level immediately before and reconsider your answer to that. If that doesn't help you solve the problem, go back up two levels. For example, if (at Level 2) you have problems deciding on a research QUESTION that interests you, check your FIELD at Level 1. You may decide that you would prefer to work in some other FIELD. If (at Level 3) you cannot formulate a precise TITLE, revise your QUESTION, and then, if necessary, check the FIELD again.

This process of revision can be crucial when deciding on the practical issues of collecting and analyzing DATA at Levels 4–9. If you cannot collect the DATA you need for a particular TITLE and QUESTION, you may need a new TITLE and ask a new QUESTION, or even rethink the FIELD.

For example, two London-based students planned to research patronage networks in Indonesia. Reliable data on patronage is difficult to find; the media seldom report it with sensitivity and most people are cautious of discussing their own experiences unless they fully trust the researcher. The first student found the resources of time and money to make the trip, and thanks to personal contacts prepared in advance was able to conduct useful face-to-face interviews. The second did not have these resources and at a distance could not create the confidence needed. Eventually he was forced to consider two options: either change his question and data sources and write on patronage from a text-based point of view, reviewing the existing literature; or, change to a new field. In fact, he chose the second route, and chose a new field and question asking how American multinational headquarters controlled the organizational cultures of their Indonesian subsidiaries. The written literature was more extensive, and the topic was less contentious. Using his contacts in American industry he contacted a range of American multinational managers on the internet, and conducted an internet survey which generated some excellent data.

What Writing Style Suits You?

Dissertation planning and writing are creative activities and different people develop individual strategies. Some people prefer to complete all reading and researching before starting to write. At the opposite extreme, others prefer to write as soon as possible and to tailor data collection and analysis to their writing needs. Most students find solutions between these two extremes.

Some prefer to start by writing the first chapter, then write the second, and so on, developing the dissertation in strict sequential order. Others start at a midpoint, then move backwards and forwards, filling in different sections as their knowledge and understanding develops. Some try to complete all writing in one or two drafts whereas others continually draft and redraft.

The factors that influence how you write include the type of project, the topic, availability and type of data, time factors, and your psychological make-up. This last may be the most important. There is no one way to research and write an extended project, and different people may follow very different strategies to write about the same topic.

Be prepared for problems to arise – they undoubtedly will. How will you resolve them?

BIBLIOGRAPHY

Adedaji, A. 1995: The challenge of pluralism, democracy, governance and development, *The Courier*, March–April, EU, Brussels, 93–5.

Adler, N. J., Campbell, N. C., and Laurent, A. 1989: In search of appropriate methodology: from outside the People's Republic of China Looking In, *Journal of International Business Studies*, Spring, 61–74.

Albrecht, M. (ed.) 2001: *International HRM: Managing Diversity in the Workplace*. Oxford: Blackwell.

Allee, V. 2003: *The Future of Knowledge*. London: Butterworth Heinemann.

Andrews, K. 1971: *The Concept of Corporate Strategy*. Homewood, IL: Irwin.

Andrews, T. G. 2005: *Future Proof: Time, Intuition, and Strategic Response*. Edward Elgar.

Andrews, T. G. and Chompusri, N. 2001: Lessons in "Cross-vergence": restructuring the Thai subsidiary corporation, *Journal of International Business Studies*, 32 (1), 77–93.

Andrews, T. G., Chompusri, N., and Baldwin, B. J. 2003: *The Changing Face of Multinationals in Southeast Asia*. London: Routledge.

Ansoff, I. 1985: *Corporate Strategy*. London: Penguin.

Ashcar, G. 2002: *The Clash of Barbarisms*. New York: Monthly Review Press.

Baetz, M. and Bart, C. 1996: Developing mission statements which work, *Long Range Planning*, 29 (4), 526–33.

Barber, B. 2001, 1995: *Jihad vs McWorld*. New York: Ballantine Books.

Barnet, R. and Cavanagh, J. 1995: *Global Dreams*. New York: Touchstone.

Bartlett, C. A. and Ghoshal, S. 1989: *Managing Across Borders: The Transnational Solution*. Hutchinson Business Books.

Bartmess, A. and Cerny, K. 1993: Building competitive advantage: a capability-centred approach, *California Management Review*, 35 (2), 78–103.

Bate, P. 1999: *Strategies For Cultural Change*. Butterworth Heinemann.

Bergen, P. 2001: *Holy War, Inc.: Inside the Secret World of Osama Bin Laden*. London: Weidenfeld and Nicholson.

Beugré, C. D. and Offodile, O. F. 2001: Managing for organizational effectiveness in sub-Saharan Africa: a culture-fit model, *International Journal of Human Resource Management*, 12 (4), 535–50.

Bjerke, B. 2000: A typified, culture-based interpretation of management of SMEs in Southeast Asia, *Asia Pacific Journal of Management*, 17, 103–32.

Björkman, I. and Schaap, A. 1994: Outsiders in the Middle Kingdom: expatriate managers in Chinese–Western joint ventures, *European Management Journal*, 12 (2), 147–53.

Black, B. 1994: Culture and effort: British and Irish work related values and attitudes, *International Journal of Human Resource Management*, 5 (4), 875–92.

Black, J. S. and Mendenhall, M. 1993: Resolving conflicts with the Japanese: mission impossible? *Sloan Management Review*, Spring, 49–59.

Black, J. S. and Stephens, G. K. 1989: The influence of the spouse on American expatriate adjustments and intent to stay in Pacific Rim overseas assignments, *Journal of Management*, 15 (4), 529–44.

Blau, P. M. 1968: The hierarchy of authority in organizations, *American Journal of Sociology*, 73, 453–67.

Blumen, J. L. 2002: The age of connective leadership. In Hesselbein, F. and Johnston, R. (eds): *On Leading Change*. San Francisco: Jossey Bass, 89–101.

Bonvillain, G. and Nowlin, W. A. 1994: Cultural awareness: an essential element of doing business abroad, *Business Horizons*, November–December, 44–50.

Bork, D. 1986: *Family Business, Risky Business*. New York: American Management Association.

Borner, S., Brunetti, A., and Weder, B. 1995: *Political Credibility and Economic Development*. St Martin's Press, New York.

Bourantas, D. and Papalexandris, N. 1999: Personality traits and discriminating between employees in public- and in private-sector organizations, *International Journal of Human Resource Management*, 10 (5), 858–69.

Braudel, F. 1984: *The Perspective of the World: Vol. 3, Civilization and Capitalism*. London: Collins.

Brummelhuis, H. T. 1984: Abundance and avoidance: an interpretation of Thai individualism. In Brummelhuis, H. T. and Kemp, J. (eds): *Strategies and Structures in Thai Society*. Antropologisch-Sociologisch Centrum, Universiteit van Amsterdam, 39–54.

Bush, J. B. Jr. and Frohman, A. L. 1991: Communication in a "network" organization, *Organizational Dynamics*, Autumn, 23–35.

Caligiuri, P., Phillips, J., Lazarova, M., Tarique, I., and Bürgi, P. 2001: The theory of met expectations applied to expatriate adjustment: the role of cross-cultural training. *International Journal of Human Resource Management*, 12 (3), 357–72.

Carney, M. 1998: A management capacity constraint? Obstacles to the development of the overseas Chinese family business. *Asia Pacific Journal of Management*, 15, 137–62.

Carter, M. 2001: *Anthony Blunt: His Lives*. London: Macmillan.

Cartwright, R. 2000: *Mastering the Business Environment*. London: Palgrave.

Cascio, W. F. and Serapio, M. G. Jr. 1998: Human resources systems in an international alliance: the undoing of a done deal? *Organizational Dynamics*. Special report: "The people side of successful global alliances," Luthans, F. (ed.), 109–20.

Chandler, A. 1962: *Strategy and Structure*. Cambridge, MA: MIT Press.

Chen, Ming-jer. 2001: *Inside Chinese Business*. Harvard Business School Press.

Chew, I. K. H. and Lim, C. 1995: A Confucian perspective on conflict resolution. *The International Journal of Human Resource Management*, 6 (1), 143–57.

Chiu, O. and Siu, W.-S. 2001: Coping with the Asian economic crisis: the rightsizing strategies of small- and medium-sized enterprises, *International Journal of Human Resource Management*, 12 (5), 845–58.

Chow, C. K.-W. 1996: Entry and exit process of small businesses in China's retail sector, *International Small Business Journal*, 15 (1), 41–58.

Chow, I. H.-S. 1988: Work related values of middle managers in the public and private sectors, *Proceedings of the 1988 Academy of International Business Southeast Asia Regional Conference*. Bangkok, A14–25.

Collis, D. J. and Montgomery, C. A. 1995: Competing on resources: strategy in the 1990s, *Harvard Business Review*, July–August, 118–28.

Cooper, G. L. and Argyris, C. (eds) 1998: *The Concise Blackwell Encyclopedia of Management*. Oxford: Blackwell.

Craig, S. 2002: *How Chinese Are Chinese Family Companies?* Unpublished MA dissertation, SOAS, The University of London.

Cross, R. and Israelit, S. (eds) 2000: *Strategic Learning in a Knowledge Economy*. London: Butterworth Heinemann.

Czarniawska, B. 1986: The management of meaning in the Polish crisis, *Journal of Management Studies*, 23 (3), 313–31.

Daft, R. and Weick, K. E. 1984: Toward a model of organizations as interpretation systems. In Weick, K. E. (ed.) 2001: *Making Sense of the Organization*. Blackwell, 241–58.

David, F. R. 1993: *Concepts of Strategic Management*. New York: Macmillan Publishing Company.

Davies, H. 1995: Interpreting guanxi: the role of personal connectedness in a high-context transitional economy. In Davies, H. (ed.): *China Business Context and Issues*. Hong Kong: Longman Asia.

Day, J. D., Mang, P. Y., Richter, A., and Roberts, J. 2002: Has pay for performance had its day? *McKinsey Quarterly*, 4, 46–56.

Dean, J. W. Jr. and Sharfman, M. 1996: Does decision process matter? A study of strategic decision-making, *Academy of Management Journal*, 39 (2), 368–96.

Delios, A. and Björkman, I. 2000: Expatriate staffing in foreign subsidiaries of Japanese multinational corporations in the PRC and the United States, *The International Journal of Human Resource Management*, 1 (2), 278–93.

East Asia Analytical Unit, Department of Foreign Affairs and Trade, Australia. 1995: *Overseas Chinese Business Networks in Asia*. Canberra, Australia: Commonwealth of Australia.

Easterby-Smith, M., Malina, D., and Lu, Y. 1995: How culture-sensitive is HRM? A comparative analysis of practice in Chinese and UK companies, *The International Journal of Human Resource Management*, 6 (1), 31–59.

Electronic Banking Group of the Basel Committee for Banking Supervision, 2001: *Risk Management Principles for Electronic Banking*. Switzerland: Basel Committee for Banking Supervision.

Elsom, J. (forthcoming): *Missing the Point* (Ms.).

Elton, B. 1999: *Blast From the Past*. London: Black Swan.

Eschbach, D. M., Parker, G. E., and Stoeberl, P. A. 2001: American repatriate employees' retrospective assessments of the effects of cross-cultural training on their adaptation to international assignments, *International Journal of Human Resource Management*, 12 (2), 270–87.

Fedor, K. J. and Werther, W. B. Jr. 1997: The fourth dimension: creating culturally responsive international alliances, *Organizational Dynamics*, Autumn, 39–51.

Feldman, D. C. and Bolino, M. C. 1999: The impact of on-site mentoring on expatriate socialization: a structural equation modelling approach, *The International Journal of Human Resource Management*, 10 (1), 54–71.

Ferris, S. P., Joshi, Y. P., and Makhija, A. K. 1995: Valuing an East European company, *Long Range Planning*, 28 (6), 48–60.

Finlayson, I. 1993: *Tangier: City of the Dream*. Flamingo.

Fisher, R., Ury, W., and Patton, B. 1997: *Getting to Yes*. Arrow.

Flood, P., Dromgoole, T., Carroll, S., and Gorman, L. 2000: *Managing Strategy Implementation*. Blackwell.

Ford, M. 1996: Why friends in high places can be a mixed blessing, *Institutional Investor*, International edition, November, 28J–28N.

Forster, N. 2000. The myth of the "international manager", *International Journal of Human Resource Management*, 11 (1), 126–42.

Forte, M., Hoffmen, J. J., Lamont, B. T., and Brockmann, E. N. 2000: Organizational form and environment: an analysis of between-form and within-form responses to environmental change, *Strategic Management Journal*, 21, 753–73.

Franko, L. 1971: *Joint Ventures Survival in Multinational Corporations*. New York: Praeger.

Fukuyama, F. 1991: *The End of History and the Last Man*. London: Hamish Hamilton.

Fukuyama, F. 1995: Social capital and the global economy, *Foreign Affairs*, September–October, 89–103.

Gannon, M. and Newman, K. 2002: *Handbook of Cross-cultural Management*. Oxford: Blackwell.

Garcao, M., Aronoff, C., and Ward, J. 1997: National survey and highlights of Arthur Anderson / mass mutual American family business survey. Kennesaw State University. http://www.arthuranderson.com

Garsten, N. 2001: An exploratory examination of the factors that determine and influence whether or not major British organizations give externally run cross-cultural awareness briefings to expatriates going to work in Asia. Unpublished MA dissertation, School of Oriental and African Studies, University of London.

Gersick, K., Davis, J., McCollum, M., and Lansberg, I. 1997: *Generation to Generation: Life Cycles of the Family Business*. Boston: Harvard Business School Press.

Gooderham, P. N. and Nordhaug, O. (eds) 2004: *International Management*. Oxford: Blackwell.

Gowan, P. 1999: *The Global Gamble: Washington's Faustian Bid for World Dominance*. London: Verso.

Grant, R. M. 2002: *Contemporary Strategy Analysis: Concepts, Techniques, Applications*, 4th edn. Oxford: Blackwell.

Grey, J. 1990: *False Dawn: The Delusions of Global Capitalism*. London: Granta Books.

Griffin, W. and Pustay, W. 1999: *International Business: A Managerial Perspective*. Addison-Wesley.

Hailey, J. 1996: Breaking through the glass ceiling, *People Management*, 11 July, 32–4.

Haines, W. R. 1988: Making corporate planning work in developing countries, *Long Range Planning*, 21 (2), 91–6.

Haley, G. and Tan, C.-T. 1996: The black hole of South-east Asia: strategic decision-making in an informational void, *Management Decisions*, 34 (9), 37–46.

Hall, E. T. 1976: *Beyond Culture*. Anchor Press/Doubleday.

Hall, E. T. 1983: *The Dance of Life*. Anchor Press/Doubleday.

Hall, E. T. 1987: *Hidden Differences*. Anchor Press/Doubleday.

Hall, E. T. and Whyte, W. F. 1961: Intercultural communication: a guide to men of action, *Human Organization*, 19 (1), 5–12.

Hamill, J. 1989: Expatriate policies in British multinationals, *Journal of General Management*, 14 (4), 18–33.

Hammer, M. 1996: *Beyond Reengineering*. HarperCollins.

Hammer, M. and Champy, J. 1993: *Reengineering the Corporation: A Manifesto for Business Revolution*. HarperBusiness.

Hampden-Turner, C. and Trompenaars, F. 1993: *The Seven Cultures of Capitalism*. Doubleday.

Hampden-Turner, C. and Trompenaars, F. 1997: *Mastering the Infinite Game: How East Asian Values are Transforming Business Practices*. Capstone.

Handy, C. 1985: *Understanding Organisations*. Penguin.

Harnett, D. L. and Cummings, L. L. 1980: *Bargaining Behavior: An International Study*. Texas: Dame Publications.

Harris, J. 1998: Globalization and the technological transformation of capitalism, *Race and Class*, 40, 2 (3), 21–35.

Harung, H. S. and Dahl, T. 1995: Increased productivity and quality through management by values: a case study of Manpower Scandinavia, *The T.Q.M. Magazine*, 7 (2), 13–22.

Harvey, M. 1998: Dual-career couples during international relocation: the trailing spouse. *International Journal of Human Resource Management*, 9 (2), 309–31.

Harzing, A.-W. 1999: *Managing The Multinationals – An International Study of Control Mechanisms*. Cheltenham: Edward Elgar.

Harzing, A.-W. 2001: Who's in charge? An empirical study of executive staffing practices in foreign subsidiaries, *Human Resource Management*, 40 (2), 139–58.

Herzberg, F. 1968: One more time: how do you motivate employees? *Harvard Business Review*, 46, 53–62.

Herzberg, F., Mausner, B., and Snyderman, B. 1959: *The Motivation To Work*. Wiley.

Hesselbein, F. 2002: The key to cultural transformation. In Hesselbein, F. and Johnston, R. (eds): *On Leading Change*. San Francisco: Jossey Bass, 1–5.

Hesselbein, F. and Johnston, R. (eds) 2002: *On Leading Change*. San Francisco: Jossey Bass.

Hofstede, G. 1983: National cultures in four dimensions, *International Studies of Management and Organizations*, 13 (1–2), 46–74.

Hofstede, G. 1984: *Culture's Consequences: International Differences in Work-Related Values*, abridged edn. Beverly Hills: Sage.

Hofstede, G. 1985: The interaction between national and organizational value systems,

Journal of Management Studies, 22 (4), 347–57.

Hofstede, G. 1991: *Cultures and Organizations: Software of the Mind*, 1st edn. McGraw-Hill.

Hofstede, G. 1997: *Cultures and Organizations: Software of the Mind*, 2nd edn. McGraw-Hill.

Hofstede, G. 2001: *Culture's Consequences*, 2nd edn. London: Sage.

Huang, T.-C. 1999: Who shall follow? Factors affecting the adoption of succession plans in Taiwan, *Long Range Planning*, 32 (6).

Huntington, S. 1998: *The Clash of Civilizations and the Remaking of the World Order*. Touchstone Books.

Ishizumi, K. 1990: *Acquiring Japanese Companies*. Blackwell.

Jackson, K. 2003: The emerging structure of trust in international HRM: case studies from the Japanese pharmaceuticals industry. Ms., kgj824@aol.com

Jackson, K. and Tomioka, M. 2004: *The Changing Face of Japanese Management*. London: Routledge.

Jackson, T. 2002: *International HRM: A Cross-Cultural Approach*. London: Sage.

Jackson, T. and Bak, M. 1998: Foreign companies and Chinese workers: employee motivation in the People's Republic of China, *Journal of Organizational Change Management*, 11 (4), 282–300.

Jaeger, A. M. 1983: The transfer of organizational culture overseas: an approach to control in the multinational corporation, *Journal of International Business Studies*, Fall, 91–114.

Jolly, A. (ed.) 2003: *Managing Business Risk*. London: Kogan Page.

Jolly, D. 2002: Sharing knowledge and decision power in Sino-foreign joint ventures, *Asia Pacific Business Review*, 9 (2), 81–100.

Kay, D. and Hinds, R. 2002: *A Practical Guide to Mentoring*. Oxford: Howtobooks.

Kelly, M. J., Schaan, J. L., and Joncas, H. 2002: Managing alliance relationships: key challenges in the early stages of collaboration, *R&D Management*, 32 (1), 11–23.

Kent, D. H. 1991: Joint ventures vs. non-joint ventures: an empirical investigation, *Strategic Management Journal*, 12, 387–93.

Kent State University. 1997: *Developments in the Understanding of Workforce Motivation*. Ohio: Kent State University.

Klingel, F. 2002: Comparison of Asian and German Family Firms on the Basis of Corporate Governance and Corporate Finance. Unpublished MSc dissertation, School of Oriental and African Studies, University of London.

Kluckhohn, F. R. and Strodtbeck, F. L. 1961: *Variations in Value Orientations*. New York: Peterson.

Knight, R. and Pretty, D. 2003. Risks that matter. In Jolly, A. (ed.): *Managing Business Risk*. London: Kogan Page, 6–16.

Kolb, D. 2000: The process of experiential learning. In Cross, R. and Israelit, S. (eds): *Strategic Learning in a Knowledge Economy*. London: Butterworth Heinemann, 313–31.

Kopp, R. 2001: Why it is so difficult to tell what a Japanese person is thinking. *Japan Close-Up*, November.

Kovach, K. A. 1987: What motivates employees? Workers and supervisors give different answers, *Business Horizons*, September–October, 58–65.

Kowtha, N. and Quek, S. I. 1999: Incentives in the Asian context: theory and preliminary evidence, *Asia Pacific Journal of Management*, 16, 95–109.

Kuemmerle, W. 1997: Building effective R&D capabilities abroad, *Harvard Business Review*, March–April, 61–70.

Kumar, S. and Seth, A. 1998: The design of coordination and control mechanisms for managing joint venture-parent relationships, *Strategic Management Journal*, 19, 579–99.

Lacey, R. 1981: *The Kingdom*. New York: Harcourt Brace Janovich.

Lasserre, P. 1999: Joint venture satisfaction in Asia Pacific, *Asia Pacific Journal of Management*, 16, 1–28.

Lasserre, P. and Putti, J. 1990: *Business Strategy and Management: Text and Cases for Managers in Asia*. Singapore Institute of Management.

Laurent, A. 1981: Matrix organizations and Latin cultures, *International Studies of Management and Organization*, 11, 101–14.

Laurent, A. 1983: The cultural diversity of Western conceptions of management, *International Studies of Management and Organization*, 13 (1–2), 75–96.

Lee, J. S. and Akhtar, S. 1996: Determinants of employee willingness to use feedback for performance improvement: cultural and organizational interpretations, *International Journal of Human Resource Management*, 7 (4), 878–90.

Lewis, D. 1998: How useful a concept is organizational culture? *Strategic Change*, 7, 251–60.

Lim, L. Y. C. 1996: The evolution of Southeast Asian business systems, *Journal of Asian Business*, 12 (1), 51–74.

Lincoln, J. R. 1989: Employee work attitudes and management practice in the U.S. and Japan: evidence from a large comparative survey. *California Management Review*, Fall, 89–106.

Lindgren, M. and Bandhold, H. 2003: *Scenario Planning: The Link Between Future and Strategy*. New York: Palgrave Macmillan.

Litvin, D. 2003: *Empires of Profit: Commerce, Conquest and Corporate Responsibility*. London: Thomson Learning.

Lowe, S. 1996: Culture's consequences for management in Hong Kong, *Asia Pacific Business Review*, 2 (1), 120–33.

Luo, Y.-d. 2000: *Guanxi and Business*. World Scientific Publishing.

Luthans, F., Marsnik, P., and Luthans, K. 2001: A contingency matrix approach to HRM. In Albrecht, M. (ed.): *International HRM: Managing Diversity in the Workplace*. Oxford: Blackwell, 83–102.

Maier, K. 2001: *This House has Fallen: Nigeria in Crisis*. London: Allen Lane/The Penguin Press.

Malone, T. W. 1997: Is empowerment just a fad? Control, decision making and IT, *Sloan Management Review*, Winter, 23–35.

Mann, L. 1989: *Beijing Jeep: The Short, Unhappy Romance of American Business in China*. Simon and Schuster.

Maslow, A. H. 1954: *Motivation and Personality*. New York: Harper and Brothers.

Maung Maung Oo. 2001: Burma's Great Depression, *Irrawaddy Publishing Group* – interactive edition, 9 (7), August–September.

McClelland, D. C. 1976: *The Achieving Society*. New York: Irvington.

McGuinness, N., Campbell, N. C., and Leontiades, J. 1991: Selling machinery to China: Chinese perceptions of strategies and relationships, *Journal of International Business Studies*, Second quarter, 187–207.

McKenna, S. 1995: The cultural transferability of business and organizational re-engineering: examples from Southeast Asia, *The T.Q.M. Magazine*, 7 (3), 12–16.

McNerney, D. J. 1995: The joy of sharing bad news, *H.R. Focus*, May, 3.

McSweeney, B. 2002: Hofstede's model of national cultural differences and their consequences: a triumph of faith – a failure of analysis, *Human Relations*, 55 (1), 89–118.

McVey, R. (ed.) 1992: Editorial, *Southeast Asian Capitalists*. Ithaca.

Mead, R. and Jones, C. J. 2002: Cross-cultural communication. In Gannon, M. and Newman, K. (eds): *Handbook of Cross-cultural Management*. Oxford: Blackwell, 283–91.

Mead, R., Jones, C. J., and Chansarkar, B. 1997: The management elite in Thailand: their long- and short-term career aspirations, *International Journal of Management*, 14.

Mendenhall, M. E., Punnett, B. J., and Ricks, D. 1995: *Global Management*. Blackwell.

Merritt, A. C. 1999: Replicating Hofstede: a study of pilots in eighteen countries. http:// www.psy.utexas.edu/psy/helmreich/hofrep.htm

Michaud, C. and Thoenig, J.-C. 2003: *Making Strategy and Organization Compatible*. London: Palgrave.

Ministry of Public Management Statistics Bureau. 2000: *Labour Force Survey*. Tokyo.

Mintzberg, H. 1975: The manager's job: folklore and fact, *Harvard Business Review*. July–August, 4–16.

Mintzberg, H. 1985: Of strategies: deliberate and emergent, *Strategic Management Journal*, 6, 257–72.

Mintzberg, H. 1994: *The Rise and Fall of Strategic Planning*. Prentice Hall.

Mittelman, J. 2000: *The Globalization Syndrome: Transformation and Resistance*. New Jersey: Princeton University Press.

Mühlbacher, H., Dahringer, L., and Leihs, H. 1999: *International Marketing: A Global Perspective*. London: International Thomson Business Press.

Negandhi, A. R. 1979: Convergence in organizational practices: an empirical study of industrial enterprises in developing countries. In Lammers, C. J. and Hickson, D. J. (eds): *Organizations Alike and Unlike: International and Institutional Studies of the Sociology of Organizations*. Routledge and Kegan Paul, 323–45.

Nevis, E. C. 1983: Cultural assumptions and productivity: the United States and China, *Sloan Management Review*, Spring, 17–29.

Ng, E. S. W. and Tung, R. L. 1998: Ethno-cultural diversity and organizational effectiveness: a field study. *The International Journal of Human Resource Management*, 9 (6), 980–95.

Nishiyama, K. 2000: *Doing Business With Japan: Successful Strategies for Intercultural Communication*. Honolulu: University of Hawaii.

O'Connell, J. 1998: International management. In Cooper, G. L. and Argyris, C. (eds): *The Concise Blackwell Encyclopedia of Management*. Oxford: Blackwell.

Ogbonna, E. and Harris, L. C. 1998: Managing organizational culture: compliance or genuine change? *British Journal of Management*, 9, 273–88.

Onedo, A. E. O. 1991: The motivation and need satisfaction of Papua New Guinea Managers, *Asia Pacific Journal of Management*, 8 (1), 121–9.

Pananond, P. 2001: The Making of Thai Multinationals: The Internationalisation Process of Thai Firms. Unpublished PhD dissertation, University of Reading.

Park, S. H. and Ungson, G. R. 1997: The effect of national culture, organizational complementarity and economic motivation on joint venture dissolution, *Academy of Management Journal*, 40 (2), 279–307.

Pascale, R. T. 1990: *Managing on the Edge: How the Smartest Companies use Conflict to Stay Ahead*. Simon and Schuster.

Payutto, Ven P. A. 1994: *Buddhist Economics: A Middle Way for the Market Place*, 2nd edn (translated by Dhammavijaya and Evans, B). Thailand: Buddhadhamme Foundation.

Perlmutter, H. V. and Heenan, D. A. 1974: How multinational should your top managers be? *Harvard Business Review*, November–December, 121–32.

Pettinger, R. 2001: *Mastering Management Skills*. London: Palgrave.

Phan, P. H. 2001: Corporate governance in the newly emerging economies, *Asia Pacific Journal of Management*, 18, 131–6.

Plutarch, 1973: *The Age of Alexander* (translated by Scott-Kilvert, I.). Penguin Books.

Pomfret, R. 1996: *Asian Economies in Transition: Reforming Centrally Planned Economies*. Edward Elgar.

Porter, M. E. 1990: *The Competitive Advantage of Nations*. New York: Free Press.

Porter, M. E. 1996: What is strategy? *Harvard Business Review*, November–December, 61–89.

Prime Minister's Commission on Japan's Goals in the 21st century. 2000: *The Frontier Within: Individual Empowerment and Better Governance in the New Millennium*. The Government of Japan, January.

Puffer, S. M. 1996: *Management Across Cultures: Insights from Fiction and Practice*. Malden, MA: Blackwell.

Renshaw, J. 1999: *Kimono in the Boardroom: The Invisible Evolution of Japanese Women Managers*. Oxford: Oxford University Press.

Revenaugh, D. L. 1994: Implementing major organizational change: can we really do it? *The T.Q.M. Magazine*, 6 (6), 38–48.

Richard, O. C. 2000: Racial diversity, business strategy, and firm performance: a resource-based view, *Academy of Management Journal*, 43 (2), 164–77.

Rieger, F. and Wong-Rieger, D. 1990: A configuration model of national influence applied to Southeast Asian organizations. *Research Conference on Business in Southeast Asia: Proceedings*. Southeast Asia Business Program, University of Michigan, 1–31.

Roberts, K. and Boyacigiller, N. 1984: Cross-national organizational research: the grasp of the blind man. In Staw, B. and Cummings, L. (eds): *Research in Organizational Behavior*, vol. 6. Stamford, CT: JAI Press, 423–75.

Robertson, C., Al-Khatib, J., Al-Habib, M., and Lanoue, D. 2001: Beliefs about work in the Middle East and the convergence versus divergence of values, *Journal of World Business*, 36 (3), 223–44.

Robson, J. 2002: Applying the Model of Scenario Planning: The Case of China. Unpublished MSc dissertation, School of Oriental and African Studies, University of London.

Rocca, J. 2000: The Internet in the People's Republic of China: Opportunities and Threats. Unpublished MA Dissertation, the School of Oriental and African Studies, University of London.

Ronen, B. 1995: Caution! Reengineering. Unpublished ms., Faculty of Management, Tel Aviv University, Israel.

Rosenzweig, P. M. and Singh, J. V. 1991: Organizational environments and the multinational enterprise, *Academy of Management Review*, 16 (2), 340–62.

Ross, H., Bouwmeesters, J., and Other Institute Staff. 1972: *Management in the Developing Countries*. UN Research Institute for Social Development, Geneva.

Rosten, K. A. 1991: Soviet–U.S. joint ventures: pioneers on a new frontier, *California Management Review*, Winter, 88–108.

Sala-I-Martin, X. 2002: The world distribution of income. NBER Working Paper 8933.

Salk, J. E. and Brannen, M. Y. 2000: National culture, networks, and individual influence in a multinational management team, *Academy of Management Journal*, 43 (2), 191–202.

Samovar, L. A. and Porter, R. E. 1995: *Communication Between Cultures*. Wadsworth.

Saunders, M., Lewis, P., and Thornhill, D. 2002: *Research Methods for Business Students*, 3rd edn. Pearson Education.

Scarborough, J. 1998: "Comparing Chinese and Western cultural roots: why 'east is east and . . .'," *Business Horizons*, November–December, 15–24.

Schein, E. H. 1981: Does Japanese management style have a message for American managers? *Sloan Management Review*, Fall, 55–68.

Schein, E. H. 1987: *Organizational Culture and Leadership*. San Francisco: Jossey Bass.

Schneider, S. C. 1988: National vs corporate culture: implications for human resource management, *Human Resource Management*, 27 (2), 231–46.

Schoemaker, P. 1995: Scenario planning: a tool for strategic thinking, *Sloan Management Review*, Winter, 25–40.

Schrage, M. 1989: A Japanese giant rethinks globalization: an interview with Yoshihisa Tabuchi, *Harvard Business Review*, July–August, 70–6.

Schwartz, S. and Sagie, G. 2000: Value consensus and importance: a cross-national study, *Journal of Cross-Cultural Psychology*, 31, 465–97.

Seagrave, S. 1995: *Lords of the Rim*. London: Bantam Press.

Selmer, J. 1996: Expatriate or local boss? HCN subordinates' preferences in leadership behaviour, *International Journal of Human Resource Management*, 7 (1), 59–81.

Selmer, J. 2001: Psychological barriers to adjustment and how they affect coping strategies: Western business expatriates in China, *International Journal of Human Resource Management*, 12 (2), 151–65.

Shane, S. 1993: The effect of cultural differences in perceptions of transactions costs on national differences in preferences for international joint ventures, *Asia Pacific Journal of Management*, 10 (1), 58–69.

Shenkar, O. and Zeira, Y. 1987: Human resources management in international joint ventures: directions for research, *Academy of Management Review*, 12 (3), 546–57.

Siddall, P., Willey, K., and Tavares, J. 1992: Building a transnational organization for BP Oil, *Long Range Planning*, 25 (1), 37–45.

Sinclair, J. McH. 1980: Discourse in relation to language structure and semiotics. In Greenbaum, S., Leech, G., and Svartvik, J. (eds): *Studies in English Linguistics for Randolph Quirk*. Longman, 110–24.

Smith, P. B. 1994: National cultures and the values of organizational employees: time for another look. Unpublished ms., Workshop of the European Institute for the Advanced Study of Management, Henley Management College, 1–15.

Smith, P. B. 2002: "Culture's consequences:" something old and something new, Review article and response to McSweeney (2002), *Human Relations*, 55 (1), 119–35.

Smith, P. B., Dugan, S., and Trompenaars, F. 1996: National culture and the values of organizational employees: a dimensional analysis across 43 nations, *Journal of Cross-Cultural Psychology*, 27, 231–64.

Sondergaard, M. 1994: Research note: Hofstede's Consequences: a study of reviews, citations and replications, *Organizational Studies*, 15 (3), 447–56.

Soon, H. W. 1995: Educational background and corporate culture: a case study of a South Korean business conglomerate, *Journal of Asian Business*, 11 (4), 51–68.

Staw, B. and Cummings, L. (eds) 1984: *Research in Organizational Behavior*, vol. 6. Stamford, CT: JAI Press.

Stern, J. 2003: The protean enemy, *Foreign Affairs*, 82 (4), 27–40.

Stewart, J. M. 1995: Empowering multinational subsidiaries, *Long Range Planning*, 28 (4), 63–73.

Strange, S. 1994 (2nd edn): *States and Markets*. London: Pinter Publishers.

Strathem, P. 2003. *The Medici: Godfathers of the Renaissance*. London: Jonathan Cape.

Sugarman, B. 2001: A learning-based approach to organizational change: some results and guidelines, *Organizational Dynamics*, 30 (1), 62–76.

Sullivan, J. J. and Nonaka, I. 1986: The application of organizational learning theory to Japanese and American management, *Journal of International Business Studies*, Fall, 127–47.

Sun, B. C. 2000: Pay and motivation in Chinese enterprises. In Warner, M. (ed.): *Changing Workplace Relations in the Chinese Economy*. London: Macmillan.

Suutari, V. 1996: Variation in the average leadership behaviour of managers across countries: Finnish expatriates' experiences from Germany, Sweden, France and Great Britain, *The International Journal of Human Resource Management*, 7 (3), 640–56.

Taylor, B. 1995: The new strategic leadership – driving change, getting results, *Long Range Planning*, 28 (5), 71–81.

Taylor, S., Beechler, S., and Napier, N. 1996: Towards an integrative model of strategic international human resource management, *The Academy of Management Review*, 21 (4), 959–85.

Thawley, S. 1996: Foreign Direct Investment and the Regulatory Environment in China. Unpublished MA dissertation, School of Oriental and African Studies, University of London.

Thomas, K. W. 1976: Conflict and conflict management. In Dunnette, M. D. (ed.): *Handbook of Industrial and Organizational Psychology*. Chicago: Rand McNally.

Torrington, D. 1994: *International Human Resource Management: Think Globally, Act Locally*. Prentice Hall International.

Tretiak, L. D. and Holzmann, K. 1993: Operating joint ventures in China, *Crossborder*, Autumn, 10–13.

Trompenaars, F. 1997 (2nd edn), 1993: *Riding the Waves of Culture*. London: Nicholas Brealey.

Tse, D. K., Francis, J., and Walls, J. 1994: Cultural differences in conducting extra- and intercultural negotiations: a Sino-Canadian comparison, *Journal of International Business Studies*, 3rd quarter, 537–55.

Tung, R. L. 1982: Selection and training procedures of U.S., European and Japanese multinationals, *California Management Review*, 25 (1), 57–71.

Tung, R. L. 1987: Expatriate assignments: enhancing success and minimizing failure, *Academy of Management Executive*, 1 (2), 117–26.

Tung, R. L. 1991: Motivation in Chinese industrial enterprises. In Steers, R. and Porter, L. (eds): *Motivation and Work Behavior*. McGraw-Hill.

Van den Bulcke, D. and Zhang, Hai-yen. 1995: Chinese family-owned multinationals in the Philippines and the internationalisation process. In Brown, R. A. (ed.): *Chinese Business Enterprise in Asia*. Routledge, 214–46.

Vaughan, L. Q. 1998: A cross-cultural comparison of business information use, *International Information and Library Review*, 30, 157–68.

Vroom, V. 1964: *Work and Motivation*. Chichester: John Wiley.

Wang, S.-Y. 1998: Recruiting to the Chinese Family Company. Unpublished MA dissertation, School of Oriental and African Studies, University of London.

Warner, M. (ed.) 2000: *Changing Workplace Relations in the Chinese Economy*. London: Macmillan.

Watanabe, S. 2000: The Japan Model and the future of employment and wage systems, *International Labour Review*, 139 (3), 161–87.

Watson, F., Corry, S., and Pearce, C. 2000: *Disinherited: Indians in Brazil.* Survival International.

Watson, W. E., Kamalesh, K., and Michaelson, L. K. 1993: Cultural diversity's impact on interaction process and performance: comparing homogeneous and diverse task groups, *Academy of Management Journal*, 36 (3), 590–602.

Weick, K. E. 2001: *Making Sense of the Organization.* Blackwell.

Whitley, R. 1992: *Business Systems in East Asia: Firms, Markets and Societies.* Sage.

Wilms, W. W., Hardcastle, A. J., and Zell, D. M. 1994: Cultural transformation at Nummi. *Sloan Management Review.* Fall, 99–113.

Wong, S.-L. 1986: Modernization and Chinese culture in Hong Kong, *China Quarterly*, 106, 306–25.

Woodworth, W. and Nelson, R. 1980: Information in Latin American organizations: some cautions, *Management International Review*, 20 (2), 61–9.

Wright, L. 1992: A Comparison of Thai, Indonesian and Canadian Perceptions of Negotiating, Working Paper 92-34, School of Business, Queen's University, Ontario.

Yavas, U. 1992: Constraints on the application of management know-how in the third world, *International Journal of Management*, 9 (1), 17–25.

Yeung, H. W.-C. 2000: Strategic control and coordination in Chinese business firms, *Journal of Asian Business*, 16 (1), 95–123.

Yoshimori, M. 1995: Whose company is it? The concept of the corporation in Japan and the West, *Long Range Planning*, 28 (4), 33–4.

Zhou, Wei-dong 2000: Chinese Business Negotiating Style: A Sociocultural Arrroach. Unpublished MA dissertation, School of Oriental and African Studies, University of London.

INDEX